More praise for *Holocaust Escapees and Global Development*

'Simon has undertaken a novel and also an unusual quest, one which sheds new light on the genius and creativity that the Nazis set out to destroy by the Holocaust.'

Reinhart Kössler, Arnold-Bergstraesser-Institut, Freiburg

'A fascinating and important book about the extraordinary contributions to global development by those who escaped the Holocaust.'

Nicholas Stern, LSE, and former Chief Economist for the World Bank

ABOUT THE AUTHOR

David Simon is Director of Mistra Urban Futures,
Gothenburg, and Professor of Development
Geography, Royal Holloway, University of London.
He specialises in development–environment
issues, with particular reference to cities, climate
change and sustainability, and the relationships
between theory, policy and practice, on all of which
he has published extensively. He is the author,
editor and co-editor of many books and journal
special issues on cities, development–environment
challenges and climate change adaptation, most
recently *Rethinking Sustainable Cities* (2016), *Urban
Planet* (2018) and *Key Thinkers on Development*
(2019).

HOLOCAUST ESCAPEES AND GLOBAL DEVELOPMENT

HIDDEN HISTORIES

David Simon

ZED

Holocaust Escapees and Global Development: Hidden Histories was first published in 2019 by Zed Books Ltd, The Foundry, 17 Oval Way, London SE11 5RR, UK.

www.zedbooks.net

Typeset in Plantin and Kievit by Swales & Willis Ltd, Exeter, Devon
Index by John Barker
Cover design by Burgess & Beech
Cover photo © Jared I. Lenz Photography/Getty

A catalogue record for this book is available from the British Library

ISBN 978-1-78699-513-1 hb
ISBN 978-1-78699-512-4 pb
ISBN 978-1-78699-514-8 pdf
ISBN 978-1-78699-515-5 epub
ISBN 978-1-78699-516-2 mobi

MIX
Paper from responsible sources
FSC® C013604

Printed and bound by CPI Group (UK) Ltd, Croydon, CR0 4YY

This book is dedicated to my late parents, Ruth and Wolfgang Simon, and the remarkable group of people whose life stories and legacies inspired and fill these pages. All their young lives were torn apart by the Holocaust (and two again by subsequent purges in Poland and Romania), yet they were determined to avoid the common survivors' traps of guilt and victimhood. Instead, they seized every moment, every opportunity, to adapt to radically changed circumstances and rebuild their lives in their countries of refuge or subsequent settlement, using their good fortune and expertise to help make the world a better place through long and creative lives. The scars, of course, remained to varying extents and it is gratifying that for some, at least, engaging with me over the course of this work helped fill in gaps or provide fresh perspectives on their formative experiences and their legacies.

CONTENTS

ABBREVIATIONS AND ACRONYMS

AAA	American Anthropological Association
AAC	Academic Assistance Council (later SPSS and CARA)
AMPC	Auxiliary Military Pioneer Corps
ANU	Australian National University
CARA	Campaign for Assisting Refugee Academics (now Campaign for At-Risk Academics)
CBF	Central British Fund for the Relief of German Jewry
CENIS	Center for International Studies (Massachusetts Institute of Technology)
CGJ	Central Council for German Jewry
CIA	Central Intelligence Agency
CSPSL	Canadian Society for the Protection of Science and Learning
ECA	European Cooperation Agency
ECLA(C)	UN Economic Commission for Latin America (and the Caribbean)
ED&CC	Economic Development and Cultural Change journal
EGC	Economic Growth Center (Yale University)
EPU	European Payments Union
ERP	European Recovery Program
FAO	UN Food and Agriculture Organization
FBI	Federal Bureau of Investigation
G24	Group of 24 countries
ICA	International Cooperation Administration (predecessor of USAID)
ICHR	International Commission on the Holocaust in Romania
IDS	Institute of Development Studies
IFIs	international financial institutions
ILO	International Labour Organization
ITDG	Intermediate Technology Development Group
JFC	Joint Foreign Committee of the Board of Deputies and Anglo-Jewish Association
KPD	Kommunistische Partei Deutschlands
KPD-O	Kommunistische Partei Deutschlands – Opposition

LSE	London School of Economics
MA	Master of Arts degree
MIT	Massachusetts Institute of Technology
NCB	National Coal Board
NGO	non-governmental organisation
NIEO	New International Economic Order
OBE	Order of the British Empire
OECD	Organization for Economic Co-operation and Development
OEEC	Organization for European Economic Co-operation
OSE	Oeuvre de Secours Aux Enfants (Children's Aid Society)
PDS	Party of Democratic Socialism
PEGS	Practical Education and Gender Support
PhD	Doctor of Philosophy degree
PNG	Papua New Guinea
PPE	Politics, Philosophy and Economics (Bachelor's degree at Oxford University)
SAP	Structural Adjustment Programme
SPSL	Society for the Protection of Science and Learning (later CARA)
SUNFED	Special United Nations Fund for Economic Development
UCLA	University of California, Los Angeles
UK	United Kingdom
UN	United Nations
UNAM	National Autonomous University of Mexico
UNCRD	United Nations Center for Regional Development
UNCTAD	United Nations Conference on Trade and Development
UNDP	United Nations Development Program
UNICEF	United Nations International Children's Emergency Fund
UNIDO	United Nations Industrial Development Organization
UNIHP	United Nations Intellectual History Project
US(A)	United States (of America)
USAID	United States Agency for International Development
USSR	Union of Soviet Socialist Republics
UWI	University of the West Indies
WEA	Workers' Education Association

ACKNOWLEDGEMENTS

It would not have been possible to write this book without British Academy funding for the small grant SG-43920 in 2006–7 that enabled the initial research project, and the almost universally enthusiastic participation of the many interviewees. These comprise the Holocaust escapees and survivors whose lives and contributions to postwar development form the principal focus of the book (see Table 1.1 in Chapter 1), along with close relatives and colleagues of those who had died by the time I undertook the interviews, and other key informants. Sydel Silverman, Odile Stamberger, Basil Yamey and the late John Shaw are cited directly in the text but Bettina and Nicholas Arndt, Piers Blaikie, Arturo Escobar, Tirril and Nigel Harris, Richard Jolly, Frances Stewart, Immanuel Wallerstein and Tom Weisskopf provided important information and/or valuable insights in the early stages of my research, not least in testing my inclusion criteria for escapees. My escapee/survivor interviewees also willingly answered follow-up questions and requests for supplementary information as appropriate, as well as checking the draft transcripts and segments of relevant draft chapters relating to them over subsequent years. Several also became champions of the project, most notably Michael Cernea and, until her death, Scarlett Epstein, urging me to complete the book and castigating me when other commitments caused long pauses.

My main regret is that, despite such encouragement, many of my interviewees and my parents have not lived to see this book in print. That reflects principally the time taken to complete the manuscript, undertaken as a labour of love in short bursts amid other professional commitments, not least as panel member for the 2008 UK Research Assessment Exercise, Head of Department (2008–11), work on other research grants and, since 2014, my secondment as Director of Mistra Urban Futures based at Chalmers University of Technology in Gothenburg, Sweden. Moreover, the sabbatical period in 2013 allocated to complete the bulk of the book was cut very short by my father's sudden death in Sydney at the age of 90 and the task of dissolving his estate. Those interviewees who are still able to appreciate the book will hopefully feel that their engagements with me and the tapestry into which their respective experiences and reflections have been woven have merited the wait.

Jenny Lunn served as my invaluable research assistant on some of the background searches, in undertaking the interview transcriptions and in interviewing Irma Adelman. Reinhart Kössler kindly read the completed manuscript very rapidly and his feedback has added to the robustness of the final product, particularly by identifying Theodor Bergmann and Andre Gunder Frank as meeting my inclusion criteria. Reports by the publisher's referees have been similarly helpful. Thanks to Shula Marks, the Campaign for At-Risk Academics (CARA) kindly granted me access to their archives held in the Bodleian Library, Oxford, which proved a rich treasure trove of records of wartime correspondence with several of my interviewees and their families before, during and after their flight from the Nazis. This access also enabled me to supply Gerry Helleiner with copies of key documents that filled a void in his and his brother's knowledge of this key episode in their escape from Vienna via the UK to Canada as young boys with their late parents.

Many others, too numerous to mention individually, bounced ideas around and made helpful suggestions at successive stages of the project and book writing, among them colleagues and former students, particularly Klaus Dodds, Nina Laurie, James Sidaway and the late David Cesarani. I also gratefully acknowledge participants in the various seminars at Royal Holloway, the University of Newcastle-upon-Tyne, University of Gothenburg and elsewhere in the UK and internationally, including annual conferences of the Royal Geographical Society (with the Institute of British Geographers) and the Association of American Geographers, where ideas contained in this book and the earlier papers from this project (Simon 2009, 2012) were presented. I am grateful for the invitations to present drafts of the latter paper at the 75th Anniversary Conference of the Council for Assisting Refugee Academics (CARA), 'In Defence of Learning: The Past and the Present', British Academy, London, 4 December 2008 and at 'Beyond Camps and Forced Labour: Current International Research on Survivors of Nazi Persecution', Imperial War Museum, London, 7–9 January 2009.

Ken Barlow at Zed Books found the manuscript of this unconventional and cross-disciplinary book – the evolution of which is explained in Chapter 1 – sufficiently engaging to add it to their comprehensive and progressive development studies list.

Finally, I owe a huge debt of gratitude for the support and forbearance of my wife, Sheryl, and sons, Jonathan and Dan, not least by tolerating frequent disappearances to my study during 'holiday' periods over recent years for intense bursts of writing.

TO HELL AND BACK – FOR MY GRANDPARENTS
VISIT TO AUSCHWITZ-BIRKENAU, 2 MARCH 1997

A very personal pilgrimage I've made
This sunny, warm spring day,
To the greatest living hell,
The biggest camp of death
This Earth has ever known.
Auschwitz-Birkenau.
The name emblazoned
On my mind –
Half a world away –
Since I was but a boy:
The place where young and old had died
By gun, torture, gallows, starvation, disease
    And Zyklon B,
In ones and twos,
Two thousand at a time.
Hans and Hilda Simon,
Erna and Rosa Stern
Among them,
Burnt to ashes too.

So how would I confront this,
The sheer enormity:
Two thousand at a time,
Twenty-four thousand in a day,
One point five million in all,
Or maybe one point four.
And yet among them
Four, five or several more,
The grandparents and great aunts
That I just never knew.
And yet,

And yet,
But for whose deaths among
The millions
I would not be living
At all or here right now.
Did they walk exhausted,
Full of fear and dread,
That late May day in '43,
Under the black iron arch
    Where 'Arbeit Macht Frei'?
Or did they disembark
Along the dreaded ramp
Beyond the red brick tower
Astride the railway line –
That special siding in Birkenau –
For selection:
    To left or right,
To slave or die,
Right from the cattle truck?

Would I find them –
Emaciated faces on the wall?
Their hair amid two tonnes?
Their spectacles perhaps?
A suitcase with a name on?
A toothbrush in the pile?
Some shoes among the millions?
Or pot or pan or shoebrush?
A shaving brush or two?
Did I want to?
    Yes!
    No!
and didn't know;
Perhaps I stood inside the gas chamber
    Yes!
    No!
(No Zyklon B today),
And the giant crematorium
Where they died,

Or walked upon their
    Ashes
Or smelt them in the air.
I do not know.
I never will.

But I came here
To grieve for them,
To walk the path with them,
Fifty-three years later
    – A flash and yet so long –
To say their names out softly,
Not barked in Nazi tongue.
I said the Kaddish
And lit a modest flame
At the end of The Line
Afront the basalt
    Memorial,
By the plaque in their native tongue
And let the tears fall.
I stood midway up That Siding,
Right by The Selection Hut.
    Alone.
I crossed Those Railway Tracks.
    And back.
A rabbit hopped the other way.

I turned and walked towards
    The Gate –
Tinged red by the setting sun –
So peaceful now, I thought.
For me The Gate stayed open,
What luck for their grandson!
And so I went back out
To join once more the living
And leave behind the dead

David Simon

1 | INTRODUCTION

Origins, Originality and Intellectual Context

This book represents the culmination of a 12-year-long endeavour initially intended as a short project funded by a small grant from the British Academy during a term's sabbatical leave from Royal Holloway in late 2006. The project arose out of my realisation, while editing the book *Fifty Key Thinkers on Development* (Simon 2006), that 10 of the luminaries selected for inclusion were child or young adult escapees from the Nazis. Although I had read and utilised some of their work, and had met three (Paul Streeten, Michael Cernea and John Friedmann) at conferences and seminars, I was unaware of this aspect of their past. The others included were Andre Gunder Frank, Alexander Gerschenkron, Gerry Helleiner, Albert Hirschman, Fritz Schumacher, Hans Singer and Eric Wolf, while an eleventh, Michael Lipton, was born in the UK to recent Nazi escapees. Several other figures who might have been included in the book but for my imperative to select as globally diverse a set of key thinkers as possible to avoid total Euro-American dominance, also shared this history.

I pondered whether the size of this group – which had been irrel-evant to their inclusion – could be purely down to chance or whether their childhood socialisation and wartime experiences may have influ-enced their subsequent career choices and professional trajectories. By extension and in consequence, might Holocaust escapees and survivors be somehow disproportionately numerous among the first generation of postwar development pioneers, just as many prominent medical, scientific and legal figures in Western Europe, North America and occasionally Australasia shared this history? The latter issue would be hard to demonstrate and a complex statistical challenge. However, the first question fascinated me and became the central research focus of the ensuing study and hence this book. It also had a particular personal resonance since I am the son of Holocaust refugees (and grandson of Birkenau gas chamber victims). I had, furthermore, been acutely aware of and discomfited by the discriminatory implementation of urban apartheid in my neighbourhood while growing up in Cape Town,

South Africa. During my childhood, I had also acquired a profound interest in environmental conservation and sustainability. Then, as a university student in that country and then the UK, I found a particular resonance in inter- and multidisciplinary engagement and subsequently gravitated increasingly into development–environment research and teaching. I will return to the issue of my own positionality later in this chapter on account of its importance to so complex and sensitive a topic (e.g. Herod 1999; Laurie 2010).

My initial intention was to use the small grant to undertake a limited set of interviews with the six living figures included in my book (Gerschenkron and Schumacher had died long before and Andre Gunder Frank and Hans Singer just months before my project commenced), a few other escapees and children of escapees/survivors, such as Immanuel Wallerstein, Thomas Weisskopf and Nicholas Stern, as well as other eminent development thinkers who might provide interesting insights and reflections on the framing and focus of my research, notably Gerry Meier, Piers Blaikie and Arturo Escobar. On this basis, I planned to publish a journal article or two as a modest contribution to the history of development. However, each of my interviewees and my own reading provided new leads and names. As a result of this snowballing, the interview process expanded and extended over a longer period than intended, while targeted archival research became appropriate to fill in particular wartime gaps, and a wider range of literature had to be consulted. I ultimately conducted some 33 interviews, including with spouses and children of deceased survivors/escapees on several continents (see below). The scope and depth of material far surpassed what could be included in the two papers I subsequently published (Simon 2009; 2012) and – prodded by the enthusiasm of many of my interviewees – I commenced writing this book.

For reasons explained in the Acknowledgements, however, its progress proved far slower and more interrupted than even I imagined. One possible consequence is that as the analysis and writing progressed, some shifts of emphasis inevitably occurred. The balance of content eventually evolved into the present chapter structure, which provides thematic coverage within a broad chronological frame. The logic is that a full analysis of the evidence and reflections of my interviewees in order to answer the main research question – as provided in the concluding chapter – requires an appreciation of each person's life story and contributions to his/her field. These have been grouped by category or key variable in order to facilitate teasing out the most salient similarities and differences in the conclusions to each chapter and the final chapter. These features include where and in what social context the subjects grew up; their ages and hence stages of formal education or early professional practice when they were forced to flee; the nature and geography of their wartime experiences of flight, refuge, internment and postwar settlement and rebuilding of lives; along with their subsequent chosen career trajectories and nature of their contributions to development.

As such, this book opens new vistas and also provides a situated ethnographic cohort biography of this distinctive group of people at the intersections between the intellectual histories of development studies and of social sciences, and Holocaust studies. The research utilised a unique opportunity in the narrow window when many in this cohort had, late in life, begun to talk and write about their traumatic pasts and while most were still broadly healthy. Inevitably, though, some key figures had already died – including the three mentioned above plus Heinz Arndt, Peter Bauer, Andre Gunder Frank, Wolfgang Stolper and Eric Wolf – while Gerry Meier and Albert Hirschman were too terminally ill to be interviewed. Fortunately, their autobiographical and other writing plus, in the case of Hirschman, earlier extensive interviews which I managed to obtain in published or transcript form, provided invaluable information on many aspects of my explorations. In other cases, I was able to interview relatives or former colleagues (see sample characteristics below). Fortunately, as a result, I could include these deceased figures fully in the study.

As revealed in the following pages, there are a few loosely comparable studies of key figures and high achievers in other disciplines or fields on other themes, not least their key contributions to their respective fields. However, this book is distinctive in assessing the formative contributions of an exceptional group of people – identified by their traumatic youthful experiences of the Holocaust – to the emergence of a new field of theory, policy and practice intended to make the world a better place, and in teasing out what role those formative traumas played in shaping their careers.

Indeed, the history and sociology of science and social science have become vibrant fields of enquiry, characterised by the deployment of research approaches and methodologies ranging from traditional narrative historical monographs and reflexive autobiographies to autobiographical hagiographies and critical 'archaeologies' based on discourse analysis and the deconstruction of key texts. This complex and innovative study involved a mixed-methods approach, including an extensive literature review and focused archival research centred around a large suite of in-depth interviews with a diverse group of Holocaust escapees and survivors who subsequently became influential figures in various elements of the emerging postwar field of ('international') development policy, practice and studies. In addition to the interview transcripts themselves, the interviewees' own corpus of professional, academic and sometimes autobiographical writing was also interrogated to provide further detail and additional insights.

Several notes of caution are nevertheless appropriate. First, the device of historical contextualisation is hardly original, being central to the (auto-)biographical genre. Moreover, seeking to discern and understand the influence of scholars' backgrounds and formative influences on the various aspects of their professional work has been a key normative challenge in the sociology of science since at least the work of Robert Merton (Merton 1973; 1979). Yet even the Holocaust, as a defining trauma and genocide of the mid-twentieth century and basis for identifying my study cohort, does not obscure the diverse contexts and experiences of my research subjects. Striking an appropriate balance between 'the big picture' and individual lifecourses, overwhelming odds and serendipity, structure and agency, and published sources versus new primary material proved challenging, and some variation within and between chapters will be evident according to the balance of available evidence and the desired emphasis. All of these issues emerged repeatedly in my interviews as well as the autobiographical writings of the cohort, and form a thread running through the book.

It would also have been easy to fill an entire chapter on diverse interpretations of the nature of the Holocaust and its broader implications as backdrop to my study and the ethical and moral compass which impelled some of my interviewees towards careers in development. Since this is not, however, the central focus of the study and the existing Holocaust literature is voluminous, I have restricted coverage to the most relevant aspects within Chapters 2, 3 and 4. The principal exception is the discussion of Zygmunt Bauman's (1989) seminal reinterpretation of the Holocaust as being fundamentally a product of German industrial modernity, which appears in Chapter 6 since it constitutes a key part of his oeuvre and contribution to the field.

Second, my interview sample was neither random (having been recruited through a combination of a priori knowledge, snowballing and secondary search) nor representative of the formative generation of development studies as a whole, since it was restricted to Holocaust survivors and escapees (and, in a few cases, their children who specialised in development) and further limited by those who were still alive (plus a few close relatives of key figures who had died). Third, inevitably, I cannot claim total inclusiveness of coverage. Although I have ultimately been able to include the vast majority of relevant people, a few potential interviewees have been omitted for various reasons and in relation to the criteria adopted, as explained in the overview of my sample later in this chapter.

Fourth, retrospective reflections from beyond the end of careers – even, or perhaps especially, by former leaders in a field – are inevitably susceptible to exaggeration, nostalgia for some sense of what may be caricatured as 'the good old days' on the one hand and a somewhat jaundiced view of the present and recent past as inferior by comparison (Simon 2009), perhaps also as having betrayed the original values and enthusiasms of their own youthful era. Regardless of whether they had already published autobiographical texts, some of my interviewees also implicitly regarded our threaded conversations as an opportunity to record or even embellish their own sense of their lives and contributions for posterity. As such I have been mindful of the extensive 'memory industry' surrounding histories of the Holocaust and in historical discourse more generally since the 1980s (see Klein 2000; Anderson 2001; and Saija 2017 for cogent reviews[1]), and I have sought to avoid adding to it.

Finally, as already alluded to, I have made no attempt to quantify the number of survivors and escapees who went into some aspect of development relative to other fields, be it the so-called 'caring professions' or beyond. That did not appear a valuable activity and was not an objective of the study, which has been concerned principally with the experiences and formative influences on this group's career choices, subsequent trajectories and achievements.

[1] There is also an intriguing discussion regarding the extent to which the 1904–7 Herero and Nama genocide in Namibia constituted a direct antecedent of the Holocaust (cf. Stone and Moses 2008; Olusoga and Erichsen 2010; Sarkin 2011; Zimmerer 2011; Kössler 2011, 2012). This is discussed in more detail in Chapter 3.

Nevertheless, the contribution of this group of former refugees to the evolution of development economics, in particular, has been immense. For instance, one of my interviewees, Kari Polanyi Levitt (daughter of Karl Polanyi and a naturalised Canadian) – herself just 10 when she arrived in London from Vienna as a refugee in 1934 – described Irma Adelman as 'probably the most serious of the American contributors … I mean, true, real American' to a book that she was working on at the time (interview, Kari Polanyi Levitt[i]). She was astonished when I pointed out that Adelman, another of my interviewees for this study, was a Romanian-born former refugee. This merely illustrates how well integrated many of the pioneering generation became in the USA and Canada – as predominantly immigrant societies – and thus far less conspicuously foreign than their counterparts in the UK, for instance. It also reflects the duration of their active careers, so that their early histories are now often forgotten or simply unknown unless they spoke or wrote autobiographically in their later years.

As already mentioned, both intellectually and practically, this cohort biography integrates elements of development studies, Holocaust studies and history of social science. Holocaust studies, broadly defined as encompassing any enquiry into the Holocaust and its causes and consequences, is filled with a substantial library of (auto)biographies of survivors and escapees in all walks of life, from ordinary people to literati and political and scientific leaders, such as Sir Hermann Bondi (1990) and the prominent international human rights lawyer, Thomas Buergenthal (2015), to name but two. Generally written late in life, as the authors overcame their fear of revisiting traumatic pasts and sought to reflect on their contributions to scientific or public life,[2] these books are most revealing of the extent to which the Holocaust shaped their lives. Until relatively recently, escapees and survivors active in development studies had not 'gone there', so to speak. Indeed, the earliest such autobiography encompassed by this study, by Heinz Arndt (1985), is notable for its complete omission of his youth and Holocaust experience. Focusing entirely on his subsequent professional life as an economist, the only mention of his origins is the opening sentence of the second paragraph, which states blandly,

---

[2] The so-called 'cultural' turn in social sciences probably played little role since it commenced after virtually all my interviewees had retired; besides, it has not influenced Economics, which is by far the most common discipline with this cohort.

When I arrived at Oxford in 1933, straight from school in Germany, it was suggested to me that 'Modern Greats' was closest to the sort of studies I had been contemplating before Hitler took over. (*ibid.*: 1)

This was partially corrected in an essay 12 years later (Arndt 1997) but it was left to his posthumous biographers to fill in some gaps. As will become evident in later chapters, several other subjects of this study wrote autobiographically or gave interviews for publication since the 1980s that covered autobiographical themes. However, the extent to which these address their childhood/youth and the impact of the Nazi era varies considerably. Equally, it is notable that, where subjects of this study appear in biographical dictionaries or compendia of economists, this key formative influence is almost never referred to. Even Paul Streeten's (2000b) autobiographical essay avoids explicit mention, referring only to the development of his social conscience as a result of growing up in interwar Vienna. (*ibid.*: 638). A notable exception is Scarlett Epstein's (2005) autobiographical monograph, which provides extensive detail of her childhood, living under Nazi occupation and her eventual flight from Vienna.

It is also important to understand that, notwithstanding their diversity of national and familial circumstances, one unifying contextual element in the background of most of this cohort is the almost pan-continental Germanic linguistic and cultural realm pervading interwar Central, Northern and parts of Eastern Europe as a legacy of the Austro-Hungarian Empire. This provided one important set of values absorbed by most assimilated, secular and modestly observant Jews, a category embracing most of my cohort, despite differences in mother tongue, national affiliation, class and the like. The historian Tony Judt's reflections on his own partially Jewish family's history in Eastern Europe provide a nuanced analysis of these issues and the associated intellectual currents (Judt with Snyder 2013: 12–31), aspects of which are echoed briefly by Paul Streeten's autobiographical essay (Streeten 2000b) and my interview with him in 2006 (see Chapter 2). Another of my research subjects, the anthropologist Eric Wolf and who, like Streeten, hailed from Vienna, captured the context particularly eloquently in the opening paragraph of his 'intellectual autobiography'. He simultaneously identified implicitly many of the roots of the rise of Nazism and the profound and traumatic rupture that it foreshadowed:

I was born in Vienna in 1923, at a time when the Hapsburg Empire had been dismantled and Austria had shrunk to a miserable remnant of its former glories, leaving the city as the hydrocephalic head of a dejected, economically depressed political unit. My father's family had been in Austria since about 1650, while my mother's family were Russians from the Ukraine, who, after participating in the 1905 revolution, were exiled first to France and then to the Mongol-Chinese-Russian borderland. My parents met when my father, an officer in the Austrian reserve army during World War I, was a prisoner of war in Siberia. He seized an opportunity to leave the barracks by volunteering to teach English (of which he knew very little) to my mother's brother, a Russian officer; rather than return to the camp, he made his way to the family home in Vladivostok. Both sides of my family were highly secularized Jews, and in my household it was the virtues of the Enlightenment that were extolled: the great German poets, morality without religion, progressive liberalism, playing the violin. In the Vienna of my childhood, violence and anti-Semitism became increasingly part of everyday life, but I also benefited enormously from the outstanding elementary school education that had been developed by the Socialists, who controlled the city government. (Wolf 2001: 1)

The field of endeavour that has come to be identified academically as development studies and its applied counterparts as development policy and practice is young – generally regarded as having been born through efforts to apply lessons from post-World War II reconstruction and development in Europe to problems of poverty, inequality and 'underdevelopment' in restless European colonies and former colonies of the global South, ideas in which postcolonial elites were often also invested (e.g. Simon and Dodds 1998; Engerman et al. 2003). However, there are other emphases. For instance, Staples (2006) focuses particularly on the role of key multilateral agencies established at the end of World War II – the World Bank, Food and Agriculture Organization and World Health Organization – in 'the birth of development'. However, Gilbert Rist (1997) regards two League of Nations' initiatives in the interwar years as more properly marking the birth of contemporary development. Several US historians have illuminated the central role of preoccupations with modernity and modernisation in the US during the interwar period, and their translation via key purposely established official committees and university centres into a strategic global mission that equated development with modernisation,[3] not least as a bulwark against communism and other anti-capitalist ideologies (e.g. Gilman 2003; Ekbladh 2010; Latham 2011; Engerman 2017). Several of the key figures in this study became engaged in these efforts to differing extents in the immediate postwar period (see Chapter 5). More broadly, Cowen and Shenton (1996) trace the intellectual origins of development much further back, to ecclesiastical notions of betterment and trusteeship for the poor in the eighteenth and early nineteenth centuries. Hans Singer, on the other hand, regarded Adam Smith as, in effect, the first development economist – because he believed in the possibility of progress – in a lineage that included Joseph Schumpeter, John Maynard Keynes and William Beveridge (Shaw 2002: 277).

Hence it is only relatively recently, prompted by the gradual demise of its founding generation and the profound crisis of identity, epistemology and purpose spawned by the sustainability debate, end of the Cold War, poststructural epistemological challenge and global justice/debt cancellation campaigns (collectively known as the 'development impasse'), that concern to document and assess the history and contribution of development studies from such critical perspectives has grown (e.g. Sachs 1992; Schuurman 1993; Escobar 1995; Streeten 1995; Cowen and Shenton 1996; Leys 1996; Rist 1997; 2001; Kössler 1998; Kothari 2005; Simon 2009; 2012).

This literature intersects with the (auto-)biographical genre of reflections on disciplinary evolution. Accordingly, the term 'development pioneers' in the sub-title of my paper in *Third World Quarterly*, which assesses just such perspectives by some of my interviewees (Simon 2009), deliberately echoes the title of a landmark book edited by Gerald Meier and Dudley Seers (1984) for the World Bank, which was a very early attempt at (re)assessment of the field. Interestingly, no fewer than three of the 10 authors who contributed essays to that volume, i.e. who were already regarded as pioneers in the early 1980s, were Holocaust survivors/escapees (Peter Bauer, Albert Hirschman and Hans Singer), although this shared history was not identified. All three have been included in this study. A potential fourth, Paul Rosenstein-Rodan, came to study in the UK just before the Nazi rise to power, and hence was excluded from my study (see below). The other pioneers were Colin

---

[3] This is also sometimes referred to as modernist developmentalism or modernisation-as-development (e.g. Simon 2003).

Clark, Arthur Lewis, Gunnar Myrdal, Raul Prebisch, Walt Rostow and Jan Tinbergen. The editors defined 'pioneering' in terms of their work having dominated development economics during the formative years of the late 1940s and 1950s and asked the contributors

> to reassess the main themes of their early work and to reconsider their assumptions, concepts, and policy prescriptions in relation to the way the course of development has proceeded since their pioneering days. Their individual chapters now recall the intellectual excitement, expectations, and activism of that unique period. (*ibid.*: jacket cover)

What does come through very strongly from my conversations with interviewees was precisely the heady atmosphere of postwar optimism, economic growth, altruism, commitment and belief that modern 'development' really did hold the potential to make a better world, free from the horrors of war and the injustice of poverty. Individual ideas and activities could make a real difference very rapidly. By contrast, today's environment for development is widely seen as crowded, bureaucratic in the extreme, endlessly complex, cynical and careerist and often filled with inertia and entrenched vested interests.

The history and sociology of science and social science, more broadly, have become vibrant fields of enquiry, characterised by the deployment of research approaches and methodologies ranging from traditional narrative historical monographs and reflexive autobiographies to auto-biographical hagiographies and critical 'archaeologies' based on discourse analysis and the deconstruction of key texts. A review of the field is beyond the scope of this book but Robert Merton's *The Sociology of Science: An Episodic Memoir* (Merton 1979) stands out as a comprehensive state-of-the-art review of the then 'emerging sociological specialty' in which he had by then been engaged for several decades (*ibid.*: 3).[4] He defined it as 'a paradigm for the sociology of knowledge' … with 'a focus on the interactions between the social structure and the cognitive structure of knowledge generally and of scientific knowledge as a specific, major case in point' (*ibid.*: 21), for which he set out to develop a conceptual framework. Of particular relevance here is the chapter on

---

4 I am grateful to Michael Cernea for drawing my attention to this landmark volume as we discussed finalisation of this text, and also to James Loeffler's (2018) new study, *Rooted Cosmopolitans: Jews and Human Rights in the Twentieth Century*, published after this book went to press, and which has interesting prosopographical and content-related intersections with it.

'The transfer of research procedures' (*ibid*.: 25–47), in which Merton surveys the evolution of the core approach of historical collective biography or prosopography (I prefer critical cohort biography) from the mid-nineteenth century, led by Francis Galton, Alphonse de Candolle, Alfred Odin and Havelock Ellis. This paralleled the evolution of quantitative and statistical analysis of outputs and trends within sociology, and Merton assesses at length the deep contestation over bringing them together in the then very recent heated debates over the *Dictionary of Scientific Biography*. Merton invokes Lawrence Stone's (1971) definition of prosopography as constituting:

> the investigation of the common background characteristics of a group of actors in history by means of a collective study of their lives. The method employed is to establish a universe to be studied, and then to ask a set of uniform questions ... The various types of information about the individuals in the universe are then juxtaposed and combined, and are examined for significant variables. (Merton 1979: 33)

This, then, constitutes a key part of the methodological tradition evident in this study, along with my training and experience in social anthropology and development studies.

A very different intellectual enterprise – perhaps best conceived of as fitting within the narrative historical tradition – but which also intersects with my study is the impressive multi-volume United Nations Intellectual History Project (UNIHP). Headed by Louis Emmerij, Richard Jolly and Thomas Weiss, this project sought – with a good measure of success – to explore the history of the UN system and its 'family' of specialist agencies while many of the key individuals who helped shape it were still alive. This is not so much a bureaucratic, institutional history as an attempt to record and understand the intellectual energies and trajectories with which these key individuals imbued the parts of the UN within which they worked. Altogether 73 extensive interviews were conducted, covering a distinctively wide range of nationalities, backgrounds and UN insertion points. Three of these people are shared with my study (Gerry Helleiner, Hans Singer and Paul Streeten), while several others were of European refugee backgrounds. Also shared with the present study is the strong evidence of the role of serendipity and that individuals make a difference, even within large institutions (Weiss et al. 2005).

The various volumes of the UNIHP are divided thematically or sectorally rather than by institution per se, but the presentation has a strongly historical narrative character, with extended interview excerpts or summaries forming the bulk of the text, which are integrated by means of very brief linking commentaries. The people-centred volume and the CD-ROM containing the full set of interview transcripts (Weiss et al. 2005) have provided valuable comparative sources for this study and enabled triangulation of interview content.

Harriet Zuckerman's (1977) cohort study of US Nobel laureates – a key exercise in prosopography closely influenced by Merton[5] – contains a particularly useful chapter for present purposes, comparing the socio-economic origins of 'American-reared Nobelists' with those of all members of the National Academy of Sciences and the scientific community at large. Zuckerman found that laureates-to-be had certain homogenising tendencies among themselves and which differentiated them from the wider population. This comparative approach, made possible by the shared national background, distinguishes it from my own single-group study within which – as will emerge later – there is considerable diversity. Zuckerman also notes the important contribution of Nazi émigrés to expanding the locally reared cohort, including eight (seven of them Jewish) who were already laureates on arrival in the USA but many more who would make their mark later (*ibid.*: 69–71). Importantly too, her evidence that Jews, who represented 3 per cent of the US population in the early 1970s, comprised 19 per cent of that country's Nobel laureates by 1972 enabled her to challenge the prevailing conventional wisdom that postwar US scientific prowess in terms of Nobel laureates depended heavily on Nazi émigrés (*ibid.*: 68–9).

The present enterprise is also somewhat different from Heather Newbold's (2000) set of commissioned autobiographical essays by eminent scientists who reflect – sometimes rather self-indulgently – on their life's work and its relevance to science and understanding the sustainability of spaceship earth. However, that book lacks any contextual matrix or other cement to link or help interpret the chapters, let alone to explore common ground or differences among the contributions. A similar recent enterprise is Haselsberger's (2017) collection of autobiographical accounts by leading planners, which has that discipline as common focus rather than sustainability. One

---

[5] Who was Zuckerman's doctoral supervisor and later her husband.

of the essays is by John Friedmann (2017), the only planner included within my study.[6] Saija's (2017) introductory essay on the use of autobiography as a research method provides some salutary reminders of the challenges and potential biases involved, as already mentioned above (see also Klein 2000; Anderson 2001).

One of the most interesting monographs on the evolving intellectual challenges and agendas of development economics – arguably the largest and best-resourced sub-field in development studies – is the *Biography of a Subject* by Gerry Meier (2005), drawing on his 50 years of engagement with it. I am not aware of any autobiographical writings by him and he was sadly too ill to be interviewed for my project, but this volume provides valuable insights into his thinking. Referring somewhat idealistically to development economists as having a role as 'trustees for the poor', he sketched his terrain in the following terms:

> Why are poor countries still poor? What can be done to remove their persistent poverty? Simply stated, these are the two fundamental questions confronting the trustees for the poor. As given by the subject of development economics, however, the answers are continually evolving. They are evolving on three levels – the theoretical, empirical and normative.
>
> My task is to interpret this evolution. In doing so, I look at the intellectual biographies of the trustees for the poor through the biography of their subject – the progress in their ideas for promoting development in poor countries. This may be best realized through an understanding of the core ideas for development, their translation into policy, and their consequences for development performance. (*ibid.*: 7)

In his schema, my concern is very much with leading lights of the first generation of development economists since World War II, namely those who led the field from roughly the 1950s to the 1970s but overlapped with the second generation (1970s–90s); we are now in the second decade of Meier's third generation (*ibid.*: vii).

Boundaries and Definitions

Development: Conceptualising and defining 'development' is complex and fraught, as evidenced by the vast literature generated over recent

[6] Fittingly, this was probably his final publication, which appeared just months before his death in June 2017.

decades. This reflects the diverse theoretical and ideological positions of protagonists as well as differences between academics, policy makers and practitioners, which in turn tend to reflect geographies of experience, time period and personal and/or institutional positionalities. Imposing a particular definition for a study such as this would be counterproductive, in view of the principal research question and the diversity of my research subjects. Instead, I have chosen to follow their self-identifications and attributions, where they have published or worked, and acceptance into the respective epistemic communities. This use of the plural form is deliberate, since there is no single or universal 'development community' but a diversity. Even the academic disciplines and specialist sub-disciplines tend to form distinct epistemic communities, with greater or lesser degrees of interaction with others. Over the last 20–30 years, for instance, development economics has become increasingly isolated from other disciplines, probably as a microcosm of how economics as a whole has evolved (see e.g. Simon 2009). There have also been extensive post-structural and postcolonial critiques and counter-critiques under the guise of anti- and post-development. Hence, 'development' here is used in the broadest sense of multidimensional positive change or progress, either autochthonous or externally derived, which can apply at different scales from the individual and household upwards. It follows, therefore, that development policy and practice are the formulation of frameworks for deliberate interventions and the implementation of such interventions respectively (cf. Kössler 1998; Simon 1998; 2006; Desai and Potter 2014; Ziai 2016).

Holocaust Escapees and Survivors: In this study, the term 'escapees' refers to people who managed to escape their countries of birth or residence by avoiding detention by the Nazis or their clients and its consequences, or who left voluntarily to escape the general repression and poisoned atmosphere, even though not (yet) under direct threat. 'Survivors' are those who were incarcerated and subsequently escaped, were released or survived until liberation. Implicit in the foregoing is that the term 'Holocaust' is used here to denote the entire Nazi era commencing with their election victory in Germany in January 1933 – the crucial watershed for this study for reasons explained in the next subsection – rather than the stricter sense of after the formal adoption of 'the Final Solution' as strategy by the Nazis.

The Appropriate Commencement Date for Inclusion in This Study: Defining precise boundaries to this study proved difficult because of the diversity of circumstances in which individuals found themselves as well as among the countries affected by Nazism and Italian Fascism. Altogether 33 potentially appropriate people were identified through a combination of literature search, key contacts and snowballing by interviewees. The group comprised twenty-two economists, five sociologists, two social anthropologists, one political economist, one planner, one agronomist and one psychologist (Table 1.1).

Following careful consideration and testing during early interviews, I ultimately resolved to use the Nazi ascent to power in Germany in January 1933, when Hitler became Chancellor, as the formal start of my focal period, since this provided the tipping point in terms of the risk of systematic arrest, persecution or worse versus other factors prompting emigration or decisions to study abroad. That said, the preceding years had already been characterised by rapidly increasing concern at rising anti-Semitism amidst the economic meltdown in Germany and the rise of fascism in Hungary, Romania and elsewhere. In consequence, emigration commenced in different directions and for different combinations of reasons, not least the dramatic political boundary changes (Frank 2009: 121, 129–30). Initially it was principally the cultural and intellectual elites and middle classes who felt most vulnerable or threatened, and left. For instance, the exodus from Hungary began soon after the end of World War I, ironically, as it later turned out, mainly towards Germany and Czechoslovakia, because of linguistic and cultural compatibility amid the ruins of the 'multi-centred world' that had been the Austro-Hungarian Empire, within which the Weimar Republic represented a vibrant hub of liberal and cultural creativity (*ibid.*: 121–3):

> Contrary to general belief, migrations were not limited to Jews
> suffering from the political and educational consequences of the White
> Terror in Hungary. Yet, Jewish migrations were a definitive pattern
> of the 1920s when the *numerus clausus*[7] law kept many of them out
> of university. The result of these migrations was the vulnerability of

---

[7] *Numerus clausus* and *numerus nullus* relate to the number of Jewish children permitted: the former had a clause specifying a quota, whereas the latter allowed none (*nullus*). See Chapters 2 and 4.

statelessness, or at least mental statelessness, the troubled existence of living long years without citizenship in a world built on nationality. Gentile Hungarians also left their country in considerable numbers in this era, for a variety of reasons. In subsequent years, many of them returned to Hungary. (*ibid.*: 130)

By contrast, the Hungarians living in Vienna apparently found it far more barren – 'disillusioned, uninspiring and lacking substance' (*ibid.*: 161), as evidence for which Frank quotes frustrated letters from Karl Polanyi (see Chapters 2 and 3) to his brother and mother in 1920. He evidently had a longstanding desire to move his newspaper to Berlin but this never came to fruition (*ibid.*: 161–2).

This broader context is extremely helpful, both in terms of understanding the consequences of the outcome of World War I on many parts of the former Austro-Hungarian Empire and in terms of the impacts initially not being focused exclusively on Jews, although they did suffer particular discrimination. Indeed, the severe economic recession and high unemployment among the urban workforce that triggered increased prejudice and anti-Semitism attest to the particularly modern dimensions of the war's legacy in terms of destruction of the Axis countries' industrialisation projects. As part of this process, several people who were subsequently to become significant figures in development left their home countries during the interwar period to study abroad, most commonly in the UK, often after an initial sojourn elsewhere on the Continent. Some, in turn, later moved to the USA.

With few exceptions (e.g. Albert Hirschman and Gerry Meier were too terminally ill to be interviewed, and Theodor Bergmann was identified by Reinhard Kössler as pertinent only shortly after his death in mid-2017, as this book was being finalised), those still alive and healthy were interviewed (two of them twice). In addition, close relatives and/or former colleagues of deceased figures were interviewed as key informants, namely the daughter-in-law and the biographer of Hans Singer (Odile Stamberger and Paul Shaw respectively); Sydel Silverman, the widow of Eric Wolf; Frances Stewart, a daughter of Sir Nicholas Kaldor; Tirril and Nigel Harris, respectively the step-daughter and son-in-law of Thomas Balogh; and Basil Yamey, the long-time collaborator and friend of Peter Bauer. As mentioned above, several former close colleagues or other authoritative commentators were also interviewed to gain their perspectives on the project's themes or particular individuals.

Following careful evaluation, several notable figures were ultimately excluded by the boundaries adopted for this study. Nicholas Kaldor, Thomas Balogh and Paul Rosenstein-Rodan did not fit the time frame. The first two had come to London from Budapest in 1928 and 1930 respectively, and Rosenstein-Rodan from Vienna in 1930, several years before the Nazis came to power, principally in order to pursue their studies or teach rather than to escape persecution.[8] Similarly, Wolf Ladejinski escaped Russia to the USA in 1922, after the Russian Revolution. Immanuel Wallerstein was born in the US after his parents emigrated there before the Nazis came to power, so he is classified as a commentator rather than survivor/escapee for purposes of this project. Brief profiles of these thinkers are provided in the next section to demonstrate the challenges of drawing a timeline boundary. Biographical sketches of these excluded figures (also mentioned in Table 1.1) are provided in the Appendix.

Detailed *relevant* information on Bert Hoselitz has unfortunately eluded me, even from discussions with several of his contemporaries or potential associates among my interviewees. However, a recent Wikipedia biography (Wikipedia 2017a) indicates that he does qualify for inclusion as he was politically active in the social democratic labour movement and fled immediately the Nazis occupied Austria. I also learned of Gustav Ranis' likely membership of this cohort only at the end of my interview process when the travel funds had been exhausted, and no appropriate autobiographical or biographical material could be traced on the basis of which still to in- or exclude him. One or two other names were suggested to me for consideration but they were deceased and no corroborating evidence was available.

Norbert Elias and Henri Tajfel were ultimately excluded on the grounds of marginality to development theory, policy and practice. Particularly in relation to Elias, this was a judgement with which some may disagree in view of the importance of his Ghanaian experience and his understanding of rural Ghanaians as a 'Naturvolk' to his world view and controversial comparative understandings of 'the civilisation process' (Elias 1939 [1969, 1976, 1994a]; 1994b; Goody 2002; 2003),

---

[8] Rosenstein-Rodan's essay in *Pioneers in Development* (Meier and Seers 1984) contains much interesting reflection on his entry into development, on his seminal 1943 paper on problems of industrialisation in Southern and Southeastern Europe that some people, including Michael Lipton (interview, Michael Lipton, Brighton, 11/10/06) cite as the dawn of development economics, and his subsequent publications, including the 'big push'.

to evolving modernisation theory and other development discourses. He was also one of the lecturers in British internment camps during 1940–41 (see Chapter 3), where he influenced the young Eric Wolf, for instance. Conversely, Zygmunt Bauman, another eminent sociologist, has been included because of the importance of his work on the Holocaust as an aberrant form of industrial modernity for the wider analysis.

Key Characteristics of the Sample

Following from the foregoing, the bulk of my analysis focuses on interviews with (or interviews and writings by or pertaining to) the 21 people whose names appear in bold in Table 1.1. Classification of the sample can be done on several cross-cutting variables, the first three of which are given in Table 1.1, namely their country and year of birth and main academic/practitioner disciplines. In addition, their family context (including degree of religious observance and political engagement), country/-ies of first asylum, higher education and ultimate residence are potentially significant in shaping their orientation, mode of professional engagement and *Weltanschauung* (world view).

TABLE 1.1 Key figures in the sample frame, by discipline and country, year of birth and (where relevant) year of death. Names in bold formed the basis of analysis; names with an asterisk are the children of escapees/survivors born subsequently and thus do not feature centrally in the study, although they may have been influenced indirectly to different extents by their parents' experience.

Economists
Fritz (EF) Schumacher (German, 1911–77)
Alexander Gerschenkron (Russian, 1904–78)
Hans Singer (German, 1910–2006)
Wolfgang Stolper (Austrian, 1913–2002)
Albert Hirschman (German, 1915–2012)
Heinz Arndt (German, 1915–2002)
Peter Bauer (Hungarian, 1915–2002)
Paul Streeten (Austrian, 1917–)
Kari Polanyi Levitt (Austrian, 1923–)
Shlomo Reutlinger (German, 1926–)
Irma Glicman-Adelman[9] (Romanian, 1930–2017)

---

[9] She was born Glicman but published professionally under her married name, Adelman; she requested that I use this double format in referring to her in this book.

Ernie Stern (German/Dutch, 1933–)
Gerry Helleiner (Austrian, 1936–)

Excluded from time frame
Wolf Ladejinski (Russian, 1899–1975)
Paul Rosenstein-Rodan (Polish/Austrian, 1902–85)
Thomas Balogh (Hungarian, 1905–85)
Nicholas Kaldor (Hungarian, 1908–86)

Excluded as children of emigrants/escapees
Michael Lipton (British, 1937–)★
Thomas Weisskopf (American, 1940–)★
Oded Stark (Israeli, 1944–)★
Lord Nicholas Stern (British, 1946–)★

Inadequate detailed information
Bert Hoselitz (Austrian, 1913–95)

Political economists
Andre Gunder Frank (German, 1929–2005)

Sociologists
Zygmunt Bauman (Polish, 1925–2017)
Michael Cernea (Romanian, 1931–)
Emanuel de Kadt (Dutch, 1933–)

Marginal to topic
Norbert Elias (German, 1897–1990)

Excluded as child of emigrants/escapees
Immanuel Wallerstein (American, 1930–)★

Social Anthropologists
Scarlett Epstein (Austrian, 1922–2014)
Eric Wolf (Austrian, 1923–99)

Planners
John Friedmann (Austrian, 1926–2017)

Agronomists
Theodor Bergmann (German, 1916–2017)

Psychologists
Marginal to topic
Henri Tajfel (Polish, 1919–82)

Year of birth is important in relation to their age at the time of the rise of Nazism and hence how much formal education they had received before their flight, as well as how nearly adult they were and hence the degree of awareness of, and potential active engagement with, public and political life they had. Familial context is also a crucial socialising influence, with most of the sample coming from middle- or upper-middle-class professional homes and the intellectual, political, educational and commercial elites. Although a few came from observant Jewish homes (and remain so today), the majority were highly assimilated and secular. In keeping with a fairly widespread custom of the early decades of the twentieth century, several Germans and Austrians had even been baptised (generally as Protestants) in the hope of gaining better social acceptance and cementing their perceived assimilation.

Country of birth is pertinent in terms of the nature and timing of the rise of fascism and Nazism and the degree of anti-Semitism and active persecution experienced. For instance, the *Anschluss* in 1938 was a sudden and crucial watershed for the Austrians, whereas in Germany, the heat was on from the minute the Nazis took power in 1933. At the other extreme, Michael Cernea managed to survive World War II inside Romania, albeit with some terrible experiences, including Romania's worst pogrom, and then attempted to contribute to building what he anticipated would be the bright new socialist world thereafter. The same applies to Zygmunt Bauman, who escaped Poland to Russia when the Nazis invaded, and enlisted there before returning to Warsaw after the armistice. It was ultimately the Communist purges and associated anti-Semitism in the late 1960s that drove them both out.

The UK (usually England) was the country of initial asylum for most of the refugees, although Hans Singer went first to Turkey, which welcomed refugee scholars as part of Atatürk's Westernisation/modernisation programme, and then to Cambridge to study under Keynes. The duration of their sojourns in the UK varied greatly, from just a few weeks in transit en route to Canada for Gerry Helleiner, then aged only three, to the rest of their lives, as for Scarlett Epstein (born Trude Grünwald). Emanuel de Kadt came to London to study at the London School of Economics (LSE) only after initially returning to his native Netherlands from Portugal, where his family saw out the war, but then stayed. For those who eventually moved on, mostly to North America (but in the case of Heinz Arndt to Australia), completion of secondary and/or higher education, with a taste of early career, was common. However, Paul Streeten left for the USA only in 1976, because his American wife preferred to live there. Hans Singer worked in the UK for some years before commencing a long career in the UN system in the USA, and then returned to the nascent Institute of Development Studies in Sussex, where he remained as fellow and then active emeritus fellow until his death in February 2006 at the age of 95. John Friedmann, Ernie Stern and Michael Cernea are representative of those who went straight to the USA from Europe, while Andre Gunder Frank and Wolfgang Stolper spent time in Switzerland before heading to the USA. Frank would later spend the second half of his life in Latin America and various parts of Europe in a highly mobile and often fraught existence. Irma Glicman-Adelman escaped from Romania to Palestine, later going to the USA to study but she stayed permanently. After wartime refuge in Russia, Zygmunt Bauman returned to Poland, and then fled to Israel in 1968 to escape anti-Semitic purges, before settling in the UK. Remarkably, Theodor Bergmann fled to Palestine in 1933, then moved back to Europe – to Czechoslovakia in 1935, before fleeing the Nazi annexation of the Sudetenland in 1938 and finding refuge in Sweden. He returned to Germany in 1946, just a year after the war ended , and remained there for the rest of his life.

Interestingly, not least in terms of the impact of their childhood experiences on their later *Weltanschauung* and professional orientations, with a predisposition towards critique and heterodox perspectives, several of the economists in my study frame (i.e. on both sides of the 1933 watershed and children of refugees) appear in the second edition of the *Biographical Dictionary of Dissenting Economists* (Arestis and Sawyer 2000), namely Balogh, Hirschman, Kaldor, Singer, Streeten and Weisskopf.

The Research and Analysis Process

Undertaking the interviews for this study presented intriguing challenges, even once appropriate candidates had been identified and approached, because the subject matter was both very personal and deeply traumatic. Indeed, this constituted a distinctive combination of researching a highly sensitive topic and elite interviewing (Lee 1993; Renzetti and Lee 1993; Arksey and Knight 1999; Herod 1999). Most interview studies involve professional researchers (academic or otherwise) interviewing 'ordinary' people who are usually in lower social strata and have less formal education and/or social power than the interviewers. Interviewing professional elites, and especially in this case, where some of the sample themselves have extensive interviewing experience, represents a relatively uncommon situation of balanced or even reversed power relations.

Except in the very few cases where this had already been revealed in autobiographical writing or by other key informants, I could not know in advance how each person had been personally affected by the rise of Nazism and the Holocaust and had dealt with the traumas over the intervening decades. I anticipated variations in response, since experience (see below) had taught me that some survivors/escapees were more willing and able to talk freely about this period than others. Indeed, I know several examples of camp survivors who 'buried' or suppressed it completely for most of their lives, and only began to 'go there' when prompted by high-profile Holocaust anniversary commemorations or direct questions by children or grandchildren. Indeed, one Auschwitz survivor I have known for many years progressed rapidly from five decades of silence to very reluctant speaker at his grandchild's school in a history class to becoming a guide in the Holocaust exhibition at the Sydney Jewish Museum.[10]

Both in the initial approaches, initially via email where possible, then followed up by phone, otherwise directly by phone) and during the interviews themselves, gaining their attention and confidence was vital. Responses were generally very positive, although a few sought clarification or expressed some hesitation. Nobody ultimately refused to be interviewed, although, as mentioned above, illness or unavailability within the relevant timeframe precluded three potential interviews. Interviews were largely unstructured but with a semi-structured element to ensure that I obtained the key biographical data and other details necessary for me to undertake the cohort analysis referred to in the previous section, and which inform many aspects of the unfolding storyline throughout the book.

Most of the interviews were undertaken between October 2006 and April 2007, with a few more added by April 2008. All were recorded with permission on an unobtrusive digital dictaphone/recorder, then transcribed by Jenny Lunn, my research assistant. I then edited them,

[10] There has been research on this and other psychological aspects of survivors'/ escapees' lives but that is beyond the scope of this study.

checking numerous unclear or ambiguous passages and in almost all cases, then corresponded with the interviewees to clarify points, obtain missing details and the like. Finally, interviewees were sent cleaned transcripts to check and approve. Most did so readily, though a few sought to made modest edits and one or two more substantial rewrites. These latter were then negotiated in order to retain the accuracy of the transcript rather than produce a publication. A couple of interviewees asked for and were given a copy of the recorded interview to share with their families.

Since my approach was qualitative, with the principal focus on the individual narratives rather than systematic quantitative or semantic comparisons of word strings and their frequencies of occurrence, I analysed the interview transcripts manually rather than by means of qualitative software such as NVivo. Later, draft chapter sections were then again shared with interviewees for checking and approval, and occasional filling in of missing details. Occasional disparities between an interview and written texts, or among different texts, were also discussed and resolved. Readers will see occasional notes about material discrepancies in footnotes later on. Negotiations were also occasioned in one or two cases where rewriting was requested to change emphasis or present things in a more formal sense than reflected in the interview discussion. Overall, therefore, while I am wholly responsible for the text of this book, my interviewees have been as fully consulted as possible in relation to coverage of them and are comfortable with my text.

My positionality proved crucial to the interview and interpretative process and hence merits explicit mention here. Having grown up as the child of Holocaust escapees, with both my parents having lost large parts of their respective families in the extermination camps, and knowing many others, including survivors of Auschwitz-Birkenau, Treblinka and elsewhere, played a role both in honing my desire to undertake the study and in establishing credibility with my interviewees. Moreover, the distinctive combination of my Jewish heritage and lifelong immersion in personal dimensions of the Holocaust legacy, so to speak, my professional status as a development specialist with social anthropological training and experience enabled me to establish empathy and build rapport with my interviewees over their traumatic pasts, to broach aspects, elicit details and sustain discussion of topics that might have been far more difficult for an 'outsider'. Indeed, most engaged fully and, in many cases, we spoke far longer than initially scheduled, covering a diverse range of interrelated topics. Many expressed their fascination with my questions and how we discussed them, admitting that they had never thought about the issues in this way or made such clear connections between their Holocaust experiences and later professional life. A few even revealed that they had never spoken as much about those traumatic years with anyone. Most were extremely modest, personable and delighted that, long after their retirement, someone should be so interested in their stories. For some, too, this represented their first or only autobiographical engagement. One or two also confessed later that their interview had stimulated them to talk or write about their life's story. Both during the interviews and for engaging with contemporary documentation and the relevant literature, my ability to speak and read German also proved invaluable.

Structure of the Book

The next chapter surveys the diverse childhoods of the study sample growing up in the various countries of interwar continental Europe later subjected to Nazism and Nazi rule from which they had to flee, namely Germany itself, Austria, Poland, Romania, Hungary and the Netherlands. Cross-cutting this national frame is an age-related assessment, since how old the subjects were when Nazism or Nazi rule dramatically affected their lives and then when they fled emerged from the start as a crucial variable, determining how far through the formal education system and/or early professional careers they had progressed and how extensive their socialisation had been.

The following two chapters address the research subjects' wartime experiences, comprising their circumstances of flight and becoming refugees, as well as their subsequent reception, treatment and how they lived out the war in the UK and in continental Europe and North America respectively. In Chapter 3, the ambiguities and ambivalences of the refugees' reception and treatment in the UK are analysed as backdrop to the supreme irony and very personal traumas bound up with the fate of German speakers being classified as 'enemy aliens' in 1940–41 and interned contentiously under circumstances of hardship within camps on the mainland, the Isle of Man and abroad. Along with those not interned, those later released made do as well as possible in often difficult personal and family circumstances in civilian life or military service in the Pioneer Corps.

Chapter 4 examines the great diversity of experiences and tracks of those who became refugees elsewhere in continental Europe or Palestine or survived the war in hiding. I was able to record or reconstruct astonishing and often emotive first-hand accounts of underground resistance fighting and regular soldiering, of internment in Bergen-Belsen and an eventual hostage swap, of flight as a child after the trauma of *Kristallnacht*[11] to transit camps and eventually a boat to Palestine, of surviving one of the worst pogroms in a small Romanian town to lying low in Bucharest, of dodging detention in the Netherlands to refuge in Portugal, and for a couple of fortunate younger refugees, relatively rapid transit across parts of Europe to secure a safe passage to the USA. By the end of the war, several others had reached there too.

In Chapter 5, attention shifts to how and where the adult escapees and survivors sought to come to terms with their lot and to rebuild their lives and restart or commence careers in the postwar period. Most eventually landed up in the USA after varying periods in the UK but one moved to Australia and one remained in the UK, while another returned there for a second career after one in UN agencies based in the US. A striking feature of this group is how adroitly they were able to use their education and experiences, including of wartime privations, to good effect just as vast new opportunities opened up in the formative years of the multilateral development agencies within and beyond the UN system, in the mushrooming university sector, and in nationalised industries and consultancy. The chapter is organised by career track, with some blending hybrid and geographically and sectorally fluid careers and others remaining in one line of work for the duration.

The postwar trajectories of the younger generation, who were but children or teenagers during the war, form the subject of Chapters 6 and 7. The former focuses on those who completed their tertiary education and pursued academic careers, mostly in the UK and USA, although two did so in newly socialist Central/Eastern Europe and then had to flee the anti-Semitic purges of the late 1960s. The latter chapter traces and assesses the careers and contributions of those who practised development within the ranks of multilateral agencies or as leading consultants, sometimes alternating with periods in academia.

---

[11] Today, in much relevant German discourse and writing, this name is avoided since it was the Nazi propaganda term and it has therefore been superseded by *Reichspogromnacht* (the night of the Reich's pogrom). I am grateful to Reinhart Kössler for this point. However, *Kristallnacht* is used here because it is the term used by my interviewees and in most of the Anglophone Holocaust Studies literature.

Finally, Chapter 8 integrates the various threads running through the narratives and critical assessments of them in order to arrive at a concluding analysis that answers as far as possible the research questions and fulfils the overarching objectives. What emerges is a fascinating tapestry of variegated complexity and texture, a blend of serendipity and steely determination, of overwhelming odds and individual agency, and of deliberate and almost coincidental entry into the emerging field of development for a variety of reasons. Some of these are indeed directly contingent on their wartime experiences, gratitude at having avoided the Holocaust, or religious and moral values but in other cases those apparently played little if any role.

Postscript

As this book neared publication, it emerged that Ignacy Sachs is also a member of the cohort covered by this book. The eminent ecosocioeconomist was a key organiser of the landmark UN Conference on the Human Environment in Stockholm in 1972 and the Conference on Environment and Development (UNCED) in Rio de Janeiro in June 1992. Born in Warsaw in 1927, he fled with his family in late 1939 and, after crossing Europe, landed in Brazil in 1940, where he completed his education and began working. Imbued with a similar socialist idealism, he and his young family relocated to Poland in 1954. While working at the Polish embassy in Delhi, he and his wife became possibly the first Europeans to obtain PhDs in India, at Jawaharlal Nehru University. Like Zygmunt Bauman and Michael Cernea, he was forced to flee again from the purges of 1968, since when he has lived and worked in Paris (see Vinaver, K. and Monteiro, M. (2019) 'Ignacy Sachs (1927–)' in Simon, D. (ed.) *Key Thinkers on Development*, 2nd edn. London and New York: Routledge, in press).

2 | EUROPEAN CHILDHOODS, NAZI RULE AND ESCAPE

In order to understand more fully the lives and contributions of the people featured in this study, it is necessary to appreciate where and how they grew up and were socialised into interwar Europe. This was a world of complex dynamics and rapid change, from the fallout of the demise of the Austro-Hungarian Empire and the World War I armistice burden imposed by the victorious Allies on Germany, to the impact of the Great Depression and hyperinflation that wiped out many middle-class and poorer families. Widespread impoverishment and a strong sense of injustice were the conditions so deliberately and successfully exploited by the Nazis to win power and forcibly extend their reach into neighbouring countries even before the outbreak of World War II. These features formed a clear backdrop to my interviewees' young lives, some-times linked to very personal experiences of victimisation, harassment and even attack directed at them individually or as part of organised pogroms and internments. At whatever degree of personal proximity or remove, such experiences left a strong mark on their psyches.

In what follows, I attempt to provide a loose schema for understanding these experiences. I also seek to strike a balance between the provision of adequate detail in order to appreciate the specific circumstances and personalities – where appropriate through the subjects' own voices – and commentaries and assessments to frame and compare these individual stories as a platform for subsequent chapters. The structure of this chapter reflects age-based differences, as well as distinguishing those who left north-Central Europe before the Nazi era from later emigrants and refugees, and highlighting country-specific issues where relevant.

With just two exceptions (**Fritz Schumacher** and **Wolfgang Stolper**), all my interviewees and the available (auto-)biographies – including of those who predeceased this study – described child-hoods quite typical of middle- or upper-middle-class professional Jewish and baptised families of Jewish origin in Northern and Central Europe during the interwar years. The large turn-of-the-century families had mostly already given way to smaller, more nuclear families and living arrangements, although elderly and widowed grandparents or an aunt or uncle sometimes shared the flat or house. The education ethic remained strong, as did professional aspirations among these highly assimilated modern communities, where women were often as well educated and qualified as men and double careers were no rarity. This applied especially in the larger cities like Berlin, Frankfurt, Vienna, Warsaw and Amsterdam, most of which were long-established seats of learning, formal 'culture', industry and colonial or imperial power, and where most of my sample grew up. Particularly in Germany, Jewish communities in smaller centres from where some hailed (**Hans Singer** and **Shlomo Reutlinger**) shared most of these characteristics, but elsewhere, especially in east-Central Europe (**Irma Glicman-Adelman, Zygmunt Bauman** and **Michael Cernea**), domestic arrangements were sometimes still more traditional. Parental careers included the medical, legal, business (all sizes and diverse sectors), educational, media and political fields.

Adult Émigrés during the Nazi Era (1933 Onwards)

Since the age at which people had to escape the Nazis has emerged in this study as a key variable explaining their experiences, it is important to distinguish here between those who had to flee as adults from those who were children or teenagers. The adults were direct targets for arrest and persecution in their own right, on account of political or other professional activities in addition to their Jewishness or Jewish origin, rather than more indirectly as adjuncts of their parents or other family members. Nine of my sample fell into this category, namely **Gerschenkron**, **Schumacher**, **Bergmann**, **Singer**, **Stolper**, **Arndt**, **Bauer**, **Hirschman** and **Streeten**. Since their stories have particular salience, they will be recounted in greater detail than those of the younger emigrants and refugees. Schumacher was distinctive in having no Jewish origins but a profound political and moral repugnance at Nazism and what it was doing to Germany.

Alexander Gerschenkron: Only three people in my study had to flee for their lives more than once under different regimes. One was Alexander Gerschenkron, the noted economist who was born in Odessa, then part of Russia, in 1904. After the Revolution, he fled to Vienna, only to have to escape rapidly from there within days of the Nazis' invasion in 1938. Whereas Paul Rosenstein-Rodan, born two years earlier, left Vienna for London as the clouds of Nazism were gathering (see above), Gerschenkron was the oldest person in my study to have had to flee twice from direct danger, this being the second such trauma by the time he had reached his mid-thirties.[1]

For this reason, because his family context and the successive cross-currents of history in which he became enmeshed are particularly interesting and since, as a result of his age, he was already well established in his career as an economist when he had to flee Vienna in 1938, his story bears telling in some detail. The following narrative also provides a broader context to the evolving situation in Vienna during the 1930s against which the experiences of the other Viennese members of my study cohort should be understood.

Both refugee experiences left their mark on the man, but the second even more than the first because he was fully adult and had family responsibilities. Gerschenkron was evidently a complex character, fond of obfuscating fact for a good or provocative tale, as his grandson recounts in his nuanced biography of 'Alex' or Shura, to use his family nickname:

> Sometimes two people would offer conflicting versions of the same Gerschenkron story. Often my grandfather turned out to be the source for both of them. When asked about his childhood, he might say that his father worked as a plant manager for a factory owner in Russia. Other times he would explain that his old man had operated an inherited family business – a huge bordello in Russia with six thousand women. It was a truly grand operation, the biggest bawdyhouse in Europe.
>
> ...
>
> When the Bolshevik revolution came, my grandfather was said to have fled by swimming an icy river with his father and then walking for hundreds of miles from Russia, through Romania, all the way to Vienna. He lived in the Austrian capital for eighteen years until the Nazi soldiers arrived from Germany. I heard various accounts of how he got out of the country. One claimed that he sped through a snowy pine forest into Switzerland on a BMW motorcycle under a hail of bullets with my grandmother hunkered down behind him on the bike, my infant mother in her arms. Another had him disguising himself as a Saint Bernard and trotting slowly past a row of Nazi sentries. (Dawidoff 2002: 19–20, also 236–8)

---

[1] As detailed later, the other two people who faced such double persecution, Zygmunt Bauman and Michael Cernea, both survived World War II in exile (ZB) or hiding (MC), and then had to flee Poland and Romania respectively during the Communist purges of the 1960s.

The Nazis reached Vienna in 1938, and the Gerschenkrons had settled there in 1920, some 3 years after the Russian Revolution, because the Bolsheviks had confiscated Paul's factory as the civil war ebbed and flowed and Paul had been caught paying dividends to minor shareholders in defiance of their policies. The story of Paul and Alexander's flight is indeed dramatic but they walked over the frozen Dniestr River to Romania rather than swimming (*ibid.*: 45–55) and were later joined by his mother and siblings.

While fleeing Russia aged 16 saved his life, he lost his country, familial and social context, language and sense of life and security:

> Whatever of his that wouldn't fit into a grain sack to be carried out of Odessa disappeared, along with most of his relatives. Whether it was Russian firing squads or Nazi death camps or the far-flung diaspora or just the daily hardship of life in the Soviet Union, by 1942 there weren't any more Gerschenkrons in Russia. (*ibid.*: 54)

But what do we know about the young man's character? Perhaps in consequence of this traumatic flight, to be repeated in 1938, the adult Alexander

> rarely spoke about his youth except to tell what were, in effect, more watermelon stories ... Later in life he set down some of his boyhood recollections and fashioned them into a memoir ... [his] descriptions of his adventures are often vivid, but what is most striking about the work is how much it doesn't explain. (*ibid.*: 28)

Nevertheless, Dawidoff's extensive chapter on Alex's youth in Odessa (*ibid.*: 24–55) provides some fascinating insights into a complex family life and the show-off that Alex became as a youngster. Like many others in this study, he attended the best, most elite, local school, in this case Odessa's Gymnasium. The family was certainly wealthy, owning a dacha and small estate outside Odessa; his father, Paul, was the manager of tobacco and match companies but 'a true Micawber – the lifelong victim of pecuniary liabilities to which he was unable to respond' (*ibid.*: 30).

Although Paul was Jewish, he married a Russian Orthodox woman, Sophie. They set little store by formal religion but both Alexander and his younger brother were circumcised and had a Barmitzvah out of deference to Paul's observant Jewish sisters:

> So Shura was the only Gerschenkron child with a true religious upbringing, albeit one that would confuse anybody. He was brought

up as a Russian Orthodox Christian by a pair of freethinkers who packed him off to the synagogue whenever his pious Jewish aunts came for a visit. Many people who have been exposed to a number of religions come to feel that the grain of all faiths amounts to the same thing – treating others with the kindness you would like them to extend to you. That was how the Gerschenkrons thought. They were enlightened humanists, far ahead of their time in Tsarist Russia, a notably bigoted country ... the unusual wealthy Russians of that time who were truly liberal, who sympathised with the workers and oppressed, dispatched their children to prisons to read to 'the little unfortunates' as Sophie called them, and made genuine friendships with people from lower classes ... Their personal ethics were also progressive. (*ibid.*: 34–5)

Alexander took time to acclimatise in Vienna, where he struggled in the very different environment to finish his Gymnasium education in German but eventually succeeded eminently in 1924. He also spent considerable periods alone, including hiking during the school holidays, and during the final year, fell in love with Erica Matschnigg, the woman he was later to marry, although she did not initially seem interested in him. When, after the end of Gymnasium, she showed a little interest, he switched his plans to study economics in Paris, enrolling instead in the school of *Nationalökonomie* in Vienna in autumn 1924 (*ibid.*: 74–81).

His decision to study economics had come as what Dawidoff describes as a 'Eureka! Moment' when he perused one of his father's economics texts in the summer of 1924 while frustratedly wiling away the time during Erica's absence (*ibid.*: 81) and because 'the job seemed to bear directly on questions of human happiness and human progress' (*ibid.*: 153). Already during his time at the university, anti-Semitism and discrimination, often violent, were increasing amid a tide of poverty, unemployment and political intolerance. The descent of the university, until recently one of the intellectual pinnacles of Europe, like the decline in the calibre of economics as taught there, is very clearly portrayed, partly through Gerschenkron's eyes, by Dawidoff (*ibid.*: 84–90).

Gerschenkron graduated in 1928, his thesis on the Austrian party system and democratic crisis winning praise from the examiners. Right after the graduation party thrown by his parents, he and the pregnant Erica went secretly to a civil registry office and got married. He then held down a succession of jobs in commerce, with some teaching and a difficult spell in politics with the Social Democrats from 1931 to 1934 as the tide of fascism and anti-Semitism increased. His political involvement originated as a protest at the suppression of democracy by the dictator, Dolfuss (*ibid.*: 84–90).

The ascent of Nazism affected every aspect of life in Vienna more and more through the 1930s, and Alexander Gerschenkron had to take what employment he could, generally in fields unrelated to his formal training. As explained above, his experience and then escape bear recounting in some detail from his biography:

> Through all of this time, he had very little sense of being what he was, a professional economist, and he wasn't alone. A second generation of exceptional Austrian economists emerged during the interwar years. They were highly creative, liberal of mind if not always liberal-minded, and some of them were Jewish – all reasons for which Friedrich von Hayek, Oskar Morgenstern, Gerhard Tintner, Gottfried von Harberler, Paul Rosenstein-Rodan, Fritz Machlup, and Karl Schlesinger, among others, were, like Shura, consigned to the intellectual penumbra. This being Vienna, however, persecution begat inspiration. The liberal Austrian economists met informally in coffeehouses and office spaces around the city, and the most dynamic of these small groups – Ludwig von Mises's Society for Political Economy, Karl Menger's Mathematical Colloquium, and Hayek's Institute for Business Cycle Research – became the economics equivalents to the Vienna Circle. (*ibid.*: 105–6)

Given his Jewish background, the Nazi persecution affected Gerschenkron increasingly personally:

> Beyond the physical terror they inflicted, the open drain of propaganda emptying into Vienna revealed a parallel Nazi gift for emotional intimidation. Hitler's views about blood reduced Shura's existence to a basic issue: was he what he thought he was? Before renouncing religion, all his religious life he had lived and worshipped as a Christian. To the Nazis, that made him even worse than a mere Jew. As the Russian-born son of a Jewish father, Shura was not only a *Judenfresser*, a devouring Jew,[2] but he was also stateless, a *Staatenloser*,

---

[2] This seems to be a mistranslation, since *Judenfresser* means a Jew devourer, whereas a devouring Jew would be a *FresserJuden*. Which way round this was intended is unclear, but the implication remains evident.

in the pitiless German. After all the years of immersing himself in the culture of his second country, there was nothing legitimately Austrian about him. He was no more than a wandering Russian Jew, and, for implying otherwise, a charlatan. (*ibid.*: 109)

Gerschenkron's younger daughter, Heidi, recalled the self-doubt that this caused in him. In addition, he grew increasingly anxious that his children were being endangered through him. Even before the Nazi invasion in March 1938, he realised the need to escape Austria and applied for travel documents. His younger brother and his girlfriend escaped to England on a train just days before the invasion but Gerschenkron's papers never materialised. Within days of the invasion, with the help of non-Jewish friends and associates, Gerschenkron's wife, Erica, and elder daughter, Susi (then nine), were accompanied on the train to Zurich using the doctored passport of a similar-aged child; the five-month old Heidi was taken by a Dutch priest (the husband of one of Erica's school friends) to Rotterdam using his own infant's passport; and then, dodging Gestapo raids in Vienna, Alexander escaped over the Swiss border on skis accompanied by one of his own school friends who had by then become a Nazi but who regarded their friendship as more important than politics. For the actual border crossing, Alexander was disguised as a Swiss salt miner sitting in a trolley, itself risky and nearly leading to detection (*ibid.*: 109–14).

Gerschenkron was reunited with Erica and Susi in Zurich, from where they travelled immediately to Britain to his parents, who had been living in Letchworth in Hertfordshire, north of London, since 1934. It took a few months to get Heidi to England, by which stage Alexander had already left for a job at the University of California at Berkeley provided by the American economist, Charles Gurlick, whom he had assisted on a research project in Vienna the previous year. After the 1938/9 academic year, he returned to his family in England but, with all of Europe at war, there was no prospect of a rapid return to Austria, so he took his family via New York to California, where they saw out the war and Alexander established his academic career (*ibid.*: 114–20). It was also where he first met and worked with **Albert Hirschman** (see Chapter 4; Adelman 2013: 205); their lives would have several parallels and intersections.

Fritz Schumacher: Ernst Friedrich (Fritz) Schumacher was born in Bonn on 16 August 1911 into a long-established Christian family which had played a civic role in Bremen from the fourteenth century, but Fritz's grandfather had served as German ambassador to Colombia and then consul in New York during the late nineteenth century. His two sons were sent to school in Bremen when he became ambassador to Peru in 1882, making them feel like orphans. The older boy, Hermann, was very bright, single-minded and authoritarian, and became an economics professor aged 31. After spells in Cologne and Columbia University in New York, he was appointed to Bonn University, from where he moved to Berlin University in 1917, just as his son, Fritz, began his schooling. The father was a well-regarded and conscientious teacher, who took a great interest in his students. Around this time, the financial hardships of World War I increased in severity and the family took in some students as lodgers to help the household budget – including Thomas Balogh (Wood 1985: 1–17), as mentioned above.

The food shortages and associated privations had a profound effect on the young Fritz (*ibid.*: 8) – something that was later to contribute to his world view and professional commitment to 'economics as if people mattered'. Over the succeeding years, he and his siblings also experienced the hyperinflation, being 'sent out to join the food queues for food, their shopping bags bulging with paper money which took up more space than the few essential which they hoped to buy. They were always afraid that prices would have been put up before their turn had come' (*ibid.*: 10). At the same time, Fritz was also exposed to high political economics since his father was part of an inner circle on government economic policy, including the decisive intervention to end the hyperinflation by replacing one billion old marks with the Reichsmark on 23 November 1923.

Fritz was urbane, congenial and extremely bright, often finding schoolwork boring, so he devoted much time to acting and writing plays. To his relief, he finished Gymnasium in 1929 but felt unfulfilled, as he recorded in a letter to his sister and a subsequent book. That autumn he commenced his studies in law and economics at Bonn University, playing much tennis and having to attend some 25 hours of lectures each week. 'Unlike most people of his age it was intellectual freedom rather than freedom from the restrictions of family and childhood that he wanted' (*ibid.*: 14). He was most impressed by the leading economics professor, Joseph Schumpeter – who also subsequently taught **Hans Singer** (see below).

He spent the first term of his second year in London, having learnt English intensively beforehand. This experience also proved formative, from attending lectures at the London School of Economics (LSE) to meeting John Maynard Keynes, another world-famous economist, and receiving a much sought-after invitation to attend the latter's economics seminars in Cambridge. He disliked much of what he experienced by way of English culture and urban life. He also found it quite disturbing to see war memorials commemorating the recent victory over Germany and local people's respect for them, and to experience their anti-German sentiments without any understanding of the postwar privations visited upon the German people by the Treaty of Versailles. He also experienced the first bout of health problems that would, in one form or another, remain with him for decades. Back in Berlin for Christmas, Fritz applied for and was awarded one of the first post-World War I Rhodes Scholarships to study at Oxford, where he moved in September 1930, having spent the intervening two terms at Berlin University (*ibid.*: 14–23).[3]

He spent two years at Oxford, an experience about which he felt remarkably negative both at the time and subsequently, on account of having to study and sit exams on a fairly general syllabus rather than focusing on what he saw as the crucial issues in contemporary economics. He also disliked the tutorial system, student mores, cultural traits he found difficult to adapt to, the cuisine and the male clubbishness that he experienced. His efforts to promote Anglo-German understanding – something very much in line with Cecil John Rhodes' ethos – extended to becoming secretary and then president of the university's German club. In that role, he became embroiled in an attempted take-over by a group of Nazi sympathisers, and although the move was defeated, it left a bad taste and he soon handed over before becoming involved in another international affairs club (*ibid.*: 24–36). The intervening summer he utilised to gain practical experience of different parts of banking operations at MM Warburg in Hamburg. This he relished and,

> It was also a lesson which held one of the keys to the rest of Fritz's life. He discovered that there is no substitute for practical experience. Gradually this unshakeable opinion hardened into a degree of contempt for academics. Fritz believed that academic training without

[3] Unfortunately, his entry in the *Register of Rhodes Scholars 1903–1995* provides no biographical details beyond his name, that he was elected from the German constituency and was a member of New College, and died on 4 September 1977 (Evans 1996: 66).

practical experience was generally valueless. To him, 'knowledge' incorporated experience of the real world. (*ibid.*: 36)

He applied for and was awarded a third year of Rhodes Scholarship funding (1932/3) to study the workings of the New York money market while based at Columbia University. That year was one of the most enjoyable of his life to date, and a dramatic contrast to his British experience. This had less to do with student life than with the social life and access to influential people he had through introductions by his father. He extended his stay for a second year after being invited to present a course of lectures and seminars at the university's School of Banking – a rare honour for someone at his stage of life (*ibid.*: 41–53).

Schumacher also remained convinced that Germany was misunderstood abroad but was greatly troubled by the rise of Nazism, trying vainly, like his father, to believe that good could come of it. He felt isolated from Europe in the USA due to the lack of press coverage and deliberate vagueness in his father's letters beyond urging Fritz not to take sides. However, Hitler's appointment as Chancellor by Hindenburg in January 1933 and what followed immediately did increasingly call into question his patriotic Germanness and made defending Germany in the USA as well as his own decision about whether to return to Germany far more complex and difficult. However, it took another two years for Fritz – by then back in Berlin and doing very well professionally – to appreciate the impossibility of being a 'good German' under Hitler (*ibid.*: 54–62). Following his return in April 1934 and consequent realisation how bad the situation had become, his father urged him to join an appropriate Nazi organisation if he were to have any future, but he resolutely refused. 'In particular, it was interference in the pursuit of truth that Fritz found intolerable, evil and not to be countenanced' (*ibid.*: 63); he also grappled with 'the dilemma of whether one could lead a moral life within an immoral system without compromise' (*ibid.*: 65).

Shortly after his return, amid his turmoil in relation to Germany, he met Anna Maria Petersen (Muschi), the woman he would later marry in October 1936. He then found work as a translator for a visiting English delegation attending a conference on prisons in 1935. This group included two leading figures in the field, Harold Scott and Alexander Paterson, who would become crucial in helping him find employment after his arrival in England a few years later (see Chapter 3). He then worked with a group of friends for a barter syndicate among major exporters and industries in Germany, affording him an intimate insider's perspective on contemporary trade problems. One by one, the group was diminished as members left the country. He also left his elite club in protest at its increasing anti-Semitism. His despair at what was happening in the country deepened and he eventually realised that the only solution was to leave, which Fritz and then Muschi did in early 1937, heading to London:

> Neither set of parents understood the real issue: that Fritz felt he had to leave Germany because of the evil presence of Hitler. Fritz was already certain that Hitler's policies would inevitably lead to war. In the next year both parents came to believe this too, but it did not occur to them that Fritz would not fight for Germany in such a war. For them [like many other non-Nazi Germans] it would become a question of the defence of the Fatherland, irrespective of Hitler. They could not understand that for Fritz the Fatherland no longer existed; and that he believed it could not exist again until the blight of Hitler had been removed. (*ibid.*: 87)

Theodor Bergmann: Born in Berlin as the seventh child of a Reform rabbi, Julius Jehuda Bergmann and his wife Hedwig on 7 March 1916, the mid-point of World War I, Theodor Bergmann had an observant Jewish upbringing in an upper-middle-class family. They lived in a five-storey apartment block typical of central Berlin, with the Tiergarten and zoo as the main nearby recreational areas. His earliest memories dated from the very early 1920s, characterised by food shortages, heating with low-grade peat, inflation and revolutionary unrest (Bergmann 2016: 9). Like many of his cohort, including others covered in this study, he was taken up with the spirit of the time and became politically conscious and active at an early age, joining the Jungspartakusbund (Young Spartacus Union) and Sozialistischer Schülerbund (Socialist Scholars' Union) as a mere 11-year-old. In 1929, around the time of his Barmitzvah, the Jewish religious threshold of adulthood, he joined the Communist movement. His interpretation of Judaic principles of justice and care for the poor no doubt led him, however, to the youth wing of the newly formed Communist Party of Germany Opposition (KPD-O) rather than the Stalinist rump of the Communist Party of Germany (KPD). He was to remain a critical Marxist with an acute sense of justice all his life (*ibid.*: 8–30; Kessler 2017; Wikipedia 2017b).

The rising tide of national socialist sympathy landed him in trouble the same year, being expelled from the Mommsen Gymnasium for a critical article in the *Schulkampf* left-wing student magazine. He transferred to the Köllnische Gymnasium, where he had many classmates from working-class backgrounds and influential teachers who impressed on him 'that the fight to defend Weimar democracy and the struggle against social injustice must be brought together' (Kessler 2017). Once Hitler had come to power, his student activism forced him into exile on his seventeenth birthday and just five days after completing his *Abitur* (final secondary school exams) in 1933 and four days after his grandmother's death. Nazi crowds mobbed mourners at her funeral, singing and chanting. After two years working on Kibbutz Geva in Palestine, which stimulated his enthusiasm for agriculture and agronomy, and refusing to become embroiled in the growing conflict with Arabs/Palestinians, he returned to Europe in early 1936. He then commenced his studies in agronomy in the Agricultural Department of the German Technical University in Tetschen-Liebward (now Děčín) in northern Czechoslovakia. He used this as a base for smuggling and distributing political leaflets to his KPDO comrades across the nearby border into Germany until having to flee once more – this time to Sweden – following the Munich Agreement and annexation of the Sudetenland (which included that part of Czechoslovakia) in 1938 (Bauer 2017; Kessler 2017; Wikipedia 2017b).

Albert Hirschman: The most comprehensive accounts of Albert Hirschman's early life are provided in the Shoah Foundation interview that he gave to Marlene Glassman in January 1996 (Hirschman 1996, Tapes 1 and 2), in a published interview (Hirschman 2001 [1998]: 45–110)[4] and Jeremy Adelman's (2013) monumental biography, on which this summary is based.

His father's family had emigrated to New York City at the turn of the twentieth century, when his father, Carl (born in 1880) was a young man, but he returned to study surgery in Berlin, which was a world-leading centre in that field at the time. He remained there permanently, later specialising in brain surgery and marrying Hedwig Marcuse (also born in 1880 into a large Jewish family). Born on 7 April

---

4 The interview was conducted and originally published in Italian but Hirschman later translated it into English for inclusion in this partially autobiographical book.

1915, Otto Albert Hirschmann, as he was registered, was the middle of three children, his two sisters, Ursula and Eva Estella being born in 1913 and 1920 respectively. He was named for Otto von Bismarck, as his scheduled birth date coincided with the centenary of the great Prussian leader's birth on 1 April, but he arrived a few days late. During his time with the French resistance during World War II, he reversed the order of his given names and that, along with the dropping of the Germanic second 'n' from his surname became legally binding when he was subsequently naturalised in the USA (Hirschman 1996, Tape 1; Adelman 2013: 187; see also Chapter 4).

In terms of religious affiliation, all three children were baptised soon after birth as an act of assimilation in an effort to enhance the children's prospects. Albert records that his mother's non-Jewish friends were influential in this regard, perhaps on account of the family's strongly Jewish surname. There was some debate over whether to have the children confirmed but Albert's was postponed as he had by then become interested in Buddhism. According to Albert's interview, despite being highly secular and assimilated Jews, their parents were never baptised, although Adelman (2013: 24) is less certain. The family celebrated Christmas rather than Chanukah, with a large family gathering on Christmas Eve. Albert has no recollection of ever attending a synagogue (Hirschman 1996, Tape 1; Adelman 2013: 21–6). Although there is no autobiographical record of how Albert felt about this issue at the time, Adelman (2013: 25) reveals correspondence between Albert and his daughter in 1982 in which he admits to ambivalence and ambiguities as between elements of Jewish and Christian belief.

The young Albert had a close relationship with his father but, due to his heavy professional commitments, they spent little time together apart from during holidays. However, Carl enjoyed reading to the children and loved literature, even being able to recite Faust by heart. His mother had a strong interest in art, which she had studied. The family often visited museums and attended concerts. They lived centrally in Berlin, at 21 Hohenzollern St (now Hiroshimaweg), near the Tiergarten. Albert's father died of cancer or an associated operation in late March 1933, shortly after the Nazis took power, whereupon Albert and Ursula left the country quickly on account of their political activities and religious background. Only decades later did Albert learn that, even as his father was dying of cancer, he was hiding fugitives from the Nazis in his clinic (Adelman and Loyer 2010: 13). Their mother and younger sister remained in Berlin until able to depart for the UK in late 1933. In the interim, their mother ran a 'lunch table' (equivalent of today's soup kitchen) for Jewish families who had been made destitute through enforced unemployment (Hirschman 1996, Tape 1; 1998: 45–9).

For the first three years of schooling, Albert and Ursula had attended a private school run by a friend of their mother's. Albert spent the final nine years of his school career at the state-run Französische Gymnasium, completing his *Abitur* in the spring of 1932 aged 16, two years ahead of the norm (Hirschman 1996, Tape 1). This is where he learnt the fluent French that was to stand him in such good stead during World War II (see Chapter 4). He then spent the 1932/3 academic year studying law and economics at the (Humboldt) University of Berlin – then the Friedrich-Wilhelm-Universität – before having to escape Germany, as explained above (Hirschman 1996, Tape 2; 1998: 45–9; Adelman 2013: 53–6).[5]

Hirschman recalled clearly how, following the Nazi party's election gains in September 1930, their flags appeared throughout the city and tension increased. Although his family had traditionally supported 'bourgeois' democratic parties, he and Ursula sought to help the anti-Nazi cause and joined the *Sozialistische Arbeiter Jugend* (Socialist Worker Youth) in 1931. In the interview, he provided details of their activities, early arrests and detentions and, after he had left Germany on 2 or 3 April 1933 for Paris via Amsterdam, reports from his associates of internment of Nazi opponents in concentration camps. His final night in Berlin was very difficult, not least because he had to leave his mother and sisters behind (though Ursula would follow three months later) shortly after their father's death, but the situation was very bad and, although he cannot recall his precise feelings, he knew that an era had ended and that his future would have to lie elsewhere (Hirschman 1996, Tape 2; 1998: 55).

Finishing *Abitur* two years 'early' attests to Hirschman's academic prowess. Another incident recounted in a partially autobiographical book amplifies this point: aged 12 or 13 he plied his father with political and

---

5 Although not really a contradiction of the Shoah Foundation interview, in the published interview (Hirschman 2001 [1998]: 46) he puts a somewhat different complexion on his reasons for leaving: 'I must say that it was the coincidence of his [my father's] death with the anti-democratic and anti-Semitic persecutions that made me decide to leave Germany and to go to France'.

semi-religious questions, some of which the latter was unable to answer. On one particular day, this inability led Albert to be amazed at his father's evident lack of global perspective or world view (*Weltanschauung*), which he immediately reported to Ursula. Retrospectively, Hirschman ponders poignantly why he recalls this moment so clearly – precocious arrogance, instant mortification at the ridiculousness of his exclamation, or uncertainty as to whether not always having clear answers is so bad (Hirschman 1995: 111–12; 1998: 56)?

Hirschman spent the next two years in Paris, mainly among the many German and then other European socialist and communist émigrés, building up networks on the basis of political and familial contacts. His sister, Ursula, had several romances with members of this circle, before in December 1935 marrying Eugenio Colorni, an intellectually engaging and action-oriented Italian anti-fascist with whom Albert and Ursula had worked politically in Berlin. They moved to Italy to continue his political work and Albert would later join them. In Paris, Albert read widely and earned money by teaching German. He became increasingly disillusioned with Marxism over time, as he pondered and debated the fate of the highly organised socialist and communist workers' movement in Germany once Hitler took power, the brutal purges in Stalin's Russia and the ideological circularity of debate among the émigrés in Paris. He was often lonely and found his studies at the École des hautes études commerciales de Paris tedious, not least because he did not intend pursuing a career in business (Hirschman 1998: 58; Adelman 2013: 85–118).

Hence, he snapped up the opportunity of a fellowship to spend the 1935/6 academic year at the London School of Economics (LSE), which he retrospectively regarded as 'decisive' for his formal education and understanding of economics. He attended lectures by Lionel Robbins and Friedrich von Hayek but was also taken with the impact of Keynes and joined the growing group of young German and Hungarian enthusiasts, including Abba Lerner and presumably Thomas Balogh and Nicholas Kaldor, although neither of these is mentioned by name. Albert also met Piero Sraffa, Colorni's cousin, at Cambridge, who was then editing David Ricardo's works. Hirschman's main focus was a research project on the French economic reforms of the 1920s, supervised by Barrett Whale and which he later developed into his doctoral dissertation at Trieste University from 1936 (Hirschman 1998: 59–60; Adelman 2013: 119–28).

In the interim, he returned briefly to Paris, experiencing emotionally difficult times as a result of his uncertainty over how to take his career forward. Although not explicitly linked in his own words, this may have played a role in his decision to enlist for the Republican side shortly after the outbreak of the Spanish Civil War: 'I realized that fascism was advancing and that I could not just sit and look on ... so, when I felt that there was the possibility of doing something I seized the opportunity' (Hirschman 1998: 61). After basic training, he saw action for several months, before leaving after growing disillusioned by the way his unit in Catalonia had been taken over by the doctrinaire Communist party. He then travelled straight from Barcelona to join his sister and Colorni in Trieste in their anti-fascist work, ironically without hindrance, on his German passport issued before he fled Berlin. He worked as a university assistant and also completed his PhD (*ibid.*: 61–7; Adelman 2013: 129–37).

Hirschman's biographer, Jeremy Adelman, notes that the fighting in Spain had a strong effect on him, with the combination of harrowing experiences and the ideological disillusionment making him reticent to talk about that period, even to his wife, Sarah (Adelman 2013: 133–5). Adelman (*ibid.*: 119–20) also summarises the years 1935–38, which had great importance for his emerging identity and orientation, somewhat floridly as being

> pendular years. Hirschmann swung between countries and languages, as well as from esoteric reading to self-sacrificing struggle, from homme de lettres to man of action, suggesting an erratic, reactive, or unpremeditated quality to his moves ... there was a great deal of restlessness to his decisions ... and the volatility of European popular fronts and their right-wing foes account for part of Hirschmann's swings as he moved around the continent searching for new coordinates. But he was not just reacting to external shifts. His personal will was at stake as well ... it is not easy to figure out what was going on in his mind as his road kept forking. This is largely because keeping these two Hirschmanns, the combatant and the thinker, in the same frame runs up against the dearth of sources.

Hans Singer: Hans Wolfgang Singer was born into a mainly secular and highly assimilated Jewish professional middle-class family on 29 November 1910 and obtained a robust classical education at the local Gymnasium. He had two younger brothers, one of whom was retarded and died young. They lived in Elberfeld (now within Wuppertal), Germany, as what Singer liked to call 'a [Jewish] minority within a [Protestant] minority within a [Catholic] minority' (Shaw 2002: 3; UNIHP 2007: Singer: 28–33). It also lay within the French sector of the post-World War I demilitarised zone; as a medical doctor, Singer's father had served with the German forces during the war, during which time his health suffered badly.[6]

His father and the local rabbi, Dr Norden, from whom he obtained training in ethics, morality and civic duty, were key influences on the young Hans. His father wanted him also to become a doctor and that is what he enrolled to study at Bonn University in 1929. However, as a teenager he became fascinated by the economic issues surrounding the hyperinflation and depression of the 1920s. Indeed, he became absorbed in the nature of these and related contemporary economic problems, and read avidly, including the *Manchester Guardian* newspaper (forerunner of today's national newspaper, *The Guardian*) through which he also taught himself English. At the recommendation of some friends, he attended a few economics lectures by the eminent professor Joseph Schumpeter, and his imagination was immediately captured, resulting in a rapid change of degree programme. Schumpeter (who left for Harvard University in 1932) and Arthur Spiethoff were the two principal academic influences on Singer in Bonn (Shaw 2002: 4–8; 2006a: 242; interview, John Shaw[i]; Singer 1997: 127–8; UNIHP 2007: Singer: 36–8), although Singer also had great personal and academic admiration for his fellow student, August Lösch, who inspired Singer's own early work on duopoly and spatial compartmentalisation that impressed Keynes in Cambridge once he arrived there (UNIHP 2007: Singer: 39–41). Lösch's work later became seminal in economic geography until the 1970s/80s.

Singer was one of a close-knit group of enthusiastic liberal, social democratic students in the faculty association, drawn from different religious and cultural backgrounds in this very mixed urban population. They could not perceive of a Nazi take-over but immediately after they took power vicious attacks were launched against the student leaders, including Singer, in particular. The fact that he stood up to the attackers made him a marked man and he had to flee very rapidly, just making it across the border to Switzerland to join his fellow student, **Wolfgang**

---

[6] See footnote 25, this chapter, on the extent of this phenomenon.

Stolper, who had gone earlier (see below). After a few weeks there, Singer went to Turkey as one of a significant group of refugees granted asylum by Atatürk (Kemal Pasha) to help with the modernisation and Westernisation of Turkish universities (UNIHP 2007: Singer: 45; see also Reisman 2006). Before long, however, through the good offices of Schumpeter and Keynes, he was invited to a scholarship interview at King's College Cambridge, to where he relocated in the autumn of 1933, having covertly entered Germany for three days en route to marry his girlfriend, Ilse Plaut (Shaw 2002: 8–9; 2006a: 242; interview, John Shaw[ii]; Singer 1997: 128–33; UNIHP 2007: Singer: 45–7).

Wolfgang Friedrich Stolper: Born in Vienna on 13 May 1913, Wolfgang Stolper was a relative of **Paul Streeten** (cousin once or twice removed, according to Streeten (pers. comm.[iii])). His family moved to Bonn in 1925, when he was a teenager, and he completed secondary school at the Arndt Gymnasium in the Berlin district of Dahlem in 1930. He then studied law at Berlin University for three semesters before moving to the more stimulating environment at Bonn University at his father's behest. There he became a fellow student and activist with **Hans Singer**, three years his senior. Like Singer, he found Schumpeter and Spiethoff exciting but also greatly appreciated Von Beckenrath and Rössle.[7] Although a Protestant rather than a Jew, he was a member of the opposition to the Nazis so that when they came to power, he had to switch to economics as he was no longer permitted to study towards his *Referendiat* (combined law and economics). Considering himself – as he continued to do throughout his life – to be principally an economic theorist, he did not appreciate the more practical or applied nature of this (Hagemann 1997a: 23; Stolper 1997: 94–7; 1998; UNIHP 2007: Singer: 41).

As mentioned above, both men had to escape Germany in early 1933, not long after the Nazi takeover. In Stolper's case, this occurred shortly before his Master's degree examinations, having submitted and passed the requisite thesis (*Diplomarbeit*). He was bidding his parents farewell in London (they were emigrating to the USA) when

---

[7] A full appreciation of Schumpeter and the intensely collegial and intellectually stimulating atmosphere in his seminar – particularly highly unusual in Germany at the time – is provided in Stolper (1998). Remarkably, Stolper observed that Hans Singer and he were apparently the last two survivors of that seminar.

he received word not to return to Germany because an arrest warrant for him had been issued. Initially, he stayed with his Swiss fiancée, Heidi, in Switzerland, because his *Diplomarbeit* was accepted in Zurich as the basis for a doctorate, which he completed in just two semesters. However, before he could formally obtain the doctorate (Dr.rer.pol), he was awarded a fellowship to Harvard University in the USA in 1934 through the efforts of his former Bonn professor, Joseph Schumpeter. Thus the teacher–student relationship that they had enjoyed in Bonn prior to the professor's emigration in 1932 was recreated (Hagemann 1997a: 23; Stolper 1997: 97; Perelman 2002).

Stolper's original plans had been to complete his degree in Bonn and then pursue his studies in Oxford on a Rhodes Scholarship, for which he had been interviewed and anticipated winning. He withdrew, however, when the Nazis took power, as he was not prepared to represent the country under that government. He had anticipated undertaking a doctorate thereafter at the University of Chicago, prior to returning to a career as editor of the *Deutsche Volkswirt* journal (of which his father, Gustav, was publisher) and a political career,

> for neither of which I was by temperament particularly qualified. So while the loss of one's fatherland and particularly of one's mother tongue is a major tragedy in one respect, emigration opened for me whole new worlds for which I seemed temperamentally and intellectually made. (Stolper 1997: 98)

He fitted in easily and thrived at Harvard, which he found equivalent to Oxford in many respects. He mixed with many of the leading American and European émigré economists, including Leontief, Musgrave and Haberler, and completed his PhD under Schumpeter's supervision in 1938 at the age of 26. Co-students and friends later to become leading economists included Paul Sweezy. He admitted to working very hard but also enjoying a rich social life. 'In short, the Americanization and integration went on simultaneously with my economics training. It was for me a wonderful life, and I felt at home in this essential medieval *communitas academica*' (Stolper 1997: 103), where he stayed until the end of his fellowship in 1941.

Heinz Arndt: Heinz Wolfgang Arndt was born on 26 February 1915 in Breslau (now Wroclaw), the leading scientific and cultural centre in the part of Eastern Germany ceded to Poland after World War II. The

family spent two years spanning the end of World War I in Constanti-
nople (Istanbul), where his father, an academic chemist and linguist,
modernised the Chemistry Department of the Ottoman University as
part of a German assistance programme. His younger brother, Walter,
was born there but his sister, Bettina, was born back in Breslau, which
was deemed healthier after Heinz developed para-typhoid. Heinz spent
the rest of his childhood and completed his schooling in Breslau (Arndt
1997: 151–3; Coleman et al. 2007: 1–12).

His family was not politically active but his father was more liberal
and less nationalistic than most of his peers (see also Coleman et al.
2007: 3). Both parents were Anglophiles, having actually met at the
city's English Club, and generally spoke to each other in English.
However, they divorced when Heinz was 12 as his mother wanted to
marry another man; Heinz later reflected that the shock of it probably
contributed to his puritanical attitude to sex (Arndt 1997: 152; further
details are given in Coleman et al. 2007: 5).

The Arndts were among the Jewish families that had embraced
Christianity in the late nineteenth century, although the historical
family name of Aaron had been changed to the Nordic Arndt already
in the mid-eighteenth century. Three of Heinz's grandparents were
Jewish, although not practising, despite one grandfather occasionally
donating money to the local synagogue.

> But of all this Jewish background we were as children barely aware. It
> did not affect our lives in any way until the rise of the Nazis ... Both
> my parents were Protestants,[8] and I was baptized and confirmed in
> the Lutheran church. But this, too, was a matter of social convention.
> Religion played no part in our home.[9] (Arndt 1997: 152)

Heinz completed his final eight years of secondary school in the
Kaiser Wilhelm Gymnasium in early 1933, just as the Weimar Republic

[8] Heinz's younger brother, Walter, told me (pers. comm., 6/9/07) that their mother
was in fact baptised only shortly before her wedding and that he doesn't believe that she
retained any Jewish identity.

[9] Walter recalled that they were indeed aware of their Jewish roots, 'like a great
many Jewish jokes and games, e.g. "Gottes Segen bei Cohns"'. ... Furthermore, 'there was
considerable interest in our later years in our Jewish origin, but it did not amount to an
exploration of Jewish history' (pers. comm., 6/11/07). These are interesting reflections that
differ to some extent from Heinz's but they do coincide with respect to formal religion or
religious (as opposed to cultural) identity, which is the issue of central concern.

ended with the Nazi election victory. Indeed, his class returned from the traditional skiing tour between the written leaving exams and subsequent orals to find that 'the Third Reich had broken out' (*ibid.*: 153). Over the final three years at school, he recalls the severe recession and rise of Nazism, with increasing nationalism among the teachers and more and more of his classmates joining Nazi organisations. He joined a small group of active anti-Nazis.

Immediately the Nazis took power, his world was thrown into turmoil and long-held plans to study law and oriental languages in Geneva and Hamburg in preparation for a diplomatic career had to be abandoned. He joined a voluntary work camp established for the unemployed by the Social Democrats, while his family kept a low profile during the early anti-Semitic violence, and detention and internment of political opponents. Within a few months, his father had been dismissed from his post at Breslau University under the 'Aryan Laws' because of his Jewish origins and, having been offered a position at Oxford University through the newly established Academic Assistance Council (AAC) (see also Chapter 3 and Simon 2012[10]), he and Heinz's stepmother and younger sister left in August. Heinz followed on 10 October, gaining admission to Lincoln College to study philosophy, politics and economics, specialising in politics (Arndt 1997: 153–4), while his brother enrolled in Oriel College. His mother and her second husband later had to flee Berlin for Istanbul, where she was widowed; she subsequently remarried and moved to Prague until forced to flee to London (Coleman et al. 2007: 11).

Meanwhile, Heinz's father and stepmother left Oxford for Istanbul after only a relatively short sojourn, despite the arrival of both Heinz and Walter from Germany. Fritz's appointment was of uncertain duration and the renewed offer of a permanent Chair in Chemistry at the Ottoman University, where Fritz had earlier been so happy, proved irresistible.[11]

[10] At the time of writing that paper, I was unaware that Fritz Arndt had been among the very first to be helped by the AAC, so his case is not covered there.

[11] He thus joined many other German refugees and émigrés who had been given sanctuary by Atatürk as part of his drive to modernise universities and the Turkish economy as a whole. Fritz Arndt remained in post there until his retirement in 1955 (Coleman et al. 2007: 10–11; Reisman 2006: 197–9; Prudence Arndt, pers. comm., 15/1/13, Miriam Arndt, pers. comm., 15/1/13).

As Heinz later reflected, '[t]hus, by a curious irony, the calamity of Hitler's rise to power in Germany brought me the incredible good fortune of an Oxford education (financed in the main by [his] rich Polish uncle) and a life spent in England and Australia' (Arndt 1997: 154).

He also reflected on his five years in Oxford as well as subsequently working at the LSE on a Leverhulme Research Fellowship from 1938. Of particular relevance to understanding his later academic interests is a comment about the impact on him of reading Karl Mannheim's *Ideology and Utopia* and coming to understand political and moral ideas as an ideological superstructure. Henceforth, how such ideas developed and what their historical functions were became 'absorbingly interesting' to him (*ibid.*: 154–7).

Peter Bauer: Peter Thomas Bauer was born in Budapest on 6 November 1915 to Aladár Dezsö Bauer, who was a bookmaker by trade, and Anna (née Grossmann).[12] Despite the range of secondary sources (including published interviews) and primary research to hand on Bauer, there is rather less information on his childhood and family life than on many others in this study. It is therefore very difficult to draw any tangible conclusions about any possible early influences on his career aspirations and thinking. Indeed, his longtime friend and colleague, Basil Yamey, confirmed that Bauer hardly ever spoke about his childhood but did mention that, in common with others seeking assimilation (including several in this study), his parents had him baptised a Catholic but he was not an active practitioner (interview, Basil Yamey[iv]).

Like most others in this study, he attended secondary school at a Gymnasium (Scholae Piae – run by the Piarist religious order). Again, as so common among middle-class families, and indeed the cohort in this study, he then enrolled for a law degree at Budapest University but after a year came to the UK in 1934 to study economics at Cambridge University. This came about on the recommendation and with the financial support of one of his father's clients (Tribe 2006: 1), who was an Anglophile and suggested that an English education would be highly advantageous (Tribe 2006: 1; IEA 2002: 20).

Very unusually at that time, he arrived in Cambridge without confirmed prior admission:

---

[12] This is a common German Jewish surname, suggesting German roots, although the earlier family history is not revealed in any of the sources I have utilised.

I then had no contacts in this country. I simply turned up here in March 1934 and presented myself at half a dozen colleges at the tutorial hours of Senior Tutors. Caius was one of them … They may have been surprised [at a complete stranger appearing from another country like this] but all were very friendly. I had provisional acceptance from five out of the six colleges, including Caius. [I chose Caius because] In 1933–34 I was already studying Law at Budapest University. I expected to return to Hungary and practice law, specialising in International Private Law, for which I thought the study of economics and law would be helpful. I had heard of Buckland and McNair. I thought that if I came here I might be taught by them. This is how I came to Caius. (Bauer 1985: 32)

He also attended some of Keynes' lectures and seminars and had Joan Robinson as tutor (IEA 2002: 22–3).

Of course, the rise of Nazism and fascism made a return to Hungary impractical and so Bauer remained in the UK and made his mark as an academic economist and later in life as a member of the House of Lords. He was the only member of my study cohort never to marry, although he had numerous heterosexual relationships, some of considerable duration.

Paul Streeten: Born Paul Hornig in Vienna on 18 July 1917, Streeten's father died before he was two, while his mother, Berta, was pregnant with his younger brother, Walter. He was too young to be much affected but recalls his mother's resultant depression. The three of them moved in with Paul's maternal aunt Annimädel and her husband Lubig, and the two young boys became very close to their two girl cousins. Berta had to earn a living by selling knitwear from a small shop in the *Judenstadt* (Jewish part of the city), so Annimädel became almost a surrogate mother during the day. Paul hardly knew his paternal family. His mother eventually remarried and a half brother, Peter, was born in 1930. He describes himself as having been a shy and dreamy child, living in fear that his mother would also die (interview, Paul Streeten[v]; Streeten 1997: 177–9).

His first primary school in the Gumpendorferstrasse in Vienna's Sixth District was a strict, boys-only school but taught him a lot. Later they moved to a co-educational school in the Eighth District, with an entirely different educational philosophy, based around games and play. He then attended the Gymnasium in the Eighth District, completing his schooling in 1935, aged 18 (interview, Paul Streeten[vi]). He then studied law at Vienna University, passing the *Staatsprüfung* (State examination) but his progress was interrupted by the Nazi *Anschluss* (annexation) in March 1938, whereupon he was expelled from the university and it immediately became clear that the family would have to get out (Streeten 1997: 181; interview, Paul Streeten[vii]).

Religious Upbringing: Although his maternal grandparents were Jewish and observed the holy days, his mother and her siblings were very secular – 'they really had removed themselves almost completely from any consciousness of Jewishness' – with the result that Paul and his brothers had very little concept of being Jewish or what it meant, although he remembers his grandfather going to the Temple (reform synagogue) on Rosh Hashana and Yom Kippur, as well as the annual family Seder on Passover (interview, Paul Streeten[viii]; UNIHP 2007: Streeten: 4). Nevertheless, many of his and the family's friends were Jewish and he recalls hitting a fellow pupil at the Gymnasium who called him a *Saujude* (literally 'Jewish pig/swine'[13]) – symptomatic of the 'rife and virulent' anti-Semitism in Austria. That said, he does not recall a specific moment, as others have, when he first became conscious of being a second-class citizen (Streeten 1997: 180).

Economic and Political Consciousness: Paul Streeten recalls some very early childhood memories regarding conversations about the hyper-inflation when he was just four or five years old. Even while still at primary school, he felt that severe poverty and sharp inequality were intolerable. In his teens, he and his brother and cousins thrived on the romantic novels of Karl May, which he interpreted as illustrating the Hegelian and Kantian theories of progress propounded by Max Adler, the eminent Austrian Marxist philosopher, lawyer and politician, some of whose lectures he attended while still at school (Streeten 1985a: 45–6; 1986a: 396–7; 1986b: 137–8; 1997: 179–80; interview, Paul Streeten[ix]: UNIHP 2007: Streeten: 1, 16).

He became active in the *Roten Falken* (Red Falcons), a socialist youth movement, which was banned by the fascist Heimwehr in 1933,

---

[13] This is a derogatory anti-Semitic term widely used in the German-speaking world since the 1880s; the reverse form, *Judensau*, and *Judenschwein* date from the early nineteenth century. However, the derogatory linking of Jews and pigs in illustrations dates back to the Middle Ages (Wikipedia 2013; my translation).

so that they had to operate underground. Following the murder of Engelbert Dolfuss, the Austro-Fascist leader, by the Nazis in 1934 for not being ruthless enough, repression increased and legitimate organisations like the Boy Scouts were then used as fronts for continuing their activities. 'We engaged almost full-time in political activities' (Streeten 1997: 181); 'we discussed and talked about national and global issues of poverty, inequality, and policies of how to remove or reduce them. We really wanted to do things rather than think or write about these problems' (UNIHP 2007: Streeten: 1). One of those active in his group, and with whom he was very close, was Hermann Bondi, later to become a scientific polymath, Chief Scientific Advisor to the British Government and then Master of Churchill College, Cambridge. Streeten also explains his own conversion from socialism and collective action to individualism and democratic reform at the age of 18 (Streeten 1985a: 46–7; 1986a: 397–8; 1986b: 138–9; 1997: 181; interview, Paul Streeten[x]; Bondi 1990; UNIHP 2007: Streeten: 1–2).[14]

Because of his Jewish background and political activities, Paul was on the Nazis' priority list for arrest. On the very day of the *Anschluss*, hours after the family had coincidentally moved from a flat in the Eighth District to a house in the Wattmanngasse in Hitzing, part of the Thirteenth District, the flat was raided and searched for him. By one of the many coincidences that characterise the circumstances under which almost everyone in this study was able to escape persecution, a British consular official happened to live in the same street as the Hornig family's new house and helped secure an entry visa to the UK. This was also facilitated by affidavits from friends in England of his then girlfriend in the Knighthood of the Blue Pilgrims Christian group active in saving persecuted Jews and who provided financial guarantees for Paul's upkeep.

Thus he became the first member of his family to leave Austria, arriving in England in April or May 1938, aged 20. He spent the first few months with the Gibson family in Cambridge, where the husband headed Ridley Hall theological college. Paul was not to see the rest of his family again until 1947 as they subsequently emigrated to Greensboro, North Carolina, in the USA on a transfer organised by

---

[14] All of Streeten's accounts give his age then as having been 18, except for 1997 (the most recent), which says 15; the earlier versions refer to a different conversion, from outdoor pursuits to learning, as having occurred when he was 15.

his stepfather's firm, the Kuhlmann chemical dyestuff firm. Even when Paul was interned as an 'enemy alien' in Canada in 1940–41, he was unable to get permission to join them (Streeten 1985a: 45–8; 1986a: 398–400; 1986b: 141–2; 1997: 181–2; interview, Paul Streeten[xi]; see also Chapter 3; UNIHP 2007: Streeten: 2–3).

Teenage and Child Émigrés during the Nazi Era (1933 Onwards)

As explained in the introduction to this chapter, teenagers and children at the time of their flight from danger were usually enmeshed in their respective families' strategies rather than those of their own making. Nevertheless, their lives before escape from Nazi rule or occupation were marred by victimisation, through expulsion from school, being ostracised by erstwhile friends, having to stand in long food queues and the like. They also suffered indirectly through seeing their parents' anguish at expulsion from their jobs, then struggling to make ends meet, and/or being attacked, beaten up or even being detained. Danger was often a daily presence. Hence, they had to grow up, so to speak, very rapidly and often assumed roles not generally undertaken by children in their normal contexts. The impacts were sometimes quite profound and, as the examples below illustrate, in some cases did influence subsequent lifecourses and career choices, occasionally strongly. The nature of their experiences and likely impact was often age-related, being stronger the closer to completion of secondary school they were.

Conversely, two others, namely **Andre Gunder Frank** and the youngest in my study, **Gerry Helleiner**, were young boys of about four when their families fled Berlin in early 1933 and Vienna in 1938 respectively, so they had no real memory of life there and there is little to recount in the context of this chapter – but see Helleiner's reflections in UNIHP (2007: Helleiner: 1–2; Helleiner 2018). A detailed account of his family's exodus to Canada via the UK, assisted by the AAC, is provided in Simon (2012). That account is based largely on the Helleiner file in the AAC archive, of the existence of which Gerry and his family were previously unaware.

Frank was born into a professional Jewish Berlin family on 24 February 1929. His father, Leonhard, was a novelist and pacifist – which made it necessary to escape immediately Hitler became Chancellor in January 1933. They settled in Switzerland until moving to the USA in 1941, where, apart from initial schooling, Frank obtained his formal education.

His early exposure to the three linguistic communities in Switzerland may have kindled his great linguistic ability – he later spoke and wrote in some seven European languages. His given name was actually Andreas, which became Andrew in the USA; Andre arose due to a librarian's error in relation to Andrés, the Spanish version of his name (Watts 2006; Mintz 2007; Wikipedia 2017c). Neither Frank's (1991b; 1997) autobiographical essay nor any other commentator mentions the extent or significance to him of his Jewish upbringing, in the light of which it seems fairly safe to assume that it played little role.

Austrian Experiences

Although anti-Semitism and discrimination in Austria had increased greatly before the German *Anschluss* (annexation) in March 1938, as outlined in relation to Paul Streeten above, most of the families of the Austrian children in this study had to leave the country soon afterwards, so their experiences are examined as a group.

That said, however, **Kari Polanyi Levitt** (born 14 June 1923) does not quite fit with the other three below because her father, the socialist lawyer and journalist, Karl Polanyi (1886–1964), did have to leave Vienna soon after Hitler took power in Germany. He was a prominent member of the editorial staff of, and a columnist for, the *Österreichischer Volkswirt*, Austria's leading weekly economic and political newspaper. By the end of 1933, he had been compelled to resign because, under Nazi pressure, the liberal editor could not continue to employ a prominent socialist (Kari Polanyi Levitt, pers. comm.[xii]). He then moved to London as a political refugee, initially becoming the newspaper's foreign correspondent. Like Fritz Arndt, he was one of the early people helped by the Academic Assistance Council (AAC) – see Chapter 3. According to the correspondence in Karl Polanyi's AAC archive file, his wife and Kari joined him in London in mid-May 1934, when she was 11, although his wife then returned to Vienna for a couple of years. By 1937, the Polanyis were receiving financial assistance to send Kari to Bedale's School in Hampshire and rented a cottage from the prominent Wedgwood family of pottery fame, to whom Polanyi's wife was related by marriage (Simon 2012: 25–6).

Kari's own recollections are somewhat different from the AAC file on several key points and we have been unable to reconcile these accounts. In terms of her own journey and stay in England, she says,

I was sent from Vienna to London in March 1934. In my recollection, I travelled alone although there may have been some adult who was asked to keep an eye on me and assist in transit from the train to the Calais–Dover ferry and back to train ... I have a very clear recollection of the two days of travel [from] Vienna to London. I was certainly not accompanied by my mother. For the first part of the journey from Vienna to the Swiss border, I was glued to the window and very sad at leaving Austria. In this two-day journey, I remember how my heart sank as the train passed through the suburban stations of South London. There was nothing green and the houses looked grey and poor with forests of chimney stacks.

...

My destination in London was the home of the Grant[15] family, whom I knew well from their prolonged stay in Vienna. My mother neither accompanied me nor visited London in 1934; she stayed in Vienna to work with the now-illegal Schutzbund after February 1934 and participated in training some of the volunteers who joined the International Brigade in Spain. She probably knew Gerry [Helleiner]'s grandfather, Julius Deutsch. I remember when she arrived in London in 1936.[16] My parents rented a room in a boarding house for overseas students where my mother was expected to assist in minimal domestic duties. The landlady imagined that coming from Vienna she would excel at cooking and baking but soon discovered that these were not among her many talents and the arrangement was soon terminated. The address was in West End Lane.

...

I won a scholarship which covered full tuition fees at Bedale's [starting in 1936] although it is possible that Janos and Rosamund (Wedgwood) Bekassy contributed to incidental expenses. To me they were my aunt and uncle in England and I spent many happy vacations at their farm in Suffolk. The reference to the renting of a cottage [mentioned above] may refer to some financial assistance for renting a small house in rural Kent after leaving the boarding house in West End Lane. (Kari Polanyi Levitt, pers. comm.[xiii])

She regards the enforced departure for the UK as 'the defining event of my life, and the source of my commitment to socialism and

---

[15] See Chapter 3.
[16] This account is consistent with that in her online autobiographical summary (Polanyi Levitt n.d.).

social justice'. Up to that point, she had enjoyed a happy Red Viennese childhood,

> participating in socialist community organizations, including gymnastic club, summer camps and the great May Day parades. I recall every day of the week in February 1934 when the government launched a military attack on the workers of Vienna. When I returned to my school, the rector and many teachers were missing because they had all been arrested. (Kari Polanyi Levitt, pers. comm.[xiv])

Since she was completing her schooling (1936–42) and university (1942–47), and became naturalised, Kari Polanyi Levitt survived the remainder of the Nazi era without problem and she is therefore not included in Chapter 3; instead, her story continues in Chapter 6.

Of the three other Vienna-born Austrians, both **Scarlett Epstein** (**Trude Grünwald**, born 13 July 1922) and **Eric (Erich) Wolf** (born 1 February 1923) were almost identical in age to **Kari Polanyi Levitt** but had very different experiences. Epstein remained in the city until July 1938, while Wolf left in 1933 because his father was transferred to Czechoslovakia by his firm. The youngest of this cohort, **John Friedmann** (born 16 April 1926), left only after World War II had started, in April 1940, aged 14.

Scarlett Epstein's autobiography (Epstein 2005) describes in vivid detail her Viennese childhood, the impact of anti-Semitism and the complex and fraught process of escape after the *Anschluss*, which eventually brought her family to England. Only the essentials for present purposes will therefore be repeated here.

Her initial childhood was very happy as the youngest of three children[17] in an extended family with many friends in the immediate vicinity – a working-class district (Brigittenau) in which many poorer Jews lived. Her father became a textile salesman for her uncle's factory in Yugoslavia since he had found it hard to obtain employment after World War I. This meant extended periods away from home. In contrast, therefore, to almost all the other subjects of this study, Scarlett came from a semi-working-class background.

---

[17] Her brothers Otto and Kurt were ten and four years her senior respectively. While she adored Otto almost as a father figure since her father travelled a lot for work, she had a complex and often fractious relationship with Kurt, who was sickly and manipulative, whereas she was independent, impulsive and hot-headed (Epstein 2005: 3).

Her father came from an assimilated Jewish family and, as a member of the Freidenkerbund (Free Thinkers' Association) was avowedly atheist, whereas her mother came from an orthodox Jewish family but became increasingly removed from ritual and observance after marriage. She later came to regret not having brought up the children as proud Jews once anti-Semitism increased (*ibid.*: 5, 11–12, 15).

When she was eight, they moved to a larger apartment in the brand new Karl Marx Hof in the Nineteenth District, part of a bold initiative to reduce the housing shortage and upgrade the stock by the socialist government, of which her father was a supporter. Apart from innovative social facilities, there was running water and an inside toilet, but still no bathroom or shower (*ibid.*: 7–8). That Epstein remarks on these features is revealing about the state of the general quality of flats in that district at the time. Almost immediately after their move, Scarlett had her first experience of anti-Semitism on her first day at the local primary school, when a group of children she tried to join stuck out their tongues and all shouted '*Saujüdin, Saujüdin!*'[18] She rapidly had to develop a protective shell since she was the only Jewish girl in the school and even to her few non-Jewish friends she somehow remained 'a stranger' (*ibid.*: 15–16). The problems intensified as anti-Semitism increased among her high school teachers as well as fellow pupils during Dollfuss' fascist repression. She found totally unfair her mother's attempts to explain that, as a Jew, she would have to perform far better than her peers to obtain the same marks:

> It was then that I began to resent that I was being persecuted for something of which I had never experienced any positive aspects. All I knew was that I was discriminated against because I differed from my non-Jewish fellow students, yet I had no positive identity of my own and I felt I did not belong anywhere. (*ibid.*: 20)

Coinciding with the onset of puberty made this even harder to deal with. Following the *Anschluss*, she also observed groups of religious Jews in their medieval garb and of assimilated Jews being humiliated and taunted by Nazi youths. Whereas the former retained a glint in their eyes throughout and were able to maintain their sense of worth, the latter looked completely defeated. Later in life, these experiences had a strong influence on how she brought up her own children as Jews: 'I swore that

---

[18] See footnote 13, this chapter, for an explanation.

if I managed to get out alive I would try my best to instil in my children a positive Jewish identity' (*ibid.*: 30; interview, Scarlett Epstein[xv]).

Life immediately became harder and more dangerous after the annexation. When schools reopened after a fortnight, Jews were thrown out and forced to attend all-Jewish schools, while Jewish teachers had been replaced by Nazis, often with no teacher training. Harassment and victimisation became daily occurrences, as did arrests and incarcerations of friends and acquaintances, including Scarlett's first boyfriend. Fortunately, her father was in Yugoslavia at the time and they managed to alert him not to return. It became necessary to wear some Nazi-affiliated youth uniform or badge in order to move about freely. Scarlett wore one when Otto sent her to apply for Yugoslav visas at the embassy. This proved a traumatic experience, not least because Hitler was making his triumphant entry procession to Vienna and she had to give the 'Heil Hitler' salute in order not to betray herself, while other Jews seeking urgent visas at the embassy looked at her with disdain. Fortunately, her contact person turned out to be the then-just-ex-ambassador, who was nevertheless helpful. Obtaining the visas would take a few months and, on account of his political activities, Otto was in real danger and managed soon to fake some documents with an English friend in order to obtain an entry visa to the UK, whereupon he departed.

Scarlett then effectively became head of the household, since Kurt was shy and her mother an emotional wreck. A while later, Kurt escaped by plane to Italy as Jews were, for some curious reason, still permitted to enter that country by air but not by surface transport. Eventually the visas for her mother and herself arrived and they left Vienna by train on 23 July 1938, feeling a profound sense of relief to leave the home that had come to feel more like a prison in recent months. Her father and uncle met them at the first station on the Yugoslav side of the border (Epstein 2005: 22–34).

Relief proved short-lived, however, since Scarlett's father had a work permit that required regular returns to Austria, which had become impossible. He was threatened with arrest and deportation, so the family managed to move to Zagreb, which was safer. Their position there also soon became untenable as their tourist visas approached expiry. Bribes provided only a short extension and just as they struggled to find a solution and her parents became depressed and suicidal, Scarlett discovered that they could obtain entry to Albania as tourists despite the large red J in their passports, to mark King Zog's jubilee celebrations. This saved their lives since other Jews who remained in Zagreb were captured when the Nazis invaded Croatia. In the spring of 1939, Italy invaded Albania, provoking much anxiety and danger, but the Italian troops regarded them as Germans and hence friends in view of the Hitler–Mussolini axis, so they were safe. Otto obtained British entry visas as menial workers for Scarlett and her mother, but it proved difficult to do so for her father; the women delayed departure until the last possible moment, and were then forced to fly there from Rome with multiple transit stops, including Frankfurt and Cologne, which provided the last terrifying ordeal that almost proved their undoing during a three-hour strip search and both physically and psychologically intimidating interrogation by Nazi officials, but eventually they arrived in England late on 21 April 1939 (*ibid.*: 49–62). Her father was eventually able to join them some time later.

Scarlett's journey to ultimate safety was remarkable, not least because she had been cast into the leadership role in her family after Otto's departure for England and, despite her tender age of 15–16, had to negotiate numerous risky situations when one or both of her parents proved unequal to the challenge. The duration, number of stops and succession of hazards en route stand out as distinctive. Throughout her life, Scarlett retained her gratitude to Albania and Albanians for saving her and her parents' lives – and spoke publicly about this.

Eric Wolf spent only the first 10 years of his life in Vienna, before moving with his family to Tannwald in the Sudetenland, then part of Czechoslovakia, where his father managed a textile factory. Eric attended a German-language Gymnasium and became very conscious of growing up in privilege relative to the children of the factory workers, something which developed his early class consciousness. He was also aware of ethnic conflict as played out between his German and Czech classmates. Return visits to Vienna continued on holiday until the *Anschluss*, but he also learnt much from hiking and cycling through the countryside. On one such trip to Munich in 1937, he recalled seeing the Nazi parades and exhibitions of both approved 'German' and 'degenerate' art. However, he regarded his early years in Vienna as formative in two interrelated but profound ways: the fluid cross-cultural family context in which he grew up and the harsh post-imperial realities of contemporary Vienna despite its grand architecture and layout reflecting its previous status as 'die Kaiserstadt' (Wolf 1992: 7; 2001: 1–2; interview, Sydel Silverman[xvi]).

His family were Jewish by descent but for several generations on his father's side had been highly assimilated and non-practising, but in the Austrian context were very conscious of being perceived as different. His Austrian father, Arthur, had travelled extensively in Latin America, then had experienced a prisoner of war camp in Irkutsk during World War I after capture by the Russians, and subsequently travelled widely in the Balkans for work, thereby acquiring an unusually international world view. While in Siberia he met and later married Mura, who would become Eric's mother. Her family was Russian Jewish (and observant) but had been banished to the Siberian-Chinese border due to her father's role in the Russian revolution of 1905 (Wolf 1992: 5; Friedman 1987: 107–8; interview, Sydel Silverman[xvii]).[19] Eric's home life in Vienna

> thus combined two different worlds: the world of my father and his friends who shared the common experience of captivity in Siberia, and the Russian world of my mother ... Thus in our apartment on the edge of Vienna's ninth and first districts the continents intersected, at least in my imagination, if not in reality. (Wolf 1992: 5–6)

At school in Vienna he learned to draw maps, which he combined with symbolic representations of different commodities as a way of representing abstract concepts concretely, something that would later prove very influential in his approach to anthropology. He also drew ancient artefacts in the Natural History Museum, which somehow 'connected up the world of my grandfather on the edge of China with our Peregringasse in Vienna' and had intensive violin tuition (*ibid.*: 6–7).

An only child, Eric clearly developed fast and was in some respects precocious. This is evident from a postcard he wrote in dialect, aged 10, to his father, who was away on business in late May or early June. Describing watching Nazis parading through Vienna, he found Hitler's affectations ridiculous: 'S'on oller Kerl, ist ja leider n'bisschen doof' (such a foolish chap; unfortunately, he is a bit silly/stupid; my translation).[20] The postscript is equally remarkable: 'Verzeih' mir. Daß ich jetzt ein bisschen politisch eingestellt bin, die Zeiten verlangens halt'

[19] In fact, Sydel Silverman mentioned that Mura's father became the head of the Jewish community in Harbin in China, when they moved there from Vladivostok a few years later (Sydel Silverman, pers. comm., email, 25/1/13).

[20] Unpublished postcard, May or early June 1933, kindly provided by Sydel Silverman, who also referred to this document as providing her 'sharpest sense of Eric the boy' (Silverman 2002: 4–5).

(Forgive me for becoming a bit political now but the times demand it; my translation).

Eric's father happened to be in Vienna at the time of the *Anschluss* and the accompanying anti-Jewish pogrom in March 1938. He thus realised that the family had no future there and used his resources and contacts to get Eric into school in England, taking him there personally that summer (see Chapter 3). Soon thereafter, his parents also moved to the UK until all three emigrated to the USA in 1940 (Wolf 2001: 2; interview, Sydel Silverman[xviii]).[21]

John Friedmann regarded his first 14 years of life in Vienna as 'decisive in terms of my political consciousness but ... I didn't really understand the situation in Austria, and Vienna in particular, and ... the background, the political background, to the turn of events that I have lived through and experienced ... until much later' (interview, John Friedmann[xix]).

His background was half Jewish in that his father, Robert, grew up Jewish and his mother, Susanne (Suzi) Martinz, as a Catholic, but when they met and decided to marry, they both converted to Protestantism (*Evangelisch*). In the liberal atmosphere in Vienna at the time, his father 'found the Jewish communalism in this ... inward-looking environment ... *engherzig* (narrow-minded) ... and so for him it was a kind of liberation'. Socially and professionally they moved in middle-class circles since his father, an engineer by original training (who had built roads and bridges on the Italian front during World War I), subsequently changed career track and studied history and philosophy and became a Gymnasium teacher and researcher (interview, John Friedmann[xx]).

On reading the draft of this text, John reflected – in very similar terms to those expressed by Eric Wolf above – on how the distinctive position of Vienna as Austro-Hungarian imperial hub was responsible for his own multinational familial background and that this also constituted a formative influence:

> My mother's birthplace was Marburg (Maribor), a small city in Slovenia; my father's parents came respectively from Hungary and moved to Vienna to study medicine. He became a medical doctor

[21] Arthur Wolf kept meticulously detailed diaries over many years, initially in German and later, in the USA, in English. Sydel Silverman learnt much about Eric's early life from Eric's comments while reading these diaries, now deposited in the Leo Baeck Institute in New York City (interview, Sydel Silverman, Irvington, NY, 6/11/06; pers. comm., email, 25/1/13).

working for the City of Vienna. His wife, my grandmother, came from Galicia. In the 19th century, everybody with aspirations turned to Vienna and German-Austrian culture. This is part of my heritage, too. (John Friedmann, pers. comm.[xxi])

After *Kristallnacht*, his father was detained for three weeks. This evidently had a profound impact:

He never talked very much about his experiences during those three weeks but it became clear then, as it hadn't been clear before, that it was really not safe for a Jew, even a converted Jew, a Christianised Jew, to remain. So he left ... we had a cousin who was married to a Swiss, [so he] went to Switzerland and then got to the UK with the help of the Society of Friends, the Quakers ... and he really came to appreciate their work, particularly their pacifist [approach]. (interview, John Friedmann[xxii])

After nine months or so, he managed to obtain visas to the USA because his sister, Mitzi, was already living in New York, having had to stay there when the *Anschluss* had made it impossible to return to Vienna from exhibiting her artwork there. After this period of uncertainty, John, his mother and younger brother, Martin, were able to leave Austria and were on the last ship to depart from Italy before that country joined the war, arriving in New York City on 14 April 1940, two days before his fourteenth birthday (interview, John Friedmann[xxiii]).

Childhood in Hitler's Germany

Shlomo (Fritz) Reutlinger is the only German-born person in this study to have lived on in Germany until after *Kristallnacht* in November 1938 and, perhaps in part because of the greater social immediacy of the relatively small-town environment, the events of that night and their consequences proved particularly shocking, not least to a boy just turning 13.

He was born on 31 October 1925 in Pforzheim, in the Black Forest, where he would live until forced to flee in early 1939. His father, Louis, born in 1894,[22] had a construction materials firm, which absorbed

---

[22] He had grown up in a nearby village, Königsberg, where Jews had lived by the grace of the local baron since the Middle Ages. Although not permitted to own land, they dominated cattle trading – which was apparently the dominant livelihood among southern German Jews over a long period. Shlomo traces his paternal family back five generations; as reflected in their surname, its origins were in Reutlingen.

most of his time and energy, so he had far closer contact with his mother, Elsa, as a child. Not unusually at that time, she was some 14 years younger than her husband.[23] She had no interest in business but had a more imaginative, artistic orientation and loved being outdoors, so the family went hiking and picnicking in the Forest each Sunday. Shlomo had two younger siblings, a brother (Erich) born in 1929 and a much younger sister (Ruthie) born in 1936. The family firm was successful, even possessing cars for the sales staff, and affording the family a comfortable, middle-class lifestyle. Shlomo takes more after his mother than his father in terms of interests and aptitudes, although he was passionate about football (Reutlinger 2005: 3; interview, Shlomo Reutlinger[xxiv]; pers. comm.[xxv]).

Among his childhood memories are the Nazi election victory in 1933[24] and the animated discussions of it among the adults, who were convinced – as so many others across the country and beyond – that it would be but a short-lived episode and could not last. At age 10, when those children deemed bright enough for a more academic school track were separated from those who would receive only eight years of schooling, he was sent to the local *Oberrealschule*, where he learnt Latin and French. Along with a few other Jewish children, he was later permitted to attend the Gymnasium, only because his father had fought for the Kaiser during World War I and had been decorated for his actions (Reutlinger 2005: 2; interview, Shlomo Reutlinger[xxvi]).[25]

He received private tuition in English and also in Hebrew since the local Jewish community was too small to sustain any classes. That said, the town had two synagogues, one Reform (of which all the members were German-born) and a Stiebel, which comprised mainly Romanian and Polish immigrants, although his was the only German family in that community (Reutlinger 2005: 3; interview, Shlomo Reutlinger[xxvii]). As right across Germany, the synagogues were attacked on *Kristallnacht*

[23] She hailed from Bavaria, where her grandfather had established a textile business and changed the original family name of Chaim to Heimann. Her mother had married a Hamburger – a very well known Jewish family.

[24] Possibly partly because his elementary school served as a polling booth.

[25] It was a reflection of the extent and depth of Jewish assimilation at the time that most German Jews thought of themselves first and foremost as Germans and therefore did not hesitate to enlist, just as in any other country. Both my own grandfathers and great uncles, along with various cousins, did likewise. Grady's (2011) detailed study estimates that almost 100,000 Jewish soldiers served the Kaiser.

(the night of glass crystal/chandeliers), Wednesday 9 November 1938 – a momentous event in Shlomo's life, as his Barmitzvah (the Jewish coming of age ceremony) was due to be held in the Stiebel synagogue the following Saturday. His vivid first-hand account bears quoting in full:

On Wednesday 9th, I went with my teacher to the synagogue to practise one more time the reading of my portion in the Torah ['*Vayera*']. We took the Torah out from the closet and with my teacher standing next to me, I did my final rehearsal ... and this was the last time I could go to the synagogue ... [O]n the same day ... a teacher [at] my school phoned my mother to tell her that it might be better not to send her son back to school the following day. He said something is 'cooking'. So what was cooking was a 'spontaneous' uprising. And I remember that this professor or teacher ... was always good to me. He was visibly unhappy with the Nazi regime. Although I was not happy at the school because every Monday morning the other students came back from indoctrination – from Nazi indoctrination [in the *Hitlerjugend*] – and they wanted to practise what they had learned on the two Jewish boys in school. So I was quite happy not to go back to that school. As it happened, on Wednesday night all hell broke loose.

They came to the door of our building – there were four apartments in the building and the [one] below ours was my aunt's apartment. Her father, my grandfather, lived with her. And he went to the door and they beat him up. So we heard noise in the hallway. My parents rushed downstairs to see what had happened. I remember that when my parents returned, they got on the phone to call a doctor, a nurse, and ... police – they called the police – they did not even suspect that it was an organised thing and, of course, nobody came but we did find out ... they said they have other calls to make. So the only one who came was the Catholic nurse, I think she was Catholic – anyway, a nun who used to do some medical work ... She came to the house to bandage my grandfather.

At that time, they took away most of the men and even young boys. A truck driver in our business suggested that my father and I don't stay home, that we go to his house and I remember my father and I went to sleep in their village, in an attic somewhere for one night. But as it turned out, they did not come for my father but, of course, my Bar Mitzvah was highly unusual ... there was no synagogue, there was no Torah scroll ... except my parents had a Torah scroll in their home ... and we had nine men and I was doing the reading at home.

[DS: On the Saturday?]

On the Saturday. We had *mountains* of food prepared because relatives were going to come from all over Germany but many of them couldn't come. A few showed up and for them it was lucky too, because the police did come to call for them in their homes – to pick them up to send them to Dachau, Buchenwald – so they were saved actually because they came to my Bar Mitzvah.

...

Both synagogues were destroyed. The big temple was burnt out and today there's only a marker there ... Our little synagogue was actually in an apartment building and they just destroyed everything ... they took out all the furniture, all the books they spread outside on the streets. I know it as an eyewitness because that night – the day after – when this truck driver took us to his home, we passed by the synagogue and we saw everything out on the street – that I remember. This weekend marked the beginning of the end of my normal life at home ... I left Germany a few months later.

...

From then on I was in a Jewish school in a neighbouring town (in Karlsruhe) and at the first opportunity I left Germany. I remember my father took me and my brother to Cologne and said goodbye and we were on a train to Brussels.[26] And my parents stayed in Germany with my little sister and they had to sell their business for, I think, one Dollar – some symbolic amount of money – to the most ... to the only employee who was a real Nazi – he had no ability to run any business, the bookkeeper – and they tried to get out of Germany. I remember they always talked about emigrating ... the talk of the town among the Jews was 'what number do you have?' You must have heard this story before – and that meant what number in the queue [for visas]. (interview, Shlomo Reutlinger[xxviii]; see also Reutlinger 2005: 4–8)

Eastern European Childhoods

Born on 19 November 1925, **Zygmunt Bauman** spent his childhood in the Polish city of Poznań (Posen). Although his father was a scholar at heart, he ran a small shop that went bankrupt during the Great Crisis of 1929. Failing to find an alternative job and with a family of four to support, he despaired and jumped into the river. He was, however, rescued by passing boy scouts and 'the first episode of life memorized and remembered by me was hard knocking [on] the door and my father dripping water brought home on a stretcher carried by ambulance

---

[26] This story is picked up in Chapter 3.

paramedics ... His unsuccessful suicide attempt made ... a stir and he was offered an accountancy job' (Zygmunt Bauman, pers. comm.[xxix]).

Perhaps paradoxically, despite being very secular in his daily life (the family attended the synagogue services only on the New Year (Rosh Hashana) and Day of Atonement each year), Zygmunt's father spent considerable time studying the holy books and was a committed Zionist (interview, Zygmunt Bauman[xxx]). Zygmunt admired his father, who lacked formal education but taught himself to read several languages and became an avid reader. By contrast, his mother was a housewife and Zygmunt was 'brought up in the kitchen', where he learned to cook (Bunting 2003).

Unlike those in my study growing up in a Jewish context, Zygmunt was conspicuous as the only Jew in his primary school and

one of the only two Jewish boys admitted to a Poznań secondary school (the only one in Poznań that practised *numerus clausus* instead of *numerus nullus*[27] as the rest of Poznań secondary schools did) in 1938. We were also the only Jewish family in the Poznań district of Jeżyce, where we lived – which made me a prize game for the local hooligans. This is probably why all my time out of school I spent at home – with books. I guess that was one of the reasons, in addition to Father's job security and Mother's first job (of restaurant cook, an occasion to display her unused culinary talents) in life that prompted me to see my situation in the USSR [see Chapter 4] as heretofore unexperienced freedom. (Zygmunt Bauman, pers. comm.[xxxi])

He and his parents fled to the Soviet Union when the Germans invaded in September 1939 (see Chapter 4). As a 13-year-old, he was still in secondary school and completed his studies in exile. He had one sibling, an older sister, who got married and emigrated with her husband to Palestine in 1938, where she lived the rest of her life on the kibbutz Givat Brenner (interview, Zygmunt Bauman[xxxii]).

Since their mothers had been childhood friends, **Irma Glicman-Adelman** (b. Irma Glicman, 14 March 1930) and **Michael Cernea** (Musi Katz; b. 14 October 1931) played together as children in Galatz, Romania, before World War II and were to meet again by chance in Stanford after a gap of some 35 years. Whereas Irma's family emigrated to Palestine to escape the fascist and Nazi oppression, Michael's lived

[27] See footnote 7, Chapter 1.

out the war as what would now be called internally displaced people in Bucharest (see Chapter 4). Both experienced Romanian anti-Semitism and fascism as young children.

Irma was the only child born to a prominent Jewish couple in the small town of Czernowitz[28] in Bukovina but the family soon moved to Galatz, which is situated on the Danube River just inland from the Black Sea. While she had no memory of the former, she did recall vividly the confectionery shop (*Konditorei*) she passed en route to school and which she was forbidden to enter by her parents – so her grandmother would sometimes take her secretly (interview, Irma Adelman[xxxiii]).

She attended Notre Dame de Sion, a Catholic convent, which practised a cross-subsidy system whereby the wealthier parents paid high fees that were then used to finance schooling for children from poor households. The two groups were segregated, however, with a mere six well-off children per class but 30–40 per class among the poor. The nuns adhered to their promise to Irma's mother not to try to convert her to Catholicism and even employed a rabbi to teach her during the religious studies lessons. This arrangement continued until Jewish children were expelled from Romanian schools and adults from their jobs under the fascist government in late 1938 or early 1939, accompanied by pogroms. It became very dangerous and her family rapidly left Galatz, where they were very conspicuous, for the greater anonymity of Bucharest – see Chapter 4 (interview, Irma Adelman[xxxiv]).

Notwithstanding her family's position within the local Jewish community, her upbringing was not at all religious beyond her convent education because her father considered himself an atheist and would strenuously have opposed any effort by her mother to 'drag religion in'. Like many at the time, he saw no contradiction between his atheism and being both a Zionist and Menshevik (socialist reformer) (interview, Irma Adelman[xxxv]; Adelman 1988/1995: 244).

Michael Cernea was born and grew up in the thriving northeastern Romanian town of Iaşi,[29] which had a total population of around

---

[28] Cernauti in Romanian and Chernovtsy in Russian. The area's long Jewish history and the local context of the times are well captured in Gila Ramras-Rauch's (1994: 3–7) biography of Aharon Appelfeld, the leading Israeli novelist, who was also born there just two years after Adelman. Ramras-Rauch describes his work as reflecting the distinctive ethnic diversity of that commercial and intellectual centre. Even the Jewish community comprised the full spectrum from ultra-orthodox Hassidim to highly secular and assimilated.

[29] The Anglicised form is Jassy.

100,000, some 40 per cent of them Jewish.[30] They belonged to no fewer than 157 synagogues, which ranged in size from single rooms to large, elaborate buildings and catered to the full diversity of Jewish traditions. Michael's father was not particularly orthodox, praying at home most days. His family lived modestly, as his father was an engineer and the country was emerging from the Great Depression. He had a younger brother and both his widowed grandmothers lived with the family, so he therefore learned and spoke Yiddish from an early age.

He commenced elementary school in the state system (there were few private schools at the time) in 1938, just as the fascist Iron Guard came to power and imposed racially discriminatory laws based in part on supposed blood lines (the so-called Blood Law) and other anti-Semitic measures. One of these forced the dismissal of Jewish professionals, as a result of which Michael's engineer father lost his job in a textile factory. Since he was the extended family's sole breadwinner, this triggered real hardship – 'so this was how I learned, quite early, what being unemployed means and what having or not having a *parnassa* [livelihood; means to earn a living] means for a family' (interview, Michael Cernea[xxxvi]).

Soon thereafter, all Jewish children were expelled from school,[31] forcing the well-organised Jewish community federation (which served the membership of all the synagogues) to organise its own schooling system. Improvised schools were rapidly opened in the synagogues, and Michael found himself in one of those. Despite the 'disaster' that mass expulsion heralded,

> [T]here was one 'saving grace' to it. The Jewish pupils were not the only ones expelled from schools: all teachers of Jewish origin suffered the same fate, at the same time. Since the town had a large Jewish population, there were many Jewish teachers, who were generally regarded as being very good. Thus, courtesy of the racial fascist laws, the public schools were suddenly deprived of full cohorts of much-needed teachers, while we could have access to a high concentration of good teachers. And despite the cramped and improper schooling conditions, we did receive an excellent school education. Into it, some specific Jewish subjects were added as well, such as moments and events of Jewish history. But we got the full usual assortment of classes – chemistry and mathematics, history and geography ... and so on. (interview, Michael Cernea[xxxvii])

---

[30] Ioanid (2000: 3) puts the figure higher, at about 50,000 or 50 per cent.
[31] See footnote 7, Chapter 1.

Young Children Growing Up in the Netherlands

The two Dutch members of my cohort share two significant characteristics. First, both were born in neighbouring countries and moved to the Netherlands with their families at a very young age but regarded themselves as Dutch. Second, they were born a week apart in 1933, the year the Nazis took power in Germany, and were thus still young children at the outbreak of World War II and the subsequent German invasion of the Netherlands on 10 May 1940. Although the consequences of the latter traumatised their lives and are remembered acutely (see Chapters 3 and 4), their prewar memories are mainly of immediate familial circumstances.

Ernie (Ernst) Stern was born on 25 August 1933 in Frankfurt am Main, Germany; his parents lived in what was then the nearby village of Bergen (Kreis Hanau) but which now forms part of the city. When he was four months old, his father, who had been working in a metal import–export firm, joined Lissauer and Co. in Cologne (Köln) but the firm moved them to Amsterdam in December that year, so Ernie essentially grew up and went to school there until the German invasion. His brother Justin (Joseph) was born there on 22 September 1937. Through work, his father became more fluent in Dutch than his mother but since his grandfather also came to live with them in Amsterdam, German was still spoken at home (interview, Ernie Stern[xxxviii]; email clarifications[xxxix]).

Emanuel de Kadt was born in Gent, Belgium on 30 August 1933, where his father, Herman, worked in his maternal grandfather's hat felt factory. However, when Emanuel was a year old, his mother, Bep (Betsy), divorced his father and they moved back to her native Holland, where she married Max Freundlich, a German Jew who had fled Germany after Hitler took power. They lived comfortably in Rotterdam, where Max was a partner in a grain importing firm, and Emanuel attended a private school. Two half-sisters, Els and Helen, were subsequently born in 1937 and 1939 respectively. At the outbreak of the war, his maternal grandparents (the van Daelens), who were visiting New York, hastened back to be with their only daughter and her family – 'a fateful decision'. Emanuel had no further contact with his natural father and discovered after the war that, as a Jew, communist and resistance member, he had fallen foul of the Nazis and died in Dachau (De Kadt 2009: 1; interview, Emanuel de Kadt[xl]).

Discussion

Despite the relative socio-economic homogeneity of the middle-class, professional families in which almost all my subjects grew up across continental Europe, one of the abiding characteristics to emerge from the foregoing pages is the diversity of socio-cultural and personal circumstances and experiences. National context and age at the time that their lives were directly caught up in the world the Nazis forged are two of the clearest differentiators. Nevertheless, what became of each person and his/her family as the noose of oppression tightened reflected the interaction of numerous contextual variables, the extent to which people anticipated what might happen and were able to exercise their agency to negotiate and effect an escape by mobilising relatives, friends or business contacts abroad, as well as their tangible and intangible assets. By definition, all those in my study were ultimately successful in escaping and/or surviving, and the remainder of this study explores the extent to which that success and the experiences en route influenced their subsequent life courses and career choices.

The families' degree of religious observance covered a wide spectrum, from orthodox (Michael Cernea) through conservative and reform/liberal[32] – the majority in my sample – to non-observant and secular (Paul Streeten, Eric Wolf) or even agnostic. In some cases, parents or grandparents – sometimes in mixed marriages – had opted to convert to Christianity (usually Protestantism but occasionally Catholicism) at some stage in the preceding decades in an effort to avoid anti-Semitism, to assimilate more easily and/or perhaps to facilitate educational and career prospects (Alexander Gerschenkron, John Friedmann, Kari Polanyi Levitt and Gerald Helleiner). It is perhaps no coincidence that these families lived in Vienna, where anti-Semitism was marked.

A similar diversity existed in relation to the degree of political involvement by parents, although, unsurprisingly, there was marked inverse covariance with religious observance. The oldest members of my study cohort (Alexander Gerschenkron, Hans Singer, Wolfgang Stolper, Albert Hirschman, Heinz Arndt, Peter Bauer and Paul Streeten) were already at university before having to flee (and the first two were already working professionally). They were politically active in their

---

[32] By then already a thriving movement in Berlin, Frankfurt and other large cities.

own right in progressive or socialist circles, making them immediate targets when the Nazis came to power, as recounted below.

It is noteworthy that all bar one (Reutlinger) of the Germans in this study were adults by the time of the Nazi accession to power in 1933 and – with the exception of Schumacher – were in immediate danger on account of their Jewish identities or ancestry or political activities and hence had to flee almost immediately. Schumacher left on account of his conscience in 1937. Conversely, apart from Gerschenkron and Streeten, the other five Austrians represented in this book were still children and teenagers, who were thus not independent actors. They therefore left or remained until after the German *Anschluss* in 1938, according to the situations facing their parents. Kari Polanyi Levitt was the only one whose father was in immediate danger, on account of his work as a leading newspaper editor. Peter Bauer left his native Hungary in 1934, but this was not principally related to the rise of fascism and religious bigotry. The numbers from other countries – one or two each – are too small to make any valid generalisations of this sort but the majority were caught up in their family dynamics prior to adulthood.

The diversity of their individual circumstances notwithstanding, the experiences of my sample are broadly representative of what befell established middle-class – and many other – victims of Nazism in their respective situations. Poorer families, exemplified in this study by Scarlett Epstein's, while perhaps less likely to have been immediate targets in large cities like Vienna since they were less visible, often found themselves even more vulnerable by virtue of lacking the contacts or resources to assist them. The suffering and ultimate escapes of all in this study therefore represent a microcosm of what happened in successive waves inside Nazi Germany and then in neighbouring countries and beyond after the respective Nazi annexations, invasions and/or occupations. The majority of my research subjects escaped before the formal declaration of war but several endured part or all of it under increasingly difficult circumstances, from which they either managed to escape (Emanuel De Kadt), had to hide after surviving a pogrom (Michael Cernea) or suffered incarceration in a concentration camp (Ernest Stern), as will be detailed in Chapters 3 and 4.

3 | SURVIVING THE WAR IN THE UK

As demonstrated in Chapter 2, flight paths were diverse, sometimes fairly straightforward but often complex and fraught. Key factors explaining the experiences of each refugee were the date of departure relative to the Nazi ascent to power or invasion of their country, and the outbreak of war; their country of origin; where they could gain admission, had relatives or could find sponsorship or other forms of support (these three often being closely linked); as well as an element of serendipity. This chapter focuses on the United Kingdom (UK), a key European bastion of resistance against the Nazi regime and a popular destination for refugees fleeing its clutches. Not only was there a long history of contact between the UK and most of mainland Europe, including previous waves of refugees, but British universities had long been highly regarded and there were many Anglophiles in German-speaking countries and those invaded by the Nazis. Although the UK was the principal destination for escapees in this study, only a few remained there permanently. As explained in detail below, despite the existence of various energetic refugee assistance organisations, the UK's attitude to the new wave of refugees was complex and, in 1940–41 in particular, highly problematic. The chapter therefore begins by examining this institutional-political landscape as context to understanding the experiences of those refugees in the study who reached the UK. Moreover, wartime and postwar privations meant that life was hard and employment opportunities were very limited. Hence many refugees ultimately headed west to the USA or Canada (though one left for Australia) after sojourns ranging from a few weeks to many years. Some were able to join relatives there or obtained employment offers, particularly after completing their university studies in the UK.

By contrast, those refugees in this study who found sanctuary away from the European theatre of war, whether in North America or Palestine, were particularly fortunate, notwithstanding often difficult conditions en route. Their physical safety was then ensured and they had the opportunity to start life anew despite a lack of resources, even as hostilities raged elsewhere and they still sought to contact and assist stranded relatives and friends. Others got by, often still under difficult and unsettled circumstances, in neutral states fringing the war zone, such as Switzerland, Turkey and Portugal. These trajectories form the subject of Chapter 4.

The UK admitted a substantial number of German-speaking refugees, who comprised the large majority of the 73,355 German and Austrian nationals who had to register with the police at the outbreak of war (Stent 1980: 36–7). London (2000: 11–12) estimated that a total of some 78,000 refugees, about 70,000 of them Jewish, were in the UK at that time, while another 10,000 who had been admitted had by then re-emigrated. At that juncture, too, visa restrictions were imposed so that only those with employment offers or sponsors agreeing to cover their full living expenses could gain admission thereafter. The same applied to Italians once Mussolini declared war. Various organisations were established from 1933 onwards in the UK to assist refugees in different ways but, in many cases, this was focused on facilitating what officialdom defined as 're-emigration', i.e. moving on as soon as possible to a third country, predominantly the USA and Canada, but also Australia, Latin America, China and eastern and southern Africa. Examples of this appear below but on southern Africa see Sichel (1966).

The majority of refugees in my study who spent time in the UK arrived between 1933 and 1939, under diverse circumstances. Re-emigration meant that the young **Gerry Helleiner** and his family, reunited in England after arriving from Vienna at different points during 1939, left for Toronto in December after he and his mother – who were on the last flight out of Vienna before the outbreak of war on 3 September – had been in the UK just three months. His father, Karl, was the first refugee academic assisted by the Canadian Society for the Protection of Science and Learning (CSPSL), established earlier that year along the lines of the British SPSL (Simon 2012: 31).

The often-fragile lives of German-speaking refugees still in the UK were then rudely interrupted by internment in May and June 1940. This fate befell five male refugees in my study (**Arndt**, **Schumacher**, **Singer**, **Streeten**, **Wolf**). Karl **Polanyi** escaped it only by virtue of having obtained British naturalisation a week after the outbreak of war, thanks to the intervention of an influential sponsor, just shortly before the introduction of internment (*ibid.*: 28). For reasons still hard to discern beyond inaccurate gender stereotyping, numerically and proportionally fewer women were interned – some 4,000 – than men (23,000) (Kochan 1993:

148) and **Epstein** narrowly avoided being detained (see below). Given the historical and political importance of this controversial but today surprisingly little-known episode, as well as its impact on the internees and their relatives, it is examined in depth later in this chapter.

Being Hungarian, **Peter Bauer** received no such unwanted attention; indeed, none of his autobiographical tracts, published interviews, obituaries or even my interview with Basil Yamey about him makes any mention of hostility or ostracism during World War II, so it seems likely that he was spared such treatment. Indeed, he was able to complete his Cambridge University studies in 1939 and begin his career. Initially he worked for Guthrie and Company, a prominent firm of rubber growers and merchants in East Asia, analysing rubber markets – a role that later provided the springboard to his early academic career, which commenced as Leon Research Fellow at the London School of Economics (LSE) from 1943 (see Chapter 5). Between these two jobs, he had a spell monitoring foreign radio broadcasts at the BBC (Tribe 2006).

Ambiguities and Ambivalences: The Reception of Refugees in the UK

There is a growing published literature on Britain's reception and treatment of European refugees from Nazism and Italian Fascism, ranging from detailed empirical accounts produced in great haste at the time in an effort to influence public opinion and hence official policy (Lafitte 1988 [1940]), to more dispassionate analyses written some decades later and benefiting from hindsight, a wider range of witness and participant testimonies and also official records of the time as they gradually were declassified in the Public Record Office (now the National Archive) in Kew (southwest London). The more recent accounts utilise then-newly declassified sources and also different conceptual perspectives and approaches in what amounts to a revisionist historiography (Kushner 1989; Cesarani and Kushner 1993; London 2000; Dove 2005).

This literature is also diverse in terms of focus. At one extreme, the contributors to Mosse (1991) adopt a much longer historical lens, illuminating aspects of, and episodes in, the reception and treatment of Jewish refugees in Britain over the nineteenth and twentieth centuries. Similarly, Sponza (1988) examines the experiences of Italian migrants in the nineteenth century. By contrast, most sources focus on Jewish refugees from Nazism (of which London (2000) is widely regarded as the most authoritative) or even particular episodes, especially internment

(Lafitte 1988 [1940]; Bentwich 1953; Gillman and Gillman 1980; Stent 1980) and specific refugee organisations and the key individuals behind them (Beveridge 1959; Cooper 1992; 1996; Kreft 2011). Shatzkes (2002) focuses particularly on the ambivalences and fissures within Anglo-Jewry during this period, with particular reference to their reception of Jewish refugees. Another strand of work examines the flight and experiences of German-speaking refugees of whatever religious and political persuasion (Hirschfeld 1988; Hagemann 2006). Other more recent studies and edited volumes have sought to broaden the focus to include the experiences of other national and ethnic groups (Cesarani and Kushner 1993; Sponza 1993; Stern 2000; Chappell 2005; Dove 2005).

Statutory controls over immigration, including particularly in relation to refugee flows and nationals of countries at war with Britain, have existed for over a century now, prior to which records were merely kept. The Aliens Act of 1905, promulgated to deal with an influx of Jews from the exigencies of Eastern Europe, represented the beginning of the 'modern' era of British immigration legislation (Stent 1980; Mosse 1991; Cesarani and Kushner 1993; London 2000: Chapter 2). Even internment of German-speakers and then Italians in 1940–41 was not a new departure, resembling very closely a similar episode during World War I, to the extent of using some of the same places of detention) (Panayi 1993).

Ultimately, although this connection is not made in the literature, British policies of 'enemy' internment had their origins in the 1899–1902 Anglo-Boer war in South Africa, when Boer civilians were shepherded into concentration camps in order to clear a hostile population from the countryside in order to deny support for Boer guerrilla warfare. Nazi concentration and later extermination camps were more sinister developments from the same prototype, by way of successful experiments by German imperial forces – most notoriously on Shark Island off Lüderitz in German South West Africa (present-day Namibia) during the 1904–7 Herero and Nama revolts and subsequent German extermination campaign (cf. the perspectives of Stone and Moses 2008; Olusoga and Erichsen 2010; Kössler 2011; 2012; Sarkin 2011; Zimmerer 2011; Kreienbaum 2015). Very sadly and ironically, and for them also profoundly shockingly, some Germans imprisoned in concentration camps shortly after the Nazis took power, who later became refugees in the UK after their release, then found themselves incarcerated once again on suspicion of being potential enemies of the British state.

The British registration and then internment measures after the declaration of war with Germany in September 1939 reflected a complex combination of contextually legitimate, if often paranoid, security concerns about 'enemy aliens' as potential fifth columnists, abiding anti-alienism (Burletson 1993; Cesarani 1993; Kushner 1993; Shatzkes 2002) and actual or latent anti-Semitism. Citing the experience of Max Perutz, an eminent refugee molecular biologist working in Cambridge (see also Ferry 2007), Lafitte (1988: xv–xvi) also points to a common British elite perception at the time that the Nazis and Mussolini represented bulwarks against the westward and southward spread of communism and that the refugees from those regimes – many of whom were active on the political left – might be dangerous communists. It is in seeking to untangle this web that the revisionist historiography differs markedly from the standard explanations among refugees (including those in my study), refugee organisations and their supporters that focus predominantly on abiding anti-Semitism and seemingly astonishing ignorance in terms of a widespread failure to understand the fundamental difference between supporters and victims of Nazism (e.g. Stent 1980: 152), as we shall see below.

London (2000: 3–5) argues that the most important earlier literature focused too heavily on the content of British policy towards Jews, while to a greater or lesser extent neglecting the context and administration of the policies. Nevertheless, this issue was not a major focus of overall government policy. Hence, '[a]t times, British policy comes across as a series of inexplicable interventions in the fate of the Jews by a succession of indistinguishable bureaucrats and politicians' (*ibid.*: 3). Equally, and in terms of the thrust of the broader refugee studies literature within which London situates her valuable book,

> for a balanced account of the responses of bystanders it is vital
> to distinguish the centrality of the Jewish experience for the Jews
> themselves from its relative unimportance for the rest of humanity and
> to locate the response to refugees within its political and institutional
> context.[1] (*ibid.*: 4)

---

[1] London's self-positioning within the refugee studies literature is particularly noteworthy in the present context, in that it demonstrates the need to integrate British refugee policy – especially in relation to Jewish refugees – into the broader comparative literature from which it had thus far remained marginal, as indeed it had from mainstream British history (London 2000: 7). Moreover, none of my interviewees

Hence, for instance, Kushner (1993) argues robustly that long-term anti-alienism provides the most convincing explanation for internment. This is evidenced by the succession of similar episodes over time (not just during World War I) and the consistent emphasis on nationality and language rather than religious affiliation/ascription and political allegiances as the basis for visa restrictions and internment.[2] The politically potent anti-alienism was manifest particularly amongst key elements of the elite whose rules of belonging reflect the membership criteria of London clubland, as encapsulated in the title of Kushner's chapter. From this perspective, the military and political situation at the time – as expressed in the changing balance of power among government departments and especially between the War Office and Home Office – merely formed the specific context to, rather than the underlying rationale for, internment:

> [M]ore fundamental was an ongoing and ever-developing battle over 'Englishness'. The crisis of spring 1940 brought into sharp focus in a most dramatic manner the question of who did, and did not, 'belong' in British society. The key to understanding this issue can be found in the world of British clubland. (Kushner 1993: 80)

> Those that excuse the internment of aliens as military necessity ignore the direction it took and the motives of those responsible. The whole episode can only be understood by examining the class and racial snobberies of those such as Ball and Crocker. (*ibid.*: 92) [These were key – and anti-Semitic – figures on the secretive Home Defence (Security) Executive Committee, also known as the Swinton Committee after its chair, which took over all relevant decisions and determined internment policies and practices after its formation in late May 1940; see *ibid.*: 91–4.]

> The internment episode needs to be examined within a domestic context of what was and was not possible. (*ibid.*: 96)

made this connection explicitly during my interviews or in their own autobiographical or professional writings, despite them all having become specialists in some aspect of development studies. Indeed, several even worked on labour mobility, remittances, forced or voluntary resettlement and the like, perhaps for reasons linked to their own previous experiences. In part, this might be an expression of methodological nationalism, largely taken for granted in that generation.

[2] Similarly, internment camps in France turned out as traps – and in the case of Gurs, it was used later to receive Jews from southwestern Germany (e.g. Feuchtwanger 1982).

Kushner's conflation of Britishness and Englishness in the first quote betrays an English positionality and demonstrates the implicit power relations and ambiguities of nationality and senses of identity within the UK. While all too common in England, this conflation is particularly unfortunate, and indeed ironic, in view of the centrality of (elite) national identity and social structure to Kushner's argument. I should point out, however, that Kushner's and other revisionist interpretations do not deny or downplay the chaotic events of the internment episode, the widespread injustices and suffering caused to internees and their families, or the harm done to Britain's humanitarian image abroad and to the country's war effort. The burden of their contributions lies in seeking to move away from exceptionalism and ignorance/irrationality as principal explanations to broader socio-structural and identity political processes within which internment was just a particular moment contingent upon the specific political and military equations of the day.

While this perspective is helpful, it does not entirely supplant other explanations or indeed, as some might interpret it, provide an implicit excuse or apologia for individual human agency. For, as the published literature and individual accounts demonstrate, even against the backcloth of unfolding internment policy, there were numerous examples of individual behaviour by government figures, middle and low-ranking officials and military and police officers, NGO staff and even Jewish community figures that spanned the full spectrum from enlightened, humane and helpful to bureaucratic and literalist to petty, obstructive, prejudiced and delight at the suffering of others. It would be a gross oversimplification – and cold comfort to the victims of such actions – to attribute all xenophobia or anti-Semitism to structural causes and identity politics. A crucial lesson emerging from post-structural debates in the social sciences and humanities is that human behaviour is highly complex and that nuanced and multi-stranded, not monocausal, explanations point the way forward.

Refugees and Refugee Organisations

Nazi persecution of political opponents, real or perceived, and Jews, in particular, commenced immediately they took power in 1933. Many were rounded up and herded into concentration camps, while others had to flee immediately. The flow of refugees to the UK commenced at that time, with professionals – particularly academics, journalists, lawyers and even politicians – prominent among them. As mentioned above, until late 1939 no visas were required and entry was relatively straightforward. Numbers were also relatively small, making their reception and assistance manageable. Various organisations were established for this purpose, by both the Jewish and Quaker communities, in particular, and non-denominational groups, including German-speaking resident and refugee scientists already in the UK (Lafitte 1988 [1940]: 54–7; London 2000: Chapter 3).

Foremost among these were the Central British Fund for the Relief of German Jewry (CBF) – much later to become World Jewish Relief;[3] the Central Council for German Jewry (CGJ); German Jewish Aid Committee (GJAC); Joint Foreign Committee of the Board of Deputies and Anglo-Jewish Association (JFC); the German Emergency Committee of the Society of Friends; the Church of England Committee for 'non-Aryan' Christians; the Catholic Committee for Refugees; and the *Notgemeinschaft Deutscher Wissenschaftler im Ausland* (Emergency Association of German Scientists Abroad) and the Academic Assistance Council (AAC)/Society for the Protection of Science and Learning (SPSL). By 1940, there were some 200 such organisations, each operating in a different way, with its own eligibility criteria based on religion, occupation and/or nationality/language; fundraising activities, and regional/provincial networks. The Notgemeinschaft was the expatriate/refugee equivalent of the AAC/SPSL, founded by Philip Schwartz (Kreft 2011) and at the time led by the dynamic Dr Fritz Demuth. The two organisations worked closely together. Initially focused on Germany alone, the Notgemeinschaft had to broaden its remit successively to include Czechoslovakia and Austria, and then even Spain and Italy, as each generated new refugee flows (Lafitte 1988 [1940]: 54). Austrian Centres were established in many cities and a non-political Council of Austrians spoke for over half the 12,000 Austrians in the UK by 1940 (*ibid.*: 54–7).

As war approached and refugee flows increased, these organisations realised the importance of enhanced collaboration through a Central Co-ordinating Committee established in 1938 (and by 1940 renamed the Joint Consultative Committee on Refugees). This was given physical effect through deliberate co-location of the major bodies in Bloomsbury House in central London in 1939, passing on cases to the

---

3 Formally the Central British Fund for World Jewish Relief.

most appropriate organisation, and sharing fundraising and other key tasks, including the organisation of provincial committees and lobbying of government when shared priorities and principles were identified. This physical proximity lasted only until the Blitz, when the SPSL, like the London School of Economics (LSE), was evacuated to Cambridge for the remainder of the war (see especially *ibid.*: Chapter 2; Cooper 1992; London 2000: Chapter 3).

Given the identity of my interviewees as a particular subset of refugees and the specific remit of the AAC/SPSL in relation to academics and scientists, it is perhaps unsurprising that the main such refugee organisation assisting the subjects of my study and their families was the AAC/SPSL[4] rather than the far larger CBF (although the latter had a specifically Jewish remit), with the Quakers' German Emergency Committee also mentioned occasionally. The history of the AAC/SPSL has been well documented over time, with key contributions from its principal actors, including particularly Lord William Beveridge, on whose initiative as Director of the LSE it was established,[5] Prof A.V. Hill and Tess Simpson, the long-serving assistant secretary and then secretary, who, for the period of concern here and long after, literally *was* the dynamo and persona of the Society in many respects (Bentwich 1953; Beveridge 1959; Hirschfeld 1988; Cooper 1992; 1996: 11–45; Hill 1996; London 2000: 47–50, 53; Coleman et al. 2007: 9–10; Seabrook 2009: Chapters 1 and 2; Marks 2011: 9–11). Shatzkes' (2002) monograph mentions the AAC/SPSL only in passing (p. 27), presumably because it was not a Jewish-focused organisation.

The more recent research listed above has been greatly enhanced by access to the Society's archives, lodged in the Bodleian Library, Oxford. The records are very detailed, including every item of the copious correspondence (and even hand-written notes of conversations) with several thousand people, by no means all of whom it could help

---

[4] Two of the three in this category, Kari Polanyi Levitt and Gerry Helleiner, were still children so it is their fathers who have files in the archive and in which they are mentioned. Only Hans Singer, then already an adult university student and later researcher, was in direct and very extended contact with the Society.

[5] The stimulus was that Beveridge and Lionel Robbins were in Vienna when newspapers carried the names of all German professors – including the father of Heinz Arndt (an eminent chemist) purged under the Nazis' racial laws – upon which they resolved to establish an organisation to assist such victims find appropriate employment in the UK (Coleman et al. 2007: 9).

since some were not academics or scientists. One case in point was Karl Polanyi, the renowned Austro-Hungarian lawyer/journalist and an editor on the authoritative *Österreichische Volkswirt* economic and financial newspaper, who was a friend from Tess Simpson's period working in Vienna from 1928 to 1933 (Cooper 1992: 29, 65)[6] and father of Kari Polanyi Levitt, one of my interviewees (see Simon 2012). In such cases, cross-referrals were made to the organisation deemed most appropriate, a task facilitated by their co-location in Bloomsbury House until the forced relocation to Cambridge.

The Society's record of achievement was remarkable, due to a combination of its clear focus, influential contacts, often proactive interventions but particularly the energy and determination of Tess Simpson, who not only persevered through the toughest of conditions but developed a personal rapport with many of 'her' scholars, as she liked to refer to them. Indeed, her persona is writ large across the AAC/SPSL's history and the accounts of some of the scholars helped by it. Her own account of the modus operandi (Cooper 1992: 33–47) is disarmingly honest, not least in terms of some of the tactics they had to deploy in relation to applicants for assistance in situations of sometimes very constrained resources and in dealing with officials under often volatile conditions (*ibid.*: 34). In fact, the archival correspondence demonstrates an often more proactive level of assistance in dealings with universities and related potential employers than the above account suggests, especially during the immediate prewar and early wartime periods when jobs were at a premium (Simon 2012: 24–5).

Despite frequent casework overload, especially when new influxes arrived, e.g. after the promulgation of the Nuremburg Laws in 1935, the annexation of the Sudetenland and then occupation of Austria, those eligible cases taken on by the Society were always treated as individuals and Simpson developed more personal relationships with some and provided emotional support when needed. That said, some she found hard to get along with, as evidenced by a terse comment or file note and perhaps a particularly bland and brief letter. Letters of gratitude, Christmas cards and samples of published work often continued to

---

[6] There are a few small inaccuracies in Tess Simpson's account: she refers to Polanyi as Budapest-born whereas he was born in Vienna but lived a long time in Budapest while growing up and in early adulthood. Similarly, he was a lawyer by training rather than a political scientist.

arrive for years after former refugees had become established in new homes and jobs in the UK, North America or elsewhere. Each of these is carefully preserved in the respective personal files in the archive and some provide fascinating glimpses of subsequent stages in the senders' lifecourses.

That said, fine judgements were often required, as well as hard decisions when funds or sponsors were under particular pressure. An initial rebuff or setback occasionally required expediency in not pursuing that line of enquiry lest it jeopardise longer-term opportunities, despite the impact on the individual person under discussion. Long hours, intolerable bureaucratic delays and obfuscations, alongside the sudden dramatic developments, occasionally wore patience thin, as particular pieces of correspondence reveal (*ibid.*: 24–5, 32–3). Personal preferences also did play a role. However, it is certainly clear from the archives that correspondence from Walter Adams (the first General Secretary) and other staff was far more formal, neutral and generally brief than most of that from Simpson.

As with all the voluntary refugee organisations, fundraising was a major and vital activity, embracing subscriptions from core members or supporters to one-off events (none more dramatic than the jointly organised public fundraising meeting at the Royal Albert Hall in October 1933 addressed by Albert Einstein; see Cooper 1996: 47–82) and regular appeals (*ibid.*: 36–43). Even for the much larger CBF, CGJ and other Jewish organisations, the increasing flow of refugees, many unable to find employment or sponsors, provided a growing burden on the Jewish community (London 2000: Chapter 3). The Austrian *Anschluss* in March 1938 triggered an immediate increase in the numbers of refugees, while prospects for re-emigration or employment in the UK declined markedly. The CGJ was unable to adhere any longer to its commitment to the government to cover the costs of new Jewish refugees, triggering the rapid introduction of visa restrictions with the objective 'to avoid creating a Jewish problem in this country' (*ibid.*: 59–60).[7]

With the outbreak of war 18 months later, the financial position of refugee organisations became untenable, even though the flow of refugees slowed dramatically, and the government was forced to cover a large proportion of the costs of these organisations, which were acting

---

[7] The quote is from a Cabinet minute cited by London (2000: 60).

almost as agents of the state in a situation of visa restrictions and then internment, when many refugees already established in jobs were summarily detained for extended periods and their dependents left with little or no reserves. To Tess Simpson, the war therefore ironically 'solved' many of the SPSL's financial problems (Cooper 1992: 45–6) even as the plight of many refugees deteriorated considerably.

As ever, though, experiences were diverse. With the start of the Blitz and the evacuation of London and other major industrial cities, many refugees (especially women) who had been placed as domestic servants lost their jobs; by this time, however, the Helleiner family was safely in Toronto, albeit not without problems and anxious delays en route (Simon 2012: 28–32). Internment had a similar impact on those still studying or working, as we shall see below. Conversely, however, war service for many British men and women did open up vacancies in factories and offices that could be filled by refugees of whatever religious inclination or none if they could be released from internment.

The position of the established British Jewish community was complex and ambivalent. On the one hand, they recognised the plight of their co-religionists and offered help, sometimes very generously, as evidenced by the financial support for the CBF and other organisations. However, some people were decidedly cool towards the refugees and there was widespread concern that too large an influx would exacerbate the longstanding latent and occasionally not-so-latent anti-Semitism in the broader society. Such voices worried that any perception of the public purse supporting the refugees or that they would obtain jobs ahead of unemployed British people in a country just emerging from the Depression, would bring opprobrium on the entire Jewish community. Some went as far as to withhold support from the refugees. The intra-communal dynamics and divergent approaches taken by various Jewish leaders at the time in dealing with the government and officials are well articulated in London (2000: 25–57).

Such attitudes mirror the arguments examined above about the basis of internment policy, demonstrating the sensitivity then prevalent within the local Jewish community as a function of their perceived vulnerability to a resurgence of anti-Semitism. They also found resonance in other contexts, including Cape Town's Jewish community in South Africa, in relation to fears of reputational damage that 'different' and especially poor and less well-educated co-religionists from other parts of Europe might induce for established local Jewish interests (Kaplan Centre

2012). Highly ironically, the same concerns were expressed in Berlin in the interwar years about fears regarding the immigration of *Ostjuden* from Poland and beyond (Adelman 2013: 22, 25–6). These instances provide powerful evidence that such ambiguities and anxieties over difference and perceived risks of hostility towards minorities under conditions of stress and discrimination are universal rather than community-, place- or time-specific.

These ambivalent sentiments of established British Jewry were certainly perceived and sometimes resented by the refugees, who felt that their plight was often of little concern to their co-religionists. In the words of **Scarlett Epstein**, who arrived as a teenager:

> The British Jewish community I felt then was not very pleased to have this large number of Jewish refugees come here, fearing that this will cause a lot of anti-semitism. The only people who made us feel welcomed were the Quakers. (pers. comm.[i])

Even within academia and the refugee organisations, such ambivalences and barely concealed anti-Semitism lurked and were experienced by refugee academics. Jews were kept off the AAC council and executive lest it deter support and funding from non-Jewish sources. Even A.V. Hill, a key figure in the AAC/SPSL and the Society for Visiting Scientists, warned against the latter being swamped by the many Jews utilising the Society's services (Marks 2011: 6).

Inhospitable Hospitality: Internment of 'Enemy Aliens' 1940–41

> The only blessing for which we can thank Britain's rounding up of its 'enemy aliens' in 1940 is that it unintentionally accomplished the genesis of the Amadeus Quartet.

With these memorable words, Lafitte (1988 [1940]: vii) commenced his immensely detailed and authoritative monograph on internment, written under high pressure and amid much official secrecy and obfuscation while the process was at its zenith, in an effort to influence public and parliamentary opinion against its injustices and self-defeating nature. Although the Gillmans (1980), Stent (1980), Kushner (1993), London (2000), Shatzkes (2002) and others have benefited from hindsight and access to a far greater range of records, thereby being able to update data and provide new insights into aspects of the process, such as the crucial role of the Swinton Committee (see above), Lafitte felt that his assessment had stood the test of time so well that he needed to make only small alterations for his 1988 edition. One of these was an addendum on explanations of why internment and deportation had been embarked upon, referring to the Swinton Committee that the Gillmans had first highlighted. Even so, he felt that his assessment in 1940 had been vindicated, with the exception of his overly positive perspective on the role of Winston Churchill (Lafitte 1988: ix).

Alien Registration and Classification: Known German and Austrian 'security risks' were arrested immediately at the outbreak of war. Other citizens of those countries had to register with the police, and all adults over 16 were interviewed by local tribunals with legally experienced chairs, starting in November 1939, with a view to classifying them into one of three key groups. The immense workload aside, numerous inconsistencies and inappropriate classifications arose, especially early on. In all, 73,355 were interviewed, 569 being placed in Class A (high security risks) for immediate arrest, 6,782 in Class B (people of uncertain loyalty to be kept under observation through restrictions on movement), and 66,002 in Class C (posing no security risk and hence to be subject to no additional restrictions). The last-mentioned category was subdivided into non-refugees and 'victims of Nazi oppression', with the vast majority (55,457) placed in the latter subcategory. Police registration books were endorsed accordingly. A significant proportion of those in Class B were actually misclassified refugees, but no appeal was possible and they later found themselves high on the internment lists (Lafitte 1988 [1940]: 37–9; Stent 1980: Chapter 2; London 2000: 170–2).

Previous undertakings notwithstanding, the commencement of the Blitz and real fears of a German invasion of Britain following those of the Netherlands and Belgium led to a decision on 12 May 1940 to declare a wide coastal zone around the country to be 'protected'. All registered aliens were to be removed from this zone and all B Class aliens within it detained. In a chaotic operation amid a volatile atmosphere and with wide discrepancies in local practice and interpretation, over 2,000 men were detained over that Whitsun weekend, including many registered as C Class, among them five subjects of this study, **Heinz Arndt**, **Fritz Schumacher**, **Hans Singer**, **Paul Streeten** and **Eric Wolf** (see below), who should have been left alone. In Streeten's words, there was real fear that '[f]ifth columnists would betray them and it was a panic measure' (interview, Paul Streeten[ii]; see also Streeten 1985a: 49–50; 1986a: 401; 1986b: 144; 1997: 191). Eric Wolf felt that a fifth column probably did exist (Ghani 1987: 350). **Scarlett Epstein** narrowly avoided internment for her socialist youth group activities, but both her father and brother were interned on the mainland and then Isle of Man, as were most of the male members of her youth group (Epstein 2005: 76).

By mid-June the internee totals had reached 7,000 men and 3,800 women; from 21 June, all men were to be arrested following pressure from military chiefs but this had to be done in stages due to lack of adequate detention facilities, and by mid-July some 13,000 had been detained (Lafitte 1988 [1940]: 70–5; Stent 1980: 53–74). Lafitte (1988 [1940]: 75–91) provides great detail on the mechanisms used and who was detained, including a series of internee profiles and experiences.

The basic process was for police to detain people from their homes – as recounted vividly in the quotations below – and deliver them to local collection and holding points, including Kempton Park Racecourse in Sunbury, southwest of London, which served the London area. There were no accommodation facilities and transfer to Liverpool or the Isle of Man occurred when space there became available. Journeys were long and conditions poor; the whole operation was chaotic, especially until the Home Office took over administration of the system from the War Office on 5 August 1940 (*ibid.*: 93–4).

I was in Aberdeen [studying at the University] from the autumn 1938 until Whitsunday 1940. In the early morning of that sunny day two friendly policemen, who addressed me as Paul, asked me to pack a few things in my bag because there was a need for temporary internment quite near Aberdeen. It turned out to be much longer, and my farewell to Aberdeen. (Streeten 1986a: 401; 1986b: 144, 1997: 191)

He had been given no notice – the un-uniformed policemen got him out of bed (Paul Streeten, pers. comm.[iii]; Wilson 2006: 254; UNIHP 2007: Streeten: 6).

On 7 May, Churchill replaced Chamberlain as Prime Minister and issued the order already cited: 'Collar the lot!' Accordingly, after lunch on a brilliant spring Sunday on 12 May 1940, the Cambridge police 'collared' Arndt. He outlined his trials in the next months in his regular letters to Ruth Strohstahl, whom he planned to marry. The letters were written daily, then weekly, and all of the regulation-length 24 lines. They did not tell the full story. Arndt chose his words with care to make sure they passed the British censors. He also tried hard, sometimes too hard, to be cheerful. But he gave a characteristically clear record of the main events and of his gradual change of mood from confidence in his early release to despair that he might remain imprisoned for years. (Coleman et al. 2007: 32–3)

Conditions were abysmal in most camps in England, but particularly Huyton, a semi-completed housing estate near Liverpool, where four of the people in my study found themselves interned. Some camps were dilapidated, lacked utilities and facilities and even unfit for human habitation. Those on the Isle of Man, where many were transferred from the mainland as space became available, especially to Hutchinson's and Onchan camps for men and the Female Camp, were considerably better. Ironically, prisoners of war (PoWs) were kept in far superior conditions, as the British government scrupulously observed the requirements of the Prisoners of War Convention lest any default be exploited by Germany to victimise Allied PoWs (Lafitte 1988 [1940]: 91–143; Stent 1980: 83–94, 134–98; Wolf 2001: 2; Shaw 2002: 29–30; Wilson 2006: 254; Coleman et al. 2007: 33–4). This sharp contrast was not lost on the internees or critics like Lafitte (1988 [1940]: 94), whose judgement, intended to influence public and official opinion, bears repeating:

> The evidence at our disposal, from reliable and carefully checked sources, is quite sufficient to show that conditions in the camps constituted an unsavoury scandal which could not be allowed to continue in a democratic community in full possession of the facts.

Not everyone wanted or was interested in full details, since the broader strategic concern with the war and threat of invasion was seen as the principal priority. The failure to understand or even sometimes to care about the vital distinction between actual or potential Nazi sympathisers and victims of the Nazis led to much indignation and incomprehension among refugees and their supporters but, as argued in the revisionist historiography explored above, they were not the central concern.

Paul Streeten concurs with Lafitte's assessment (interview, Paul Streeten[iv]):

I remember that exactly. The houses weren't quite finished, there was hardly any heating in the very cold winter and the food was extremely scarce – we had very few rations – and one wasn't allowed to receive very much from outside – so I think it was a pretty bad situation.[8]

And reflecting on how it felt to be interned in Huyton again upon returning from Canada at the beginning of 1941, he commented:

But still ... I was happy to be back in England, in spite of the bombardment, in spite of the bad conditions of the camp because at least one could establish – it had been established – that we were not fifth columnists or enemies of the country.

...

I remember again, you see, the English officers on the Isle of Man (because I went to the Isle of Man before I went to Canada) ... I remember the day that Paris fell to the Nazis and somebody brought us the news – we were not allowed, of course, any papers – and we said 'what is the news?' And they were clearly worried and terribly concerned and that stupid English officer said: 'Well good news for you; bad news for us – Paris has fallen to the Nazis!' He thought it was good news for us. It showed you the stupidity of some of these people. (interview, Paul Streeten[v]; see also Streeten 1997: 191)

All the ex-internees ascribe such crass and incomprehensible comments to ignorance and hence the inability to understand the fundamental difference between the refugees and their former Nazi oppressors; at the individual level, no doubt, this was accurate but it is pertinent to recall the revisionist interpretation that such distinctions were of far less consequence in the broader strategic context than to the refugees themselves.

Hans Singer was luckier than some, gaining release from Huyton after only six weeks or so, and thus without missing work as it was the university summer vacation. This reflected the nature of his 'useful' employment, whereas **Streeten** and the others were somewhat younger and thus still students. Singer's detention was made more bizarre because he and his wife had already applied for naturalisation in 1938 but this had not yet been processed, and because he had highly influential figures, including the Archbishop of York (William

---

[8] Heinz Arndt's letters to his intending wife also corroborate such details (Coleman et al. 2007: 33–4).

Temple), John Maynard Keynes and the vice-chancellor of Manchester University acting as advocates for his cause (Shaw 2002: 29; Simon 2012: 33).

Ironically, too, around that time he had turned down an invitation from Alvin Johnson, the president of the New School for Social Research in New York and founder of the University in Exile (which later became the School's Graduate Faculty) to join the School. Alvin had been alerted to Singer's abilities and likely plight in the event of a German invasion since he was on a Nazi blacklist that had been published in the *Manchester Guardian* newspaper (Singer 1997: 137).

Eric Wolf, who had been attending the Forest School near Epping Forest in Essex[9] for two years since arriving in England from Vienna in the summer of 1938 until completing A-levels, was also interned in Huyton but released after no more than a few weeks – although his autobiographical essay and *American Ethnologist* interview (Ghani 1987) provide no details of this or his initial arrest – because in late June 1940 he and his parents embarked for New York on one of the last civilian ships to sail west, to start the next phase of his life there (Wolf 2001: 2–3). However, his widow, Sydel Silverman (2002: 7), records that Eric had been classified as a B Class alien by the tribunal because when asked to confirm that all Nazis were wicked or suchlike, the 17-year-old had replied 'It's more complicated than that'.

Despite its brevity, internment had a profound impact on him, in terms of his subsequent career track in social sciences and an abiding concern with networks and relationships of power:

> I was organised [by veterans of the Spanish Civil War and German communists] with several other kids into a group that would go and steal stuff from the officers' mess – food, medicine, and newspapers – collect bricks that were lying around this housing project, pieces of wood and tar, so that people cold build shelter. The other side to this was, of course, people in this camp who had just arrived in England after losing their shirts in the Continent, and had opened up shops and found themselves once again without any kinds of means of support. They were very depressed; several committed suicide. Or people who would fight over the one piece of meat that swam in the soup. I learned a lot about people under stress. And then, of course, the

---

[9] This is now very much part of urban east London; the school still exists (www.forest.org.uk).

third thing is, when intellectuals get together they organize seminars. We ran the symposia on topics on everything under the sun. One man preached vegetarianism; I had written a paper on Frederick the Second of Prussia in school and I talked about Frederick. [Norbert] Elias talked about social networks. That was an entirely new idea to me. (Ghani 1987: 350; see also Wolf 2001: 2)

This quote provides explicit evidence for one of the key questions underpinning the research that informs this book, namely to assess the extent to which childhood socialisation and wartime experiences influenced my research subjects' subsequent career directions. I examine such evidence in detail in Chapter 8. In Wolf's case, the intensity of his internment experience, in terms both of the process and its implications but also of exposure to the 'camp university' at a critical stage in his life and education, is particularly noteworthy. Indirectly, it also points to the speed following their arrival with which the internees had organised and launched their educational activities, when they might still have believed that their internment would be of only short duration. Elias' lectures on social networks also addressed power relations, providing the young Wolf with his first exposure to social scientific concepts that would become central to his own academic career. Eric also presented his first scholarly paper in the camp university (Wolf with Silverman 2001: 2; Silverman 2002: 7).

Although not Jewish and being older and already a professional of some years' experience, internment also had a profound impact on **Fritz Schumacher**. Having moved with his wife from Berlin to a prestigious job in London in late 1936 to escape the Nazi regime and how it was destroying his idea of the enlightened, world-leading society that Germany should be, he resigned shortly after the outbreak of war over office feuding that may have been linked to his nationality. He and his wife were then registered as enemy aliens and had to vacate their large house in Weybridge, Surrey when that area was included in the 'protected' zone. After lodging with friends, Fritz was found a farm labourer's job with tied cottage at Eydon Hall estate in Northamptonshire, enabling them to move with their two small sons. Shortly after the move, he was detained and interned for three months at Prees Heath, near Whitchurch, one of the worst mainland tented camps (see Lafitte 1988 [1940]: 104; Stent 1980: 92, 151–2; Wood 1985: 108–15; Binns 2006: 219). His health suffered initially but he rallied and was later elected camp leader, in which capacity he organised improvements to sanitation and cooking arrangements, including efforts to diversify how the staple diet of herrings was prepared. This was his first experience of non-intellectual work and group leadership, as well as exposure to the diversity of 'ordinary' people. As in other camps, some of the inmates engaged in intellectual discussions and lessons for mutual benefit and to retain their sanity. Schumacher discovered Marx's work and was struck by its relevance to conditions there and on the farm. This was to prove an enduring influence on his thinking and writing (Wood 1985: 108–15; Binns 2006: 219).

As with all internees, the intervention of well-placed friends or employers proved crucial in obtaining Schumacher's release. Among those acting on his behalf were Harold Scott, Deputy Secretary at the Home Office, and Alexander Paterson, a highly experienced Quaker prison governor and leading penal reformer, who visited Fritz in Prees Heath and was appalled at conditions. They had first met and become friendly during a conference on prisons in Berlin in 1935, when Schumacher acted as Scott and Paterson's translator (Wood 1985: 75, 114). Paterson's visit to Prees Heath and his experience of how internship affected a friend were soon to acquire greater significance in terms of his opposition to the indiscriminate nature of the system and determination to help as many refugee and anti-Nazi internees as possible (see below). This provides another instance of the serendipitous interplay between the personal and the processual – the role of happenstance – in shaping the courses of events and lives.

The capacity problem in the internment camps was to be tackled through deportations to two agreeable Dominions, Australia and Canada, with four vessels sailing from July 1940. The second of them to Canada, the *Andorra Star*, was sunk by a German U-boat in a notorious incident with huge loss of life. It was made worse by lack of information and incorrect reports to relatives of those thought to be on board. However, records were inaccurate in the chaotic situation at the time and there was no definitive passenger list. Overall, Lafitte's (1988 [1940]: 74–5) indignation captures the mood of many:

> News began to filter out about the indiscriminate character of internment and deportation and about the bad conditions in the internment camps. The main feature of July [1940] was the growth of a mighty feeling of dismay and indignation among well-informed people in all walks of life, not against the principle of interning and

deporting *suspects*, but against the tactless, stupid and unimaginative measures which had actually been adopted. The lumping together of Nazis and non-Nazis, of enemies and friends, soon made it clear that measures had been taken which were tinged with panic, and which were so wholesale and so lacking in common sense as to extend far beyond what national security required.

Cross-party protests in parliament had little effect, and it was only decades later, as we have seen, that the hidden hand of the Swinton Committee was uncovered. One of the most outspoken critics of government policy and actions at the time was Sir Josiah Wedgwood, who, with his family, played a prominent role in support of refugees and indeed facilitated the naturalisation of Karl Polanyi's family, including Kari, in May 1940, very shortly before the commencement of internment (Simon 2012: 27–8):

> I know that that is a fact because we had a family relationship with the Wedgwoods. And Sir Josiah Wedgwood was, of course, a Labour Peer and a very decent fellow who did an awful lot for people to help them to get out of Austria, Germany etc., and in this case to have my father … obtain British naturalisation probably two or three weeks before he would otherwise have been interned. (interview, Kari Polanyi Levitt[vi])

Together with Eleanor Rathbone, Josiah Wedgwood, then a member of parliament and not yet knighted, was very outspoken on behalf of refugees, not least during the increasingly xenophobic parliamentary debates on immigration policy and then the chaotic internment and deportation processes (culminating in an enquiry and courts martial over the treatment of internees sent to Australia on the *Dunera*) during the period 1938–41 (see Lafitte 1988 [1940]; Stent 1980; Shatzkes 2002: Chapter 5; Inglis et al. 2018). **Paul Streeten** and **Heinz Arndt** were the only internees in my study to have been shipped west across the Atlantic, both having been on board the *Ettrick* in early July 1940, where conditions were appalling and health and sanitary problems therefore severe (Streeten 1985a: 51; 1986a: 403; 1986b: 145–6; UNIHP 2007: Streeten: 6–9; Wilson 2006: 254; Coleman et al. 2007: 34–6). Indeed, Streeten found this a formative experience that would later resonate in a key phase of his career, leading a team undertaking seminal work on poverty and basic needs at the World Bank: 'Curiously the least disagreeable feature of this voyage was the crammed space. It is then that I discovered that, while food, water and sanitation are basic needs, shelter and housing are not, but are an acquired taste' (1986b: 146). This therefore constitutes important evidence for my inquiry.

Streeten expounded in detail on his Canadian experiences and their impact during our interview:

PS: The first camp was near Québec – you could see the Hotel Fotonac, is it?,[10] from the camp – and then we went from the camp inland to Sherbrooke which I think is near ... I believe, Montreal.

DS: [O]ne of the main streets in Montreal is called Sherbrooke Avenue.

PS: Sherbrooke, yes it must have been, because ... Canadians didn't really know much about the war – they didn't know about refugees ... – they thought that we were extremely dangerous as economists! And they came out ... it was one of the Sunday afternoon entertainments to look at the Prisoners of War behind ... behind many layers of barbed wire and observation towers and searchlights and so on (in day time, of course, the searchlights weren't on). But the Sunday Montrealers came out to look at these strange animals. Now my colleagues wanted to make sure that they understood that we were not their enemies; we were not fifth columnists, we were their friends. So they put up a large sign (I didn't see it because I would have corrected it – I knew enough English) but that sign said in a somewhat ambiguous way: 'We in this camp hate the Germans as much as you French Canadians', which is a bit ambiguous!!

But ... physically in terms of nourishment, food was much better, more plentiful; it was warmer (it was a very cold winter in Huyton and in the Isle of Man because fuels were scarce); but the psychological treatment one got ... First of all we were completely robbed of all the few possessions we had like watches and things by the Canadian military who emptied [our luggage] and filled their pockets.[11] And later on, their whole attitude ... in fact I remember that they used these observation towers to shoot at us and there was a curfew at night – you're not supposed to ... move outside the hut – but one of these poor guys, he was mentally disturbed, and he didn't quite

[10] Hotel Frontenac – which still exists as an impressive castle-like hotel overlooking the St Lawrence River; see www.fairmont.com/frontenac (confirmed to be the place by PS in email 5/2/12).

[11] See Stent (1980: 111, 225–6) for corroborative details.

know what was happening, and he was shot by these people when he walked out at night, out of the hut into the camp. So psychologically it was not a very pleasant period and, of course, we felt that war was going on without us and we wanted to be in it (some of us) [see also Stent 1980: 216–23].

So they sent out ... a very good man called Alex Paterson, a Quaker who was a Prisons' Commissioner and he interviewed us and he was supposed to select kosher prisoners, if you like, to be returned. And we talked to him and a few selected groups of us were supposed to go back on a ship in ... early January or mid-February 1941, I guess it must have been – and we were put onto this ship.[12]
...

We came back during the height of the Liverpool blitz. I remember Liverpool being bombarded by the Germans and still being interned again – once again in Huyton. There was a German ex-spy from the First World War called [von] Rintelen – he wrote a little Penguin book in English[13] – he was also amongst those interned – I think he was one of those German spies (he was not a Jew but he was against the Nazis) and he, I remember, gave lectures on spying – 'it doesn't matter who you spy for, it's much the same whoever it may be' [see Stent 1980: 64]. He was quite an interesting man ... but eventually sooner or later we were released and the funny thing, you know ... while I was still in Aberdeen University I had volunteered for the Royal Air Force (RAF) – and I had my calling-up interview notice sent into the internment camp ... by ... post (that was one of those odd paradoxical situations). But we went along to join the Air Force – in those days we were allowed to join the [Auxiliary Military Pioneer] Air Corps, which I don't know whether you know – very lowly digging duties and putting up walls and tents and similar things. But still it was freedom – freedom was greatly appreciated

[12] This is the Alexander Paterson who had visited Fritz Schumacher in Prees Heath internment camp a few months earlier (see above). Stent (1980: 216–28) provides details of Paterson's thorough investigation, his humanitarian approach (which confirm Paul Streeten's comments) and the impact his report had in the UK. In later email correspondence (18/1/12), Paul Streeten confirmed that he thinks he left Canada in December 1940, arriving back in Liverpool in January; the return ship was the *Thysville*. This is indeed confirmed in Streeten (1986a: 404; 1986b: 147) and corroborated by Heinz Arndt's account (see below).

[13] Von Rintelen's book was entitled *The Dark Invader* (Stent 1980: 64; Streeten 1986b: 147).

after nearly a year in internment, which ... seem[ed] much longer than a year seems nowadays.

DS: How did it feel being interned as a potential enemy when you had just escaped from Austria – escaped all that?

PS: Well it felt like being completely ... completely without any roots, you know. You had, of course, no roots in Austria or Germany any more because they had been completely cut off. You thought you were trying to get new roots in England but *they* had been cut off ... so you really felt without friends in the world, which was a very unpleasant and unkindly feeling. (interview, Paul Streeten[vii])[14]

Of course, that merely drove as many of the refugees as had anything in common closer together. Both in Huyton and Sherbrooke, the academics and scientists organised classes for anyone interested. This has been widely documented (Stent 1980; London 2000; Bondi 1990[15]) but Paul Streeten's recollections bear quoting at length for their immediacy and subsequent influence (interview, Paul Streeten[viii]):

> I do remember meeting very many distinguished [people] including Perutz and future Nobel Prize winners in the camps. In fact, in Canada we started a university – there was a very wonderful art historian in Canada, an elderly man called Wilde. I remember both in camp, on the ship and in Canada, there were very distinguished people – (people who later became distinguished; they were not yet distinguished in those days) – scientists and so on. There was, of course, my best friend (but I had known him already in Vienna), Hermann Bondi, who became Her Majesty's Chief Scientific Advisor ... but he was in a class in the elementary school together with my brother – he was in the same year as my brother Walter. Hermann Bondi, Tommy Gould was in the camp, and Max Perutz. There was a wonderful economist who did not become famous but be would have had he not committed suicide later – A. Radomysler.[16]
>
> ...

---

[14] This sentiment inspired the title of the (1986b) penultimate version of Streeten's autobiographical sketch, in which he also refers to the irony of internment after being forced out of Austria – see below.

[15] Bondi's file in the SPSL Archive contains further corroborative evidence on this period.

[16] See also Streeten (1997: 191).

Many of the Canadians, of course, stayed in Canada. In fact, I only looked up on the Internet the other day some of the people who were in camp with me in Canada. There was, for instance, a very distinguished (later he became a very distinguished) rabbi called Emil Fackenheim and there was another guy who was with me (they were both with me in Aberdeen too) called Rotfeld, Kurt? – I forget his first name now … he was a very nice man – biologist – he did lots of work on the *drosophila*, the fruit fly …; many stayed on in Canada and were eventually released into Toronto University. When I came back to Toronto University and looked at the telephone directory of the people there, I was astonished at how many people from the internment camp had become professors at the University of Toronto.

In his final – and longest – autobiographical essay, Streeten (1997: 191–2) mentions **Heinz Arndt** as being among the economics faculty in Sherbrooke camp, and – quite remarkably – as having given a highly impressive lecture on John Locke at the railway station before they embarked on the *Ettrick* for Canada. Streeten also remarks with hindsight that 'His origins, fate, manners and, up to a point, intellectual development have parallels with mine. But he has become very conservative'.

Arndt's letters and the commentary of his biographers (Copeland et al. 2007: 34–41) provide very similar testimony, from the details of the appalling conditions on board the *Ettrick*, which took him to Quebec, to the double robbery on arrival and the initial discrimination suffered at the hands of the Canadians, the role of the aristocratic non-Nazi internee, Count Lingen (a grandson of the Kaiser and cousin of King George VI) (see also Stent 1980: 64–5; Streeten 1997: 191–2), the camp university and the rest. Arndt was active in representing other internees and negotiating on their behalf with complaints about conditions such as the inadequacy of ophthalmic and dental treatment. This earned him the displeasure of the camp commandant, who informed him after some months that, bizarrely,

> his name was now included on a list of internees suspected of
> 'communist leanings' and therefore of being pro-Hitler and 'hostile'
> to Great Britain and the Empire. Fearing that these suspicions might
> jeopardise his hope of returning to England or of being naturalised
> as a British subject, Arndt demanded to see the evidence against him
> and he put in writing his loyalty to the British cause. He did not and,
> because of censorship, could not write to Ruth any of these worries.
> (Coleman et al. 2007: 39)

Although he was indeed going through his communist phase and was close to the communist cell headed by Colonel Kahle in internment, he was not a formal party member (*ibid.*: 42–3). Neither Arndt nor his biographers commented on the extraordinary assumption by the camp commandant that communists would be pro-Hitler when communists had been among the very first to be detained and murdered systematically after the Nazis took power.[17] This is presumably yet another example of the extent of ignorance among Canadian forces – and perhaps the population at large – like their British counterparts, in respect of the differences between German and Austrian Nazis and their sympathisers on the one hand, and victims of their oppression on the other. When encountered in such crude form in the very different Canadian context, where there was no Blitz or threat of German invasion and the entire war at that time was a very distant phenomenon, it does pose a challenge to the revisionist British historical interpretation examined above.

Naturally, Arndt also responded with joy and relief to Alexander Paterson's enquiry and report, which led directly to his release. As he wrote to Ruth on 1 December, 1940:

> Good news today for the first time in 6 months. I shall probably be back in England shortly and may be free again in 2 or 3 months. Last week a high civil servant of the H.O. [Home Office] was here to sort out those, among C cases only, who will be sent back to England and those who want to join the A.M.P.C. [Auxiliary Military Pioneer Corps]. He was very nice to me, advised me strongly not to join up but to go on with my academic work. He said he would try to send me on the second ship, possibly soon after Xmas. We shall go to an English internment camp and have to apply for release from there. (*ibid.*: 41)

Like **Streeten**, he returned to Britain on the *Thysville*, which reached Liverpool on 11 January 1941. In sharp contrast to the disgraceful conditions on the *Ettrick* en route to Canada, '[t]here were no guards, the food was good, the cabins warm, the sheets clean' (*ibid.*: 41).

Inevitably, the eight months of internment, comprising the humiliating arrest and deportation, the dreadful passage to Quebec and subsequent hardships, his role as leader in constant negotiation with

---

[17] However, Reinhart Kössler (pers. comm., 4/8/17) has pointed out to me that many communists actually found themselves in a terrible predicament in terms of the Hitler–Stalin Pact, because of the imperative of obeying party orders.

the camp authorities, and his stigmatisation for his communist sympathies, had a profound impact on Arndt. On release, he was 'a changed man' – tougher and more mature: those months 'had not destroyed his pro-British idealism, but they had indubitably tempered it. On his return to England, he was no longer the uncertain scholar. He was his own man. He was 25' (*ibid.*: 42). Perhaps in consequence, his politics also began to shift markedly – see below.

The use of the Auxiliary Military Pioneer Corps as a principal route for internees to win their freedom – cited by both **Streeten** and Arndt – had become Home Office policy from July 1940. This was part of the process requiring internees 'to prove not merely that they were not a threat to security but also that furtherance of the war effort would result from their release – a far more difficult task. The threat of continued detention became an instrument of manpower control' (London 2000: 171; see also Lafitte 1988 [1940]).

The evidence presented above is more than adequate to give the lie to some revisionist historians' and even ex-internees' claims – as **Paul Streeten** (1986b: 145) articulated particularly forcefully:

Some authors have recently maintained that the internees were quite happy with their lot and regarded it [internment] as an enforced by welcome holiday. This is quite wrong. All of us hated and resented the enforced idleness. And it was humiliating to have been rejected by the Austrians as a Jew, and imprisoned by the English as an Austrian.[18]

Making the Best of Hard Times in 'Civvy Street'

Together with the experience of working as an agricultural labourer at Eydon again after his release from internment, and examining critically many aspects of farm organisation and operations in the process, **Fritz Schumacher**'s time in Prees Heath proved an important influence on his subsequent career (Wood 1985: 105–19) and his interventions in development theory, policy and practice. At Eydon he worked manually by day and cerebrally at night, reading prodigiously and writing. A crucial element of this was his research on inequalities in international trade and detailed proposals for an international clearing house. This paralleled John Maynard Keynes' research at that time and brought

---

[18] A slightly different version appears in Streeten (1986a: 402), particularly the use of 'annoying' instead of 'humiliating'; that particular sentence does not appear in the earlier text (Streeten 1985a: 50).

them into contact during the later war years. They formed a relationship of mutual but somewhat competitive respect (*ibid.*: 120–35).

In 1942, Schumacher joined the Institute of Statistics in Oxford, working with Michal Kalecki and other European refugees as well as British economists. Although providing some intellectual relief from his isolation on the farm, this was a difficult phase in his career, both intellectually and personally. His arrogance and emotional suppression formed a difficult combination. It also came at some marital cost since his wife and sons remained at Eydon for many months until he found family accommodation in Oxford (*ibid.*: 150–7). His name and reputation were enhanced by regular newspaper articles intended to supplement his income. These led indirectly to his next career markers in 1944 through his involvement in two important works on unemployment, which formed part of an initiative that sought to anticipate the return of a problem of the Depression but temporarily eliminated by the war. His drafting of *Full Employment in a Free Society*, with contributions from other noted economists, for Sir William Beveridge proved controversial on account of its argument for socialisation of large enterprises, reflecting the influence of his exposure to Marxist ideas during and since internment (*ibid.*: 136–49, 158–67).

Beveridge had up to then held strongly contrasting views to Schumacher but Fritz was able to win him over. Nevertheless, in a somewhat unexpected outturn, the process had a longer lasting impact on Fritz, one that would affect how he saw the world and on his later landmark contributions to development thinking and practice:

> Although Fritz won all the economic arguments in his tussle to get Beveridge to accept his draft, the force of Beveridge's compassion, the ability he had to feel for the plight of the poor, had a profound effect on Fritz's own thoughts. His newly acquired socialism became the foundation for a more humane way of thinking, an attempt to put himself into the position of the poor and the deprived. He realized that if full employment affected the industrial strength and bargaining power of the workers then some thought must be given to secure their respect and understanding for what the Government was trying to achieve. At all costs, crude tampering with economic freedom had to be avoided; subtlety was necessary. (*ibid.*: 164–5)

As mentioned above, **Hans Singer**'s release from internment came in good time for him to return to Manchester University for the start of the 1941/2 academic year, when he again bore a heavy teaching load in the absence on war service or related duties of many British colleagues. He continued his research on poverty, unemployment and the unemployed, which he utilised in support of Beveridge's seminal studies that laid the foundations for the postwar British welfare state. Particularly influential in focusing his interest in and empathy with people in this predicament was his two-year involvement with the 1938 Pilgrim Trust report, *Men Without Work*. This experience, in turn, inspired him to join the United Nations after the war to work on economic development in poor countries, so there is in part a direct career link (see Chapter 5).

He also turned his attention to the German war economy at the behest of Keynes, publishing, amongst others, a series of 12 authoritative articles in consecutive issues of the *Economic Journal* between 1940 and 1944 on diverse topics, contrasting the German and British approaches. Given the topicality and importance of the subject, these greatly enhanced his reputation (Singer 1997: 135–8; Shaw 2002: 28–9, 30–4, 2006a: 242–3; UNIHP 2007: Singer: 50–1). All this while, however, he remained a 'friendly alien' and was greatly frustrated and at times felt depressed by the interminable delays in obtaining naturalisation for his wife and himself, despite his research being so pertinent to Britain's war effort; this status was finally conferred only in June 1946 (Simon 2012: 33).

Upon release from 'several months "on government business" in Canada in January 1941' as he termed internment, **Heinz Arndt** completed his interrupted Leverhulme-funded studies at the LSE but found himself increasingly frustrated by political science and sociology as 'intellectual flabbiness' and also with the loss of his intellectual integrity that being a loyal communist entailed. Three watersheds in his shift to social democracy appear to have been the total communist support for the Soviet Union following the Nazi invasion of that country, the impact on him of reading Arthur Koestler's newly published *Darkness at Noon* (which described intellectual self-destruction of the sort he felt himself to have experienced), and also his professional contact with Paul Rosenstein-Rodan, as whose research assistant as Secretary to the Committee on Postwar Reconstruction at the Royal Institute of International Affairs (Chatham House), Arndt commenced work shortly after his marriage to Ruth Strohsahl in July 1941 (Arndt 1985: 4; 1997: 158–9; Coleman et al. 2007: 43–4).

This turned out to be a decisive experience. His junior status and lack of economic experience paradoxically provided his first big break: to publish the Committee's preliminary historical report under his sole name as a book, *The Economic Lessons of the Nineteen-Thirties* (1944) because of the strong disagreements among the Committee's eminent but ideologically and theoretically diverse membership, both economists (including A.G.B. Fisher, Roy Harrod, James Meade, Joan Robinson and Barbara Wootton) and politicians, over the most appropriate economic policies to stimulate recovery. Stimulated and/or 'protected' by Rosenstein-Rodan, a convinced structuralist, the young research assistant was able to draw on lessons from his native Germany and other parts of Europe during the Depression – in very similar ways to **Fritz Schumacher** and **Hans Singer** in contemporaneous research programmes – to inform the debate and advocate the need for state initiatives and controls rather than free enterprise. The ensuing controversy, sometimes very uncomplimentary to Arndt, merely spread knowledge of his work and hence his reputation. Friedrich Hayek, the free trade advocate and who had, ironically, taught Rosenstein-Rodan in Vienna, was particularly acerbic (Arndt 1985: 5–7; 1997: 159; Coleman et al. 2007: 44–55). Those who had departed or escaped from fascism and Nazism were clearly just as ideologically diverse a group as any other.

This turn of events was particularly ironic since, as the opening paragraph of Arndt's (1985: 1) autobiography points out, although it is not uncommon for eminent economists to come to economics from other disciplines, 'to embark on a career as an economist with little formal training in Economics and virtually none in Mathematics is not sensible'. Yet that is precisely what he did, to the initial annoyance of many others. As he recorded,

> What made the decision at once impertinent and momentous was the fact that it was a research assistantship in Economics: impertinent because I knew virtually no Economics and momentous because it proved to be the starting point of my career as an economist … Apart from its presumed relevance to important concerns of the day, Economics promised more solid mental nourishment [than politics and sociology]. (*ibid.*: 4)

Arndt also claimed to have been so impressed by Rosenstein-Rodan's approach and the work of the study group of Eastern European émigré economists considering postwar development options for that region that 'I also pride myself on having badgered Rosi' into writing his famous *Economic Journal* article on the industrialisation challenges in Eastern and Southeast Europe (1943) that many consider marks the birth of development economics (*ibid.*: 7; Coleman et al. 2007: 47) – but see Hirschman (1981a), Arndt (1987), Singer (1997: 136), Meier (2005) and Simon (2009) for broader assessments of the origin of the sub-discipline.

Following the end of his Chatham House contract in September 1943, Arndt planned to volunteer for military intelligence, but was instead appointed an assistant lecturer in Economics by another eminent economist, John Hicks,[19] at Manchester, where he worked for three years alongside **Hans Singer** and Hla Myint. He also taught energetically through the Workers' Education Association (WEA). Following the return of permanent staff from wartime duties, including John Jewkes (who was one of Singer's referees for naturalisation and who disliked Arndt's approach) and Ely Devons, prospects of obtaining a permanent post vanished and he began a worldwide job search. Following their eventual naturalisation in July 1946, the Arndts and their infant son set sail for Sydney, arriving in October 1946, where he took up a senior lectureship in economics at the University of Sydney. He never regretted the move, rather enjoying being a big fish in a small pond, and despite having 'persuaded my wife to agree, very reluctantly, to a 2–3 year stint in Australia' (Arndt 1985: 9), they were to spend the rest of his career and their lives there. From Australia, he later began working in Asia and moved increasingly into development economic research and consultancy (*ibid.*; Arndt 1997: 158; Coleman et al. 2007: 55–67).

The only German-speaking wartime refugee to the UK in my study who both avoided internment and was to settle permanently here was **Scarlett Epstein** (born Trude Grünwald).[20] Arriving in London with her mother in late April 1939 and reunited with her older brothers, who had fled there considerably earlier (see Chapter 2), she faced the

[19] And with whom, as Sir John Hicks, and his equally eminent wife, Lady Ursula Hicks, I shared fascinating lunchtime conversations about the competing theories and the evolution of economic thought as a doctoral student at Linacre College, Oxford from 1979.

[20] Although Paul Streeten did live in the UK until emigrating to the USA, his wife's home country, in 1976, while Hans Singer returned to the UK after retiring from the UN in 1969 to pursue an academic career (Chapter 5).

challenges of learning English, of which she then spoke not a word, and
earning some money.

For a proud, middle-class 16-year-old girl aspiring to a medical
career, coming to terms with marginality and the harsh realities of
unskilled manual labour in a foreign country the language of which
she understood very little, represented a harsh lesson, despite having
had to grow up fast during the increasingly oppressive years in Vienna
and then the time she and her parents spent as refugees in Albania and
Yugoslavia (Chapter 2). Rejecting the paltry wages of the hairdressing
apprenticeship that had served to gain her the British entry visa, she
soon landed a job, along with many other Jewish refugee women, as a
machinist in a large East End clothing factory (Epstein 2005: Chapter
6). Starting on 15 shillings per week, within a month she was classed as
'experienced' and earned upwards of three pounds weekly on piecework,
although this varied according to the time taken for particular types of
garment. In this environment, she also learned English fast, augmented
by evening classes organised through a local Quaker group, and made
friends.

> Soon working in the factory became not only a source of income
> [to support her and her unwell mother] and self-respect but, more
> importantly, a social occasion. I enjoyed listening to the different
> experiences my friends had in their attempts to escape from Hitler's
> fascist regime. (*ibid.*: 69–70)

Especially early on, she found her elder brother, Otto, who was
active in communist circles and trying to help others escape from Nazi
occupation, sometimes overbearing and unsympathetic, perhaps acting
too much like her absent father, who had not yet managed to reach
England. She also found it difficult dealing with the steady flow of
escaped concentration camp victims arriving at their London flat with
shaven heads and 'hollow, sunken eyes' – needing to hear their horror
stories but also somehow despising them for having allowed themselves
to be thus dehumanised (*ibid.*: 72). Her father finally obtained an
entry visa and joined the rest of the family but shortly thereafter, Otto
emigrated to Australia, leaving a large void in her life since they were
close, despite an ambivalent and sometimes strained relationship, and
he had been a key source of advice. Karl, the other brother, lived in
Manchester. Her father soon became depressed again and she found
herself looking after both parents and running the flat (*ibid.*: 73–4).

After the outbreak of war, the family joined Karl, who found them a house in Salford; Scarlett quickly found work there as a machinist. Karl introduced her into the Young Austria in Great Britain socialist youth group, which became her social focus. During the internment period, she found having sole responsibility for her neurologically fragile mother – who suffered a fall and mild stroke during one of the frequent air raids – very difficult, especially as she was also studying after hours. Plans to have refugee friends move in to help and also to contribute to the household income through rent, with Scarlett reducing her work hours, were frustrated by the police refusing permission to register the address change under the alien registration regulations. They cited the building as a known location for underground political meetings, which were clearly perceived as an enemy threat amid the paranoia of the time. Scarlett was then interrogated by the police and, fearing arrest, decided on a radical course of action – a marriage of convenience with a fellow youth group member to create the fiction that she would then be focusing her energies on her husband and family and no longer on politics. Her family were surprisingly supportive, and with her father and brother released from internment, the synagogue wedding went ahead on 21 June 1941, a few weeks short of her nineteenth birthday, despite her own increasing anxiety at the implications as the day approached. Indeed the 'sham' caused her great anxiety, affecting her health for several months thereafter, until Ken left to join the army, whereupon her health recovered. At least the police harassment had ceased with her marriage, thus somehow validating her decision. She soon fell in love with and wanted to marry a fellow refugee (also by then in the army) but the complexities of the situation led to a traumatic climax in which she fell out badly with her brother, lost her intending husband before a divorce could be arranged and became even more estranged from her husband. She found it difficult to trust men thereafter and vowed never to become so vulnerable again (*ibid.*: 82–7; interview, Scarlett Epstein[ix]).

In a very immediate way, this narrative reveals the great personal trauma and human cost to German-speaking refugees of British refugee policy and especially the internment programme during the 1939–41 period. Coming on top of the trauma of Nazi persecution, flight and the struggle to start a new life during wartime, it broke some people and would have done many more but for their steely determination. Although very different from those interned, such experiences proved formative for them all, hardening them and sharpening their ambition to succeed against all the odds, as so vividly evoked in the title of Epstein's autobiography, *Swimming Upstream*.

Thereafter, despite her marital and related traumas, life improved in other respects, through gaining higher-paid salaried work as a wages clerk, while her father also found manual labour as a packer that brought in additional income. The end of the war seemed strangely anticlimactic for a 21-year-old legally married but de facto single woman living with her parents and without the education required to progress in life. She declined to give her marriage another chance when her husband was demobbed. While some other refugees began to consider returning to their home countries, she 'could not face living where I suspected everyone of having been a Nazi and party to all the terrible atrocities I had witnessed' (Epstein 2005: 90). That feeling was soon compounded by the new trauma of discovering the fate of the family's many relatives and friends who had not escaped in time:

> Like many others, Mama and Papa went into a state of shock and were like zombies. It was impossible to conceive what had taken place in Germany, the magnitude of the cruelty. When we heard that my grandmother had been marched into a gas chamber, Papa went white and sat with clenched fists, unable to speak for hours. I had a strange cloak of general grief, as I hardly knew the numerous relatives … I did not mourn their loss any more than I mourned the millions of other Nazi victims who had been murdered. I hated to see my parents' misery and instead of grief I felt anger. (*ibid.*: 90)

This prompted her to establish a new identity, discarding everything associated with Austria, including her name. She dropped Trude for Scarlett after the heroine of *Gone with the Wind*, then recently a hit in both book and film formats (*ibid.*: 90–1). Thus began a new phase in her life.

Military Service

Of the then UK-based people, only **Paul Streeten** saw active military service. Having had his intentions of serving in the Royal Air Force at the outbreak of the war frustrated by internment (his call-up papers reached him in the camp!), the AMPC provided his route out of internment in 1941, although that had its own frustrations:

> I had set my heart on something more active and more interesting than digging trenches and painting sheets of corrugated iron, but I

accepted the condition. The Pioneer Corps was much better than internment, but it had some similarities. It was recruited from mental defectives, criminals, conscientious objectors and enemy aliens: some of the best and worst human material. I was a private ... The work was tedious. But we had our evenings off, and, though not free, were not behind barbed wire. (Streeten 1985a: 52; 1986a: 404; 1986b: 146; see also Streeten 1997: 192)[21]

Among those serving with him in 251 Company was Arthur Koestler, whom Streeten admired for refusing certain privileges, although 'he was a bully: selfish, anti-social, always jumping meal queues' (Streeten 1985a: 52; 1986a: 404; 1986b: 147–8). After two years in the Pioneer Corps, Streeten was one of those individually selected for a combat role once this was permitted. As a distinguished long-distance runner, he was sought out for the commandos and joined Commando X and underwent training in various parts of the UK. 'It was great fun, more like a super holiday camp with a lot of diversified exercise. One of the happiest days of my life was when I was promoted to Lance Corporal' (Streeten 1985a: 52; 1986a: 405; 1986b: 148). During the training, he and other German-speakers were instructed to adopt English names and think up false life histories in order to avoid them being treated as traitors and shot by the Germans should they be captured. He instantly chose the name of his two adoptive 'maiden aunts', as he knew it would please them, and thus Paul Hornig became Paul Streeten (Streeten 1985a: 52; 1986a: 404–5; 1986b: 148; interview, Paul Streeten[x]).

He was then attached to 41 Royal Marine Commando and prepared for the invasion of Sicily, where they landed on 9 July 1943. After a few weeks, he was severely wounded in action behind enemy lines in an operation to prevent the Germans withdrawing with their weaponry and too many troops. Not initially expected to survive, he was evacuated by sea to Catania and thence via Alexandria to Cairo, where he regained consciousness after a few days. His bed in the Fifteenth Scottish General Hospital afforded him a view of the pyramids in one direction and the Nile in the other, but he was never able to walk, let alone explore these wonders. At Christmas, he was evacuated back to the UK on a hospital ship, where he spent several further months of rehabilitation in hospital (Streeten 1985a: 53–4; 1986a: 405–6; 1986b:

[21] My interview with Paul Streeten (7/11/06 @ 49–65 mins) covered this ground in similar vein.

150; 1997: 193), which thus took a year in total. He never regained full power in his left foot and arm and 'I still carry pieces of shrapnel in my neck, skull and arm as mementoes' (Streeten 1985a: 54; 1986a: 407); in one of our conversations, he told me that occasionally a piece works its way to the surface, quite painfully, and has to be removed. These injuries qualified him for a full disability pension and put an end to his favourite outdoor pursuits like mountaineering and skiing, although limited walking and swimming were possible. 'But fortunately, you see, the mind was, on the whole, left untouched!' (interview, Paul Streeten[xi]; UNIHP 2007: Streeten: 9–11).

Thus ended Streeten's war and after being discharged from hospital, he returned to Aberdeen to collect his MA. Having given up the idea of further study on account of his injuries and lengthy hospitalisation, he had accepted a job on the *Financial Times* but before starting there he won acceptance to Balliol College, Oxford to read PPE (politics, philosophy and economics) in October 1944, under a new further education programme for which he qualified. One of his economics tutors there was Thomas Balogh, one of the potential subjects of this study but who had arrived from Hungary to study at the LSE before the Nazis came to power. Prior to that, Balogh had studied economics in Berlin under **Fritz Schumacher**'s father and had been a lodger in the Schumachers' home (Wood 1985: 9). While this particular connection is clearly coincidental, it provides further evidence of the degree of international integration and mobility among the professions and upper classes within prewar Western Europe. Streeten's comment on Balogh amounts to an emphatic backhanded compliment:

> From Frank Burchardt[22] I learned a lot of economics because he was always crystal clear; but from Balogh more because he was so confusing that I had to go back to my room and work it out myself. The best tutors are not the clearest. (Streeten 1985a: 55; 1986a: 407; 1986b: 151; see also Streeten 1997: 196)[23]

---

[22] Yet another eminent German-speaking refugee economist, who arrived in Oxford in 1936. He later became director of the Oxford University Institute of Statistics (Wood 1985: 151).

[23] His fulsome obituary tribute to Balogh elaborates in vivid terms that I cannot resist reproducing here:

> listening to him was like wandering through a well-stocked department store. One never quite knows what wares will turn up next, but each department presents an

Thus, in late 1944, Paul Streeten was ultimately able to return to 'normal' fulltime higher education, which extended beyond the end of the war and set him on the path to his career as a distinguished economist embracing both several branches of mainstream economics and the emergent postwar field of development economics. Ironically, having found refuge in Britain from Nazism and been able to resume his studies, British aliens policy and then his war injuries cost him another four and a quarter years, and very nearly his life.

Reflections

Conditions in the UK for newly arrived refugees from Nazism were complex and their reception was ambivalent and inconsistent over time and according to particular circumstances, not least bureaucratic complexity, political fluctuations and serendipity. Particularly for non-naturalised German speakers, internment in 1940–41 represented an initially incomprehensible affront and slap in the face. The duration of internment for each of the five people in this study (Heinz Arndt, Fritz Schumacher, Hans Singer, Paul Streeten and Eric Wolf) caught up in the net, varied according to how rapidly the required evidence could be assembled to convince the authorities that the person in question was 'useful' and posed no threat. Yet, inconsistencies and possibly discrimination existed and affected Hans Singer, for whom there was ample high-level support, particularly badly. Polanyi Levitt and Epstein narrowly avoided internment. After release, ex-internees resumed employment (Singer) or studies, while Arndt and Streeten joined the Pioneer Corps, the latter being severely wounded in combat. This further delayed his studies and ability to commence a career.

For several of the people treated in this inhumane and insensitive way, ironically after narrowly escaping arrest by the Nazis or related forces and thus deportation to a concentration or extermination camp, the experience was highly disturbing. Surprisingly, it didn't spur most

array of beautiful and useful items. The moves were sometimes vertical, sometimes horizontal, sometimes diagonal, but always unpredictable. Behind the ideas, the inspiration, the provocation, there was the readiness to offer affection and loyalty to those who opened themselves to him: his friends. (Streeten 1985b: 18)

While such a style clearly did not appeal to all, Balogh and many of his generation would certainly have fallen foul of the UK quality assurance inspection regime to which British higher education teaching is subjected nowadays.

to leave the country in disgust but the privations did have a clear impact on morale and perceptions, in Paul Streeten's case also contributing to his later formative work on basic needs strategies. Before exploring the unfolding careers of these escapees and survivors, however, I turn in Chapter 4 to the wartime experiences of those in my study who spent part or all of the war years elsewhere in Europe after escaping their home countries, or who reached the USA and Canada during the war.

4 | WARTIME TRACKS IN EUROPE AND NORTH AMERICA

Any periodisation inevitably has an element of subjectivity and does not 'work' effectively for all aspects of the relevant dynamics and processes. This applies even to as dramatic, momentous and readily definable a period as World War II. For, although it had life-changing implications for the subjects of my study, especially but not exclusively those who were still in the Nazis' path when war broke out on 1 September 1939, fascist and Nazi persecution had increased to such an extent over the preceding months and years that 'normal' life had perforce already been long abandoned in most cases. Those in my study who had managed to escape by then were able to continue rebuilding their lives in their new homes (especially in North America), seeking security, education and/ or employment as refugees or contributing to the resistance and military campaigns elsewhere in Europe and North Africa. For them, escape and sanctuary represented the most critical watersheds, as discussed in Chapter 2, although the experience of most of those in the UK, which formed the subject of Chapter 3, demonstrated the impact on them of the outbreak of war even beyond the reach of the German military. The people featured in this chapter had such diverse experiences and across a wide range of places that it is necessarily structured very differently from Chapter 3, with more individualised narrative and less scope to draw on coherent secondary literature and to generalise. In at least one case, that of **Albert Hirschman**, who (like **Hans Singer**) had fled Germany as soon as the Nazis took power in 1933, the outbreak of war nevertheless also represented an element of continuity in his life. He had by then already crossed several boundaries, literally and figuratively,[1] since, in addition to work and study, he had been active

---

[1] Indeed, the title of his book, *Crossing Boundaries*, in which his English translation and extension of an earlier autobiographical interview appears, reflects this: 'Crossing boundaries is not only characteristic of the physical moves I have undertaken (or had to undertake) in the course of my life; it is also distinctive of the interdisciplinary travels I have engaged in ever since I started to write' (Hirschman 2001 [1998]: 8).

in the anti-fascist struggle in Italy and participated in the Spanish Civil War (see Chapter 2), so he took up arms again.

Alexander Gerschenkron: An Unlikely Shipbuilder and Wartime Advisor

Gerschenkron found it hard to re-establish himself yet again, this time in the USA, his third country, but, like many of his generation, sought to do so by focusing on the present and future rather than dwelling on the past. However, his bearing and manner, clearly compounded by the burdens he felt himself to be carrying, did not facilitate new friendships or endear him to many colleagues at Berkeley. His wife struggled even more to adapt. He also felt disadvantaged relative to bright younger local scholars, many of whom overtook him in career terms. However, things looked up academically when he was belatedly promoted from associate to lecturer and his monograph, *Bread and Democracy in Germany*, was published shortly afterwards (Gerschenkron 1943). It was to remain his longest publication and became a classic (Dawidoff 2002: 121–7, 134–5).

Nevertheless, he still felt becalmed and took a summer job helping the war effort by building Liberty Ships in the shipyard near Berkeley, where he enjoyed the very different social dynamics and physical work, as well as the pay, which was superior to that from the university. 'Right there in Richmond Shura became a hopelessly besotted American patriot – fell into an American swoon that would last a lifetime' (*ibid.*: 130).

In 1944, Gerschenkron was recommended to the Federal Reserve Board and employed as a European economic analyst. He grasped this offer in the hope and expectation of becoming more centrally involved in the war effort and associated economic policy debate. He became one of many immigrants employed for their knowledge of one or more European countries, including two others he had known in Vienna, Fritz Machlup and Gottfried Haberler. Although employed for his expertise on Germany and Austria, it rapidly became clear which way the war was turning and the Fed needed his attention focused on the Soviet Union in anticipation of postwar scenarios. His substantive report on 'Economic Relations with the Soviet Union' (Gerschenkron 1945) and a secret report for the Office of Strategic Services while on assignment there espoused a pragmatic approach of reintegrating the USSR into the world economy, arguing that Soviet leaders were less ideologically committed to communism than widely assumed. This gained him much press coverage and prominence. Following another 'loan' stint at the State Department, Gerschenkron returned to the Fed, where he was promoted to head the International Section in 1946. He found this very fulfilling professionally but accepted a post in the Economics Department at Harvard in 1948 (Dawidoff 2002: 231), a position that Walt Rostow had been offered and declined, electing instead to remain in the United Nations (*ibid.*: 136–51). Becoming a fulltime academic brought to an end Gerschenkron's policy engagements.

Hirschman's War: Military Service, Resistance Work, Escape, University Research and a Different Army

Having narrowly escaped detention in Trieste following Italy's introduction of racial laws in 1938 and his public denunciation as an anti-fascist collaborator and German Jew by leaving for Paris, Hirschman enlisted in the French Army, which, in 1938, had made it possible for foreigners to sign up for service in the regular army (as distinct from the Foreign Legion) in the event of war. His company, comprising Germans and Italians, was soon surrounded near Le Mans and this necessitated a rapid abandonment of their identity documents and assumption of French names, with ID cards to match, lest they be executed as traitors if captured. Hence Albert Hirschmann (at that stage he still used the German spelling) became 'Albert Hermant, né á Philadelphie' – the false birthplace intended to preclude the possibility of the Germans checking local birth registers in France (Hirschman 2001 [1998]: 69–70; Hirschman 1996, Tape 3 @ 9–12 mins).[2]

He set off towards Bordeaux on a bicycle and avoided incarceration only because the advancing German forces were so intent on reaching the Spanish border as fast as possible that they were not rounding up individual French soldiers, merely telling them to report to the nearest prison camp. Instead, he fled to the Vichy zone, obtaining demobilisation papers from the army in Nîmes, and later moving to Marseilles with the intention of joining a group of others needing to escape from the country. There he soon met Varian Fry, then just arrived from the USA on behalf of the Emergency Rescue Committee set up by American trade unions and academics (some of the latter themselves recent refugees from Europe) to assist at-risk anti-fascist

---

[2] A photo of his false French identity card appears in one of his earlier books (Hirschman 1995: 98) as part of another autobiographical vignette.

and anti-Nazi refugees to escape.[3] Hirschman worked with Fry for six months, seeking routes through Iberia and obtaining (often with great difficulty) transit visas through Spain and Portugal once entry visas to third countries had been obtained for key people. Among those he helped were Hannah Arendt and her husband, Heinrich Blücher, the latter an old friend from Berlin who had once courted one of Hirschman's sisters! Walter Benjamin, the renowned intellectual and member of the Frankfurt School of sociology, committed suicide after being refused a French visa. Finally, the police came after Hirschman and, having serendipitously avoided arrest by being out of town when they went to his hotel, he had to depart Marseilles immediately in December 1940, using a route through Iberia on which he had previously assisted others (Hirschman 1995: 123–6; 2001 [1998]: 70–3; 1996, Tape 3 @ 16–30 mins, Tape 4 @ 0–13 mins; Adelman 2013: 171–86).

His earlier contacts and networks, in the form of a New Zealand economist who had employed Hirschman in Paris in 1938–39 but by then was a professor at the University of California at Berkeley, and the American consul through whom US entry visas were channelled, proved instrumental in getting him to safety in the USA in January 1941. Working at the University of California at Berkeley, he shared an office with **Alexander Gerschenkron**, who had himself left Austria some years before (see above and Chapter 2; Adelman 2013: 205). When Hirschman's fellowship ended after two years, he enlisted in the US Army because '[i]t was the only thing foreigners were able to do at the time, if they did not want to abandon their liberty', and soon became a naturalised American, at which point he dropped the second 'n' from his surname (he had abandoned his false identity as Albert Hermant as soon as he left France). By that time, he had married Sarah, an American, in June 1941; their first daughter was born in 1944, while he was fighting in North Africa (Hirschman 1998: 74–5). After North Africa, he spent the remainder of the war and six months afterwards in Italy, with the Office of Strategic Services and then in a counter-espionage unit. Among his postwar tasks was translating during one of the first trials of a German general, who had ordered the shooting of captured uniformed American

---

[3] For details of the Committee's work, see Varian Fry's (1945) *Surrender on Demand* and (1968, 1993) *Assignment: Rescue – an Autobiography*, the 1993 reprinting of which has an Introduction by Albert Hirschman, which is, in turn, reprinted as Chapter 10 in Hirschman (1995: 120–2).

soldiers. He returned to his wife and daughter in the US in December 1945 (Hirschman 1998: 76–7; Adelman 2013: 221–51).

A more diverse and remarkable war would be hard to imagine: evading arrest on several occasions, avoiding injury while on military duties with two different armies, commencing his professional career in the USA and starting a family. Serendipity and good fortune clearly played their part. In terms of the theme of this book, one of the distinguishing features – along with those refugees interned in the UK in 1940–1 – was his age. As the oldest living person at the time of my main research, he was an adult and by the outbreak of the war had completed his studies to doctoral level and was able to begin professional work in between his several military and underground involvements. Indeed, **Paul Streeten** and he were the only two of my research subjects to experience active war service and, overall, suffered the longest interruptions to their civilian lives. Hence by the start of 1946, when he returned to the USA, he was able to resume family life and progress his career. As we shall see in Chapter 5, his experience in different parts of Europe during the 1930s and first half of the 1940s would immediately prove invaluable in one of the seminal undertakings not just of postwar reconstruction but also nascent development policy in a decolonising world. The 'reach' and impact of this work probably distinguish him from my other research subjects in this remarkable cohort except **Hans Singer**, who was also instrumental in the design and establishment of key elements of the emerging postwar development institutional architecture.

Theodor Bergmann

Having narrowly escaped the Nazis in the Sudetenland in 1938, Theodor Bergmann landed up in Sweden after an unsuccessful attempt to continue his studies in Norway, but academic study there also proved impossible. Hence, he found work on a farm west of Stockholm and, together with one brother who had also sought refuge in Sweden, published a KPDO newspaper and worked in a committee of German trade unionists. Another brother and various other relatives were captured by the Nazis and exterminated, prompting Theodor to commit himself to ensuring that Jews would never again be subject to such barbarity. After the end of the war, and despite his family's losses, he was determined to return to his devastated native Germany to continue his studies and political work. The British occupation authorities, however, refused to permit this until intervention by influential friends and the British Labour Party politician, Fenner Brockway. After working in the Swedish mining industry in the interim, he finally returned in April 1946 (Kessler 2017). This made him distinctive in this study; as explained later in this chapter, **Zygmunt Bauman** was the only other person in this study to return to his native country (Poland) after the war, and that was one occupied by the Nazis rather than where that regime developed and took power. It also makes Bergmann highly unusual among German Jews, only a tiny number of whom returned soon afterwards. His political commitments to the labour movement and extensive networks among KPDO members and other anti-Stalinists who had somehow survived the war were central factors in his decision.

Shlomo Reutlinger: A Teenager Dodging the Nazis and Escaping to Palestine

As explained in Chapter 2, Shlomo Reutlinger, then aged 13, was sent from Pforzheim together with his nine-year-old brother, Erich, to live with their uncle in Antwerp in March 1939, a few months after *Kristallnacht* and his unforgettably disrupted Barmitzvah. Six months later, at the outbreak of war, the uncle, who was in the diamond trade and hence commercially mobile, decided to emigrate to Canada. Not knowing where Shlomo's parents would land up – they had applications pending for both the USA and Palestine – it was decided to leave the boys in Europe in the interim, and so arrangements were made for them to board with another Jewish family in Brussels. This necessitated shifting from a Flemish-speaking to a French-speaking school, with associated educational disruption in addition to the dislocation of successive changes in living arrangements (interview, Shlomo Reutlinger[i]).

As the threat of German invasion increased, it became essential to move again. A place was found for Shlomo on the Transport of Children to Palestine (who made the arrangements is unclear) in March 1940, two months before the Germans crossed the Maginot Line:

> I, together with another hundred children or so were off to Marseilles and from Marseilles to Palestine. I remember on the boat with us were French Foreign Legion – we picked [them] up ... in Algiers and they were on their way to Syria and we got off in Haifa, Palestine. And so there was this very charitable Dutch lady – I think she was Dutch, or Danish – who accompanied the children's transport. (interview, Shlomo Reutlinger[ii])

Only teenagers could qualify for Youth Certificates that were a prerequisite for entry to Palestine under this evacuation scheme; his brother was too young and had to remain in Brussels with the host family. Following the invasion, they were all deported to Auschwitz, 'and that's the last we heard of Erich' (interview, Shlomo Reutlinger[iii]).

Some months following the German occupation of Poland and France, his parents and infant sister, along with the other Jews from the state of Baden, were deported westwards for unknown reasons to the Gurs camp on the Franco-Spanish border in the Pyrenees that had originally been built to house Spanish Republican prisoners during the civil war. There they were incarcerated in separate camps for men and women for 11 months from October/November 1940 until they managed to obtain entry visas for Cuba[4] and were allowed to leave by the Vichy authorities. However, the winter of 1940/41 was particularly harsh and the privations in the camp proved severe. They had been allowed to take only one suitcase of possessions with them, so were virtually destitute by the time they reached Cuba:

> My parents never wanted to tell me much about what happened
> during that whole year – a terrible year they went through – I mean
> they got sick but survived. But the children, my children, they couldn't
> refuse – they went after them with a microphone and they recorded
> and they talked about the war. (interview, Shlomo Reutlinger[iv])

One remarkable anecdote about their deportation and incarceration bears repetition in full, both because it illustrates the religious family context in which Shlomo grew up and because it has a bearing on his parents' survival. Very unusually, his family had their own Torah (holy scroll of the Pentateuch) but how or why Shlomo does not know. On the day of deportation, his parents had already reached the railway station with their single suitcases when Shlomo's father recognised a local policeman who had occasionally been a customer of his business in town and asked him,

> 'I have one favour to ask Germany: could I go back? I forgot
> something' and he may have told him it was the Torah scroll. Anyway,
> he took a little boy with him – a ten-year-old boy – and they went back

---

[4] Along with some other Jewish refugees, they managed to obtain visas through corrupt payments to President Batista by intermediaries.

to the house. The house was [already] sealed – German punctuality [efficiency] or whatever – they made sure the houses got sealed when they took [the residents] away and took an inventory. Anyway, so he put this little boy into the window of the house and he got back in and he brought out the Torah scroll. And so they took it with them to the camp and it was one of two Torah scrolls that were taken [there] ... And in the vicinity of the camp there were small Jewish communities, but not [big] enough to have synagogues, so whenever they had a Bar Mitzvah or something they had heard that there was a Torah scroll in the camp and they asked to use [it] ... My father insisted that he would not let the Torah go without him, so he managed to get out on many Saturdays and he was able to bring back some food for my mother, I understand, so that helped them to survive. My children wrote this story up [as] 'my grandfather saved the Torah and the Torah saved him!' (interview, Shlomo Reutlinger[v])

Again, for uncertain reasons, the Torah never went with his parents to Cuba but remained with one of the local Jewish communities. This emerged only in the 1980s through another remarkable coincidence. The ten-year-old boy who had retrieved the Torah from the Reutlinger home as they were being deported had been rescued from the camp by the OSE organisation along with other children and finally reached Palestine in 1946. Shlomo heard about him and made contact but was unable to find out anything much about camp life or his parents because the boy refused to discuss his experiences. Only decades later did curiosity drive him to return to the area of the camp and, on enquiring from the local Jewish community about the scrolls, was told that they have two from the camps, one of which was in poor condition so was taken out only on the Simchat Torah festival – which marks the end of the weekly readings of the Torah and starting again – each year. He persuaded them to donate both scrolls to the Yad Vashem Holocaust Monument and Museum in Jerusalem, where they now reside and Shlomo and his family – who all live in Israel now – occasionally go there to see them! (interview, Shlomo Reutlinger[vi]).

On arrival in Palestine, Shlomo went to stay with relatives in a village but 'I was a city boy – I hated it there – there was no indoor plumbing in their house – I just didn't want to stay there'. Through the family's Zionist connections, he managed to gain admission to a Youth Aliyah (immigration) school called Kfar Hanoah, where he spent two years, becoming an enthusiastic member of the Haganah

(Jewish armed resistance group against the British occupation) and developed an interest in agriculture: 'I became a vegetable grower in my first career and a very good teacher!' The Youth Aliyah programme prepared the immigrants for life on a kibbutz (communal farm) and after overcoming an initial aversion, he became keen on milking the cows as it was seen as a high status job by the boys. After moving among various kibbutzim, he was a member of the pioneer group that established Ein Hanatziv, in the Bet Shean area in 1946. Soon after arrival in Palestine, he changed his given name from Fritz to Shlomo (interview, Shlomo Reutlinger[vii]) as a symbolic break with his German past and adoption of a Hebrew identity.

After four years on the kibbutz, he resolved to go to see his parents and sister, who had gained admission to the USA from Cuba after the war and were by then living in New York. He had not seen them for 11 years. Accordingly, he left Palestine 10 years after arriving but with the intention of returning soon (interview, Shlomo Reutlinger[viii]). However, this didn't happen permanently until 1993, after he had retired. As will be revealed in Chapter 6, his kibbutz experience was to determine the direction of his American university studies and subsequent career.

Youthful Transits through Europe to the USA

Apart from the very young **Gerry Helleiner** passing briefly through the UK en route to Canada (see Chapter 2; Simon 2012), two other young Viennese arrived in the USA in 1940 as teenagers via different routes. **John Friedmann** reached New York from Vienna with his mother and brother by train and ship just before his fourteenth birthday, whereas the 17-year-old **Eric Wolf** moved with his family after two years in London, during which he obtained his A-Levels and experienced internment (see Chapter 3). While Friedmann spent the remainder of the war completing his secondary schooling, Wolf commenced further study.

John Friedmann: Friedmann represents an intermediate situation in terms of his 'flight path' as between those who spent time in the UK, however brief, and those in other parts of Europe and beyond. Although his Jewish father, Robert, had converted to Christianity around the time of his marriage to his Catholic wife (before John was born), he was, of course, deemed Jewish in terms of Nazi ideology. Hence he was arrested in Vienna in the aftermath of *Kristallnacht* in late 1938 and spent three weeks in detention. 'He never talked very much about his experiences during those three weeks but it was clear then, as it hadn't been clear before, that it was really not safe for a Jew, even a converted Jew, a Christianised Jew, to remain' (interview, John Friedmann[ix]).

As a result, he left for Switzerland in early 1939, his entry facilitated by a cousin who was married to a Swiss national. From there, he was assisted by the Quakers to get to the UK, where he spent roughly nine months until he procured a US immigrant visa through the sponsorship of his sister, Mitzi Friedmann, who had been in New York since 1937.[5] She was also instrumental in subsequently obtaining visas for John, his mother and younger brother in early 1940. They left Vienna by train through Italy and caught the final ship to New York before Italy entered the war and that route was closed, arriving, he thought, on 14 April 1940, two days before his fourteenth birthday. Hence, although his father found intermediate refuge in the UK, John never did.

John's father, hitherto a secondary school teacher in a Vienna *Gymnasium*, found a temporary post as librarian in Goshen College, a Mennonite institution in Goshen, Indiana and the family moved there. However, John completed his secondary school education as a boarder for three years (1940–43) at Mount Hermon School for Boys in Massachusetts[6] on a scholarship arranged by a friend of his father. His entry was facilitated by his having been raised a Christian. Although he had learned a little English in Vienna, he basically acquired the language while at Mount Hermon, 'but I never lost my accent' (interview, John Friedmann[x]).

After Mount Hermon, John studied for a year at Bowdoin College in Brunswick, Maine, before conscription into the army in the summer of 1944. Having obtained fast-track citizenship that November and then completed his officer's training as a second lieutenant, he was sent to Germany in December 1945, six months after the end of the war in Europe, to work in military intelligence as part of the occupying force until his discharge in late 1947, the year he married his first wife. They then returned to the USA, where he resumed his higher

---

[5] An artist, she had gone there to exhibit some of her work and when the *Anschluss* occurred in March 1938 realised the perils of returning to Austria and had managed to remain in the US.

[6] The school, along with a girls' seminary on the opposite bank of the Connecticut River, had been founded by Moody, a wealthy evangelist, at the turn of the century.

education, spending a year at Western Michigan State University (WMSU) in Kalamazoo, where his father was by then teaching history and philosophy (and where he remained until retirement) (John Friedmann, pers. comm.[xi]).

Eric Wolf: Not long after being released from internment (Chapter 3), Eric Wolf and his parents left England for New York in June 1940 on one of the final passenger liners able to make the crossing before German U-boat attacks effectively closed that route. That autumn he enrolled in Queens College but struggled to find an academic direction that suited him until he was inspired by a course on Asian anthropology by Joseph Bram since it 'actually dealt with the cultural miscellany that had always fascinated him'. He thus opted to major in anthropology and was advised by Hortense Powdermaker (Silverman 2002: 8). Volunteering on a rural reforestation project at a folk school in Tennessee one summer proved important to his intellectual development by exposing him to the 'impoverished underbelly of the South but also to the potential of grassroots social activism and democratic idealism' (Wolf with Silverman 2001: 3).

In 1943, he enlisted in the US Army (thereby also gaining immediate naturalisation) and served in the Mountain Division, an elite ski unit, where he led a platoon but refused commission as an officer. He was proud that, as 'a book-loving Jew, once a promising violin student at the Vienna conservatory – [he] could shoot with the best of them' (*ibid.*: 8–9). His unit saw action in the Italian Apennines and he had a lucky escape when a bullet narrowly missed his brain. Although he opposed various specific wars, he was not anti-war per se. After the war in Europe ended, he was responsible for debriefing German prisoners before returning to Queens College with funding provided by the 'GI Bill' to help train and then reintegrate returned war veterans into the civilian economy (*ibid.*; interview, Sydel Silverman[xii]). He completed his BA in Sociology and Anthropology in the spring of 1946, prior to commencing graduate work at Columbia University (see Chapter 7; Friedman 1987: 108). According to Silverman (2002: 9), Wolf retrospectively regarded his army time as important in showing him the practical impact of military power, about which he had heard theoretically from Norbert Elias in the internment camp in 1940 (see Chapter 3). Power relations would come to constitute a central concern throughout his career.

The Netherlands: Occupation and After

As explained in Chapter 2, both **Ernie Stern** and **Emanuel de Kadt** were born in August 1933 and arrived in Amsterdam and Rotterdam as infants from Germany and Belgium respectively. Their wartime experiences following the German invasion when they were just seven years old were, however, very different.

Emanuel de Kadt – Childhood Torn Asunder. The German invasion of the Netherlands on 10 May 1940 brought to an abrupt end the innocent childhood of Emanuel de Kadt, then aged seven. Four days of heavy aerial bombardment sent the family repeatedly into the basement for shelter; on 14 May the blanket fire-bombing of central Rotterdam triggered the Dutch surrender and the following day German tanks rumbled past their front door at the start of the occupation (de Kadt 2009: 1).[7]

With knowledge of what had already happened to the Jews of Germany and Poland, some – including his father's brother and family (apart from an infant baby) committed suicide. Anti-Jewish measures were soon implemented and, as a German Jew who might thus 'know too much' and impede the occupation, his step-father was forced to leave Rotterdam for Doorn, a village near Utrecht. Emanuel's mother accompanied him so the young boy was given the choice of going with them, and hence having to attend a village school, or remaining in Rotterdam with his maternal grandparents so that he could continue in his current 'good school'. He chose the latter, visiting his parents during school holidays, but by early 1941 was forced out of that school to an all-Jewish one as part of the Nazi anti-'contamination' measures. On one visit to his parents, he had to help them remove anti-Semitic stickers that said 'Jews out!' plastered to the ground floor windows of their home (*ibid.*: 2).

His mother became increasingly ill and was misdiagnosed with rheumatism; the treatment worsened her condition. Only later, as a refugee in Portugal, was the problem correctly diagnosed as tuberculosis, for which there was then no ready cure, and she suffered a slow decline, dying in 1944, when Emanuel was 11.

Jews were subject to ever more intrusive and restrictive measures from 1941 onwards, having to register with the authorities – whereupon a large J for *Joode* (Jew) was stamped on their identity documents;

---

[7] This manuscript is a revised version of an earlier one that I had been sent in advance of my interview with Emanuel and on the basis of which we were thus able to discuss relevant issues and ideas without repeating the detail contained therein.

ownership of radios, bicycles and cars was forbidden, they could use the shops only for three hours in the afternoons, the wearing of a yellow Star of David with *Joode* on it became compulsory, and so forth, very much as in Germany itself. Round-ups of wanted people were frequent. By mid-1942 people started receiving summonses to present themselves for transport to 'work camps', to which they could take along only one rucksack of personal belongings and two blankets. Emanuel and his grandparents had theirs packed in case. Some people managed to obtain exemption stamps (*Sperrstempeln*) from deportation on grounds of usefulness, such as work for the puppet *Joodsche Raad* (Jewish Council) which, as in Germany and other occupied countries, had been established by the Nazis to facilitate administration of ghettos, schools and eventually deportations. Emanuel's family obtained one on grounds of possessing a permit to emigrate (*Ausreise*) but these were not guaranteed to remain valid (*ibid.*: 3–4).

Those not yet deported struggled to maintain some social and cultural life, even improvising a synagogue in a disused garage workshop, since the main synagogues had been bombed in 1940. Eventually in early 1943, there were too few remaining to make up the Minyan, and it closed. 'On the last day it was suggested that I take a 'tallith' or prayer shawl which had belonged to a deported congregant: that would be better than having it thrown out by the Germans. I still use it when I go to synagogue' (*ibid.*: 4).

His grandparents' house was used as an office by the local branch of the *Joodsche Raad* from 1942 till early 1943, but the Germans wanted to requisition the large house and visited regularly on various pretexts to try to find grounds to claim it. Over this period, Emanuel had several close escapes from being detained and deported. On one occasion the police came to arrest him at 2am but a reasonable Dutch policeman was in charge and eventually relented when his grandfather promised to go to the relevant German office the next morning. The issue was that, as a child, Emanuel did not have identity documents and hence had no *Sperrstempel*. On another occasion, he and a friend just avoided arrest at a road checkpoint by appearing to be racing each other on their mopeds through it with their chests flat on the handlebars to conceal their yellow stars (*ibid.*: 5–6).

The family's *Sperrstempels* had been obtained through an imaginative scheme thought up by his grandfather in anticipation of a forced sale of his business to a German industrialist who had shown interest in buying the firm (which made felt for hats). In the interim he created imaginary American investors and an appropriate false paper trail to show that they had bought a majority stake in the business; when the time came, the grandfather 'negotiated' with the investors to agree a sale in exchange for an *Ausreise* (exit visa) for the family from the occupied territories to a neutral country. This was ultimately arranged, which in turn led to the issuing of the *Sperrstempeln*, and the sale went through; in the process, the German became fairly friendly with Emanuel's grandfather, even coming for dinner; he divulged, at some personal risk, that he disapproved of the persecution of the Jews (*ibid.*: 6–7).

Obtaining Cuban entry visas to join Emanuel's grandfather's brother, who had left some time earlier, took a long time, and they eventually departed only in June 1943 (when Emanuel was 10 years old), by train via Paris, to Spain and then Portugal, where (as with the escapees from Germany helped by Varian Fry's Emergency Rescue Committee in France) they were to board a ship to Cuba. They were allowed to take luggage, not just a single rucksack each, and were escorted as far as the Spanish border by no less than the head of the SS in the Netherlands. Despite this, they managed to conceal jewellery in the luggage without detection. Their large home they left in the care of a non-Jewish couple, the wife of whom had child-minded Emanuel, who cared for his elderly great-grandmother who was too frail to escape with them. She died the following year but, remarkably, the house remained safe and was returned to the family after the war (*ibid.*: 8–9).

The family never departed for Cuba because Emanuel's grandfather deemed the journey too risky, so they saw out the war in Portugal. Most of the family lived in Caldas, one of two towns where people with expired visas or no papers were forced to live. Emanuel's stepfather accompanied his mother to a sanatorium in Guarda, where she died in 1944. Emanuel boarded at an English-style public school, St Julian's, in Carcavelos, near Estoril, which provided him with his first exposure to British education and he learned English. He thinks that he was the only Jewish pupil. He returned to Caldas during holidays and found it difficult to identify with the local Jewish community, mostly orthodox refugees from Poland (*ibid.*: 10–11; interview, Emanuel de Kadt[xiii]). The leader of that community was unsympathetic to the young Emanuel after his mother's death, forcing him to read the mourner's prayers in unfamiliar Hebrew rather than Dutch. 'Maybe that experience is at the root of the aversion I now feel to anything that is coercive in religion, and of my profound dislike of being told to take ritual and belief literally and as God-given and unalterable ... It is undeniable that those war years have marked me forever' (de Kadt 2009: 11).

Following the end of the war, they returned to Rotterdam in October 1945. '[I]t was totally clear that we would go back as soon as we could' and no initial reconnaissance was undertaken, perhaps because of contact with Emanuel's former childminder (still living in the family house with her husband), from whom they knew that they could simply return and take occupation since it had not been ransacked (interview, Emanuel de Kadt[xiv]). In this respect, they were particularly fortunate and must have been in a very small minority. By contrast, gaining restitution of Emanuel's grandfather's business took a couple of years because the Belgian state had taken over the factory at the end of the war as an enemy business and were very bureaucratic about the process (interview, Emanuel de Kadt[xv]). Interestingly, and in contrast to many accounts of survivors returning to Germany and Austria, Emanuel experienced no residual anti-Semitism in school, to which he quickly returned, or elsewhere in Rotterdam.

Throughout the war, despite the rather traumatic experiences, he had never stopped feeling Dutch (interview, Emanuel de Kadt[xvi]), and the lack of subsequent anti-Semitism would have facilitated reintegration after return. Again, this experience differs from that of many Holocaust survivors/escapees from Germany and Austria, who had been persecuted and deprived of their citizenship by the government of their own country rather than by a foreign occupying force. In discussing what impact his whole wartime experiences had had on the rest of his life, Emanuel was a bit more cautious than in the unpublished manuscript: 'Someone who's 12 at the time the war ends ... it's there in the back of your mind because you have consciously lived through it, but it's a different thing from if you were 18 or 20 or 25' (interview, Emanuel de Kadt[xvii]).

Ernie Stern – 'A Guest of the Third Reich': Ernie Stern recalls the worsening restrictions, arrests and deportations as outlined by **Emanuel de Kadt**. Indeed, Ernie's grandfather, who lived a few doors away in the same street in central Amsterdam, was picked up in one such raid in February 1943 and sent to Westerbork Transit Camp[8] and then

---

[8] Originally established in the northeast Netherlands in mid-1939 to receive German Jewish refugees fleeing the Nazis, Westerbork received its first arrivals on 9 October

Auschwitz, from where he didn't return. In late 1942 or early 1943, the remaining Jews who had not been deported were compelled to move into a ghetto (*Joodsche Wijk*) in the old part of the city that had been established in February 1941 (Pinto n.d.). The Stern family managed to remain in their apartment for a while longer because the 'good German' administrator who had been appointed to run Ernie's father's import–export business sought pretexts to keep him there in order to ensure the smooth operation of the business. Thereafter, they lived for about six months in the ghetto before they too were picked up on the eve of Rosh Hashana (the Jewish New Year) 29–30 September 1943 and sent to Westerbork. As a transit camp, conditions were not nearly as bad as in concentration camps.[9] From there they were deported to

---

1939, just over a month after the start of the war. The German occupation authorities took control there on 1 July 1942 and renamed it *Westerbork Durchgangslager* (Transit Camp) – which betrayed its new role as a collection and holding camp for deportations to 'the East', i.e. the concentration and extermination camps. The first trainload of 2,030 left on 16 July, destined for Auschwitz/Birkenau, which was the principal destination for subsequent deportations, but some also went to Sobibor, Theresienstadt and Bergen-Belsen. Far smaller numbers also went to Buchenwald and Ravensbrück. By the time transports ended in September 1944, almost 107,000 Jews – the great majority of the Dutch Jewish community – along with 245 Sinti and Roma and a few dozen resistance fighters had been deported in 93 trainloads. Although the numbers to be deported were set centrally by the Nazi High Command in Berlin, actual selection was the responsibility of the camp commandant, but – as in other camps – was often done by a team of Jewish assistants (akin to the *Sonderkommando* in death camps). Only some 5,000 ultimately survived and returned (Kamp Westerbork 2012). Conditions in the camp were designed to leave inmates with some hope and hence to avoid trouble during the weekly train deportations. Adrian Vanas, a Christian member of the Dutch resistance who had gained the position in charge of food distribution at the camp and who saved over 1,000 Jews through an escape mechanism between mid-1942 and its liberation by Allied forces, when he was appointed by the Dutch government-in-exile to take control of the camp, reports that 988 prisoners were in the camp at liberation (Vanas 2012). His account of the camp and his work provides a vivid and new dimension to our understanding of this transit camp and the deceptively reassuring environment created by the Nazis in order to entice some internees to catch the trains east of their own volition despite warnings against so doing (Vanas 2012: 47–52). Vanas was subsequently declared a Righteous Among the Nations by the Yad Vashem Jewish Holocaust Centre in Jerusalem and was an honoured resident of the Montefiore Jewish retirement home in Randwick, Sydney, Australia until his death on 23 January 2014, aged 92.

 9 Adrian Vanas confirmed to me that, since most of the actual administration of the camp was in Jewish hands, families were deliberately kept together. Moreover, initially at least, deportations to Bergen-Belsen were only of people eligible for exchanges and the like, enabling them to go to Palestine: 'There was in the beginning a real effort made but it failed later on' (pers. comm., email, 7/5/12).

Bergen-Belsen on 15 February 1944 (interview, Ernie Stern[xviii]; Vanas 2012) where conditions, especially for young children, were poorer still. The remarkable story is best told in Ernie's own words (ES), answering questions from me (DS):

ES: I was indeed a guest of the Third Reich.

My father ... wasn't always very decisive – he didn't like dislocations – and so he applied for immigration to the United States when it was too late. But then he did have the foresight to ask cousins of his who lived in Switzerland to see if they could help out. And while they were not able to produce US visas, they did get us Honduran passports. I'm not sure how much this cost her but I'm sure the Honduran consulate was happy. Of course, there was no possibility to get transportation. Nonetheless, the passports are relevant because they ultimately saved our lives. We never saw those passports, of course, but only received photocopies after the war. But the Germans had intercepted them and, being German, they also retained them in the files.

In February 1945, the Germans organised a transport to go to Switzerland to be exchanged for German prisoners of war. We were selected to go on the transport. We always attributed that to our Honduran 'citizenship'.

DS: Would many people have got out of Bergen-Belsen on that kind of basis?

ES: No. Reportedly there had been an earlier transport of people with British papers entitling them to emigrate to Palestine.[10] But that transport and ours are the only ones I know of.

They selected large families – and we were five. And we didn't make it all the way to Switzerland. The train stopped in Biberach, a small town near Ulm, where there was a German prisoner of war camp, operated by the Red Cross, with British citizens from the Channel Islands who had been interned there. A group of people, including our family, were removed from the train and were replaced by the Channel Islanders from the camp. There was of course, a lot of concern that they would ship us back to Bergen-Belsen but in those days the transport system was otherwise occupied. So, in fact, we spent the last three months of the war in the Red Cross camp where the Germans didn't enter. There was food ... it was

---

[10] This tallies with the account above by Adrian Vanas.

our salvation – thanks to those passports. We were liberated by the French at the end of April 1945 and it took till December 1945 for us to be repatriated to Holland.

DS: Do you still have the documentation and so on from the camps? Yellow star?

ES: I have a Xerox of the passports … and I believe I have a picture somewhere of me with the yellow star.

DS: That must be, if not unique, then certainly very very unusual – both the Honduran angle and being taken out as a family and exchanged in that way.

ES: Decidedly. My … youngest brother (I've got two), he was born when the Germans were already in Amsterdam … and they kept us together in Westerbork and in Bergen-Belsen. And there was another miraculous event – which we've never been able to explain – in Bergen-Belsen: there were two or three occasions when Red Cross parcels arrived (not just for us but we were among those recipients) … My parents tried hard after the war, to find out who put us on this list but we never figured it out … my father had a brother in New York [but] it wasn't him. Nor did we ever understand why the Germans would deliver food parcels to people in a concentration camp where people died daily from starvation. But the parcels were very helpful and also helped us survive. They contained the usual items – powdered milk, ham, etc.

DS: Kosher ham, of course! [joke]

ES: My father was diligent about *kashrut* and he tried even in Bergen-Belsen. He traded the ham for more milk, which of course was a big help with the baby. And so yes, we were very lucky as these things go.

DS: Did he – your father, that is – find work in the camp in one of these ancillary activities, orchestra or …?

ES: No, he was not exactly a musical type. No he went out on work detail every morning but it was in the forest, I think, I'm not really sure. (interview, Ernie Stern[xix])

This story is truly remarkable: for a whole family, including three young children, one of them about three years old at the start of the ordeal, to have managed to remain together and survive four and a half months in Westerbork and then a year in Bergen-Belsen must have been exceptional. Yet, as in every survivor's case, the interplay of *force majeure*, particular circumstances and serendipity is evident. Survival as a family will naturally have reduced the trauma at the time and extent of any post-traumatic stress, while also aiding the subsequent process of recovery. Nevertheless, the impact of what he had lived through and seen as a boy of not yet 12 when their prisoners' camp was liberated should not be underestimated.

As with **Emanuel de Kadt**'s family, repatriation to the Netherlands and a desire to rebuild and resume normal life there was the natural thing to do.

Zygmunt Bauman – Flight from Poland: For a complex set of historical, political, social and cultural reasons, the wartime situation in Eastern Europe was markedly different from that further west. In particular, the proximity of the Soviet Union as eastern opponent of Nazi German expansion and exemplar of a radically different socio-political system had a profound impact on constraints and opportunities in the face of Nazi-fuelled anti-Semitism and oppression. Of course, situations varied greatly over time and space, as exemplified by the experiences of the three people in my study from Eastern Europe, one from Poland and two from Romania.

Just as routes westward represented key escape pathways for refugees fleeing the Nazis in Germany and Austria (with the UK and USA as principal destinations, along with the Netherlands and France before they themselves were invaded), so eastward escape to the Soviet Union appeared attractive – or at perhaps the least unattractive option available – and practicable to many in Poland and its neighbouring countries.

Among them were the 13-year-old Zygmunt Bauman and his parents, who fled from Poznań on the last eastbound train on 3 September 1939, when the Germans invaded.[11] They found refuge in Mołodeczno (Maladzyechna), some 70 km northwest of Minsk (at the time part of Poland but subsequently incorporated into Belorus), but later had to escape the German advance once more – also on the last possible train, on 22 June 1941. The statist nature of the Soviet Union meant that arriving refugees had no say in where they landed up. The train was unloaded in the middle of a forest and the occupants were allocated to various places. The Baumans went to Wakhtan, a very small forest

---

[11] His only sibling, an older sister, had married and emigrated to Palestine – where she was to spend the rest of her life – in 1938.

settlement in the Viatka region of European Russia's extreme north (now the Khmelevitzy District of Gorkij Region). Zygmunt completed his secondary schooling there, learning Russian from scratch. His parents remained in Wakhtan throughout the war, his father practising his profession as bookkeeper while his mother was employed as a cook. He joined the Polish Army in Exile[12] in late 1943 and 'I participated in frontline actions starting from the summer 1944 till wounded in the battle for Kolberg in March 1945. But I left military hospital in time for the battle of Berlin' (pers. comm.[xx]). He then returned with the army to Poland at the end of the war, taking his parents along (interview, Zygmunt Bauman[xxi]; pers. comm.[xxii]; Bauman and Tester 2001: 2).

Although these experiences are likely to have influenced his thinking and work to some extent, Bauman believes that social thought and writing should not be seen as enframed and determined by autobiography. By contrast, he emphasised during my interview how profound an impact on him his wife's (Janina's) wartime autobiography had had, teaching him a great deal about the Nazi occupation of Poland and its treatment of the Jews. Her book relates movingly the hardships and terrors of life under occupation, especially survival in the Warsaw Ghetto, to which she and her mother were consigned, and how they avoided deportation (J. Bauman 1986). Indeed, Zygmunt Bauman made clear that this book triggered his curiosity about Nazism as a project of modernity and thus led to his landmark monographs (Bauman 1989; 1991). Hitherto, he had felt removed from this experience, having been in exile and because of how it had been dealt with by other sociologists. As he put it in the Preface to *Modernity and the Holocaust*, 'Having read Janina's book, I began to think just how much I did not know – or, rather, did not think about properly. It dawned on me that I did not really understand what had happened in that "world which was not mine"' (Bauman 1989: vii). Essentially the same points are made in Bauman and Tester (2001: 4–5). This issue is assessed in greater detail in Chapter 6.

Irma Glicman-Adelman – Escape from Romania to Palestine: By an astonishing coincidence, both Romanian-born figures in my study, Irma Glicman- Adelman and **Michael Cernea**, were childhood friends at an

---

[12] This was also known as the Polish First Army, which was under Soviet control (Wikipedia, Zygmunt Bauman, accessed 17/1/16).

early age, before circumstances forced them apart. They subsequently remet some 35 years later in the USA. But that remarkable story must await a later chapter.

As explained in Chapter 2, Irma Adelman attended a primary school run by Catholic nuns in Galatz. This came to an abrupt end when the Romanian regime ordered the expulsion of all Jewish children from schools in late 1938 or very early 1939.[13] Thereupon her family, who were prominent Jews in Galatz and hence felt very vulnerable, not least because they lived directly opposite the police station, left hastily for the anonymity of the capital, Bucharest.

Before departure, Irma recalls vividly, 'I remember witnessing from the window of our house as Jews were gathered into the police station and shot – nice folk!' She and her parents then took refuge four or five houses down the street, with the family of a Romanian Army colonel whose daughter was one of Irma's school friends. Then a childless Romanian innkeeper and his wife who lived opposite the Adelmans said, 'Give us your daughter; we will save her and cherish her' – so Irma's mother agreed and they even put a cross around her neck. However, that evening, Irma's non-Jewish uncle, who was a prominent figure in the army, and his wife passed through en route to Bucharest and it was decided that Irma and her parents should travel with them as her uncle's status would provide some safety (interview, Irma Adelman[xxiii]).

Thus they reached the capital, where they spent approximately six months awaiting immigration visas for Palestine, before departing in September 1939, just after the start of World War II. The visas were delayed repeatedly, causing much tension as the situation worsened. Eventually, her father resolved that they should, after all, head for Cuba (for which they already held immigration visas) unless the Palestinian visas arrived that week, whereupon they duly arrived. Then they were effectively held hostage for Turkish transit visas, for which they were charged 'a king's ransom at the time' of some US$15,000 per person. Having no option, her father paid (interview, Irma Adelman[xxiv]).

After arriving in Palestine, she was immediately sent to school and learned fluent Hebrew through the total immersion system within six

---

[13] Ioanid's (2000: 28–9) authoritative study and ICHR (2004) date numerical restrictions on Jewish pupils and then exclusion to late 1940 – by which stage Irma reported that the Adelmans were already in Palestine. Radu Ioanid is of the view that such expulsions during the Royal Dictatorship under King Karol would have been locally rather than centrally instituted (pers. comm., email, 16/5/13).

months. She duly completed her schooling and then briefly attended the Hebrew University in Jerusalem, before leaving to study at the University of California, Berkeley (interview, Irma Adelman[xxv]).

In an autobiographical essay many years later, she summarised the profound impact of her wartime experiences thus:

> World War II left an indelible mark, even though I escaped comparatively unscathed. My father had had the foresight and courage to leave Roumania in 1939 for Palestine, so that the entire nuclear family survived intact. The main impact of the war on me was the wrenching break in personal attachments involved in becoming a refugee, and the experience of mass religious hatred. I remember my father telling me when I was six that I might be reviled for being Jewish, but that I should be proud of this fact. Since I knew not what being Jewish was, and had been taught by the nuns that pride is sin, this talk left me totally bewildered. The War imbued me with a sense of rootlessness, a suspicion of mass ideologies, a sense of the impermanence of any state, a lack of attachment to possessions, and a sense of personal worthlessness. It also induced a sense of belonging nowhere and everywhere,[14] that is the mark of the cosmopolitan, and a feeling of 'There but for the grace of God go I' towards the less fortunate, akin to Rawls' initial state of ignorance. On the positive side, I learned that the only thing one can rely on is one's human capital – one's knowledge, skills, and character – because all else can be taken away at the bellow of a demagogue. My later fascination with stochastic shocks, with nonlinear dynamics, and socio-political view of economic development also have their roots in my World War II experience. (Adelman 1988: 244–5; 1995: 4–5)

As with several others of my research subjects, the link between wartime experiences and subsequent career direction in Irma Adelman's lifecourse is therefore explicit and direct.

Michael Cernea – Survival by Anonymity: As explained in Chapter 2, Michael Cernea commenced elementary school in Iaşi (Jassy) in northeast Romania, in 1938, just as the fascist grip on the country tightened and a series of anti-Semitic laws was enacted, in terms of

---

[14] This perception, resembling very closely indeed the words of Paul Streeten cited in Chapter 3, are commonly regarded as typical of refugees who have moved multiple times; how cosmopolitan one feels may depend more on one's class characteristics and how one manages to assimilate in a permanent context afterwards.

which his father lost his job, and he was expelled from school (see also Irma Adelman above). He found himself in a school hastily organised by the town's Jewish community federation, some aspects of which he experienced as positive.

Following the occupation of Poland, he also vividly recalls the 'caravans of refugees' fleeing to Romania, among them many Hassidic Jews (ultra-orthodox), who carried on their ecstatic worship and dancing wherever they were, maintaining a sense of cheerfulness despite their perilous situation (interview, Michael Cernea[xxvi]).

Being only some 20 km from the Romanian-Soviet border since 1940, Iaşi was the fulcrum of politico-military friction and later hostilities during World War II. Following the Molotov–Ribbentrop Pact, Germany and the Soviet Union had pressurised Romania to return to the latter the region of Bessarabia that it had held since World War I. This imposed agreement was implemented in 1940. In 1941, following the accession to power of the dictator, Ion Antonescu, and the defeat of his erstwhile fascist allies (who fled to Germany, enabling Hitler to use them as a bargaining chip for leverage over Antonescu) he made common cause with the Germans in their preparations for war on the Soviet Union. With the commencement of hostilities on 22 June 1941, Romanian forces invaded the former Bessarabia, which had a dense Jewish population, and began massacring them in revenge for the loss of that territory the previous year (interview, Michael Cernea[xxvii]; Ioanid 2000: 90–108; 2017).

Within a few days, a vicious pogrom (planned religiously/ethnically based attack) was organised against the Jewish population of Iaşi, based on fabricated allegations of treachery. This turned into one of the worst pogroms in Romanian history, despite a long legacy of anti-Semitism, and of World War II (Ioanid 2000: 63–90; 2017). Given a long history of such hatred, Ioanid (2000: 63) opens his authoritative and extremely detailed and distressing account by likening the city's position in Romanian anti-Semitism to that of Vienna in the Nazi equivalent. Michael's own experiences of it, as a young boy, are best captured in his own words:

MC: The *pogrom* consisted of Jews from the entire city being rounded up and collected from house to house and marched to the ... central police station. So [o]n that fateful Sunday of June 29, 1941 we saw that there were columns of Jews on the street and then one of these columns stopped in front of our courtyard and a number of hooligans and some policemen, *gendarmes*, came in and knocked at the door and pulled us all out – my father, my mother, one of my grandmothers, me and my [two-year old] brother ... They left in our house only one grandmother who was in ... bed and she was a fat woman ... so large that they couldn't move her out of the bed and they pulled her out of the bed by the hair. As it happens, she was [very] orthodox and she [wore] a wig so when they pulled the hair, the wig came off and the guy got scared; he threw [down] the wig – I [saw] this scene – and abandoned her there! This is how she was left at home.

But we were marched in a column from our home all the way to the central police station with a column full of Jews, stopping at every courtyard and collecting all the Jews – elderly, children – everyone – men, women ... And we were marched with [our] hands up. So I was not yet ten in '41; I was nine and a half and I [can still vividly remember] ... the scenes of our column marching on the street which was so familiar to me and then on the main street ... and I see bodies strewn left and right because of even more killing before[hand]. And we came to the police station and there was a triage – they kept men, and the police station was big but still there were so many columns coming from all sides [that] they couldn't keep everybody so they let the women and the small children ... return home, and they kept my father and all the other men and young [adolescent] boys ... I was still kind of small of stature and [therefore was allowed to go] home.

And the fear was that my father would be killed there and so my mother developed a scheme to try to save him and she was a beautiful woman and dressed herself very elegantly – painted her lips (wanted to look Romanian) – made the little bundle to take to him: soap and some shirts and some sugar to make a little thing for him to have as a survival kit. Fortunately, in the meantime (that took hours) while we ... were return[ing] home we were caught – just a few hundred metres from our home, [which] we'd just about reached – by other hooligans who said: 'You escaped from the police. You are Jews; will we kill you' and they lined us up against the wall and we saw them as preparing to kill us until somebody, one of the leaders, said 'Let them go; let them [go]back, not here'. So all of a sudden they allowed us to go. That was one of the small miracles because we saw bodies strewn here and there from other [killings].

DS: So what was going through your mind as a nine-and-a-half-year-old at that point?

MC: We were scared to death. My brother was two years old; he also had to keep his head up on the way down. On the way back, my mother kept him in her arms; she was bitten by mad women who beat her all the way back ... and we had to run and [then] hide and [then] run until we were caught again and lined [up against] the wall. In the meantime (as I learnt later from my father) the courtyard of the police station was chock full and they couldn't absorb any more so, [on] one hand they kept absorbing the columns and [on] the other hand they set up a table to register people with their address, and the people who were in front ... started to receive little pieces of paper with a stamp with the[ir] name after registration and told to go home, that they will be called and collected [later]. People thought that they [we]re going to be put into a labour camp so my father was able to get to be in front and to get the little piece of paper. He gave his name and address in full and ran home. Exactly when my mother was ready to go after my father, my father appeared. He was ... bloody but he got that little piece of paper and he came home and that was our salvation because if my mother would have left five minutes earlier, I would have gone after her, and I wouldn't ever have seen [either] of them. So immediately my father was home, [he] went into hiding and left the [house] again – it was already night – and went into a kind of ... valley behind our home where people either collected garbage or cultivated corn in summer and where we children played with our sleds because it was a ... steep slope. And at that time, it was full of corn so my father went there and hid with the garbage and the corn ... for three days and three nights. And, of course, on the first night they came after him and they knocked – almost destroyed the front door – and when we heard [that], we ran away [out of] the back of the house, but not [to] where my father was because we were afraid to give him away. Our neighbour, who was a Romanian ... accepted to shelter us, and we stayed that night and we came back [to] the house in the morning; they had broken windows and things were missing but they didn't find anybody in the house so they left. They didn't find my father, who was in hiding. At the same time ... the people who were there, the Jews who were there [at the central police station], not only were they beaten but at night many tried to escape [by] jumping the fence – they were machine gunned and pushed back and a lot died on the spot. Survivors later told how the blood was flowing in the courtyard. (interview, Michael Cernea[xxviii]; a less detailed account also appears in Cernea and Freidenberg 2007)

Michael then related what happened in the ensuing days, summarising the harrowingly detailed report (then recently published) of the International Commission on the Holocaust in Romania (ICHR) (2004) (see also Ioanid 2000; Zionism and Israel 2009).[15] Two 'death trains' crammed with 2,300 and 2,500 men and older boys respectively like sardines in box wagons – just as were being used by the Nazis in other parts of Europe – left Iaşi the following day and covered very little distance over the ensuing several days of excruciatingly hot summer weather, during which they were allowed neither water nor food, save for the courageous efforts of a handful of villagers at one enforced stop. Most of the occupants perished, with bodies being thrown out at each stop, to be buried locally. The survivors were interned in camps for several months and eventually released, whereupon their experiences became known. Altogether over 11,000 of Iaşi's Jewish population, and a further 2,000 from the surrounding area, perished over those few days. As numerous photos, including one on the ICHR report's front cover, attest, the streets were literally strewn with bodies; local people can be seen walking past without even looking at them.

After the three days of hiding in the ravine, Michael's father returned home and the situation calmed down rapidly because the Romanian Army advanced so fast into Russian territory, that all troops left the Iaşi area. Killings on the street also stopped, although tension remained and the surviving Jews continued to fear for their lives for a considerable time. Although some of the Jewish schools reopened that autumn, Michael was kept at home and tutored by his parents for a full year, before resuming school in the autumn of 1942. As he reflected,

> Well those are things in life which you don't ever forget and you know that you are at home, and you know that you are afraid for your life, and you know that you are afraid for your life because you are Jewish, and they are killing Jews like they are killing … flies and animals. And I had the yellow star and having to go out meant to put the yellow star

[15] A very moving personal reflection by the son of Iaşi's then chief rabbi, himself a rabbi in the USA, is available online (Safran 2011).

to identify yourselves so you [had] better stay in the house as much as possible. Get food, things which you need and make some living and that was what my father ... he was badly beaten and suffered all his life for the beating he got there. Well, after a year I went back to school ... That was '42. The atmosphere was very bad. I remember that one day on my way back from school, close to my house, on the street ... I s[aw] a young man – a boy, bigger than me – coming and was taking off one of his gloves as he was approaching me. He took off his glove to be able to punch me – and he punched me so hard I fell and he didn't say a word and [walked on]. So the impunity of such acts and the humiliation, it imprints in your heart ... in autumn of '42 better things started to come from the Front Line and Stalingrad started in the spring of '43. The Germans and the Romanians were defeated in Stalingrad so things started to look a bit more hopeful for us. (interview, Michael Cernea[xxix])

However, the changing tide of the war jeopardised their safety again in 1944. The Antonescu regime changed sides in August that year, joining the Allies, as a result of which the German forces were quickly overpowered and retreated, drawing the Soviet Army towards the Romanian border again, and a likely invasion route through Iaşi. Fearing another massacre during that instability, they resolved to flee south to the capital, Bucharest, in order to become inconspicuous. The family and one other widow crammed into a taxi with just what they could carry and had to pay no fewer than 15 different bribes at major junctions, where they were stopped by military and other roadblocks, during the 24-hour journey. Four days later, the Americans began bombing the city as part of their ill-conceived effort to prevent the country falling to the Soviets. The widow who had shared the taxi with them was killed in one such raid, but her two sons survived under the rubble of the house until dug out two or three days later[16] (interview, Michael Cernea[xxx]).

After those bombing raids, life quietened down since the battlefront had moved far westwards. He and a friend were prepared by a religious teacher (*melamed*) for their Barmitzvot; Michael had his in the very large Malbim synagogue[17] in October 1944, close to his thirteenth birthday as is the custom. With the king in power and the restoration of multi-party politics at the end of the war in May 1945, Jewish children

[16] They left for the USA as soon as possible after the war and, remarkably, Michael managed to trace them both in California when he arrived there in 1970.

[17] See Krinsky (1985: 152); it also served as a shelter for refugees in 1945.

were readmitted to state schools but Michael stayed to complete his education at the Jewish school in Bucharest. They never moved back to Iaşi as they expected to find nothing left in their house, and they might have faced risks if trying to claim the house back.

Especially at such an early age, these harrowing, dramatic and, at times immensely life-threatening experiences of violent and murderous anti-Semitism to him and his immediate family (as well as cousins and other relatives living in the contested territory of Bessarabia but which space precludes coverage here) clearly had a profound impact on Michael Cernea. Indeed, the above account leaves little to the imagination and Michael himself is very clear about his perceptions then and subsequently. Of course, it is very difficult, if not impossible, to separate out the immediate reactions from subsequent post hoc reasoning, informed by later experiences, higher education and research into the past, in this case such as the authoritative report of the International Commission on the Holocaust in Romania, which has evidently answered longstanding questions and debates, and which has clearly fed into Michael's account. This brings us back to methodological considerations in relation to ethnography and autobiography as discussed in Chapter 1. However, in a profound sense, perhaps it does not really matter, especially as it has been possible to triangulate his accounts with other authoritative sources, which check out and don't, in any case, affect the personal and affective dimensions of the experiences.

Reflections

While comparison of extremes is invidious, Michael Cernea's wartime experiences were the most dramatic and immediately life-threatening of all those recounted in this and the preceding chapters, on the basis of the accounts as related to me and that I have obtained from (auto)biographical writings. His case also demonstrates how sometimes life 'in situ' at home among the neighbours and townsfolk, many of whose derision and hatred simmered barely below the surface, became as perilous as the trauma of uprooting, deportation and incarceration in concentration camps experienced by Ernie Stern.

More generally, the range of experiences of my research subjects was very diverse, representing a microcosm of the persecuted populations as a whole. From the Iaşi pogrom and its aftermath, and deportation to Westerbork and Bergen-Belsen at one end of the spectrum, the accounts in this chapter embraced working for the underground at great personal risk to fighting for the French and Polish armies; sequential flight as the German forces occupied initial countries of refuge; children being left in the care of strangers in a foreign country and then losing a brother in Auschwitz/Birkenau; obtaining exit visas in the nick of time to escape to Portugal or Palestine; and relatively orderly but still highly stressful departure across Europe for the USA once visas had been obtained.

Age, stage of education, likelihood of being regarded as an adult and potential threat to Nazi or anti-Semitic actions, geographical location, family circumstances and connections all played a role, as, in each case, did courage and initiative, chance and outrageously good fortune, in the person's survival or escape. The vivid accounts demonstrate this clearly, often through my interviewees' own words.

In terms of the focus of my enquiry, some of these accounts also make explicit the impact of their wartime experiences on them personally, often with lasting consequences, and also connections between those experiences and their subsequent lifecourses, including career directions. Where apposite, these have been highlighted in the text and the issue will be taken forward in later chapters of this book. For current purposes, however, it is merely necessary to point out that there is no necessary relationship between the extremeness of those experiences and the likelihood of particular career choices since, for example, Michael Cernea regards the connections as strong and direct, whereas Ernie Stern is very clear that he landed up in development purely by coincidence.

5 | ADULT ESCAPEES: REBUILDING LIVES, (RE)SHAPING CAREERS

Just as the outbreak of World War II had constituted a dramatic historical moment but that was not necessarily the most defining rupture in the lives of those who had been forced to flee earlier, the end of fighting, first in Europe and then in Asia, was profoundly important contextually yet not necessarily to the individual lives of all in this study. While the end of the Nazi regime, in particular, came as a huge relief to them, it also enabled the traumatic process of tracing missing relatives and friends to commence. The demographic and human costs of the war everywhere had been dramatic. However, the transition from war back to a peacetime economy was complex and geographically variegated. North America had not suffered destruction of its material infrastructure and, indeed, had benefitted economically from the large-scale armaments industry. The UK had suffered widespread bomb damage and economic dislocation, while many people, especially children, had been evacuated from the large cities. Nazi-occupied Europe and Germany itself had also suffered varying degrees of physical destruction, displacement and trauma. Reabsorption of returning young men into the civilian economy following demobilisation, return of displaced people, and reconstruction became major priorities. In continental Europe, the US commenced a massive programme of reconstruction and development under various labels, most notably the Marshall Plan, as explored below. Since several of the refugees in this study became involved in different facets of the postwar reconstruction and development efforts in Europe, which in turn provided inspiration for development engagements in the global South, this context has particular salience.

The end of the war found the subjects of my study in very different circumstances, according to their age, gender, nationality, individual or family contacts, personalities and wartime experiences. The younger ones had been able to attend school or university, perhaps alongside part-time work to help make ends meet from soon after finding stable refuge and regularising their immigration status. The older German-speaking subjects in the UK had survived internment, with or without shipment abroad, and had then either resumed their studies or professional work with varying degrees of satisfaction. Two Germans had undertaken farm work to earn an income and benefit from tied housing: **Fritz Schumacher** in the UK both before and after internment, prior to obtaining more skilled academic employment at Oxford University in 1942; and **Theodor Bergmann** as a double refugee in Sweden, before spending a few months in the mining industry prior to his return to Germany in 1946. Two others had seen active military service. **Paul Streeten** had enlisted in the Pioneer Corps and then the commandos, before sustaining life-threatening wounds that required extended convalescence before being able to return to his university studies. **Albert Hirschman** spent the latter years of the war in the US Army, first in North Africa and then Italy, before returning to his American wife and daughter in December 1945. As explained in Chapter 4, **Alexander Gerschenkron** remained at the US Federal Reserve until taking up his chair in Economics at Harvard in 1946.

This chapter explores the postwar trajectories of the older generation within my study group, which can be divided most straightforwardly on an approximately age-related basis between the older cohort who had already completed or nearly finished their studies and commenced careers, and the younger cohort who first went to university and, in some cases, completed secondary school. The latter group forms the subject of Chapters 6 and 7.

Among the older group, who had already chosen academic or related research careers before the Holocaust, the dominant trend was to pursue those directions, although the postwar period offered unique opportunities to engage with European reconstruction and development via the Marshall Plan and related schemes, and to contribute to the establishment of specialised humanitarian and development agencies within the UN system and Bretton Woods institutions (the International Monetary Fund (IMF) and World Bank (WB)). **Fritz Schumacher** found himself in his native Germany as part of the immediate postwar American-led survey of the German war economy and then, after a short break back in the UK, as a member of the British Control Commission. Given his unrivalled European experience and linguistic abilities, **Albert Hirschman** was sought out to join the Marshall Plan team, while **Hans Singer** gave up his academic career in 1947 to join the UN, initially on a temporary assignment. Although principally an academic, **Paul Streeten** spent several years at the World Bank and worked for other agencies, while **Theodor Bergmann** completed his much-delayed studies before pursuing a career as an academic while always remaining a political and labour movement activist in his native Germany.

The Marshall Plan became the template for concerted and co-ordinated aid and technological assistance to decolonising or recently independent states in what became known as the 'underdeveloped' or 'developing' world, while the IFIs and specialist UN agencies assumed leading roles in such efforts once established. Accordingly, this programme and these institutions constitute logical starting points for this chapter since much else in the official development policy and practice realms over subsequent decades followed from, or arose in reaction to, the logics, rationale and experiences of these foundational initiatives.

Involvement in Landmark Postwar Development Programmes and Institution Building

Schumacher in Postwar Germany: Such was the demand for scarce skills and relevant local expertise, that Fritz Schumacher found himself returning to Germany immediately World War II ended to work on the American Bombing Survey of Germany, led by John Kenneth Galbraith, another youngish economist later to become renowned. The survey's initial focus was how Germany had managed to maintain its military strength despite the massive allied bombing campaign, although it soon evolved into a broader history of the German war economy. Inevitably, undertaking this work and travelling extensively across his native country, seeing at first hand the physical and psychological impact of the war on people, including his own family – within which the resentments at his prewar departure (seen as a form of desertion) still ran deep – made an indelible mark. His frequent letters to his wife back in London chronicle his perceptions and reactions in detail (Wood 1985: 168–83).

From this intense experience in July–August 1945, Schumacher became even more convinced than previously that his mission should be helping to overcome the Nazi propaganda and material legacy in order to rebuild a civilised Germany society. He sought to undertake this role by working for the British Control Commission in the British Sector but could do so only after his British naturalisation came through in

April 1946. He was initially based in Berlin, which he had not managed to visit in 1945. The destruction in his home city shocked him, just as he had to confront the family fissures at first hand. Nevertheless, he felt at the centre of things and was convinced that he was playing an important role. Later the Commission moved him to Frankfurt after the commencement of the Russian blockade of Berlin, but he found the context less fulfilling. His observations are very telling, as was the way in which he sought in his planning interventions to provide the foundations of a socialist state, taking the historical opportunity of the loss, flight or removal (as part of the de-Nazification process) of the erstwhile industrial barons and the fact that most economic assets were now controlled by the Allies. He argued that the masses needed to understand the defeat of Nazism as also constituting defeat of the long-standing forces of aggression and militarism (*ibid.*: 195–6).

He also brought his previous research on unemployment reduction to bear, arguing for large-scale investment and employment creation to avoid another postwar slump. However, his recommendations were not adopted by the German politicians and instead an overtly capitalist economy was rebuilt as a pre-emptive effort against Stalinist communism. From 1948 he became centrally involved in planning for the establishment of the European Payments Union (EPU) but again his proposed scheme – based on his earlier proposals for a global multilateral clearing system – was not accepted and he became increasingly frustrated and disillusioned with the route being followed. His grand vision of being central to German reconstruction was failing and he resolved to return to the UK, against the wishes of his wife, who was happier back in Germany, fulfilling many roles in her extended family. At the end of 1949, he took up the position of economic advisor to the National Coal Board (NCB) in London, a role he filled for the remainder of his career. Eventually Muschi and the children joined him in May 1950; they moved into a large house with an extensive garden in Caterham, Surrey, where they were to live for the rest of his life (*ibid.*: 184–219).

His work on the EPU at the same time as the Marshall Plan was being launched raises the intriguing question of whether Schumacher came into contact with his fellow ex-Berliner, **Albert Hirschman**, who was also involved with the negotiation of these schemes at the Organisation for European Economic Co-operation (OEEC) in Paris, as detailed below. However, neither Barbara Wood's (1985) biography of Schumacher nor Jeremy Adelman's (2013) tome on Hirschman contains any index entry or mention of the other, and neither Adelman (pers. comm.[i]) nor I have found any other hint or evidence that they were in contact.

Hirschman and the Marshall Plan: Albert Hirschman's retrospective perspective on this momentous initiative is set out in an essay written for the fiftieth anniversary of its inauguration, in which he reflects on two of its driving forces as he recollected them and as recorded in their respective posthumous memoirs. Commencing in 1947, the Marshall Plan[1] for the economic recovery of Western Europe as a whole piggy-backed on a pre-existing French plan for 'Equipment and Modernization' headed by Jean Monnet and his deputy, Robert Marjolin, an economist and editor. Marjolin became secretary general of the Marshall Plan representing Europe, while Richard Bissell, a former economics professor at the Massachusetts Institute of Technology (MIT), joined as Deputy Marshall Plan Administrator to represent the USA, and was rapidly recognised as the intellectual leader (Hirschman 1998: 34–5). The two men were both about 40 years old when recruited and had strongly Keynesian backgrounds 'and a consequent belief in the value of government activism' (*ibid.*: 35), but came from very different social class contexts and educational backgrounds. Hirschman had first met Marjolin in Paris in 1938, after having to flee Italy, when the Frenchman had given him his first job (*ibid.*: 36–7). Their re-acquaintance was thus fortuitous.

Hirschman's role in the Marshall Plan focused initially on the negotiation of the EPU – something on which he had gained expertise while working at the Federal Reserve Board in Washington after leaving the US Army upon his return from war.[2] His role was to monitor

---

[1] This is named after the then US Secretary of State, General George Marshall, who initiated it. The broader context into which it fitted was outlined in Chapter 1 (see also Engerman et al. 2003; Gilman 2003; Ekbladh 2010; Latham 2011).

[2] Already at this stage of his career, contacts (here within this refugee cohort) proved important: it was Alexander Gerschenkron, with whom Hirschman had shared an office in Berkeley in 1941 (see Chapter 4; also Adelman 2013: 205) and who was now employed at the Board, who invited him to work there. This is the kind of action that increased the visibility and impact of my subjects as a cohort. Gerschenkron then left the Board to teach at Harvard in 1948 (Hirschman 1998: 77–9). Surprisingly, however, neither Gilman's (2003) nor Ekbladh's (2010) detailed accounts of the US's postwar modernist developmental mission mentions Hirschman; only the latter author mentions

French and Italian – and then all Western European – economic and financial trends:

> To the extent that the Federal Reserve had a role in U.S. foreign economic policy, the Marshall Plan became my area of competence. In particular, I became interested in the plans for Intra-European Payments and in the various attempts to move away from the strict bilateral channels to which trade and payments in Europe were then still confined. (*ibid.*: 38)

Perhaps unsurprisingly, Hirschman derived pleasure from the strong praise for and importance attached to the EPU in the memoirs of both Marjolin and Bissell. Indeed, they regarded it as possibly the most crucial achievement of the Marshall Plan because it restored the mutual convertibility of the members' currencies. However, in order to allow temporary discrimination against imports from the US to Europe, this convertibility did not include the US dollar. In Hirschman's view, this therefore represented 'a different and higher form of aid than simple commodity aid, which had been the essence of Marshall aid' (*ibid.*: 41–2). Weiss et al. (2005: 158, 159) refer to it as 'perhaps the most generous manifestation on record of enlightened self-interest' by the USA and 'a concrete demonstration of Washington's capacity to frame its national interest in an imaginative and forward-looking fashion'.

This initial focus on rebuilding multilateral trade on the war-ravaged continent was the beginning of the European integration project still under way today through the European Union. Hirschman also explains how he deliberately got to know the key policy makers around Richard Bissell in Washington and learned how they passed ideas to the Economic Cooperation Agency's (ECA's) Paris office, as the Marshall Plan agency had become known. In late 1949, Hirschman prepared a 'Proposal for a European Monetary Authority', setting out detailed common fiscal, monetary and exchange rate policy directions for a future European central bank to steer – anticipating by several decades the process that eventually led to the introduction of the Euro as common European currency in the late 1990s (Hirschman 1998: 39).

Gerschenkron, and just once in passing, as a leading authority on international economics. Perhaps, as immigrants, they were less visible within the US inner circles and agendas on which these studies focus. If a plausible explanation, it underscores the value of multiple research perspectives to understanding such complex endeavours.

Hirschman drew comfort from these very positive retrospective assessments of the EPU by the Marshall Plan leadership, noting that his own position created great discomfort since it was contrary to that of the US Treasury and Federal Reserve Board, his employer. Indeed, he took an opportunity to leave Washington, 'with much relief', when he was recommended by the World Bank to become an economic and financial advisor to the Colombian government in Bogotá (*ibid.*: 42–3; also p. 80 for further reflections on reasons for this decision). He ended the chapter poignantly – but for purposes of this book also very pertinently:

> Little did I appreciate then how this move would start an entirely new phase of my life. Yet, some of the key notions of my later writings on development, such as a 'Passion for the Possible' and a 'Bias for Hope', may go back to Marjolin's concept of 'an apparently absurd, but successful wager', [i.e. the EPU regime] which for him was a principal characteristic of the Marshall Plan. (*ibid.*: 43)

Several very significant points for this study emerge from Hirschman's account. The first is the remarkable ease, especially by comparison with today, with which a recent European refugee, with only a short professional economics pedigree, was able to gain employment and a very prominent role in such a high-profile US aid programme for Western Europe. Second, this inclusion reflected a combination of his polylingual abilities and unparalleled first-hand experience and expertise in financial and economic situations in several core European countries. The flipside of this coin is that, in part due to the human cost of the war, there was a severe shortage of such expertise but the willingness to have a European at the heart of the US Plan staff in part also reflects the relative opportunities afforded by the nature of the US as an immigrant society. Third, many of Hirschman's ideas were ahead of their time and found resonance in institutional developments within Western Europe only some decades later.

Fourth, Hirschman makes no mention of the geopolitical dimension of the Marshall Plan, namely that economic recovery in Western Europe was seen as crucial to the strategic objective of ensuring political stability and preventing Soviet influence or communism more generally gaining a stronger foothold there. This less well-known rationale for the Plan was quite explicit (see Hogan 1987; George C. Marshall Foundation 2013) and related directly to the Truman doctrine of controlling communism adopted by that US president in 1947, after General Marshall had returned from a European tour convinced that this was a very real danger in view of the widespread poverty he encountered. Czechoslovakia taking the communist path in 1947 proved crucial in persuading the US Congress to approve the $17 billion package after initial indecision. The Marshall Plan also set the tone for subsequent official development assistance (ODA) or aid packages to poor countries, in that it simultaneously provided a sharp boost to US exports via the device of tying the majority (approximately 70 per cent) of the funds to the purchase of US-produced goods and equipment. In other words, it was by no means solely the altruistic package that is often portrayed. Indeed, this programme greatly facilitated the transformation of the US economy back from a war footing to civilian production. These omissions presumably arose simply because they didn't link to Hirschman's personal role at the time and hence the focus of his reflections in 1998, because in the 1993 interview published in English in the same volume, he demonstrates clear awareness of the interrelated economic and political dimensions and their relative importance. Referring approvingly to the idea of 'large-scale grant giving' as he saw the Plan, he commented:

> this was *an original idea ... It represented the invention of a new type of cooperative relationship between nations*, a relationship that became possible because of the Soviet threat. But this threat was not the original motivation. The most profound reason for the Marshall Plan was the desire to strengthen European democracy, in addition to the equally important idea of contributing to the process of European unification. (Hirschman 1998: 78; my emphasis)

Whether it was actually such a new idea is a moot point, although it probably seemed that way at the time. Gilbert Rist (1997, 2001) has, more recently, traced such modern large-scale development co-operation back to the League of Nations' programme of assistance to China's Four Modernisations programme in the 1930s, although I have no data on the extent of its grant element. However, implicitly, at least, Hirschman is reaffirming how the Marshall Plan was understood and that this 'new relationship between nations' was subsequently pursued through aid programmes to poor countries.

Fifth, Adelman and Loyer (2010: 13) confirm Hirschman's motivation for engagement with the Marshall Plan: 'Hirschman wanted to make a difference. To some extent, he was. Rebuilding Europe, expanding its possibilities in the wake of its self-inflicted horrors was both an ethical commitment and a practical cause'. This is perhaps a clearer and more explicit linkage between his expatriation and wartime experiences, and subsequent career engagements than Hirschman has made himself. Sixth and finally, and notwithstanding my previous observation, Hirschman himself retrospectively made the explicit connection between his Marshall Plan experiences and his subsequent development engagements in Latin America and other parts of the global South.

Following the Marshall Plan Thread – Hirschman in Colombia: Hirschman undertook one of the first such assignments of anyone in this cohort, spending the period 1952–56 in Colombia. As mentioned above, this followed immediately after his period working on the Marshall Plan. Whereas he himself portrayed it as an opportunity to escape the uncomfortable situation of supporting positions regarding the European Payments Union that contradicted those of his employers and also what he perceived as the boredom of living in Washington DC (Hirschman 1998: 42–3, 80), Jeremy Adelman (2012 @ 42–43 mins) cast it in a different light. He found evidence that Hirschman's planned move back to Paris to work there for the State Department required a full security review, which revealed that the Federal Bureau of Investigation (FBI) had been tracing Hirschman since 1941 on account of concerns at his underground contacts and resistance work – in short, he was a 'suspect character'. Although Hirschman was apparently unaware of the review, which led to his being denied a transfer to the Treasury or any future government employment, he was concerned about being shadowed (Adelman and Loyer 2010: 14; Adelman, pers. comm.[ii]; Adelman 2013: 284–94).[3]

Taking the economic advisory post in Colombia resolved this problem. Although recommended by the World Bank, Hirschman was contracted directly to the Colombian government to advise its new planning council on the basis of his Marshall Plan experience. The situation on the ground was complex, with a coup, conflicts with other advisors, including Laughlin Currie, who led the first World Bank

---

[3] Despite this history, he apparently never had any trouble during the McCarthy era from the Committee on Un-American Activities (Hirschman 1998: 80).

mission and then stayed on to avoid the McCarthyite witch hunt, and his successor whose views were too rigid and taught Hirschman 'how not to plan!' (Hirschman 1998: 81). Hence, he did not renew his two-year contract but stayed in Bogotá as an independent consultant, often assisting private firms and parastatal bodies seeking funding from the World Bank. Given the paucity of expertise on Latin America, this immersion (even with limited travel to Ecuador and Venezuela in the region), made him a leading authority, although he was conscious of being isolated from academia. Participation in a 1954 conference on tropical economic planning problems at the MIT aroused wide interest as he was the only participant able to ground his conceptual analysis in practical experience. Nevertheless, he felt very much off the pace intellectually. Led by Max Millikan and Walt Rostow, MIT was a hub of emergent liberal anti-communist development thinking with close ties to the US State Department and Central Intelligence Agency (see below) (Adelman 2013: 321–4).

Hans Singer in the United Nations: Hans Singer's career involved several phases of differing durations in government, universities and the United Nations. Following about a year at the end of World War II working for the UK government's Ministry of Town and Country Planning (1945–46), he spent the next academic year as an economics lecturer at the University of Glasgow (Shaw 2002: 34–6), before commencing a long career-within-a-career at the United Nations. This was not Singer's plan, but what John Shaw (*ibid.*: 35) calls 'another twist of fate [that] redirected Singer's career as a development economist'. David Owen, the newly appointed head of the nascent UN Department of Economic Affairs, approached the principal of the university to release either Alec Cairncross or Hans Singer for two years to help him launch the Department. The former was otherwise committed to postwar reconstruction, so the principal insisted that a reluctant Singer, who really wanted to consolidate his academic career, took a two-year leave of absence to undertake the work (*ibid.*: 35–6; Shaw 2006a: 243).

Although Singer had been keenly interested in economic development since his Bonn student days under Joseph Schumpeter, and had studied under Keynes at the time when the latter's seminal work was highlighting that economic laws were not universal truths but affected different countries and areas differently, Singer at that stage had no particular interest in development economics as such.

However, the American deputy to David Owen misinterpreted his year's experience at the Ministry of Town and Country Planning by taking Country Planning to mean national planning and hence assigned him to the Department of Economic Affairs' fledgling development section, which then had only two other members.

Thus began Singer's 22-year UN career working on poor countries, in the halcyon days of postwar enthusiasm and commitment, with the novelty and privilege of establishing and diversifying new institutions with important missions. In particular, Article 55 of Chapter IX of the UN Charter, adopted in 1945, and the 1948 Universal Declaration of Human Rights contained explicit commitments to equality; universal respect for human rights; the promotion of higher living standards, employment levels and standards; the solution of worldwide health, educational and other social problems; 'and conditions of economic and social progress and development'. These constituted ethical commitments for the UN and its new specialist agencies to serve humankind by improving different dimensions of the quality of life.

Eminent economists and others worked on diverse development topics, in the early days often alone in pursuit of projects that most interested them because of the lack of institutional structures, mechanisms and processes (Singer 1984; Shaw 2002: 39–42; 2006a: 244–5; see also Emmerij et al. 2001; Weiss et al. 2005: 145–85). This is one of the key reasons why the early postwar development pioneers were able to set their own parameters and why their publications often became foundational, especially when based on early interventions and subsequent critical reflections during the course of academic work or other engagements – a theme to which I return in later chapters.

Just how novel and strange this situation seemed to many 'mainstream' economists is evident from the discouraging reaction of Joseph Schumpeter when Singer visited him in Harvard shortly after arriving at the UN and told him that he would be working on problems of poor countries: 'But I thought you were an economist – isn't this more a matter for anthropologists, sociologists, geographers, etc.?' Having later heard Singer present a paper on part of his seminal work on terms of trade theory, Schumpeter conceded that 'there were interesting problems there after all' (Shaw 2002: 43). Of course, this was still some way short of admitting either that development economics should be considered part of the mainstream discipline since it relates to the majority of the world's countries and people, or – by extension – that 'mainstream' economics could and should be informed by advances in development economics. Sadly, this situation still pertains all too widely today.

In his interview for the UN Intellectual History Project (UNIHP), Singer also noted how the Marshall Plan experience was absorbed and adapted within the UN and how it served as a precedent for food aid under the right circumstances. He realised, however, that the impact of the Cold War meant that many such national development interventions, like five-year plans, were viewed with suspicion by American and many Western governments as potential evidence of the influence of Soviet-style central planning (Weiss et al. 2005: 159: UNIHP 2007: Singer: 12–13). This suspicion became so intense that in order to continue promoting strategies such as import substitution and export diversification, Raúl Prebisch and Hans Singer

> always had to be very careful to say that what we were talking about was not Stalinist-type central planning. It was not connected with political prisoners or labor camps, or anything of the kind. We had in mind the Indian type of five-year plan. But this distinction was sometimes very difficult to maintain in the mind of critics. (UNIHP 2007: Singer: 13; also Weiss et al. 2005: 159)

During his time at the UN, Singer worked in various capacities, including as Director of the Development Section within the Department of Economic and Social Affairs, and played a central role in the early development of the World Food Programme, Special United Nations Fund for Economic Development (SUNFED) and African Development Bank, as well as helping to initiate the World Employment Programme for the International Labour Organization (ILO). The last of these overlapped with his departure from the UN and commencement of his main academic career with the Institute of Development Studies (IDS) at the University of Sussex in 1969. In addition, he regularly undertook missions on the UN's behalf and acted as consultant to various international organisations and individual governments; such assignments continued from his IDS base. Singer also wrote a seminal paper for the UN International Children's Emergency Fund (UNICEF) on the role of children in economic development, which he recalled as being the young agency's first foray beyond postwar reconstruction and refugee-related issues. He had been inspired by a leading nutritionist's lecture on the importance of infant nutrition to physical and mental development (see Shaw 2002: 44–152; UNIHP 2007: Singer: 51,

61–141). Shaw's biographical account of this period encompasses detailed assessments of each of these stages, and the policy and political bones of contention among the various staff members and consultants – which fall beyond the scope of this study.

Singer found an ally in Raúl Prebisch, champion of Latin American development and head of the UN Economic Commission for Latin America (ECLA), who was able to use Singer's analyses in formulating more appropriate industrialisation strategies for the region. Their parallel work on differential demand elasticities and terms of trade for primary and secondary commodities led to the famous Prebisch–Singer Hypothesis. In turn, a number of other UNIHP interviewees, including Fernando Henrique Cardoso (much later to become Brazilian president), Sridath Ramphal and Gamani Corea, reported being encouraged or inspired by Singer's work during their time in the UN (Weiss et al. 2005: 197; Kay 2006; Shaw 2006c).

During his UNIHP interview, Singer enumerated the key influences on his commitment to Third World justice and progress as being his experiences of growing up in a multiple minority situation in provincial Germany (see Chapter 2); and his work on the Pilgrim Trust study and then the early UN reports, including the famous ILO Kenya study – which taught him to see the world from the perspective of the underdog, which reveals things invisible from above:

> For instance, one of the first things I did in the UN ... was a study of the terms of trade. When after looking at the facts of life, I thought if you look at foreign trade from the point of view of the poor countries, exporters of primary products, what does it look like? And it appears an unequal system that is weighted against them. That was the same way the unemployed in England looked at the unemployment insurance system. (UNIHP 2007: Singer: 57)

The third important influence on Singer was anticolonial and anti-imperial feeling among Indian and other Third World elite figures studying in Cambridge as his contemporaries – for which he also felt great sympathy: 'If I had been in charge of affairs, I would have given India independence in 1936' (UNIHP 2007: Singer: 58).

Even while working at the UN, Singer took time out for many years to teach graduate classes at the New School for Social Research (now the New School) in New York City; he also utilised this as an opportunity for reflection on his and the UN's practical engagements, particularly in relation to problems of international trade. This led, in turn, to several notable publications under his own name[4] on what he termed the seven pillars of development, as well as the mechanics of, and barriers to, economic development, as well as investment in human capacity. At the end of his time at the UN, Singer still believed that tackling pervasive poverty remained the most justifiable value judgement underlying economic policies. He also found it remarkable that, unlike in other sub-disciplines of economics, no coherent theory of economic development had yet emerged (Shaw 2002: 123–52; 2006a: 244–5; 2006c: 407; interview, John Shaw[iii]; Schiavo-Campo and Singer 1970: 3–14) – a situation with which many would still concur today.

Nationalised Industry Economic Advisor and Cross-cultural Explorer

The NCB as Platform for Alternative Livelihoods and Non-Western Explorations: On his return from Germany, **Fritz Schumacher** found his new job at the NCB, as 'the one person in the industry who was paid to think', enjoyable initially, and his home life balanced his work commitments. In particular, he became an enthusiastic organic gardener/farmer and member of the recently formed Soil Association, even making his own compost and seeking to make his family self-sufficient at a time when these were very much fringe 'niche' concerns (Wood 1985: 220–7). He also used his daily train commute into central London for private study, exploring non-Western societies and belief systems and finding a resonance in their holistic approaches to life that chimed with his organic gardening understandings. Gradually this evolved into a deep engagement with spirituality, the teachings of G.I. Gurdjieff, Edward Conze, Buddhism and the search for enlightenment and a desire to explore the East (*ibid.*: 228–39).

As her father's biographer, Barbara Wood poses a crucial question for the purposes of this investigation, namely how it was possible for a man who had, until shortly before, championed the power of the intellect and science over everything else suddenly to take such a turn towards non-materiality and spirituality. She ascribes it in part to the impact on him of the distressing postwar years in Germany in relation to both family and work, the emotional shocks of which

---

4   This was not possible within the UN.

had begun to awaken the world of his heart and of feelings, and thereby introduce questions in his mind about the condition of man which fact, science and reason did not seem to be able to answer satisfactorily. Yet many people experience such uncomfortable nigglings without paying them any attention. Why did Fritz? Fritz himself had quite a simple answer ... it was his work in the garden, working with the soil. [In contrast to his Eydon Hall days of farm work during the height of his rationalist phase,] The crucial factor he felt lay in the methods which he was now employing. Occupation with organic husbandry had opened his mind to the possibility of new vistas. His acceptance of the organic approach rather than the conventional chemical approach was, in a sense, an act of faith. (*ibid.*: 236–7)

His work at the NCB included comparative research into the range of power and energy sources as part of efforts to increase efficiency and output of coal. He was struck by the extent to which Western industrial society had come to rely so heavily on non-renewable energy resources and realised the long-term consequences, as a forerunner of the quantitative modelling 'limits to growth' thesis of 1972 (Meadows et al. 1972). His first articulation of these ideas, couched in terms of raiding nature's larder at an increasing rate, at a conference in Germany met with disinterest as postwar economic growth was increasing and,

> there was a vision of the future when technology would ensure that there was plenty for all. No one was interested in listening to an economist who told them that the future was built on dreams. His vision of industrial society containing the seeds of its own destruction in its dependence on finite resources had repercussions on another area to which he had been giving some thought. (*ibid.*: 242)

Burma, Buddhist Economics and Intermediate Technology: That area was the growing imbalance in global trade and the realisation that this could create instability and represent a new threat to international peace. He argued for 'a reasonable international division of labour' to help reduce the disparities, coupled with development assistance that blended altruism and self-interest (*ibid.*: 242–3). A three-month UN-funded advisory visit to Burma in 1955 proved crucial to the subsequent formulation of his development ideas. His mission was to evaluate advice provided by a team of American economists and to advise on the country's trade and fiscal situation but he soon came to understand that the problems were deeper than just policy instruments, lying with the mismatch between the underlying Western philosophy and the radically different Buddhist world view. Here the differences between Germany's rapid postwar economic recovery with an appropriately skilled and experienced population and Burma's challenges in trying to modernise on a Western model from a totally different starting point and without such skills became all too clear.

He rapidly developed a critique of the American advice and its effects, arguing for a Buddhist approach to economics which would be based on two interconnected principles, the recognition of the importance of limits in terms of adequacy rather than surplus ('Economic "progress" is good only to the point of sufficiency, beyond that, it is evil, destructive, uneconomic') and the difference between renewable and non-renewable resources. An economy based on the latter is superior to one driven by the former because it 'co-operates with nature' rather than robbing it and can thus last. This was the foundation of his landmark 1955 paper, 'Economics in a Buddhist Country', later expanded in a chapter entitled 'Buddhist Economics' (Schumacher 1966) and subsequently included in his landmark volume (Schumacher 1974). As Wood argues, this was a remarkable position for a Western economist to take in 1955 in a world focused resolutely on growth based on the exploitation of non-renewable minerals and energy. Both that paper and his reports to the government fell on deaf ears, rather as had his earlier recommendations in postwar Germany (Wood 1985: 247–9).

Schumacher's Burmese assignment typified the kind of overseas opportunity to engage at the highest level at what – perhaps appropriately in his case – might be termed the coalface of development in non-Western contexts that arose for this cohort of people on account of their different experiences and expertise at a time when the universalising modernising ethos was paramount. In many cases, such assignments contributed importantly to shaping their ideas and later research and policy directions, but the profound extent of the impact of this single experience on Schumacher – further deepened by later work in India and his inspiration by the work of Gandhi – was exceptional. It is also all the more noteworthy in that Schumacher was already mid-career at that stage rather than a young professional.

Indeed, it spawned an abiding interest and passion in a radically different approach to economics that would lead eventually to his magnum opus, *Small Is Beautiful* (Schumacher 1974), while also inspiring him to embrace Buddhism and to lecture and write on Buddhism and comparative religious philosophies, including his notable book, *A Guide for the Perplexed* (Schumacher 1977), published just after his death[5] and which sets out the philosophy underpinning *Small Is Beautiful*. Much of the groundwork for these publications was laid during the 1950s, a period of frustration for Schumacher at the NCB, when his advice was not favoured and he felt undervalued, even as overproduction rather than shortages became the principal concern for the nationalised industry. This afforded him the time to pursue his own interests (Wood 1985: 268–83).

Fortunately, this changed around the time that his wife, Muschi, died of cancer in late 1960, and he was able to immerse himself fully once again in his work at the NCB from early 1961 under the new Deputy Chair, Alf (later Lord) Robens, who valued Fritz's expertise in the struggle to save the Board from economic crisis; his ideas also found support within the National Union of Mineworkers. He became a regular churchgoer, taking his late wife's place at their local Congregational Church. In late January 1961, he also remarried – taking his housekeeper, Vreni Rosenberger, who was some 30 years his junior, as his new wife. He had a totally different relationship with her from that with Muschi. She was unable to match him intellectually, but provided the home support for him to emerge increasingly as a public figure and to travel widely professionally. The marriage divided his children initially; eventually another four children joined the family by 1974 (*ibid.*: 294–9). His newfound favour at the NCB was not universally appreciated but he became central to decision making during this tumultuous period in the coal industry (*ibid.*: 300–11).

Schumacher's acquaintance with J.J. Narayan, the prominent Indian politician, facilitated by Ernest Bader, proved another instrumental link in the chain that led to *Small Is Beautiful*. Narayan had Fritz's 1955 paper on Buddhist economics published in India and then encouraged him to visit, which he did briefly first in early 1961, and then more extensively later on. This brought him face to face for the first time with devastating and pervasive poverty, conditions very different from

---

[5] He did, however, receive advance copies a few days prior to his death, about which he remarked that this was what his whole life had been leading up to, and he gave one to Barbara with the inscription, 'To Barbara Wood, whose existence fills me with admiration and delight, from E. F. Schumacher, alias Papa' – from which the title of her biography of her father derives (Wood 1985: 366).

what he had seen in Burma, and drove him to question the reasons for it (*ibid.*: 316–18).

He was highly critical of conventional economic theories and policy prescriptions, including particularly modernisation theory and its proponents like Walt Rostow, arguing that the apathy and passivity he observed resulted from the impact of the Western modernity on profoundly different societies and cultures. It reinforced his commitment to Buddhist economics and focused his attention on different, more locally attuned and appropriate production processes and technologies for the majority of the poor, who lived in rural villages: 'Fritz began to think more deeply about the question of technology and technology transfer, and its implications for job creation' (*ibid.*: 319). Thus his concept of intermediate technology was born and he pursued it with vigour as soon as he returned to the UK, delivering a paper on the subject at a high-level conference in Cambridge in 1964, attended by his former Oxford colleagues and friends, the prewar Hungarian émigrés, Tommy Balogh and Nicholas Kaldor. The paper proved highly controversial, with Kaldor amongst the fiercest critics, but this merely intensified Fritz's commitment and criticism of conventional economists. In August 1965, wide support for his ideas, as published in an article in *The Observer* newspaper one Sunday, provided the platform for establishment of the Intermediate Technology Development Group (ITDG),[6] which Schumacher was permitted to lead without resigning from the NCB because of Robens' support (*ibid.*: 319–29).

The rest, as the saying goes, is history. He was finally doing work in which he believed profoundly and which was having real impact. In early 1971 at the age of 60, he left his fulltime work at the NCB, retaining only a modest advisory role, which he supplemented with consultancy elsewhere. He travelled widely and became a world-renowned figure until his untimely and sudden death on 4 September 1977 on a train journey in Switzerland (*ibid.*: 330–70), leaving a legacy that sets him firmly in the pantheon of heterodox development thinkers and practitioners (Toye 2012). The ITDG (now Practical Action) continues to thrive as a major international development agency promoting appropriate technologies at the village and household scale in low-income countries and communities.

---

[6] This became a separate entity from the African Development Trust, where Schumacher had initially found an outlet for his ideas.

Given when Schumacher was professionally active and how long ago he died, **Paul Streeten** is the only one of my interviewees to have known him. He remembers Schumacher as 'a very warm person, concerned with the underdog, the weak, the poor and the neglected. Very friendly. We were at a conference together in Germany and we were talking about *Small Is Beautiful*. I said, sometimes large is appropriate. Schumacher said I was playing with words' (pers. comm.[iv]).

Academic Careers Blended with Consultancy and Official Advisory Work

The most common track for the adults in this study who had commenced or resumed careers by the end of World War II was to work predominantly in universities and to undertake regular or occasional consultancy and advisory work from that base. The opportunities for such engagements in policy and practice were almost limitless at that time, since postwar reconstruction in Europe overlapped with the early decolonisation process in South and Southeast Asia, where the incoming governments and new planning and development departments and offices lacked expertise and experience. Everyone, be they national officials or elected representatives, foreign advisors or staff of the new Bretton Woods institutions (Word Bank and International Monetary Fund) were quite literally learning by doing.

Albert Hirschman: The Move into Academia – Yale and After: The interest shown in Hirschman's experience-based conceptual analysis at the 1954 MIT conference (see above) also led to an invitation in 1956 to spend time at Yale University – where a number of his former Marshall Plan colleagues were then on the faculty – to write up his experiences by expanding the ideas in his MIT paper. The result became his landmark volume, *The Strategy of Economic Growth* (Hirschman 1958), for which he is most widely known (see McPherson 2000; Brohman 2006: 128–30; Adelman 2013: 325–52) and often criticised, sometimes unfairly. This became an early landmark treatise in development thinking, offering a less deterministic and one-dimensional formulation than Walt Rostow's (1960) own monograph, *The Stages of Economic Growth: A Non-Communist Manifesto* published two years later. Because of and/or notwithstanding its overt ideological orientation, the latter subsequently became the foundational text of modernisation theory. In fact, one of Hirschman's earlier trademark 'self-subversions' was a critical revisiting of that book 25 years later in his contribution to the World Bank's *Pioneers in Development* volume (Meier and Seers 1984). In retrospect, he regarded the principal contribution of that chapter's critiques of both old and new orthodoxies to have been the fomenting of debate that has taken the field forward (Hirschman 1984).

Hirschman never returned to Colombia from Yale as planned, instead taking up academic posts successively at Columbia University in 1958, then Harvard and, in 1974, at the innovative Institute for Advanced Study at Princeton, where he would remain for the rest of his active life (Hirschman 1998: 81–2; Brohman 2006; Adelman 2013: 353ff.). He subsequently wrote two more books on development, *Journeys Toward Progress* and *Development Projects Observed* (Hirschman 1963; 1967), each time expanding the range of countries and project experiences in major contributions to ex-post development project evaluations; he regarded the three volumes as forming a trilogy (Hirschman 1995: 127–8). The latter involved extensive travel and research into 13 World Bank projects spread across Latin America, Africa and Asia at a time when the Bank did not yet have its own independent evaluation capacity. In line with his approach to political economy, Hirschman also sought to distil generalisable elements from the extended histories and particularities of the individual projects. His findings focused on risk and uncertainty, as well as the often important and unpredicted indirect effects of projects, which were at the time rarely accorded much attention, especially over the longer rather than immediate term. Hence, he favoured moving away from cost–benefit analysis, which was too narrow and rigid to cope with such ramifications. The critical nature of his conclusions did not endear him to Bank officials (Alacevich 2016b: 467–8).

This development-oriented segment of Hirschman's career, which more or less came to an end after *Development Projects Observed*, illustrates clearly how opportunities presented themselves based on previous experience and contacts. In this manner, the opportunity to join the Marshall Plan staff reflected his background and unique wartime credentials and, in turn, provided a highly distinctive platform for his later trajectory. His Marshall Plan experience was then refracted through the lens of his Colombian exposure and MIT and Yale connections to produce a seminal book on economic development and planning, facilitated by his former Marshall Plan colleagues. This demonstrates clearly in more personalised terms the point made above about how the Marshall Plan came to serve as reference point for the nascent venture of national development planning in low-income countries, initially in Latin America and then Asia, the Middle East and Africa as the tide of decolonisation swept away the remaining European empires.

Sometimes such close ties and serendipities can prove double edged. The MIT connection outlined above and close links with Rosenstein-Rodan and other key figures from the Marshall Plan days now associated with that university as the context to his 1958 book, led to Hirschman subsequently becoming unfairly closely associated in many later critics' minds with modernisation theory and the postwar anti-communist geopolitical project led by the US government. In reality, his fiercely independent mind refused to follow any dogmatic ideological or theoretical line. Indeed, he moved away from concerted theoretical engagements after his 1958 book, focusing increasingly on action and practice: as he once put it, 'I like to understand how things happen, how change actually takes place' (Hirschman 1998: 67). His political economy became concerned with pragmatic reform rather than wholesale or revolutionary change. He also constantly challenged his own preconceptions and earlier positions – what he liked to call his 'propensity to self-subversion' – which even became the title of one of his later books (Hirschman 1995) (see also McPherson 2000; Adelman 2013).

Critiques of his approach and publications but also his strong perception that development economics had had its heyday and was in terminal decline because of its failure to match optimistic theoretical possibilities and predictions with practical results (Hirschman 1981a; Alacevich 2016a; 2016b: 470–1) then led Hirschman away from the sub-discipline. Most of his subsequent writing addressed broader economic issues and business behaviour. Particularly notable in this respect was his extensive research on how people behave as customers and employees in relation to the strategies of firms, organisations and even governments – responses which he dubbed exit, voice and loyalty (Hirschman 1970). He also formulated a particular pragmatic approach to political economy, eschewing reductionist ideological orthodoxies, evidenced not least in his critical historical account of capitalism, which examines its intertwined positive and destructive features (Hirschman 1977; Brohman 2006: 131; Adelman 2013). Much of this work was built around the notion of 'trespassing' across often-taboo intellectual boundaries, such as between economics and politics, or the public and private spheres, often deploying his penchant for 'self-subversion' by challenging his own earlier perspectives in order to advance debate (Hirschman 1981b; 1995; 1998; Brohman 2006; Adelman 2013; Alacevich 2016a).

Perhaps surprisingly, given his earlier focus on development, Hirschman himself didn't explicitly develop arguments as to how these behavioural insights might relate to poorer countries and contexts, or North–South politico-economic relations. Only now are some aspects of his theory of exit and voice, for instance, finding such broader applications (e.g. Gonzalez 2015). As a result, Hirschman's later work remains surprisingly little known in development circles, even though his oeuvre as a whole undoubtedly establishes him as one of the most original and reflective thinkers on development and broader sociological and economic issues during the second half of the twentieth century. He died, aged 97, in New Jersey, on 10 December, 2012, after suffering from Alzheimer's disease for some years (*The Economist* 2012; Kavanagh 2012; Yardley 2012).

Hans Singer's Second Career – The Institute of Development Studies: When Singer retired from the United Nations in 1969, just short of his sixtieth birthday, an age at which most diplomats and civil servants contemplate a more leisured retirement, Hans Singer moved to the Institute of Development Studies (IDS) at the University of Sussex as Professorial Fellow (and also as a professor in the University of Sussex), commencing another career that was to last – a second formal retirement notwithstanding – until his death on 26 February 2006. Although he slowed down in his nineties and following the death of his wife in 2001, he remained active and was working on his latest paper when he died after a short illness, aged 95 (Shaw 2006b; 2006c).

His UN experience of rapid drafting in accessible prose style stood him in good stead for IDS consultancies but did not impede academic publishing. He continued working across a wide range of themes within development studies, especially development economics, maintaining his interests in the terms of trade, aid, food security, educational investment and child welfare first developed at the UN, but also opening up new themes.

In particular, his joint leadership with Richard Jolly of the International Labour Organization's (ILO's) Employment Mission to Kenya in 1972, was instrumental in changing perceptions – both official and academic – of the so-called 'informal sector' of the economy. Far from being largely economically irrelevant and possibly harmful and parasitic, it provided widespread employment and practical training that could, with encouragement rather than neglect or suppression, contribute to poverty alleviation and less inequitable economic growth and development. Indeed, the World Bank and other international agencies later adopted this perspective. Singer also opposed the structural adjustment policies of the IFIs and bilateral donors in the 1980s as undermining of the development potential of countries subjected to them. He continued to believe in the value of food aid for poor people in food deficit situations as a productive use for the sustained global food surpluses that were stockpiled as 'food mountains'; his co-authored book (Singer et al. 1987) represents a balanced assessment of the literature and debates up to that point. Singer was also convinced of the importance of redistributive policies to avoid the instability and other problems associated with wide socio-economic disparities (Shaw 2002: 155–249; 2006c: 412; Jolly 2006: 6–7; Toye 2006a: 920–1; 2006b). Indeed, Toye (2006b) argues that Singer's work on 'redistribution with growth' can be seen as the antecedent of the 'pro-poor' policies adopted by the IFIs and bilateral donors since the turn of the millennium.

His energy and active engagements were legendary. Unprecedentedly, he became President of the Development Studies Association in the UK for two years just before his eightieth birthday and was no mere figurehead. He continued to lecture and consult widely, and was the recipient of numerous awards, honorary degrees and a knighthood from the Queen in 1994. By the time of his death on 26 February 2006, he had published over 450 items of all categories, including some 260 refereed journal articles, over about 70 years – a truly distinctive oeuvre spanning a uniquely wide range of issues[7] in his distinctively authoritative yet modest style. If his influence on development thinking was immense, so too was his legacy in terms of policy instruments and UN and related development institutions (Shaw 2002: 261–4, 267–76,

---

[7] Including disarmament and economic development, technology transfer, and South–South co-operation. Like Hirschman, he often revisited earlier work, regularly modifying his position on issues in the light of changed circumstances and the evolution of his thinking.

303–37; 2006c: 404–5; Jolly 2006: 6–7; Toye 2006a: 920–1; 2006b). He is also almost certainly the only economist, let alone development economist, to have had both Schumpeter and Keynes as teachers and mentors, blending their respective perspectives into his own distinctive approach.[8]

Returning to the key research question for this study, it is clear that Singer remained firmly conscious of his German Jewish upbringing and particularly the training in ethics and civic responsibility he received from Rabbi Dr Norden – the importance of which he stressed explicitly to John Shaw during the process of writing his biography (interview, John Shaw[v]) – and wartime experiences throughout his life. In addition, his postwar exposure to severe poverty during the course of his Pilgrim Trust and then early UN work profoundly affected his outlook, no doubt reinforcing the Jewish ethical commitment to aiding the poor. This can be traced through his abiding concerns with tackling poverty, reducing socio-economic and international inequality and in providing the poor with food aid and the means for self-advancement through investments in education and health. People were always central to his approach to development.[9] Yet, Singer always emphasised the role of chance or 'twists of fate' through his life course, including the opportunities that arose and he took, including that by which he was invited to join the UN (Shaw 2002: 265–6; interview, John Shaw[vi]; Singer 2000: 606–7).

Like several other leading economists in this cohort, not least **Schumacher, Hirschman, Bauer** and **Streeten**, Singer was something of a heterodox figure, sometimes termed a 'dissenting economist', not afraid to take unpopular positions and to argue for causes and issues in which he believed. He himself lists his enduring minority views on

---

[8] Indeed, Singer regarded them, along with Beveridge, the third key academic influence on him, and all born in the early 1880s, as the first generation of development economists. Among the second generation, born around the turn of the century, Colin Clark, Rosenstein-Rodan, Gunnar Myrdal and Jan Tinbergen were important influences. Singer himself and his contemporaries in this chapter would constitute the third generation (Shaw 2002: 277). This is a very different lineage of development economics from that commonly traced back to Rosenstein-Rodan (see Chapter 1).

[9] In sharp contrast, his own familial relationships were mostly difficult and fraught, with one son estranged. He and his wife were very reticent in this regard, although one factor was probably his devotion to all aspects of his work at the expense of family time (interview, Odile Stamberger (daughter-in-law), 5/10/06; interview, John Shaw, 17/10/06 @ 29–30 mins).

the efficacy of food aid, and his prediction that food surpluses would arise in more countries as they pursue appropriate policies as distinctive examples (Singer 2000: 610–11). Most of these dissenters also worked across the theory–policy–practice divides, regarding theory and academic debate alone as inadequate. Their upbringing and formative experiences no doubt also played a key role in this.

Wolfgang Stolper: Wolfgang Stolper's career progressed very smoothly following his Harvard fellowship (see Chapter 2), initially driven by his ambition to become a pure theorist and moving in elite New England economics circles. In Paul Samuelson he found a second mentor (after Schumpeter), who soon became co-author of a seminal paper that articulated what remains known as the Stolper–Samuelson theorem on the relationship between the prices of a good and its principal factors of production under conditions of perfect competition (Stolper 1997: 105–6). That said, he found the war intellectually trying but for three special friends including the poet W.H. Auden, and he was relieved at being able to travel again afterwards.

He spent the summer of 1946 working at the International Labor Office, then still in its wartime temporary headquarters in Montreal, and – as was standard practice in those days – he was assigned to co-author a report on industrialisation in Southeast Asia despite a total lack of previous experience or expertise in the field. Although published anonymously the following year, he was very satisfied with what constituted 'the beginning of my interest in economic development, and makes me accidentally a pioneer in this field'. As if to amplify this point, and astonishing as it seems today, '[i]t was possible for me to read the whole literature on development in one month, admittedly working hard and reading a book a day plus some articles'. His central observation on this body of work comprised just one rather critical sentence: 'The central weakness of most of the literature was that everyone seemed to believe in balanced growth which seemed already then a *contradictio in adjecto*' (*ibid.*: 109) – a view shared by **Gerschenkron**, Rosenstein-Rodan, **Hirschman** and Rostow and which found expression in their espousal of different versions of 'big push' and other forms of sectorally and/or spatially unbalanced growth, at least initially. He clashed with Tommy Balogh on the value of import controls, and became immersed in location theory, even translating the second edition of August Lösch's (1954 [1940]) seminal text on

The Economics of Location (*Die Räumliche Ordnung der Wirtschaft*) into English, adding at the same time the mathematical proofs omitted by the author (Stolper 1997: 111–13).

Following work on East Germany, Stolper's first exposure to African economies came as a member of an MIT project in 1957–59. Invited by Max Millikan (see Hirschman above), he visited several European countries to assess and collect data but not Africa itself. Then, as Economic Advisor to the Nigerian Ministry of Economic Development (1960–62), he gained first-hand experience of 'how a modern economy arose' (*ibid.*: 119) and took pride in having been trusted for his honesty, so that he was later welcomed back (see Stolper 1966; 1997: 115–19).

In Stolper's own words, this experience changed his life, as he returned to the University of Michigan to become director of its Centre for Research on Economic Development for seven years, despite his dislike of administrative work. His philosophy was to focus the Centre on field-based research in Africa, recruiting specialists and leaving them to their own devices in line with his thinking at the time 'that underdeveloped countries presented not so much a special well-defined discipline but a kind of cameralistic problem where one combined everything from other fields as required in the special case' (Stolper 1997: 120–1).

He also undertook numerous consultancy assignments for USAID and occasionally the UN, working in several West African countries plus Turkey, Syria and Tunisia. His motivation was not private profit but to gain invaluable practical experience and to raise money to fund his students' studies (*ibid.*: 121). He remained active as a lecturer and writer well into retirement. In retrospect, he regarded himself as having been

extremely lucky. I have never planned anything, and what was planned by and for me in my youth was undone by Hitler. I have worked hard all my life, but so have many others. I have enjoyed doing so. I am grateful that I never was arrested, escaped concentration camp – by chance and at the last minute – that I never had to kill anybody, that I was never unemployed and had only good jobs at good universities and never had to suffer hunger and deprivation. I am grateful that I always had good and faithful friends … There is no merit to have been in the right place at the right time. There is at most some small merit in recognizing an opportunity and grasping it. Thus my life has truly been a series of facts without planning. And yet it has somehow been a unit too. (*ibid.*: 125)

These final reflections inspired the title of his autobiographical chapter, 'Facts without Planning', which also served as a witty inversion of the title of his book about his Nigerian experiences, *Planning without Facts* (Stolper 1966), to reflect the empirical vacuum or deficiency in which he felt that political imperatives drove policy. In today's parlance, this would amount to policy-led evidence rather than evidence-led policy.

In relation to the central research question of this book, the extent to which socialisation and wartime experiences influenced subsequent career choice to engage in some part of development, the available evidence suggests a negligible link in Stolper's case. Apart from the passing references above to Hitler and his narrow escape from internment in a concentration camp, he made no mention of such a connection. His formal education and then career were relocated from Europe to the USA after a short, albeit dramatic, interruption (see Chapter 2) but followed a course seemingly unrelated to that episode. He makes no reference to his religious affiliation, so that is also unlikely to have been a factor.

Heinz Arndt: Heinz Arndt moved from Manchester to Sydney University in 1946, ostensibly for a 2–3-year contract but he was ultimately to remain in Australia for the rest of his life, mainly at the Australian National University (ANU) in Canberra and its antecedent college, to which he moved four years later. His autobiographical accounts of his evolving career (Arndt 1985; 1997) explain how he became interested in development economics in the 1950s. This was stimulated by a long and animated conversation with Gunnar Myrdal on an intercontinental flight heading to sabbatical leave in the USA via London, followed almost immediately by meetings with many of the world's leading economists, some of whom were engaging in development work, during visits to Oxford, Boston, New York, Washington and Stanford. Personal connections again proved important, with Tommy Balogh reintroducing him to **Paul Streeten** in Oxford, and **Hans Singer** hosting him at the UN, where he gave a seminar and met many of the senior staff (Arndt 1985: 39–43; 1997: 162–4).

On his return to Canberra, he commenced teaching an undergraduate course in development economics but lacked first-hand experience. At Myrdal's instigation, Arndt was invited by Mahalanobis to spend the summer vacation of 1957/58 at the Indian Statistical Institute in Kolkota, where he worked with Ian Little and others on resource mobilisation from agriculture as a contribution to India's Third Five-Year Plan. This whet his appetite. He got to know the top Indian officials and also the Myrdals (then living there) when Gunnar was setting up the massive research initiative that eventually resulted in his landmark volume, *Asian Drama* (Myrdal 1968), as well as the eminent Danish economists, Ester Boserup and her husband, while on a visit.

This is indicative of how small and interconnected the relevant academic/intellectual circles were in those days, enabling even newcomers to integrate and establish themselves rapidly. The same point has already been made above with respect to **Hirschman**, **Singer** and **Stolper**. Arndt (1985: 47) did admit to having been powerfully affected by the vast scale of poverty he encountered in India and that, when asked to return for a longer period of work, 'I declined mainly for fear that I would never get away if I allowed myself to be further emotionally involved'. He gave no further hint of any emotional or ethical connection with his own background.

Accordingly, he became immersed in Indonesia, which became his principal research focus for some 20 years. As the most populous and important of Australia's Southeast Asian neighbours, it was vital for the ANU Research School to become active there and to fill the large research void, a problem exacerbated by the political tensions and economic mismanagement under Sukarno's authoritarian government. Once Suharto assumed power, Arndt launched the ANU's large Indonesia Project and visited the country four or five times annually. He also launched a new journal, the *Bulletin of Indonesian Economic Studies*, publishing 'empirical studies of aspects of the Indonesian economy ... which addressed analytically interesting and preferably policy-relevant questions' (*ibid.*: 60). For most of this period, he also wrote an annual *Survey of Recent Developments*. Such engagements were not without their critics on the political left in Australia and beyond, concerned at the implicit support for the Indonesian government's broad economic policies, and at the growth orientation of the research focus rather than on distributive and equity issues (*ibid.*: 52–66; 1997: 164–5; Coleman et al. 2007: 257–73). Arndt admits that his own philosophy had shifted over the years from youthful Marxism to Fabian Socialism and then a more individual libertarian position, the latter perhaps enabling him so readily to accommodate the Indonesian government's official discourse. However, there is no mention of religious affiliation or wartime experiences as seminal or contributory factors in the evolution of Arndt's development engagements beyond the point in the previous paragraph about having been deeply moved by the poverty he encountered in India.

Until his retirement in 1980, he also undertook numerous visits for conferences, research and consultancy assignments for the UN and various international agencies (especially the UN Conference on Trade and Development (UNCTAD), the UN Industrial Development Organization (UNIDO), the Organization for Economic Co-operation and Development (OECD) and World Bank) in many other East and Southeast Asian countries (Arndt 1985: 52–66; 1997: 164–5; Coleman et al. 2007: 274–92).[10] All these activities both established and reflected his standing as a leading 'Western' economist of Southeast and East Asia; he was certainly the doyen of Australian economists working in the region.

Peter Bauer: As indicated in Chapter 2, Peter Bauer withdrew from Budapest University and came to the UK to study in 1934 without any prior offer of admission, despite having suffered no particular anti-Semitism or political hostility. He landed on his feet and his career evolved without any real legacy from the Nazi era beyond having been a foreigner during a difficult period in the UK. There is no clue from his writings or the recollections of his former colleagues and biographers about whether and to what extent his background may have influenced his strong engagements in what became development economics but it seems unlikely that there was a strong connection. Let us, nevertheless, assess his career track in this light.

As with the other figures profiled in this chapter, Bauer did not so much immerse himself in development economics as contribute to its emergence as a distinct field. He chose to specialise in it without being confined by it, and later in his career he used it as a platform to engage with international economics and trade, industrialisation and comparative economic systems. Nevertheless, according to Basil Yamey (1987: 21–2), Bauer became interested in development almost by accident. During World War II, he had researched and written

---

[10] In Arndt (1985: 63), he claims to have done such consultancy on only on occasion, but his later autobiographical essay refers to frequent assignments (Arndt 1997: 164–5); the latter is accurate.

on interest and depreciation, monopoly and the British agricultural marketing systems. He also worked for a London-based company heavily engaged in the Malayan rubber industry and then took advantage of a research fellowship to study that industry and was simultaneously commissioned by the Colonial Office to examine rubber smallholdings in Malaya. Following an article in the *Economic Journal* on regulation in the rubber industry, the main study and report were both published in quick succession (Bauer 1948a; 1948b) and rapidly established his scholarly credentials and spurred him on to continue in this field.

The evolution, operation and implications of monopolistic commodity markets and marketing boards became one of Bauer's principal interests and research foci, both in itself but also as a basis for research into income and price stabilisation for agricultural and related producers. Based on extensive field and desk research, his benchmark study of *West African Trade* (Bauer 1954) cemented his reputation but his analyses often proved controversial and heterodox, and he never shied away from robust academic debate in person or in writing. Indeed, as he broadened his concern to development economics as a whole, he relished being able to challenge or refute conventional wisdoms – as evidenced by his *Dissent on Development* (Bauer 1971). He discussed these and his other major contributions in an interview shortly before his death in 2002 (IEA 2002: 37–40) but didn't add any observations particularly pertinent to this assessment.

According to Yamey (1987: 26), one of Bauer's main distinguishing hallmarks was his 'insistence on the crucial importance of cultural and political factors in economic development'. Based on his Malayan and West African field experience, he emphasised the relevance of customs and practices of individuals and groups as well as the more conventional factors like resource endowment, investment and educational levels. Rereading Bauer's (1984: 33–4) own summary of his perspective is instructive in terms of its reference to the 'economic qualities of the people' as well as official policies in determining the cultivability of land:

> Although the discussion of them has been largely taboo in the postwar development literature, the reality and importance of group differences in economic performance cannot be disputed ... Discussion of the reasons for group differences in performance and of their likely persistence would be speculative, and economic reasoning is not informative on these questions. But this provides no excuse for the systematic neglect of group differences by economists.

Importantly, Bauer (*ibid.*: 32–3) argued that such differences could not be ascribed to the distinctions between migrants and indigenous residents since his Malayan research revealed radical differences between the Indian and Chinese smallholder communities there, despite the strong similarities in their respective (lack of) formal educational exposure, their landholdings and production technology. He also invoked a longer economic historical perspective on this observation and then pointed out (*ibid.*: 34) that population pressure was not absolute or universal but had to be understood contextually in relation to such considerations.[11]

Moreover, and very revealingly in terms of his self-positioning relative to modernisation theorists à la Rostow, he argued that these issues,

> have reinforced my reluctance to attempt to formulate a theory of economic development, and also my rejection of theories based either on sequential stages of history or on the conventional type of growth model. The inadequacy of these theories is in any case revealed by their inability to account for the well-attested phenomenon of economic decline. (*ibid.*: 34)

In other words, he eschewed universalising theories in principle on account of non-economic values (although he understood and referred to them in what nowadays seem Eurocentric and indeed deterministic terms) and because they were unable to account for observed realities. These are bold statements based on empirical observation in Southeast Asia and West Africa, in particular, and on understanding of the literature. Perhaps, too, his Jewish background (which he openly acknowledged despite having been baptised) and experience of having come to the UK as a foreign student from Hungary and having had to make the grade in an educational milieu rather different from that

---

[11] He elaborated on these ideas in a published interview shortly before his death (IEA 2002: 23–5), but in which he seemed to emphasis individual rather than group differences, even citing British examples to argue that, the class system notwithstanding, the UK is an open society. Moreover, in response to a question about markets producing inequalities, he responded that differences are a more appropriate term, 'because difference is a neutral term, and inequality is a loaded term. Inequalities are often equated with inequity. Except this leads to the idea that the poor are poor because the rich are rich, i.e. that the rich have extracted their incomes or wealth from the poor, which is not true'. Accordingly, his views appear to have sharpened in favour of individualism since his 1984 reflections.

in the Budapest of his youth, contributed to that sensitivity to socio-cultural difference. He never mentioned this but there might just be a modicum of evidence linking his professional engagement to his socialisation and observation (albeit from the safety of the UK) of what fate befell some of his relatives and other victims of Nazism. This is naturally speculative but there is no evidence for anything stronger, let alone a causal link with his career choice and direction. He even went to Cambridge specifically to study economics as he thought it would enhance his prospects for subsequent employment as a private international lawyer in Hungary (see IEA 2002: 21).

Notwithstanding Bauer's unusual sensitivity – especially for an economist – to 'group differences' and the importance of government policies in determining outcomes, in the immediate postwar period, his autobiographical essay reveals a curious lack of political economic perspective, at least by today's standards. Instead, he appears to have retreated into a narrower econocentric approach probably consistent with the trend within the mainstream discipline which eschews engagement with power relations and political determinants.

Two other distinctive elements of his work for which he is rarely credited, despite (and perhaps in part because of) having been well ahead of his time, deserve mention here. First, his book on *West African Trade* (Bauer 1954) drew attention to the shortcomings of formal occupational statistics that claimed most households to be engaged in agriculture in contexts of what he called 'the prevailing incomplete occupational specialisation', where many other activities, especially trade and transport were widely undertaken alongside farming (*ibid.*: 35). This phenomenon of what are now commonly referred to as 'multi-activity households' remains common but became a subject of significant research interest only three decades later, as the hardships wrought by structural adjustment programmes (SAPs) in the 1980s forced greater economic diversification by households. Similarly, too, the literature expressing concerns at the inadequacy of official statistics in reflecting such realities fails to acknowledge this far older origin. Second, this portfolio of activities comprised many livelihood strategies that fell partly or wholly beyond the reach of formal controls and taxation. As such this book and related publications quite possibly constitute the first systematic observations about the nature of what many years later became known as the 'informal' sector (Yamey 1987: 22) – long before Keith Hart's (1973) study on these activities in Ghana, the publication of which is often credited as the birth of 'informal sector' studies.

Third and perhaps ironically in relation to the first observation, his research on monopsonistic (he called them monopolistic) agricultural marketing boards demonstrated how institutions intended to stabilise and enhance the incomes of primary commodity producers rapidly became tools of systematic exploitation and profit extraction through taxation. They depressed producer prices and often imposed other restrictions on production decisions, thus reducing incentives to increase production and impeding producer livelihood security and specialisation. The pervasiveness of such practices internationally contributed to his aversion to monopolistic practices and market regulation and underpinned his advocacy of market competition since even poor producers were flexible and adept at taking advantages of marketing opportunities. He was probably the first prominent figure to draw attention to these problems. Decades later, his influence as economic advisor to Margaret Thatcher and her Conservative government that took office in the UK in 1979,[12] would contribute to the formulation of SAPs. While indeed breaking such monopolies and facilitating increased producer prices, these programmes caused widespread hardship to some producer and most non-producer households in the global South.

Essentially, Bauer contested deterministic and structuralist explanations for poverty and its perpetuation, going to great lengths to demonstrate what he saw as the distorting effects of burgeoning aid policies and the dependence culture they spawned. Indeed, in his later career and in his speeches in the UK's House of Lords after his ennoblement by Margaret Thatcher in 1983, he spoke out strongly in favour of individual freedom and choice, and market-based trade rather than aid as a key driver of development – becoming what Yamey (1987: 26) rightly calls 'the most prominent academic critic of this policy'. Even as a broadly fellow traveller, Srinivasan's (1984: 54) commentary on Bauer's autobiographical chapter in *Pioneers in Development* was critical of Bauer's

---

[12] This role extended beyond his retirement from the LSE in 1983. However, according to Basil Yamey (interview, Basil Yamey[vii]), he soon felt marginalised in the Lords, even by Thatcher and her government, who no longer consulted him. He was thus less active in the Lords than he might have been and eventually remarked memorably to Yamey that 'Mrs Thatcher is like somebody who buys a dog and then barks herself!'

work.[13] While agreeing with the appropriateness of greater marketisation, Srinivasan found 'in his writings more polemics and debating points than depth'. This might help explain some of the common hostility to Bauer's perspective, for which he was often vilified.

Conversely, those who shared Bauer's perspective were fulsome in praise of his consistency. In concluding his tribute, James Buchanan, another former LSE colleague and friend, argued that 'Peter Bauer felt that he had a moral obligation to expose the lies being told by his peers. And while he surely did feel that his own ideas were vindicated by the turn of history, he remained pessimistic about prospects for a viable liberal order' (IEA 2002: 59; Buchanan 2002: 234). In a posthumous tribute by Milton Friedman and Thomas Sowell, the latter's opening compliment was that 'The thing that strikes me most about Peter Bauer is how he stuck to his guns through decade after decade – when he was outside the mainstream, all by himself. And then, by the end of his life, the mainstream had moved over to where he was (Friedman and Sowell 2005: 441).[14] Helen Hughes (2002: 64), a former colleague of **Heinz Arndt**, drew attention to the curiosity that Arndt and Bauer were both born in 1915, although in different parts of Europe, and died in May 2002, by when their initially diametrically opposed economic perspectives had converged closely.

Bauer's anti-aid stance was already regarded as his principal contribution when I was an economics and development student in the late 1970s. It has indubitably also become his most lasting legacy, with the important work outlined above often ignored. In this sense, both he and **Albert Hirschman** (see above) acquired somewhat unfair reputations based on only parts of their work. Bauer's derived from his later publications and position, whereas Hirschman is remembered most, and in a somewhat jaundiced way, for his early landmark book despite his voluminous subsequent writings, which were consistently original and challenging.

[13] This is unsurprising. Bauer and Yamey were longstanding colleagues at the LSE and worked together closely, not least as authors. Indeed, Bauer (2002: 26–7) speaks equally complimentarily about Yamey, suggesting that the latter was a proponent of marketisation before him and had a clear influence on his own thinking. They had originally been introduced by R.H. Coase when Bauer sought help in collating the material for his Colonial Office-funded study of West African trade.

[14] This issue of *The Cato Journal* contained nine posthumous tributes, including one by Amartya Sen.

Paul Streeten: Following his long convalescence from war wounds (Chapter 3), Paul Streeten resumed his academic studies at Balliol College, Oxford in 1944–45, while still registered as disabled and in receipt of a 100 per cent disability pension. Although 'they did quite a good job suturing the nerve of my left leg and my left arm' (interview, Paul Streeten[viii]), he was left with a pronounced limp and still has some shrapnel pieces embedded in his body.

He took to the Oxonian mores extremely well and has written numerous accounts of his student days, learning from many of the leading economists of the day (including Maurice Allen, Michal Kalecki and Frank Burchardt) and benefiting from the influence of his philosophy tutors, Donald McKinnon and David Falk, and politics tutor, John Fulton. He also mixed with peers who would become prominent figures in diverse fields. Eccentricities and exploits are recorded with dry humour. Of note is that Streeten's tutor at Balliol was Thomas Balogh, who later became his mentor, a close friend and co-author, with Streeten having to apply and polish some of Balogh's sharp insights into publishable form. Balogh was notoriously sharp-tongued and disorganised, so that people tended to react strongly for or against him. Later as fellow tutors, Balogh focused on applied economics and Streeten on theory. His tutorial load was heavy and broad, which might have contributed to his aversion to narrow research specialisation (Streeten 1985a; 1986a; 1986b; 1997; 2000a; 2000b; interview, Paul Streeten[ix]; UNIHP 2007: Streeten: 16).

Following completion of his studies,[15] Streeten became a Fellow and remained at Balliol – its democratic fellowship of equals representing his conception of the ideal society (Streeten 1997: 197–8) – until moving to the USA, his wife's native country, in 1976. Initially this was on research leave but it became permanent. He had met and married Ann during earlier sabbatical leave in the USA on a Rockefeller Fellowship (1950–51), which he divided among Harvard, Washington, DC and Stanford – to him the most interesting centres of economics research at the time. To everyone's surprise, he therefore returned to Oxford with a family (including Ann's son from her previous marriage) (interview, Paul Streeten[x]; also Streeten 1997: 202).

His first four years in the USA after immigration were spent at the World Bank and proved highly significant careerwise, as well as

---

[15] He abandoned his DPhil thesis at Nuffield College under John Hicks upon election to a Fellowship at Balliol (Streeten 1986b: 152; 2000b: 199).

in terms of the innovative approach to poverty reduction in which he played a leading role (see below). Thereafter he worked mainly at Boston University until retirement, although punctuated by important assignments at and for the World Bank and ILO, in particular (see below). He retained his esteemed role as chair of the board of the journal, *World Development*, of which he had been founding editor in 1972–73, until 2003, well into his eighties (Wilson 2006: 255).[16]

Like most of the other figures in this age cohort (see above), Streeten worked across a wide swathe of economics, not just the emerging specialisation of development. Indeed, he attributes his interests in the latter – which he regards as a field of study in its own right rather than an economic sub-discipline – to four influences, the third of which pertains directly to the subject of this research:

- writing critically about economic arguments for European integration, including Rosenstein-Rodan and Nurkse's balanced growth thesis, at about the same time as **Alexander Gerschenkron** and **Albert Hirschman**, who favoured unbalanced growth as optimal economic stimulus (Streeten 1961, 1995: 351–2; see above). This Streeten regards as having been his first contact with development economics, linked to meeting and discussing the issue of (un)-balanced growth with Hirschman during his Rockefeller Fellowship in 1950–51; they had reached their positions separately but found themselves in close agreement;[17]

- being invited by Gunnar Myrdal, who became his other great mentor, to work with him on the monumental study eventually published as *Asian Drama* (Myrdal 1968);[18]

[16] Robert Maxwell, the proprietor of Pergamon Press, invited him to start the journal. Streeten's reflections on a long friendship and professional relationship, and on Maxwell's later notoriety, can be found at UNIHP (2007: Streeten: 49–51).

[17] During my interview, Streeten acknowledged how much he had been influenced by Hirschman (interview, Paul Streeten[xi]). They remained lifelong friends since their first encounters in 1951, with occasional professional interactions, although never actually working together (Streeten 1997: 204; Adelman 2013: 352, 595–6).

[18] The two had met and worked together from 1951 when, while on sabbatical, a mutual friend asked Streeten whether he would be interested in translating Myrdal's recently published book from German (into which it had been translated from the original Swedish by Mackenroth) into English. This was published as *The Political Element in the Development of Economic Theory* (Myrdal 1953) (interview, Paul Streeten[xii]; Wilson 2006: 252; UNIHP 2007: Streeten: 17, 30–32).

- a natural affinity with the field of enquiry on account of his 'social concern for poverty eradication [see Chapter 2], combined with objections to nationalism and a feeling of solidarity with the world community'; and

- the attraction of its inter- and multi-disciplinary nature (Streeten 1997: 199; see also Wilson 2006: 254–5; interview, Paul Streeten[xiii]; UNIHP 2007: Streeten: 2, 17).[19]

Among the numerous issues to which he has made important contributions are planning and India (Streeten and Lipton 1968), foreign aid (e.g. Streeten 1972a), international interdependencies (Streeten 1972b), basic needs (Streeten 1974; Streeten et al. 1981) and – in his final book, which I regard as one of his finest but which failed to receive appropriate attention – his Mattioli Lecture series about global development challenges and limitations at the end of the twentieth century. It contains possibly the earliest authoritative and reasoned voice calling for the restoration of effective resourcing and power to governments rendered incapable of effective governance by structural adjustment and economic recovery programmes of the international financial institutions and bilateral donor agencies (Streeten 1995; interview, Paul Streeten[xiv]).

This kind of perspective and willingness to challenge conventional wisdom marks Streeten out as another dissenting economist (included in the Biographical Dictionary of that name) regarding his perspectives on most fronts, including the theory of the firm, the compensation principle in New Welfare Economics, and those already discussed above (Streeten 2000b: 638–9). That said, he wisely cautions that the gulf between the heterodox and orthodox positions is easily exaggerated and that, much as dissenters might like the idea of forming an alternative paradigm by working together, the very temperament of habitual dissenters may militate against it. Indeed, he considers the main role of heterodox dissenters as being 'to serve as an intellectual muscle therapist, to cure us of intellectual cramps, to prevent the premature crystallization of flawed orthodoxies' (*ibid.*: 641).

After his first visit to India in 1963, for *Asian Drama*, he gained further experience in Malta, India and Pakistan through work with Dudley Seers

---

[19] An earlier version of his autobiographical essay cites only the first three influences (Streeten 1986a: 408–9).

(Director-General) and Barbara Castle (Minister) as Deputy Director-General of the Economic Planning Staff in the Ministry of Overseas Development in the mid-1960s. This also gave him an understanding of the political and practical challenges of policy implementation and the need to mobilise support. He also served on the boards of the Commonwealth Development Corporation, the Royal Commission on Environmental Pollution and other bodies outside the UK. He was also involved in setting up the Asian Development Bank. His first four years in the USA (1976–80) were spent at the World Bank at the invitation of his friend Hollis Chenery (Vice-President), one of the early champions of poverty-reducing development. This was during Robert McNamara's presidency of the Bank (Streeten 1986a: 408–9; 1986b: 158; 1997: 200–1; interview, Paul Streeten[xv]; UNIHP 2007: Streeten: 30–2, 41–2, 49).

Although Streeten's published memoirs merely refer to this period in passing, it proved seminal in at least one respect. Following the ILO World Employment Conference in Geneva in 1977, at Mahbub ul Haq's[20] instigation, Streeten led a key task team that formulated the policy of basic needs and converted Bank staff to its virtues so that it was adopted as a key programme (Streeten and Burki 1978; Streeten et al. 1981; Weiss et al. 2005: 243–4; Wilson 2006: 255). Streeten had actually done his innovative thinking and writing on basic needs while still at Oxford (Streeten 1972b; 1974), so this was an exercise in refinement and translation into programmatic agendas. During my interview, I was able to draw him out more. The key to the Bank's mainstreaming of basic needs was that the approach caught McNamara's eye and got his enthusiastic endorsement. The actual process was typical for the Bank – creating a small study group to write papers, hold seminars and explain how the approach could be incorporated in practice into the work of the various departments and branches:[21]

> [A]t first [the Bank was] completely resistant but eventually it was a little bit brought around – not very much because it's a ship that moves very slowly and changes direction very slowly. But from that point of view, you see, that was one of my great achievements, I think. (interview, Paul Streeten[xvi])

---

[20] Who later became the progenitor of the UNDP's *Human Development Reports* from 1990 until his death.
[21] Getting sign-off at a higher level, and some of the perils of that process, are discussed by Streeten in UNIHP 2007: Streeten: 62–3.

With typical modesty, he did recognise the importance of this achievement in terms of its downstream impact for the next decade or so. Although he didn't mention it in this discussion, during his UNIHP interview (UNIHP 2007: Streeten: 32–3) Streeten did acknowledge Pitambar Pant, who worked under Mahalanobis at the Indian Statistical Institute, as having probably been the progenitor of basic needs through his concerns with minimum human needs in India during the 1960s.

Having later been superseded by other fashions and foci, basic needs re-emerged under a different label with the highest possible profile at the turn of the century: at my prompting, Streeten agreed that 'It seems to me that the Millennium Development Goals are a basic needs strategy – very much' (interview, Paul Streeten[xvii]).

Nevertheless, Streeten felt happiest as an academic, able to be more independent and, as he himself put it, 'better as a critic than as an apologist, propagator or advocate', although he readily agreed in my interview that his exposure to the policy and practical implementation contexts had been highly beneficial to his academic perspectives and vice versa in terms of 'mutual fertilisation' (Streeten 1985a: 55; 1997: 204; 2000b: 639; interview, Paul Streeten[xviii]). To wit, Wilson (2006: 255) recalls that Streeten's keynote lecture at the conference of the Second Carnegie Inquiry into Poverty in South Africa,[22] held at the University of Cape Town in 1984, raised serious shortcomings regarding the ability of the basic needs approach to challenge power relations through mobilising the poor (Streeten 1984).

Finally, for purposes of this study, I explored with Paul during my interview whether it was more than coincidental that he came to specialise in development economics. Part of the answer has already been given above in relation to his socialisation, broadly socialist outlook but keeping people centrally in focus and his strong moral urge to tackle poverty. He found the question very interesting:

> I would say that the Jewishness was never in any sense very conscious because in Vienna we were already very highly assimilated and I …
> was never a Zionist – I never thought that a special state is needed for

---

[22] Which Wilson organised and at which, as a new postdoctoral researcher, I presented some of the material from my DPhil thesis. I was honoured to meet Streeten for the first time and I recall his lecture for its accessible style and relevance to contemporary challenges to apartheid economic and development doctrines.

the Jews ... but in terms of my thinking or my choices in life I never really would put the Jewishness very high. In a way, I think it is a thing the Nazis to some extent forced on us – if it hadn't been for them I think I would have amalgamated [i.e. assimilated] readily and very easily. (interview, Paul Streeten[xix])

More broadly, he responded to my question about why such a significant number of Holocaust escapees and survivors landed up working in the development field as follows:

[Y]ou could construct a large building on the fact that everything is completely coincidental and not planned, and not worked out, not arranged, but coincidental ... I don't really know – I'm very puzzled by this – everything seems like an accident or like coincidence looked at from one point of view; from another it looks like a grand wonderful plan. That sounds almost theological but it isn't meant as such. (interview, Paul Streeten[xx]; see also Streeten 1985a: 86; 1986a: 409; 1986b: 159)

The Activist Academic: Theodor Bergmann

Like **Streeten**, Theodor Bergmann was able to complete his higher education only after the war, it having been delayed by his flight from Germany and then badly interrupted by his equally precipitate escape from Czechoslovakia after the *Anschluss*. He enrolled at the University of Bonn, completing his agricultural sciences degree in 1947, before embarking on his PhD at the University of Hohenheim. This drew on his Swedish agricultural experience in addressing changes in Swedish agricultural structure. It was completed in 1955, followed by his Habilitation from 1965 to 1968 on the functions and activity boundaries of production unions in developing countries. All this time, he worked outside the university context, initially as an unskilled metal factory worker, then in the Hannover Chamber of Agricultural Affairs and then leading a project in Turkey.

He was also very active in the labour and communist movements. On returning to Germany, he briefly considered moving to the Soviet Occupation Zone but was dissuaded after illegally crossing into it to meet KPD-O colleagues. He then joined the *Gruppe Arbeiterspolitik* (Workers' Politics Group) and edited its newspaper from 1948 until he resigned from the organisation over internal conflicts in 1952. The secretary's salary of his new wife, Gretel Steinhilber, a fellow party member, kept them afloat while he was unsalaried. They had no children. He later nursed her through a long illness before her death in 1994 (Kessler 2017). Following this loss, he continued his work with increased vigour.

Kessler (*ibid.*) also records that the Danish economists, Morgens and Ester Boserup, lent political support to Bergmann during the *Arbeiterspolitik* period. This is a significant connection for purposes of this book, since Ester Boserup worked in India and, along with **Heinz Arndt**, participated in the landmark *Asian Drama* project led by Gunnar Myrdal in the 1960s, as explained earlier in this chapter. This connection may well have facilitated Bergmann's research in India. Whether Bergmann and Arndt met or collaborated is doubtful, both because their politics were by then very different, and because Bergmann is not mentioned in Arndt's autobiography (Arndt 1985) or biography (Coleman et al. 2007). It is unclear whether Bergmann ever encountered **Paul Streeten**, an economist just one year his junior and another of Myrdal's collaborators.

As indicated by the subject of his Habilitation thesis, Bergmann had, during the 1950s and 1960s, expanded the geographical range of his interests beyond Europe, to developing countries and especially those experimenting with different forms of socialist transition. He focused particularly on agricultural and agrarian transformation efforts in China and postcolonial states, especially India. However, he never lost interest in the Israeli kibbutz movement, which comprised many socialist collective experiments, although some later evolved into more individualised models. He returned to that country frequently – partly to visit his extended family – and published regularly on the subject (e.g. Bergmann and Liegle 2002). On all these subjects, he became a leading international authority and regularly undertook consultancies for the UN's Food and Agriculture Organization (FAO). He published widely on these issues in both German and English (e.g. Bergmann 1960; 1966; 1971; 1975; 1977; 1979; Bergmann et al. 1984; Bergmann and Ogura 1985). The 1977 comparative analysis of the development models of India, China and the Soviet Union is possibly his most important contribution to the international development literature.

In his autobiography, Bergmann (2000, 2016) records the great professional difficulty he experienced throughout this period in the face of both residual anti-Semitism by former Nazis in various parts of German society and the pervasive anti-communist ethos. As Kessler (2017) puts it, 'West German post-war society had little room for independent Marxists of his type'. He finally obtained a permanent academic post five years after his Habilitation, as Professor of Comparative International Agricultural Policy at the University of Stuttgart-Hohenheim until 1973. This followed a visiting position at the University of New England (Australia) in 1971–72. He retired in 1980 and remained in Stuttgart, continuing his academic and political work independently again, publishing at a prodigious rate until very shortly before his death.

During this final phase of his career, which lasted almost as long as most people's entire careers, he developed his strong historical sense of the importance of the long view, producing histories of the labour movement and international socialism/politics, particularly in relation to Israel, China and the communist movement (e.g. Bergmann and Gräff 1987; Bergmann 2004a; 2007a; 2007b; 2009a; 2009b; 2011; 2012). His oeuvre also comprised biographies of several prominent socialist and Zionist families, including his own remarkable lineage (e.g. Bergmann 2004b; 2014). From 1983 onwards, he was also instrumental (with Gert Schäfer) in organising a series of conferences on key Marxist thinkers, from Engels and Thalheimer to Bukharin, Trotsky and Lenin to Rosa Luxemburg. Indeed, he was a strong and longstanding supporter of the Rosa Luxemburg Society (Kessler 2017).

Politically, he changed parties according to how well their programmes reflected his interests. In the embers of the Cold War, he joined the Party of Democratic Socialism (PDS) in 1990, standing unsuccessfully for them in that year's Bundestag elections and became president of the Baden-Württemberg regional association. In 2007 he joined the new Left party (*Die Linken*) and was actively organising against the right-wing *Alternative für Deutschland* until his short final illness in 2017.

Remarkably, for most of his career, both before and after his university appointment, Bergmann undertook many of his frequent international research and solidarity travels without institutional or other grant-funded support – to China no less than 14 times (until the age of 97) and Israel yet more often – even celebrating his centenary birthday there (Kessler 2017). Altogether, he wrote, edited or translated some 50 books and several hundred journal articles and journalistic contributions. Two years before his death, Wladislaw Hedeler and Mario Kessler (2015) co-edited a tribute volume, entitled *Reformen und Reformer in Kommunismus* (Reforms and Reformers in Communism), and, like several of Bergmann's own books, published by the Rosa Luxemburg Foundation.

His energy, determination and commitment were remarkable. His intellectual reach was as broad as it was deep, facilitated by his fluency in five languages and working knowledge of six more. The importance of his legacy lies partly in the combination of his distinctive anti-Stalinist and critical communist stance with his longevity and sharp memory, which enabled him to draw on personal experience of key episodes and acquaintances or friendships with people over a century. Indeed, he was almost certainly the last living link to the German labour and democratic communist political movements of the interwar Weimar Republic. Equally noteworthy, though, was his personal commitment to his cause and the fiercely independent way in which he refused to be hemmed in by dogma, especially in its nationalistic forms. Hence, he pursued internationalism both as a political commitment and in order to study and learn from penetrating comparative analysis of socialist/communist experiences worldwide in the agricultural, labour and broader political arenas. Fittingly then, his final book, published just months before his death, was entitled *Der chinesische Weg. Versuch, eine ferne Entwicklung zu verstehen* (The Chinese Way: An Attempt to Understand a Distant Development) (Bergmann 2017).

The Archetypical Academic: Alexander Gerschenkron

Upon his return to academia at Harvard in 1946, Gerschenkron's Soviet expertise earned him the role of the Economics Department's resident specialist and he was encouraged by the political urgency of understanding what the new superpower's real strength and global strategy would be. He thus devoted much energy to deciphering and comparing Soviet production and other data to those of the US and other Western countries, particularly the extremely rapid economic growth rates it had claimed since the Great Depression of the early 1930s. In the course of this work, he discovered how Soviet data had been officially exaggerated and formulated what became known as the Gerschenkron Effect, namely that the choice of base year for a statistical growth index determined the calculated growth rate (Dawidoff 2002: 155–61; Gerschenkron 1947).

Partly out of interest and partly because of his distaste for the Soviet regime, Gerschenkron turned his attention increasingly to economic history and from the late 1950s this became his main focus (Dawidoff 2002: 168). A key stage in that process was the work which made his reputation internationally and remains his main legacy. He sought to understand how backward economies like Russia and Austria had transformed themselves through industrialisation. Stalin's determination to make a great industrial leap forward at any cost required the oppressive dictatorship he established. At other levels, however, Gerschenkron argued that economic backwardness was not necessarily a disadvantage in that latecomers could learn from earlier mistakes elsewhere and benefit from newer technologies to progress more rapidly. He belonged to the school of unbalanced growth and the big push à la Rosenstein-Rodan that was then unfashionable, along also with Rostow and **Hirschman**. Although his major collection of essays on the subject (Gerschenkron 1962)[23] shares the notion of successive and rather linear stages of economic development with Rostow's classic treatise (1960), it is much less universalising and simplistic, allowing for the importance of diverse local contingencies of institutional architecture (Dawidoff 2002: 173–87; Gwynne 2006).

Paradoxically, given the importance of this last point as the basis for theory building, Gerschenkron's contribution (including his 1968 volume of important essays) remains much less well known outside of economic history – and especially within human geography and related fields – than those of Rostow and **Hirschman**. Gwynne (2006: 120) posits that this might be due to Gerschenkron working in a historical ideographic mode when the *zeitgeist* was more nomothetic. However, Rosenstein-Rodan's (1943) seminal essay, widely regarded as constituting the foundational text of development economics, has suffered a similar relative interdisciplinary obscurity. Moreover, given the Cold War tenor of development theoretical debates from the early 1960s onwards, it would not require a total cynic to realise that opponents would have found Rostow's mechanistic schema a far easier target to attack as the apostle of modernisation theory than the more nuanced and culturally and locally flexible formulations.

Probably through a combination of the increasingly historical focus to his work and his personality, Gerschenkron didn't engage in policy work to any significant extent from Harvard and so the balance

---

[23] This collection took its name from Gerschenkron's first essay on the subject, originally written in 1951 (Dawidoff 2002: 176).

of his contribution to development thinking remains the set of ideas outlined here, together with some of the ideas in *Bread and Democracy in Germany*. Although Dawidoff (2002: 236–7) is explicit about Gerschenkron's strong aversion to any discussion of religious views or beliefs, even with close friends and colleagues, he was observed by family members occasionally to visit a church or let unguarded comments slip out at times of stress. His successive experiences and flights from Russia and Austria, and particularly the anti-Semitism he experienced in the latter, clearly remained strongly evident in his character and mind throughout his life, and informed his professional engagement with Russian economic history. However, I have found no evidence to suggest a direct link with his choice of career in economics since that decision was made in Vienna (see Chapter 2).

Conclusions

This age cohort is small and cohesive enough that, individual differences notwithstanding, some clear generalisations emerge. Although with the exception of Stolper and Schumacher, all the members of this cohort came from Jewish backgrounds, some, like Hirschman and Arndt, had been baptised as part of the common desire to avoid discrimination and to see social advancement, while others like Streeten, were brought up in highly secular and assimilated families. As a rabbi's son, Bergmann apparently had the most observant Jewish upbringing but the other more knowledgeable Jews like Singer and Bauer lived largely secular lives. The younger cohort which forms the subject of Chapters 6 and 7 represents a broader spectrum of religious belief and observance but for this older group, socialised in interwar Europe before the rise of the Nazis, such a *Weltanschauung* was entirely consistent with the times. Indeed, but for the Nazis, formal religion or religious beliefs would have featured in their consciousness to only a very small extent, probably principally in terms of basic ethical values and concern with justice and charity.

For most of them, contemporary political developments and involvement with politically social democratic or more socialist and communist (rather than religiously based) youth groups and political parties or movements were far more important. Some, like Hirschman, Bergmann and Streeten, were active and sufficiently prominent to be in immediate danger under Nazi rule. Others, like Schumacher, felt moral outrage at the uncivilised behaviour of the Nazis and felt compelled to leave for their own sanity (see Chapter 2).

Apart from Bergmann, who had just completed secondary school, they had all at least started their tertiary education (and some had finished) before Nazi rule in their home countries and so had already made their basic career choices. The oldest, namely Gerschenkron, Schumacher and Hirschman, were thus able to use their professional expertise underground during the war and after escape and/or internment. Accordingly, too, they were subsequently able to resume or assume appropriate careers, taking advantage of available university posts left vacant by conscription and of new opportunities such as European reconstruction and development.

None of these oldest three, who all landed up working on immediate post-World War II reconnaissance and reconstruction in Germany for the Marshall Plan and European Payments Union (EPU), would have anticipated such roles before or during the war. However, their decisions to take the opportunities when they arose reflected their personalities, backgrounds, training and wartime experiences as well as a desire to help improve the world in tangible ways. These values and experiences, in turn, fuelled their subsequent perspectives and development engagements and are therefore highly germane to this enquiry.[24] This pragmatic approach to life is also echoed explicitly by Paul Streeten in his autobiographical reflections and interview with me (see above).

Personal connections and networks were often highly important to the availability of such opportunities. This is exemplified by the links between Gerschenkron and Hirschman in the USA during and immediately after the war, among the ex-internees in the UK (some of whom, of course, knew one another from childhood), or the relationships that led to Streeten collaborating with Myrdal, and the

---

[24] Indeed, Hirschman's biographer, Jeremy Adelman, described Hirschman's approach to life in precisely these terms in a seminar at St Hugh's College, Oxford on 9 October 2012: as not looking back and bemoaning past tragedies but moving forwards opportunistically, to make the opportunities that arise work for oneself (Adelman 2012 @ 42–43 minutes). This motivation is explained in greater detail in Adelman (2013: 188): 'Hirschman did not heal the incision from his past by gazing backward, fixated on the "German question". New York was filling with intellectuals with just this obsession. Rather, once more, exile provided grounds for reinvention. Hirschman did not dwell on the traumas he left behind – and was determinedly tight-lipped about it with others. Rather, he sought out new opportunities. In America, he could become the intellectual he'd dreamed of being in Europe'. Adelman (*ibid.*: 189) is also careful to qualify his use of the term 'opportunistic', making clear that Hirschman was not a narrowly self-serving opportunist in the conventional sense.

former's friendship with Chenery that led to his spell at the World Bank working on basic needs.

Singer spent longest in international agency service but then enjoyed a full second career as an academic. Gerschenkron remained an academic for the whole of his career after his time in Washington during and immediately after the war, while Hirschman became an academic after his Colombian consultancy experience, which had followed his Marshall Plan work. The others were mainly academics who undertook periodic consultancies or secondments. Schumacher was the exception, who made his decisive interventions from his position as economic advisor within the British nationalised energy industry, before taking early retirement to establish and develop his Intermediate Technology Development Group (ITDG).

Whether by chance or not, all bar one of this cohort were economists, perhaps reflecting the pre-eminence of economics among the social sciences during the period that they received university education and commenced their careers.

Importantly too, as has emerged clearly throughout this chapter, their training, the shortage of academics during and after the war, coupled with the nascent state of development economics, gave them a good grounding in the discipline. They were also required to teach and/or research across a wide range of sub-disciplines, which gave them an aversion to narrow specialisation. As such, they retained relatively holistic perspectives that proved important at key moments in terms of understanding complex interrelationships and retaining a clear focus on real people's lives and struggles as being at the heart of development. Their religious and/or political principles and wartime and early postwar experiences may have helped guide them towards a concern with poverty but none admitted to any central impetus from their socialisation or a eureka moment. This is a clear contrast to at least a few of the younger cohort, to whom Chapters 6 and 7 are devoted. The single and signal exception to this on all counts was Bergmann, who trained as an agricultural scientist as a result of his prewar interests being kindled by kibbutz work in the 1930s. He had a strong egalitarian socialist/communist ethos and secular Jewish identity that drove the rest of his life, personally, professionally and politically.

6 | THE YOUNGER GENERATION: POSTWAR EDUCATION AND CAREERS IN HIGHER EDUCATION

To do justice to their careers and contributions and to explore the key influences on their respective trajectories in relation to the main themes of this book has required two chapters, divided between those who were academics all their careers (this chapter) and those who were employed by development agencies (as distinct from undertaking occasional consultancies) for some or all of their careers (Chapter 7). Both these chapters are structured in a similar way to Chapter 5, blending relevant chronological and thematic coverage of their unfolding lives after World War II with reflection and analysis in relation to the central questions of how their Holocaust-era experiences influenced their subsequent career choices and professional trajectories. These chapters thus pick up the respective threads from Chapters 3 and 4, which cover the period up to the end of World War II. This chapter comprises sections on those trained in the UK, US and Poland.

Although there is only a relatively small dividing line in terms of age between the older and younger cohorts in this study, it is significant in terms of the stage of life at which they were caught up in or had to escape the Holocaust and its stranglehold on their countries of birth. Thus, **Paul Streeten** (born in 1917) was the youngest of those already undertaking tertiary education at the outbreak of World War II and whose trajectories were analysed in Chapter 5. Conversely, **Scarlett Epstein**, born just five years later, was the oldest of the cohort addressed in this chapter and who were still legal minors at the time. The older among them – **Scarlett Epstein** (b. 1922), **Eric Wolf** and **Kari Polanyi Levitt** (b. 1923), **Zygmunt Bauman** (b. 1925), **Shlomo Reutlinger** and **John Friedmann** (b. 1926) – were attending secondary school or Gymnasium when oppression forced them out or into exile with their families. **Irma Glicman-Adelman** (b. 1930), **Michael Cernea** (b. 1931), **Ernie Stern** and **Emanuel de Kadt** (b. 1933) were at primary school, while **Gerry Helleiner** (b. 1936) was still a young child and hence has no memory of his first years in Vienna and flight via the

UK to Canada (see Chapter 2). Several of this cohort moved more than once, either before or after university (Adelman, Polanyi Levitt, Reutlinger) or were forced to flee again many years later from renewed persecution in their countries of birth (Bauman, Cernea).

Higher Education in the UK as Prelude to Academic Careers

In contrast to the older cohort, for many of whom the UK was a key refuge and where many completed their tertiary education, **Scarlett Epstein**, **Kari Polanyi Levitt** and **Emanuel de Kadt** were the only three of this younger group to undertake some or all of their university studies in the UK. Epstein and De Kadt were then to remain there permanently and forge academic careers, while Polanyi Levitt emigrated to Canada two years after the end of the war and later resumed postgraduate research prior to becoming an academic there.

This difference between the cohorts can be explained simply: Epstein and Polanyi Levitt were the only Nazi-era refugees to the UK whose families remained there; as explained in Chapter 2, the remainder either moved on to North America with their families quite soon or never came to that country in the first place. Uniquely among those in this study, De Kadt arrived in London only after the war specifically to attend university after completing his secondary schooling once back in the Netherlands from the family's wartime refuge in Portugal (see Chapter 4).

Scarlett Epstein's experience was unusual for this cohort but reflected the premature termination of her secondary school education, the need to improve her formal English ability and her financial situation, which had necessitated working as a machinist and wages clerk during the war. She had become the main breadwinner for her family, so could not afford to give up work and enrolled in a four-year night school diploma course in Personnel Management at Manchester University of Technology (1945–49). This she completed successfully – winning the best student of the year prize in her final year – while working as office manager for a textile machinery export firm. That role afforded her more study time than her previous, less skilled jobs. Her economics lecturer persuaded her to apply to study the subject for a diploma at Ruskin College, Oxford (run by the Workers' Education Association) in 1949–50 as the stepping stone to a university degree. She was granted a place and hence a scholarship, which enabled her to study fulltime, although it was difficult for her parents to have her leave home.

Being older than the other students and, as an Austrian refugee, from a very different background, she found it socially quite isolated. She was also working very hard, achieving the then unprecedented feat of completing the two-year diploma in just one. She applied for admission to St Hilda's College, Oxford University, but was rejected on grounds of her social class despite being described as academically gifted – something she naturally found very disheartening and angering in itself but especially in view of the very hard road she had travelled to get that far. Both other Ruskin female students who sat the entrance exam suffered the same fate and Scarlett struggled to prevent a demonstration outside the College by Ruskin students (Epstein 2005: 91–8; interview, Scarlett Epstein[i]).

Instead, she won a scholarship to study Economics at Manchester University, where she found herself among like-minded people, and moved in with her parents again. Studying at Manchester, among many specialists on and from poor countries, marked the beginning of her engagement with development issues that would absorb her throughout her career (interview, Scarlett Epstein[ii]). She took summer jobs as a tourist courier in Austria, the second of which enabled her to return to Vienna for the first time – inevitably a very strange and poignant experience. However, she returned to Manchester 'with much of my hatred and desire for vengeance dissipated. I knew I could not change what had happened, but I also knew that my fate now lay in my own hands' (Epstein 2005: 105).

She was forced to take her final exams in May 1953 in pain and discomfort in hospital after suffering third degree burns the previous week, when her nylon dress touched an unprotected electric heater in her room and caught fire. She was in such distress during her social anthropology exam that she wanted to give up but the invigilator sent to the hospital, who happened to be her lecturer in that subject, the eminent Professor Max Gluckman, implored her to continue after immediate medical attention, for which he would allow her extra time. She managed to complete it and as they chatted afterwards, he encouraged her to apply for a graduate scholarship to undertake a doctorate under his supervision. Despite thinking him crazy to assume that she could do well enough under the circumstances, she agreed and was successful. Her burns became infected and she eventually required extensive skin grafts but then recovered and commenced her doctorate that autumn (*ibid.*: 107–20; interview, Scarlett Epstein[iii]).

Following her first year in Manchester, she undertook two years' fieldwork in south Indian villages, investigating the effects of irrigation canals on socio-economic development in two contrasting villages (one on a canal and the other not) in the hinterland of Mysore in Karnataka. The decision to work in India, a country that had long fascinated her, was encouraged by the Indian anthropologist, M.N. Srinivas, while on a visit to Manchester. This disappointed Gluckman, whose interests lay in central Africa, but he accepted it and supervised her to successful completion in 1958, at the age of 35 (Epstein 2005: 121–37; interview, Scarlett Epstein[iv]). Scarlett was the first student Gluckman had seen through from undergraduate to postgraduate status (interview, Scarlett Epstein[v]). Both men became her mentors.

In 1957, she married the anthropologist Arnold Leonard (Bill) Epstein, who had also joined the anthropology department. After several romantic disappointments, this marked a watershed in her personal life (Epstein 2005: 138–54). They left for the Australian National University (ANU) shortly after her graduation, taking up fellowships in the anthropology and economics departments respectively, and undertaking research in Papua New Guinea (PNG). After four years, they returned to Manchester, where Bill took up a lectureship at the university and Scarlett was offered a senior lectureship at Salford College of Advanced Technology. From 1966 to 1972 they had another spell in Canberra, with more research in PNG, before returning to permanent professorships at the University of Sussex, Bill in social anthropology and Scarlett in the Institute of Development Studies. Although she later moved to the same department as Bill, they remained at Sussex until early retirements, he in 1982 and she in 1984, whereafter they continued with research and publishing (*ibid.*: 155–69). Despite each suffering several bouts of serious ill-health, they remained happily married until his death in 1999, which left her bereft.

Partly to keep occupied and overcome her grief, Scarlett accepted all invitations to work abroad, and remained research-active. She even revisited her doctoral research area in south India again in 2004 and 2008 (the latter at the age of 85, and for which she obtained a Nuffield Foundation small grant – quite possibly the oldest such grant holder ever) for follow-up studies on rural-urban migration. She undertook numerous consultancy assignments for international agencies such as the World Bank, Asian Development Bank, UN, ILO and various NGOs, including in Bulgaria, Laos and China, where she had no previous experience. She continued to promote action research and run training workshops through her own NGO, Practical Education and Gender Support (PEGS) (see www.pegs.org.uk/44.html).

She published 14 books and some 75 articles, most on aspects of action research, as well as driving and featuring in four film projects. Apart from her autobiography, her most widely known books are the published version of her doctoral thesis and the subsequent restudies of her two research villages after several decades (Epstein 1962; 1973; 1998) along with the co-authored study of Tolai economic life (Epstein et al. 1980) and a book addressing local female fertility planning (Epstein and Jackson 1977).

Shortly after her husband's death, she revisited Vienna properly for only the second time since her flight as a 16-year-old girl. This inevitably prompted complex feelings and memories, not least when giving a lecture at the University of Vienna, where she had aspired as a child to study medicine (Epstein 2005: 206–9). **Eric Wolf**, another native of Vienna, experienced very similar emotions on returning to the city to deliver a lecture many years later (see below).

Scarlett Epstein was best known for her research on economic structure, rural development and social change in Karnataka and the Gazelle Peninsula on New Britain, PNG, as well as for the joint study she and Bill undertook of Tolai culture in the latter during their spells based at the ANU.[1] She regarded herself mainly as an applied development anthropologist (interview, Scarlett Epstein[vi]) and received wide acknowledgement and honours for her pioneering work. Her 'services to rural and women's development, especially in Papua New Guinea' formed the citation of her OBE awarded by the Queen in 2004 after nomination by the PNG government, while she was awarded the Royal Anthropological Institute's Lucy Mair Medallion in 2012 for her pioneering poverty-oriented action research (www.boloji.com/index.cfm?md=Content&sd=Writers&WriterID=3741, accessed 4/03/2014).

Her achievements and their public acknowledgement constituted very satisfying affirmation of her determination, on escaping and surviving the Holocaust, to contribute to making the world a better place

---

[1] Their fieldnotes and related papers, and much of Bill's professional correspondence, are now deposited in the Melanesian Archives in the Geisel Library, University of California at San Diego (interview, Scarlett Epstein[vii]; see also The Register of Arnold Leonard and Trude Scarlett Epstein Papers 1949–1995, http://orpheus.ucsd.edu/speccoll/testing/html/mss0022a.html, accessed on 28/09/2006.

(see Chapter 2). Yet that same experience helped to keep her active, as she pointed out in the concluding sentences of her autobiography:

> I envy those with strong religious faith who have the comforting thought of an afterlife. But because God had forsaken me many years before, and because the prayers of so many were not answered, I feel religion can offer me no solace. So instead I stave off death by being ever busier ... I work out at the gym every day ... and it feels good that I am still breaking new ground. I continue to take on new projects. Everyone asks why I don't just put my feet up and enjoy myself. But they do not realize that swimming upstream is the only way I know. (Epstein 2005: 209)

Active virtually till the end despite cardiac problems and open-heart surgery in her final years, she died at the age of 91 on 27 April 2014. Fittingly, she was remembered in obituaries published in both India and Papua New Guinea (*The Hindu* 2014; PNG Institute of National Affairs 2014).

Kari Polanyi Levitt completed her secondary schooling at Bedales in 1942 (see Chapter 2), from where she moved straight to university at the London School of Economics, graduating with a distinction (first class honours) in statistics in 1947. Having been naturalised with her parents a week after the outbreak of the war (see Chapter 3), she avoided internment or any other direct harassment as a German-speaking refugee. However, her LSE studies were interrupted by two years of wartime service spent with the research department of the Amalgamated Engineering Union (a prominent trade union) in south London. This experience turned out to be a precursor to her later professional industrial and trade union employment. While still at the LSE, she formed part of a team led by Nicholas Kaldor[2] in 1946 studying the effects of Allied strategic bombing on the German war economy and which concluded that it actually *increased* rather than decimated production – a finding corroborated by a larger parallel American project led by John Kenneth Galbraith (see Chapter 5, p. 140). Kaldor had lectured her in her second year at LSE (following Arthur Lewis in her first year) and they clearly got on well and became friendly, and

---

[2] As explained in Chapter 1, Kaldor had arrived to study in London from Hungary in 1928, several years before the Nazi rise to power in Germany, and was thus excluded from this study.

she assured me that, had she not then emigrated to Canada, she would certainly have followed Kaldor to the European Commission or UN (Polanyi Levitt n.d.; interview, Kari Polanyi Levitt[viii]).

Kari met and fell in love with Joseph Levitt, a Canadian historian serving in Europe with the Canadian armed forces during the war, whom she had met during his periods of leave in London. He returned to Canada after the war ended and she followed him after graduating from LSE in 1947. They were married in Toronto in 1950, where their two sons, Tom and Harry, were born in 1952 and 1954 respectively. Bringing them up caused her some difficulty in relation to religious and ethnic affiliation. She even enrolled the boys in the Unitarian Sunday School since they yearned to attend something when the other children went to one of the church-run Sunday schools. Having herself grown up in a socialist home, she had no active religion and felt no particular ethnicity, yet in the immigrant society that is Canada she and the children were constantly expected to have such a hybrid identity. By virtue of the Levitt surname, they were assumed to be Jewish and to identify as such but she/they felt uncomfortable with that badge:

> Montreal is a little like New York: it had a very, very strongly defined Jewish community here that immediately claimed me and my children to be part of them but I really was not enthusiastic. I really didn't want to be part of that community or any other ethnic community. (interview, Kari Polanyi Levitt[ix])

Kari found employment in industry, trade union research, journalism and other forms of activism prior to enrolling for graduate studies at the University of Toronto in 1957. She obtained her MA in Economics in 1959 and completed her doctoral courses but, before commencing her thesis, joined the academic staff of the Economics Department at McGill University, so the family moved to Montreal in the Canadian summer of 1961. She taught a diversity of classes but increasingly specialised in two main arenas. The first was economic planning techniques (especially input–output analysis and linear programming), in which she by then had considerable expertise, and in which field she directed a major project from 1965 to 1975 for Statistics Canada constructing input–output tables for the Atlantic provinces (interview, Kari Polanyi Levitt[x]; Polanyi Levitt n.d.). She was duly advised to convert some of this work into a PhD thesis 'but I saw no good reason to do that because after ten years of work with a team of four or five researchers employed by this project, there was nobody in the world more knowledgeable of this particular area of work' (pers. comm.[xi]).

The second area was her growing fascination with the emerging subdiscipline of development economics, an interest kindled by lectures given during her MA by a Greek-Canadian, Stephen Triantis, and two particular books that he recommended. These were an edited collection by Agarwala and Singh[3] and a monograph by Ben Higgins on development based on his experiences in Indonesia.[4]

> I found this simply a more interesting field ['than all the Canadian economic history that I had to learn']. And then there were familiar names like Arthur Lewis, who, as I'm sure you know, gave the lectures in the first year that I ever encountered economics. I was just drawn to this. I also had a background in mathematics. I specialised in statistics at LSE because I wanted somehow to make use of the fact that I liked mathematics. So I was interested in economic planning, which was all the vogue at that time. (interview, Kari Polanyi Levitt[xii])

In further discussion several years later about Arthur Lewis' influence on her, she added fascinating detail about his course, on which,

> I first learned about the deteriorating terms of trade of Latin American and other primary commodity-exporting countries. This made a lasting impression because at the age of six, I saw in a children's cartoon tons of coffee being burned in Brazil and didn't understand

---

[3] This was Agarwala and Singh (1958), which must have been one of the first such leading books published on development by Indian or any non-Western economists; it was reissued in 1968 and 1971.

[4] Higgins (1959), which became a widely used textbook worldwide. Ben Higgins was a leading early development economist, with particular interests in urban and regional dynamics. Born and educated up to first degree level in Canada, he too trained at the LSE during its illustrious pre-World War II period, taking the MSc (Econ) in 1933–35 under many of the leading economists who feature repeatedly in this study. This attests to the extraordinary international role and influence of the LSE at that time and the significance of it being there that the AAC was established and where several of both the older and younger cohorts in this project studied. Higgins then worked at Canadian, US and Australian universities, publishing some 30 books. He developed a longstanding interest in and commitment to Indonesia and, like many of his generation, blended academic life with numerous consultancy assignments (Mackie 2001). Polanyi Levitt later met him during the 1960s, when he returned to Montreal to hold a chair at the Université de Montreal during the 1960s. He had previously held a chair at McGill but left before Kari arrived (pers. comm., email, 7/3/14).

why they were doing that. This lecture course was later published as *Economic Survey: 1919–1939* [Lewis 1949]. (pers. comm.[xiii])

The resonance with attending Arthur Lewis' lectures was further enhanced by her contact and collaboration with Nicholas Kaldor for, although he never specialised in development economics, he was very much in demand and advised many governments of newly independent states on economic policy. She regards both Lewis and Kaldor as key inspirational influences on her engagement with economics and subsequent professional orientations. Interestingly, although Paul Rosenstein-Rodan and **Peter Bauer** were also teaching at the LSE at that time, Kari never attended their lectures or had any contact with them (interview, Kari Polanyi Levitt[xiv]; pers. comm.[xv]).

Around the same time, she encountered and became fascinated by the West Indies. This stimulated her research interest to evolve towards national economic development of the decolonising island states, especially Trinidad and Jamaica. She forged relations with local economists and students, and undertook research there, even though she still taught Canadian economic planning and statistics as well. Indeed, for much of the 1960s and 1970s, she researched and published in both arenas, including one of the early benchmark studies of transnational corporations (Levitt 1970). She has also devoted considerable time and energy to her late father's legacy, as institutionalised through the Karl Polanyi Institute of Political Economy at Concordia University in Montreal, and by editing two major volumes of his works (Polanyi Levitt n.d.).

Gradually her research career shifted increasingly into development economics in and of the Caribbean, and she spent several periods of sabbatical or secondment at the University of the West Indies (UWI) campuses in St Augustine, Trinidad and Mona, Jamaica. Following her retirement from McGill in 1992, she spent five years at UWI Mona, during which her well-known volume of collected works, *Reclaiming Development: Independent Thought and Caribbean Community* (Levitt 2005), written over a period of some 30 years and charting the evolution of relevant thinking over that period, was put together. In 2008, the UWI awarded her an honorary doctorate in recognition of her contribution over more than 40 years, and she chose to have the award ceremony on the Trinidad campus (interview, Kari Polanyi Levitt[xvi]; Polanyi Levitt n.d.).

Her first major works on the Caribbean were a jointly authored book on relations between Canada and the West Indies (Levitt and McIntyre 1967) and collaborative research with Lloyd Best on externally driven economic growth, which included innovative models of the plantation economy (Best and Levitt 1975), much of which remained unpublished for decades until Kari returned to it in the 2000s (Best and Levitt 2010). This offers a comprehensive analysis of the historical and geo-economic evolution and ramifications of the distinctive Caribbean plantation economic models. Along with *Reclaiming Development*, I am confident that this will become her best-known work in development economics. She also co-edited a volume of essays in honour of Colin Beckford (Polanyi Levitt and Witter 1996) and edited for publication some of Beckford's own papers (Beckford with Levitt 2000).

She naturally met and got to know many of the other leading development economists, especially those concerned with the Caribbean and Latin America, including **Hans Singer** and **Paul Streeten**. She became particularly friendly with Dudley Seers, who is best known for shifting attention away from economic growth towards redistribution. His role in challenging prevailing wisdoms, not least his posthumously published book, *The Political Economy of Nationalism* (1983), she regards as greatly underrated by the international development community, perhaps because he was something of a maverick (see also Escobar 2006). She also knew and greatly admired the late Brazilian economist and intellectual, Celso Furtado, whom she regards as one of her sources of inspiration together with Lewis and Kaldor (interview, Kari Polanyi Levitt[xvii]; see also Braga 2019).

So, in contrast to **Scarlett Epstein** and several others who had catalytic personal and career-defining Holocaust-related experiences, Kari Polanyi Levitt was spared such trauma. Instead, her engagement with development evolved during her university studies, stimulated by inspirational early development economists and reading some of the then-new seminal texts. She and **Irma Adelman** are the only female development economists in this study.

Following the end of hostilities, **Emanuel de Kadt** returned to Rotterdam in October 1945 and completed his schooling at the Gymnasium, where he became best friends – and remains so today – with Jaap Polak, a fellow Jewish boy whose parents had died in the camps. Emanuel's grandfather 'threw himself into the rebuilding of the Jewish community', only five per cent of whom survived or returned after the war, although some East European camp survivors settled there (De Kadt 2006).

After the Gymnasium, Emanuel spent 'a wholly unsuccessful year' at the Technical University in Delft, before transferring to the predecessor of Nijenrode University, one of the first Dutch tertiary institutions to prepare students for a business career, since his grandfather hoped and/or expected that he would join the family hat felt firm. However, Nijenrode had whetted his 'academic appetite', and he was tempted to go to study at the Sorbonne in Paris. However, his late mother's cousin, Gerhart Riegner, already then a leading light in the World Jewish Congress, convinced him to study sociology at the London School of Economics (LSE), where he would receive more individualised tuition than at the Sorbonne, so he moved to London in 1956 (*ibid.*). His grandfather may have been disappointed but never said so, perhaps hoping that Emanuel might still return to the business at a later stage. However, his grandfather died in 1958, while Emanuel was still at the LSE, and the business was sold (interview, Emanuel de Kadt[xviii]).

After graduating in sociology in 1959, Emanuel took his MA in Sociology at Columbia University in New York (1959–60), where he met and married his first wife, Ellen. He then returned to a teaching post at the LSE in 1961, while working on his PhD on Catholic Radicals in Brazil, which he completed in 1969 and published the following year (De Kadt 1970). This research was facilitated by his fluency in Portuguese from his wartime years as a refugee in Portugal. From 1964, he also held a research post at Chatham House, the Royal Institute of International Affairs, and published his first book, on British defence policy and nuclear war (De Kadt 1964). Following completion of his doctorate, and by then married to Pola Valdivieso, his second (and non-Jewish) wife, he took up a post at the Institute of Development Studies (IDS) at the University of Sussex but retained his Chatham House role with responsibility for its Latin America Department until 1973.

At IDS, he held various positions, including Deputy Director (1970–76), Acting Director (1978–79) and Academic Director (1988–91). Most of his IDS research related to health and development but also dealt with tourism and with the organisation of the state in developing countries. He co-edited a leading early collection on *Sociology and Development* (De Kadt and Williams 1974). Of his journal articles, three stand out for me as having made important contributions at the time: two were published in *World Development* (De Kadt 1980; 1985;

the latter indeed contains some antecedents of his recent monograph), while the third provided information about the poor in the *IDS Bulletin* (De Kadt 1994).

Since it was not a focus at IDS and having failed to persuade colleagues of the importance of researching fundamentalism and development, he did not undertake any further research on religion until after his retirement in 1994 (De Kadt 2006; interview, Emanuel de Kadt[xix]). He then returned to the topic of religion and society, publishing a series of articles and a major work on religious intolerance in a multicultural world (De Kadt 2013). After his appointment to a chair at the University of Utrecht in 1998, he published a few articles in Dutch. On his retirement in 2003, he became an Emeritus Professor. He still holds that position and plays an active role in teaching and researching there on short trips from Brighton, where he still lives.

De Kadt's Jewish identity has always remained strong, although it has had little to do with religion for him. On arrival in London in 1956, he explored the diversity of synagogues and found the separate traditions there a sharp contrast to the Netherlands, where – immediately after the war – all had belonged to a single (Orthodox) community regardless of the extent or depth of their beliefs. Consequently, he found the atmosphere in the Liberal Synagogue in St John's Wood cold and 'un-Jewish'. He also became active in Jewish student life, eventually being elected Chair of the LSE Jewish Society, and in student politics more generally. He attributes this in part to the welcome contrast he found with the predominantly apolitical nature of Dutch student life (interview, Emanuel de Kadt[xx]; De Kadt 2006). His most distinguished moment came during the heated debate in the Students' Union in 1957 over the proposal to invite the British Fascist Leader, Oswald Mosley, to address it:

> Speaker followed upon speaker, one for, one against. When I rose
> to speak I had pinned my bedraggled [yellow] Jewish star from
> the war days in Holland onto my jacket. I gave perhaps the most
> impassioned speech of my entire life. Yes, I could see some merit in
> allowing Mosley to hold forth on his pernicious view from a soapbox
> at Hyde Park Corner, but why on earth give the man a prestigious
> platform such as ours? And why trample on the feelings of many? I
> was probably the only person present who had actually experienced
> Nazism and lost members of my family as a result of fascist rule, but
> there were many others for whom Mosley represented all that they

loathed. To my great relief, the motion to invite him was lost. (De Kadt 2006)

One of De Kadt's early publications during his LSE period was for the *Jewish Journal of Sociology*, comparing different methods of locating Jewish university students. This was before he became fascinated by the emerging field of Latin American Studies and began research on the Catholic Church in Brazil.

Given his strong Jewish identity, it is interesting that he married a non-Jew, although they have always celebrated the major festivals. Only when their elder son, Gabriel (born in 1970), approached his thirteenth birthday and decided to have his Barmitzvah along with his best friend, did Emanuel join a synagogue, the Brighton and Hove Progressive Synagogue, because it accepted children of non-Jewish mothers (according to Halachic principles of Jewish law, Jewish descent is matrilineal). Their younger son, Joe, was born in 1972 and also had his Barmitzvah. Emanuel remains a member there and has served on its Council, including as Chair. Even though he regards himself as agnostic, he enjoys the community and shares the views expressed in sermons by the rabbi (*ibid.*).

Synthesis: Two of these three social scientists studied at the LSE, albeit a decade apart, Kari Polanyi Levitt in the 1940s and Emanuel de Kadt in the late 1950s. That was in some respects a significant gap in terms of the *Zeitgeist* (spirit of the time), for the immediate postwar austerity experienced by Polanyi Levitt had given way to greater optimism and student political activism in the very different global situation and late imperial dilemmas, such as the Suez Crisis, which characterised De Kadt's time there. They also came from rather different backgrounds, had different wartime experiences and studied different subjects: economics and sociology respectively. Hence, beyond a certain LSE ethos, there is little commonality to be discerned, even though they later specialised in adjacent regions, the Anglophone Caribbean and Latin America respectively and both adopted broadly critical socialist analytical perspectives. Scarlett Epstein studied in the very different contexts of night school, Ruskin College, Oxford and then Manchester University, and became an anthropologist specialising in South Asia and Papua New Guinea. Her principal work was rurally based in the context of development impacts but she later undertook some urban work as well, particularly in relation to her gender-focused action research. Although also concerned fundamentally with justice and making the world a better place, she never adopted such overtly socialist perspectives. Hence, overall, even the three people who completed their schooling during and after the war and then undertook most or all of their university studies in the UK are quite different in discipline, research area and outlook.

US Education and University Careers

Eric Wolf: Although he described the state of ferment and associated comings and goings in Columbia University's Anthropology Department as 'a shambles' (Friedman 1987: 108), Eric Wolf's graduate studies there exposed him to many of the leading scholars and academic currents in the subject at the time. From his own detailed accounts (Friedman 1987: 108–9; Wolf with Silverman 2001: 3–5; Silverman 2002: 10–12), he thrived in this environment, not least through a postgraduate study group he set up with 'interesting' fellow war veteran students on the political left. His sensibilities – heightened by his Jewish and cross-cultural background, experiences of flight from the Nazis, of completing secondary school near London, and of poverty and grassroots capacity in Tennessee (see Chapter 4) – were not compatible with the then-dominant 'culture-and-personality' approach, which he found deficient on account of its lack of engagement with political and economic contexts.

Instead, he was drawn towards the emerging perspective of cultural ecology, introduced to the department by Julian Steward, who became Eric's dissertation supervisor by dint of having recruited him and a few other students, including Sidney Minz, as research assistants on a project on ecological adaptations by different communities in Puerto Rico. His work encompassed coffee haciendas in the highlands that were shifting towards tobacco production, and the surrounding smallholder communities which supplied them with seasonal wage labour. Into this work he infused Marxian understandings inspired by the work of Karl Wittfogel, Paul Sweezy and CLR James, in particular. Thus he sought to differentiate categories of 'peasant', a term hitherto used uncritically by anthropologists, and to distinguish cultivation from other livelihoods, something that kindled his ongoing keen engagement in so-called 'peasant studies' (Wolf with Silverman 2001: 5; see also Wolf and Minz 1957; Wolf 1959a; Kössler and Schiel 2006: 271).

His postdoctoral project was based in Mexico, enabling him to develop and diversify his expertise further – as reflected in his *Sons of the Shaking Earth* (Wolf 1959b) – which he described as adopting a 'strictly historical-transformational approach to Mexico' and regarded as one of his best publications. His predictions in it of failed peasant revolts, partly because they were not particularly revolutionary, later proved remarkably prescient (Friedmann 1987: 111). Following successive stints in the very diverse anthropology departments at the universities of Illinois, Virginia, Yale and then Chicago – which, despite supposedly being the country's leading department, he found 'to be a gerontocracy, with long meetings devoted to trivia and an overload of ritual and obeisance to the ancestors' – he 'fled by taking up a new field project' in 1960 (Wolf with Silverman 2001: 7). Thus commenced his research engagement in the South Tyrol, rekindling memories of childhood summers and conveniently close to where his second wife, Sydel Silverman (see below), undertook research in Umbria and Tuscany (Sydel Silverman, pers. comm.[xxi]).

Then followed ten years at the University of Michigan, where he collaborated with historians and flourished in a group of cultural ecologists including Roy Rappoport and Marshall Sahlins. This was also where he became more directly politically active in civil rights (building on earlier academic freedom activism during the McCarthy era while at Illinois and Virginia) and Vietnam War issues, to which he felt anthropology was apposite. The anti-war teach-ins that he helped to launch in 1965 'had a special influence on my professional work: my interest in peasant movements began with a briefing paper on Vietnam, in which I tried to figure out for myself what was going on there' (Wolf with Silverman 2001: 8). The Vietnam conflict and the role of some anthropologists in supporting the US war effort polarised the profession as never before (or perhaps since),[5] culminating in the American Anthropological Association (AAA) appointing an ethics committee to seek evidence and formulate a code of ethics with clout. Eric chaired it and when a student group broke agreed confidences by publishing secret documents and the names of the anthropologists

---

[5] Coincidentally, Sydel Silverman pointed out (pers. comm., 8/1/16) that the current schism within the AAA over a proposal to boycott Israeli academic institutions reminded her of that episode and she was 'outraged that some pro-boycotters cite Eric's anti-war activism as comparable when he would have detested the very idea of a boycott'.

assisting the government, open conflict arose within the AAA. Eric and a colleague resigned from the committee (Silverman 2002: 20–21) and 'at one anthropology meeting where he was under attack for being unpatriotic, he wore his Silver Star [awarded for bravery in battle during WWII] ... Of course, not everyone knew what it was but then he was really a hero' (interview, Sydel Silverman[xxii]).

A new investigative AAA committee, chaired by the eminent Margaret Mead, found nothing untoward in the work of the anthropologists serving the war effort, and was roundly critical of the Ethics Committee. Although the report was rejected by the Association's membership at large, '[t]o Eric, it was a hollow victory; the whole affair had robbed him of the illusion that anthropology could only be a force for humanity and justice, and that what he had thought of as his "church" – a unified anthropology – was irreparably torn apart' (Silverman 2002: 21). As a result of this extremely painful and disillusioning experience, he withdrew considerably from overt political engagement in favour of academic writing in his brand of anthropology.

His professional and personal life also changed dramatically in other respects. Having met and fallen in love with Sydel Silverman, who worked in the anthropology department at the City University of New York (CUNY), he moved back to CUNY (of which his alma mater, Queens College, was by then a constituent) in 1971. There he found a group of kindred spirits committed to his style of humanistic, critical and politically engaged anthropology (Wolf with Silverman 2001: 8). Sydel and Eric married once his divorce from his first wife had been finalised.

Work on peasant issues dominated his research during the 1960s and beyond, with two important and influential books (Wolf 1966 and 1969). The former constituted a landmark in anthropological engagement with peasant studies, while the latter examined the revolutionary role of peasant movements. Bringing his Marxian and cultural ecological insights to bear, he developed the perspective on which he had been working since his doctoral research, exposing differentiation, ambiguities and manoeuvrings within what had hitherto been regarded as a somehow homogeneous mass (Wolf with Silverman 2001: 8). In Sydel Silverman's words, 'Eric saw peasants in terms of the exigencies of their production and their relationship to a state and to power-holders whose claims over peasants are guaranteed by a state' (Silverman 2002: 15–16). He himself attributed his abiding interest in the peasantry to having grown up in Vienna and encountered peasants 'as one's other' in the Tyrol and Carinthia during summer holidays (Friedman 1987: 111).

His research in the South Tyrol in the 1970s explored the role of cultural differences and ethnic conflicts between geographically proximate communities and in their relationships with the state. This also linked to his longstanding interest in nationalism and the state, spawned in part by his own childhood experiences of having to flee Nazi-occupied Austria (Silverman 2002: 16–17). This work then expanded over the final phase of his career to tackle questions of how such local cultures and groups were embedded into different modes of production (kin-ordered, tributary and capitalist) and hence the world-system, as examined in *Europe and the People without History* (Wolf 1982) and then *Envisioning Power* (Wolf 1999). In the latter, he used the three contrasting examples of the Kwakiutl, Aztecs and Nazi Germany to explore the relationship between particular modes of production and their ideological underpinnings (Friedman 1987: 113–14; Wolf with Silverman 2001: 9–10; Silverman 2002: 22–7; Kössler and Schiel 2006: 272–4).

Wolf died of cancer in March 1999, having just about completed work on *Pathways of Power*, an edited collection of previously unpublished papers written throughout his career and which his widow, Sydel, then finalised and saw through publication.[6] Marcus (2003) provides an extensive and very insightful posthumous assessment of Wolf's final three books and ultimately his entire oeuvre, describing him as the foremost interpreter of Marx in US anthropology.

Although Eric Wolf never thought of himself as working in or on development, and hence Sydel expressed surprise during my interview with her that I had included him in *Fifty Key Thinkers on Development* (Simon 2006), his major contributions to peasant studies speak directly to key components of the field.[7] The same is true of the

---

[6] Although Eric and Sydel supported each other directly in their respective endeavours, he encouraging her to add historical depth to her work and she helping him organise his thoughts while writing and then editing afterwards, the closest they came to direct collaboration was actually in the production of *Pathways to Power* during his illness. Nevertheless, she believes that they would have been successful had they undertaken joint research (interview, Sydel Silverman[xxiii]).

[7] Indeed, the couple spent a year's sabbatical at the School of Oriental and African Studies in London in the mid-1970s, which provided very fruitful engagements and interactions with the Peasant Studies group there and at the London School of Economics, most of whom worked within development studies (interview, Sydel Silverman[xxiv]).

nuanced interpretation of power and history – in a manner with distinct postcolonial resonances – in *Europe and the People without History*. Distinctively, perhaps, his anthropological perspective shaped his strong emphasis on human culture and agency even within his Marxian and world-systems writing, something which contrasts strongly with the conceptions of **Andre Gunder Frank** and Immanuel Wallerstein and was a source of disagreement between them.

Perhaps surprisingly, therefore, Wolf felt himself more pessimistic about the future of the world than, say Wallerstein:

> I've never been optimistic. I think that socialism is a good thing, that where and when it is honestly applied and works well it does good things for people. But where we find it in reality it always needs considerable improvement ... [and with reference to Perry Anderson's thesis that socialism will, like capitalism, take a long time to develop through various stages] Now, you can't get any enthusiasm out of me if we have to wait three centuries. (Friedman 1987: 117)

Finally, I must return to the question of how important his Jewish heritage, Viennese childhood and experience of flight from the Nazis were in shaping his world view and intellectual endeavours. Perhaps paradoxically for a socialist and highly political anthropologist, the short answer appears to be considerably. Like many of his generation, he came from a religiously and culturally mixed and non-observant family background but was well acculturated and thrived in the cosmopolitan atmosphere of interwar Vienna. Nevertheless,

> being marked as Jews in Vienna, although no one in our family was religious or had been for generations,[8] we were immediately involved in the question of who we were in relation to others. It was a time of growing anti-Semitism. I say 'growing' since Austria has always been much more anti-Semitic than other German-speaking areas. It was sort of 'in the air'. There was a great deal of street fighting. (Friedman 1987: 107)

This interview with Jonathan Friedman and his autobiographical introduction to Wolf with Silverman (2001) contain various mentions of Jewish identity, cultural and/or historical references and even idioms

---

[8] In fact, his mother's family had been at least partially observant of the Sabbath and festivals.

as he described his approach or explained his work. As noted above, his return to undertake research in South Tyrol, which resonated with some childhood memories of peasant encounters, and his choice of German national socialism as a key case study in *Envisioning Power*, provide further clear markers. The latter case also demonstrates how he sought throughout his life to explain and understand, to his own intellectual and emotional satisfaction, the tragedy in which his family was caught up and from which they were lucky to escape.

Andre Gunder Frank: The Frank family moved state several times after arriving in the USA from Switzerland in 1941. Andre completed his secondary schooling at Ann Arbor High School, Michigan. Thereafter, he studied economics at Swarthmore College, becoming, in his own words, 'a Keynesian' as he was unaware of Marxism and would remain so for a long time (Frank 1996). Then, ironically as it turned out, given Frank's subsequent theoretical and ideological orientation, and 'not knowing what I was letting myself in for', he undertook his doctoral studies from 1950 to 1957 at the University of Chicago, including a semester studying at the University of Michigan under Kenneth Boulding and Robert Musgrave. Already isolated on the far left of student politics in the McCarthyist atmosphere of rabid anti-communism, he became active for a time in the US National Student Association. He completed his thesis on growth and productivity in Ukrainian agriculture under the noted neoliberal monetarist economist, Milton Friedman,

> who in the political climate of the time did not yet have the opportunity to preach his monetarist gospel to many more than his capite student audience. I also remember Friedman's dismissing Kenneth Galbraith, who then still had more opportunity, as a mere 'popularizer' rather than an economic 'theorist'. (Frank 1997: 97)

His introduction to development occurred 'through the back door' in Bert Hoselitz's (see Chapter 1) Research Center in Economic Development and Cultural Change at the University of Chicago, where he obtained a research assistantship in 1953:

> In Bert's absence on leave, the planner and acting director Harvey Perloff [who was **John Friedmann**'s doctoral supervisor – see Chapter 7] hired me to evaluate the early World Bank reports on

Ceylon, Nicaragua, and Turkey, to which I gave barely passing marks. In response, Perloff told me to his dismay that I am 'the most philosophical person' he had ever met. (*ibid.*)

In today's terms, this would have been a most unusual introduction to conventional approaches to development,[9] soon to be systematised as modernisation theory, and which was also Hoselitz's perspective. Indeed, Hoselitz established the first academic journal in the development field, with the same title as his centre. It became globally influential for decades and remains so in (neo-)liberal development economic circles. Frank subsequently met Walt Rostow, the best-known advocate of that approach,[10] during a three-month visit to the Center for International Studies (CENIS) at MIT in 1958. Frank's colourful recollection of this formative episode is also worth quoting for present purposes:

What an opportunity that was. There I met W.W. Rostow and the others. He had just written his *Process of Development*[11] and was working on his celebrated *Stages of Economic Growth: A Non-Communist Manifesto*, not to mention his still clandestine work for the CIA with CENIS Director Max Millikan, *A Proposal. Key to an Effective Foreign Policy* [Millikan and Rostow 1957]. Although Rostow and Co. dealt with Keynesian type macro economic and even social problems, they did so to pursue the neo-classical explicitly counter revolutionary and even counter reformist cold war ends, which were newly in vogue. The quintessential modernization book, Lerner's [1958] *Passing of Traditional Society: The Modernization of the Middle East*, appeared at CENIS in 1958 while I was there ... all of which translated the 'conditions' of naked cold war ideological orthodoxy into euphemistically saleable social 'scientific responses' ... While at CENIS, Rostow 'confided' to me that since the age of 18 he made it his life's mission to offer the world a better alternative to Karl Marx. I did not understand then what that was supposed to mean.

---

9   At the time, with almost no development literature or teaching material available, it was common to throw research students in at the proverbial deep end, both to test their acuity and because supervisors were often grappling with the new challenges of working in 'developing countries' themselves and welcomed fresh ideas. Indeed, many PhDs at the time had such origins.

10   For an assessment, see Menzel (2006).

11   This would appear to be an erroneous reference to *The Process of Economic Growth* (Rostow 1953).

After reflecting on the fate of Marxism and 'really existing socialism'
I now wonder why Rostow wanted to dedicate his life to offering an
alternative to them. (Frank 1997: 80)

Frank's narrative exposes the covert collaboration with academics
in CENIS with the CIA in pursuit of the Cold War, which was one of
the key influences stimulating his enduring critiques of conventional
development theory and practice, honed subsequently during his time
in Latin America. Interestingly for present purposes, both Frank and
Friedmann, the two Chicago PhDs in this study, cut their teeth on
modernisation theory there but later became fierce critics of that and
related market-led approaches.

After short spells teaching at the University of Iowa and University of
Michigan, Frank resigned in 1962 in frustration at both the impact of
the Cold War on universities, and at what he saw as the problematic role
of much social science research. This marked a turning point in his long
process of radicalisation and the start of the peripatetic second half of his
life. His aspirations to teach at the universities in Leipzig and Havana
having been frustrated, he moved to Latin America, teaching first at the
University of Brasilia, where he met Marta Fuentes, who would become
his wife for 30 years and with whom he would have two sons, and then
at UNAM in Mexico City. A short spell at George William University
in Montreal was followed by a position with the International Labour
Organization in Chile, from which he was dismissed, whereupon Salvador
Allende facilitated an appointment in the University in Santiago (Frank
1997; Mintz 2007; Watts 2006).[12] Frank's time in Latin America, which
proved seminal to his thinking and subsequent work, ended abruptly with
the Pinochet coup against Allende's government in 1973, whereupon
he and his family fled, ironically enough, to Germany, as he still held
German nationality (Frank 1997: 82). However, the option of returning
to the USA had been foreclosed by a ban on entry imposed in 1965 for
supposedly supporting the Chinese government's position in an article in
the *Monthly Review* (as quoted in Frank 1997). This prohibition would
last for many years.

He did or could not settle in Germany, and after three years
spent between Berlin, Munich and Frankfurt, he moved to a chair in

---

[12] Although these sources are not explicit about the reason for Frank's dismissal, the
implication of Allende then helping him find a university appointment is that his radical
views conflicted with the ILO's line in Chile or more widely at the time.

Development Studies at the University of East Anglia in Norwich, UK, in 1978 before accepting a chair at the University of Amsterdam in 1983. Sustained attempts to obtain a post in the USA proved fruitless, so this was to be his final appointment before compulsory retirement in 1994, aged 65, a year after the death of his wife. He later married an old friend, Nancy Howell, but they divorced four years later and he then married Alison Candela, who survived him when he succumbed after a long fight with cancer on 23 April 2005.

As mentioned above, Frank underwent a long process of radicalisation, but his time in Latin America, and especially Allende's socialist Chile, proved instrumental in his emergence as a sharp critic of conventional development approaches. Indeed, he became one of the leading advocates of dependency 'theory', who argued that former European colonial territories were held virtual captive by unequal structural power relations with corporations, institutions and governments in the global North, not least the former colonial powers. These relations were not amenable to major rebalancing and the only way to achieve locally appropriate national development was therefore to break these relations in favour of autarchy. Frank's (1967; 1969; 1991b) two major elaborations of this position paralleled independent work by Samir Amin (1970; 1973) on Africa and by Immanuel Wallerstein at the global scale. Frank (1980; 1981a; 1981b) also wrote at the global scale, and these three subsequently collaborated on world-systems theory (Amin et al. 1982; see also Frank 1997 and Watts 2006: 92–3).

Despite his peripatetic life – holding posts in ten disciplines within multiple universities – he was phenomenally productive, with an oeuvre comprising over 1,000 items, including some 44 books, 169 chapters and 400 journal articles in, and translated into, many languages.[13] Much of this work was challenging and controversial, generating heated debate and proving polarising in that people tended to support or oppose his analyses sharply. His often-combative style contributed to this, and he would even fall out spectacularly in print with colleagues and former collaborators. One dramatic spat was his falling out with Immanuel Wallerstein in the pages of *Critique of Anthropology* (Frank 1991a; Wallerstein 1991), and another with Samir Amin, over his reinterpretation of world history over 5,000 years rather than the 500

---

[13] A full bibliography is available online at http://rrojasdatabank.info/agfrank/IISG_Pubs.html, and up to 1997 at http://wsarch.ucr.edu/archive/gunder97cd.html.

years of European capitalist domination as articulated in their earlier collaborative work on the world-system. Frank's reinterpretation culminated in *ReOrient* (Frank 1998), his final major book, in which he developed this thesis fully.

Watts (2006: 92–4) helpfully discerns five overlapping themes in Frank's voluminous output, which was framed entirely in Marxian terms (but rarely in relation to more recent Marxist theory), namely the Soviet bloc; social and anti-systems movements (the work with Fuentes and Amin et al.); world-system development and underdevelopment; contemporary international political economy; and world history. Frank's own words from the opening paragraphs of 'The Cold War and Me' (Frank 1997: 79) provide a succinct and different synthesis:

> My personal life and experience was long and intimately shaped by the cold war and its relation in turn to 'area studies' especially of the Soviet Union, Latin America and 'Third World development' policy and studies generally. Therefore, my own experience is an ineluctable prism (prison?) for me. But both may also contribute something to the general political sociology of knowledge of this period, much of which still remains to be analyzed and written.

However, in the current world order of the 2000s, he concluded his autobiographical note rather pessimistically, anticipating that his fate would be

> to disappear into politically irrelevant oblivion. Indeed, my global theory and praxis to 'ReOrient' and to promote 'unity in diversity' is likely to have no appeal whatsoever for the many who in the present political climate now rush instead to promote all manner of separatisms from post-modern ethnic identity to real ethnic cleansing. (*ibid.*: 84)

Nothing could be further from the truth. His work continues to be cited very frequently in debates on several of his research themes, especially dependency and world-systems theory. However, his autobiographical essays (Frank 1996; 1997) offer no insights into a possible influence or legacy of his Jewish roots on his life, ideological commitments and work, although values such as his commitment to justice at national and global scales could have such an origin, implicitly if not explicitly.

Irma Glicman-Adelman: After completing her schooling in Palestine, Irma Glicman-Adelman entered the Hebrew University in Jerusalem in 1948. Unable to major in economics, which was not available at the time, she opted for a minor in social sciences while majoring in French and English literature to nourish her artistic interests. She recalls frequenting the city's museums and economising on her subsistence budget from her parents in order to buy art postcards and to give some to the many street beggars at the time. This provides early evidence of her concern with poverty, which came to represent an abiding professional focus of her life as an economist.

However, the university was closed after the first armistice that ended Israel's War of Independence (known as *al Nakbah*, the catastrophe, to Palestinians) and, desperate to pursue her intellectual studies, Irma was keen to move to a US university. Her parents were unenthusiastic about their only child heading off to another continent so her father set her what he called a maturity test: he would pay for her studies and travel to the US if she could obtain an exit permit herself, since these were very hard to get at the time. By befriending the Yemeni tea seller who supplied the officials dealing with such permits, she was able to short-circuit the queues and delays and obtain one, thus enabling her to commence studies at the University of California, Berkeley, in 1949 (interview, Irma Adelman[xxv]).[14]

Rather than pursue her literary interests (ideally, she would have opted for French and German literature and art history), she enrolled for business and public administration,

> because of my perception of the primary needs of the nascent State
> of Israel, the furthering of whose interests I was dedicated to. But this
> was not to be! Shortly after coming to Berkeley I met my husband,
> [Frank,] an American Physics PhD candidate, fell in love, married,
> and stayed. (Adelman 1988: 245; 1995: 5)

She switched to economics at graduate school and, although she described Berkeley as having been 'very weak in economic theory and in mathematical training', she completed her PhD on a general equilibrium analysis based on Walrasian monetary theory in 1955. She attributes her success to being tutored by Robert Dorfman (the

---

[14] After her father's death in Israel in 1956 or 1957 and the birth of her son, Alex, in 1958, her mother opted to join her in the USA; she died in the early 1960s but her son was old enough to remember her (interview, Irma Adelman[xxvi]).

originator of linear programming) in statistics and George Kuznets in econometrics, while also learning much from her husband (*ibid.*; interview, Irma Adelman[xxvii]).

In response to my question about whether Irma's experiences escaping from Romania and completing her schooling and first year of university in Palestine/Israel and then becoming a mother in the US had affected her religious beliefs or practices, she affirmed not. She had become agnostic when 700–800 passengers on the MV Struma, a ship carrying refugees, including her paternal uncle and cousins, from Romania to Haifa drowned off Istanbul when it sank after hitting a mine[15] and the Turkish fishermen in the area made no effort to rescue anyone. In Palestine, she had merely formed part of the secular majority, while her husband was also an atheist Jew (interview, Irma Adelman[xxviii]).

In her autobiographical chapter (Adelman 1988: 244; 1995: 4), she put it far more powerfully with reference to having started school as a Jew being educated by Catholic nuns:

> The Jews are said to own 'guilt' and the Catholics to have a lifetime lease on it. My early education therefore left me with a mammoth sense of primordial guilt that was later reinforced by the guilt of a survivor of the Holocaust. The expiation of this guilt through the only mechanism it can be expiated – service to humanity – has been a primary driving force in my life.

Professionally, these experiences and sense of guilt

> certainly motivated the orientation and the focus of my research. Anti-poverty was the main motivating force and I felt a personal obligation to do whatever was in my powerless power to further egalitarian and poverty-oriented government approaches. So it certainly has had a lasting impact on me.

That motivation was strong from the outset:

> Before economic development was a field and I had to take the next best thing, namely international trade, till [that] field ... emerged. The

---

[15] This occurred on 24 February 1942 although it was apparently a Soviet submarine torpedo that caused the sinking, a fact determined only decades later. Only one person survived, making it the worst purely civilian maritime loss in the Black Sea during WWII. The behaviour of the British and Turkish authorities towards the ship and its passengers in the period culminating in this disaster in turn helped spur Jewish underground resistance against British rule in Palestine (Wikipedia 2016).

first textbook was [by] Buchanan and Ellis [1955] and both ... were teaching at Berkeley. (interview, Irma Adelman[xxix])

Hence Irma was 'in' at the beginnings of development economics as a distinct sub-discipline. Her first book (Adelman 1961), published six years later while at Stanford University on the final of several one-year temporary posts,[16] was a textbook addressing economic development theories but, like Buchanan and Ellis, seeking to capture the interplay between economic development and the socio-cultural and institutional dimensions, issues on which she felt she was perhaps too inexperienced to write about authoritatively and so delayed its publication (Adelman 1988: 247; 1995: 7). Whether because of or despite this initial hesitancy, the book provided the launchpad for one consistent theme of Irma's research throughout her career, namely seeking to understand such processes of interaction better, based 'on empirically generated hypotheses and stylized facts' (Adelman 1988: 247; 1995: 7).

In this endeavour, she collaborated over much of her career with Cynthia Taft Morris, whom she first met and worked with at the Brookings Institution in Washington, DC, during summer 1962, where they both had just moved in following their husbands' careers (Adelman 1988; 1995). I return to their lengthy and deep research partnership below. In the autumn of 1962, Irma commenced teaching at Johns Hopkins University in Baltimore, juggling two careers and a young child. She struggled to achieve tenure there in the face of gender discrimination and eventually moved to a tenured chair at Northwestern University in Evanston, Illinois, in 1966 because she liked the interdisciplinary focus on offer there, which matched her approach to economic development. Hence the move was a positive decision rather than out of spite at Johns Hopkins' short-sighted policy in having told her to find another job so that they could, in effect, test her marketability and then match the salary (interview, Irma Adelman[xxx]; Adelman 1988: 260; 1995: 17–20).

Despite her professional and personal happiness at Northwestern, her husband's employment proved problematic and so they moved

---

[16] She attributes this to the blatant gender discrimination that was pervasive at the time, since her qualifications and publications would have gained her a tenured position at any good university had she been male. She managed somehow to avoid becoming bitter, and did at least remain fully employed and gain experience of different institutions (see below).

again, initially for one year to the Center for Advanced Studies in Behavioural Sciences in Palo Alto, California, and then, when finding jobs together during the incipient recession in higher education proved impossible, they returned to Washington, where he worked on a book project and she became the principal breadwinner through a one-year position at the World Bank. Continued attempts to find joint appointments caused tension and he eventually found a position in his own field. She then took a chair at the University of Maryland but, since it was a commuter campus, she missed the collegial atmosphere of non-urban campuses.

Following her divorce in 1980, she moved back to her alma mater, Berkeley, which had offered her a post in the Department of Agriculture and Resource Economics. She would remain at Berkeley for the rest of her career, continuing as a professor in the UCB Graduate School from 1994. The initial attraction behind her move had been to learn more about agriculture, including agricultural economics and technology, since she had come to realise its importance through her anti-poverty work. Late in her career, her research focused on interactions between agriculture and industry (Adelman 1988: 259–60; 1995: 19–20) and her final book applied economic modelling to the village scale, where livelihoods including both agricultural and non-agricultural components are increasingly normal and vital to community survival (Taylor and Adelman 1996).

Three of Irma's most prominent books arose from her long collaboration with Cynthia Taft Morris, which transcended her successive institutional relocations and also shaped her career path in important ways. *Society, Politics, and Economic Development: A Quantitative Approach* (Adelman and Morris 1967) provided an innovative statistical comparison of data from USAID country reports to explore these social, economic and political interactions in an era predating published international GNP or other comparative tabulations and data sets. The idea for this work originated in Irma's exploration of the agency's files and reports in search of research inspiration at the behest of Hollis Chenery, then head of the agency's research division (Adelman 1988: 247–8; 1995: 7–8).[17] Thereafter, they worked on an historical counterpart

---

[17] An extensive and technically detailed discussion of the econometric methods underpinning this and much of Adelman's other work referred to here is provided in Grossbard-Shechtman (2002).

international comparative volume, examining similar processes during and since the Industrial Revolution, an endeavour that took some 23 years (Morris and Adelman 1988).

In between, they published a third book, *Economic Growth and Social Equity in Developing Countries* (Adelman and Morris 1973), which examined the breadth of participation in development processes by the populations of poor countries in receipt of USAID funding. It was produced for the agency in response to criticisms from Congress. The paucity of income distribution data made the work challenging but, unlike Kuznets' U-curve regarding the share of national income obtained by the poor over time, they established a J-curve, showing that the poor's share of income initially declined rapidly but that this rate then gradually tapered off and then either levelled out or began to increase, depending on the policy choices made. This reflected the increasing size of, and income share accruing to, the middle classes at the expense of both the elites and poor. These were important and unexpected results, both to them personally and to wider development debates:

> We were deeply shocked by our findings. Up to then we had
> believed in the benign view of economic development offered by
> modernization-scholars and in the trickle-down hypothesis imbuing
> mainstream writings on economic development. Were it not for the
> function-free statistical technique we adopted for our study, and were
> it not for our inductive empirical approach, we would have adopted an
> *a priori* specification confirming the modernization-cum-trickle-down
> theories. We would then have ascribed the poor statistical fit to poor
> data and small sample size. (Adelman 1988: 249–50; 1995: 10–11)

Their report to USAID was submitted in 1971 but they then delayed publication out of fear that the findings would be used to bolster political arguments in favour of cutting aid resources rather than to reorient programmes and projects towards poverty agendas. The latter was to take far longer. By 1973, aid budgets were already being cut, while 'new evidence concerning increasing urban unemployment despite rapid growth was making it clear that all was not well with the development process'. Hence they felt that publication would do no harm (Adelman 1988: 249–50; 1995: 10–11).

Adelman's shock at the findings spawned her second major research focus for the rest of her career, namely descriptive and policy approaches to income distribution and poverty, starting with a very critical reassessment of the achievements and purpose of development economics (Adelman 1974; 1975). In the first of these two provocative articles, appropriately published in the inaugural issue of the *Journal of Development Economics*, she identified four key failings that are now regarded as 'old hat' but which are still all too evident in practice. These were the failure to monitor development project results adequately, the failure to adopt a sufficiently broad systems approach, and yet an obsessive search for panaceas and for simple or simplistic guidance rules, and insufficient humility and professionalism. The second paper, in the US discipline's leading journal, the *American Economic Review*,

> argued that the goals of development should become the creation of the social and material conditions for the realization of human potential by all. This goal should replace the goal of self-sustained growth; rather, growth should be viewed as an instrument for the achievement of poverty reduction – a goal to which I referred as 'depauperization'. (Adelman 1988: 251; 1995: 11)

That paper concluded with an outline strategy for depauperisation, based on her comparative study of processes in non-communist countries that had managed to improve the incomes of the poor simultaneously with rapid economic growth, namely Israel, Japan and three of what later became known as the Asian Tigers – Singapore, South Korea and Taiwan.

The significance of Adelman's 'conversion' merits comment. It is relatively unusual in development economics to be able to demonstrate such profound problems using international econometric data as to precipitate a fundamental questioning of one's field and the proposal of different objectives. It had considerable impact and contributed in no small way to her global reputation as a leading postwar economist, earning her inclusion in several widely used directories, where she was among very few women (e.g. Blaug 1998; Kregel 1989; Beaud and Dostaler 1995; Grossbard-Shechtman 2002).[18]

What her autobiographical account does not convey, however, is the extent to which the late 1960s and early 1970s were a time of widespread

---

[18] Inexplicably, though, she was omitted from Dimand et al. (2000), a directory devoted exclusively to women economists.

ferment in development circles. The end of the long economic boom and period of heady optimism amid ongoing decolonisation, coupled with evidence from various sources around the world of widespread failures of conventional development initiatives and associated 'white elephant' projects, fed debates and searches for alternatives. These ranged from various strands of Marxian political economy to basic needs, to more holistic approaches to development than the prioritisation of economic dimensions that underpinned modernisation approaches, and to various forms of 'alternative development'. In various of the last-mentioned category, many other figures in this study, including **Hans Singer**, **Paul Streeten**, **John Friedmann**, **Eric Wolf**, **Michael Cernea** and **Emanuel de Kadt**, were involved in diverse ways. However, because of the particular institutional source of her data, the nature of her findings and her subsequent arguments, Adelman moved debates and agendas forward within some important corridors of power far more than more politically or ideologically driven critics were able to. One of her subsequent books (Adelman 1978), provided evidence-led arguments for asset and income redistribution *before* growth and also demonstrated her ability and willingness to challenge World Bank and other mainstream formulations about redistribution *with* or *after* growth (e.g. Chenery et al. 1974).[19]

Notwithstanding the foregoing and her acknowledgement of the importance of radical critiques of mainstream development economics at the start of her 1974 article, Irma Adelman eschewed Marxism, as she found the hierarchical and dogmatic aspects of Marxist-inspired movements too restrictive for her individualistic instincts. However, like many others in this study, she was sympathetic to socialism and always felt her allegiance to be to humanity in tackling poverty, rather than even to a single man, as she told her husband before accepting his proposal of marriage (interview, Irma Adelman[xxxi])!

Her change of research direction in the early 1970s, outlined above, also spelled the end of her direct policy advisory work because she 'lost all popularity' with planning agencies in developing countries. While her income distribution findings and policy implications gained her consultancy roles with the ILO, OECD and other international agencies, those offers dried up as the emphasis later shifted towards

[19] By this time, following his stint at USAID and then a period at Harvard University, Hollis Chenery had become the World Bank's first Chief Economist (Uitto 2006).

trade and debt issues (Adelman 1988: 257; 1995: 17), apart from with the FAO on her agriculturally focused work at Berkeley.

Her engagement in development planning consultancy had actually commenced early in her career, focusing initially on Vietnam for USAID and where her recommendations went unimplemented in the face of military priorities during the war. Thereafter, she fortuitously became involved in work on South Korea's Second Five-Year Plan, which heralded that country's shift to export-led growth. Once the then president became an oppressive despot, she ceased work there. Her final direct involvement with policy work was during her year at the World Bank in 1971/2, when a working paper summarising her and Cynthia Morris' findings on income distribution provided the context for the then Bank President, Robert McNamara, to herald a change in Bank lending towards poverty alleviation (see Adelman 1969; 1988: 255–7; 1995: 15–17; Adelman and Robinson 1978; interview, Irma Adelman[xxxii]).

With policy work, Adelman always found it important to ensure that her values and those of her clients were compatible for both ethical and practical reasons. With respect to the Korean policy establishment, she found no conflict because Jewish and Confucian values both favour equality and value human capital – hence education and scholars rank highly (interview, Irma Adelman[xxxiii]; Adelman n.d.: 5).

This highlights the ongoing importance to Irma Glicman-Adelman of her Jewish heritage and values in her professional work, despite her lack of religious observance and total secularism. As evident from the previous sections in this chapter and throughout Chapters 5 and 7, this is a widely shared characteristic among both the older and younger cohorts in my study. Survivor guilt, expressed so clearly by Irma in one of the quotations above, also became a driving force in focusing her career on the service of humanity and tackling poverty, although for some others it was a more positive emotion of gratitude at having escaped and survived. After a period of increasing ill health, she died in Berkeley on 5 February 2017 (Berkeley Department of Agricultural and Resource Economics 2017; Zilberman 2017a; 2017b).

Poland: Postwar Communist Oppression and Subsequent (Re-)Exile

Zygmunt Bauman: Zygmunt Bauman was famously reticent about autobiographical details, something remarked upon in almost every published interview with him. This appears to have reflected a combination of a predilection for personal privacy, a lack of a sense of a story to his lifecourse and a strong desire to avoid his intellectual work being read off as a function of particular experiences and who he was – 'the paralysing straightjacket of displays of *ersatz* intimacy', he is quoted as saying (Bunting 2003: 2). Both Smith (1999) and Bauman and Tester (2001: 1–6) actually address his enigmatic persona under the heading of 'Who is Zygmunt Bauman?' Perhaps, therefore, I was fortunate but we discussed the interplay of factors fairly freely and the biographical sketch in the following paragraphs comes mainly from my interview, augmented as appropriate from the other sources cited.

After returning to Poland with his parents at the end of World War II, Bauman moved around the country on active service as a political officer in the Internal Security Corps (KBW) until finally being posted to Warsaw in very early 1947. He would remain there until forced to flee the country again in 1968. Being an officer entitled him to a flat and enabled him to study. Initially he studied part-time through evening classes until his sudden expulsion from the army in 1953 during a political upheaval enabled him to become a fulltime student of philosophy and sociology at the University of Warsaw. He attributed his choice of disciplines to study to his wartime experiences and 'dedication' to rebuilding the devastated country: whereas prewar Poland had been wracked by poverty and neighbourly hatred and jealousy, the new communist postwar order appeared to hold the possibility of constructing a new and wonderful world, so philosophy and sociology held the keys to understanding the agency of society. Jewishness or a Jewish ethic played no role. He gained his MA, then PhD and ultimately Habilitation[20] degrees and rose through the ranks to become Head of the Sociology Department, a post he held until the purge of Jewish intellectuals in 1968 triggered his second flight from Poland (interview, Zygmunt Bauman[xxxiv]). This experience mirrors that of **Michael Cernea** in Romania (see above).

Having met while studying at Warsaw University, the Baumans married in 1948, after an intense nine-day courtship. Their first child, Anna, arrived the following year, while twin daughters, Irina and Lydia, were born in 1955. Since both parents were totally secular and their respective wartime traumas did not engender any upwelling of religious

---

[20] Poland follows the teutonic tradition of requiring a second, post-PhD, thesis, known as Habilitation, as a prerequisite for tenure and promotion to a chair.

belief, practice or an urge to pass on Jewish traditions to their children, the girls were brought up in a secular household.

Ironically, therefore, Zygmunt attributed both his education and marriage indirectly to Hitler and the Nazis. Strict prewar quotas on Jews entering university would have precluded him, while his family would never have been able to afford to send him abroad to study. Similarly, the social gulf in their respective familial statuses before the war would never have brought them together or permitted a relationship. Whereas he was from a provincial background (both his parents had grown up in Yiddish-speaking settlements, known as *shtetls* (lit. small towns)) and fitted the social category of *Ostjude* (lit. eastern Jew), Janina came from an established, wealthy and cosmopolitan Warsaw Jewish family (Bunting 2003: 3; interview, Zygmunt Bauman[xxxv]).

For both Zygmunt, having previously been exiled in the USSR during World War II, and Janina, who survived the Warsaw Ghetto and avoided deportation to the extermination camps, forced exile in 1968 proved traumatic. Obtaining an exit visa from Poland at the time was exceedingly difficult and obtaining an Israeli entry visa was one of the very few options. Janina was determined to join her mother, who was already there (as was Zygmunt's only sister – see Chapter 2), and they were thus able to secure visas and leave. Zygmunt then had to learn Hebrew from scratch, much as he'd done with Russian on reaching the USSR some 29 years previously. They didn't find it easy to settle or assimilate in Israel, finding it too nationalistic, albeit in a different way from Poland. Unhappy at the consequences of ongoing occupation of captured lands on the national psyche, they emigrated after just three years. He turned down several offers in favour of a chair in sociology at the University of Leeds, UK, where he stayed until his retirement in 1990 and beyond, publishing far more prolifically once he was free of the administrative burden of Head of Department (see below) (interview, Zygmunt Bauman[xxxvi]). One of his daughters married and remained in Israel; the other two moved to the UK with their parents and later married and have remained in the country.

Interestingly, Bauman subsequently developed deeper and more extensive relations in Poland than perhaps is true of any other of the escapees in this study. He first returned in 1988, 20 years after fleeing, and found a contingent of old acquaintances waiting to welcome him at the airport and they picked up almost as if he had been away merely on holiday. He had good relations with both the older and younger generations but was conscious that the middle cohort – those who fled and others who replaced them in the universities – were missing from his contacts. He attributed the resumption/establishment of warm relationships as possibly reflecting, in many cases, a subconscious collective Polish guilt over what happened and the associated theft of Jewish property not too dissimilar to that felt by younger Germans regarding the Holocaust for several decades until recently (interview, Zygmunt Bauman[xxxvii]).

While discussion of the wealth and diversity of Bauman's sociological output is beyond the scope of this book and exists elsewhere (e.g. Smith 1999; Bauman and Tester 2001), his work on modernity and postmodernity and on the Holocaust has direct relevance and, indeed, constitutes the rationale for including him in this study despite the bulk of his work not speaking directly to development issues. The Holocaust focus of his work he attributed to his realisation, on reading his wife's autobiographical account of life in the Warsaw Ghetto and beyond (J. Bauman 1986), how little he actually knew or understood of the traumas and suffering that she and many other Jews who had been unable to flee had experienced. Hence he set out to try to understand the Nazis and the basis for the Holocaust more fully and more convincingly than others had done. His essential thesis – which marks out his account from almost all of the innumerable others – is that this was a perverted exercise in industrial modernity (Bunting 2003; Bauman 1989; Bauman and Tester 2001):

> The unspoken terror permeating our collective memory of the
> Holocaust (and more than contingently related to the overwhelming
> desire not to look the memory in the face) is the gnawing suspicion
> that the Holocaust could be more than an aberration, more than
> a deviation from an otherwise straight path of progress, more than
> a cancerous growth on the otherwise healthy body of the civilized
> society; that in short, the Holocaust was not an antithesis of modern
> civilization and everything (or so we like to think) it stands for. We
> suspect (even if we refuse to admit it) that the Holocaust could merely
> have uncovered another face of the same modern society whose other,
> more familiar, face we so admire. And that the two faces are perfectly
> comfortably attached to the same body. What we perhaps fear most, is
> that each of the two faces can no more exist without the other than can
> the two sides of a coin. (Bauman 1989: 7; see pp. 17–23 for a fuller
> explanation of the crucial argument)

In the context of the subject of this book, and the engagement of my interviewees as Holocaust escapees and survivors in the evolution of development theory (including modernisation theory), policy and practice as forces for good and improving the world, this analysis is both shocking and illuminating. Paradoxically, moreover, Bauman explained his approach to liquid modernity as having arisen over time through his frustration with modernisation theory, which – with particular reference to the Middle East – formed an obligatory part of his sociology studies. He found it tautological and the idea that any country would or could stop modernising absurd: 'Modernity without modernisation is very much like wind which is not blowing or a river which is not flowing – it's nonsense!' ... 'Modernity has become a sign of distinction and esteem ... everybody wants to be modern without necessarily doing things that modernity requires'. Equally, he found Eisenstadt's notion of multiple modernities or its derivative, alternative modernities, inadequate – in fact a form of escape because anything or anyone who wishes it can apply the label to themselves or others. 'So I prefer now to speak about liquid modernity, which emphasises that it is still modernity but modernity which is not bent on creating a new better, solid but ... which is reconciled to its own liquid nature' (interview, Zygmunt Bauman[xxxviii]).

For similar reasons, he disliked 'multiculturalism' as expressed in British and German government policies during much of the 1990s and 2000s, for instance, through tolerance of behaviours and practices by ethnic/migrant minorities that run counter to or offend values and even ethics in the majority communities. As he argued in *Modernity and Ambivalence* (Bauman 1991) arising out of his work on the Holocaust and its legacy, such tolerance is

> mostly a matter of reaffirmation of hierarchical relationships and also expression of ethical indifference ... The term I prefer is interculturalism ... because that's what going on. Whether you like it or not, you may have 60 different ethnic enclaves in London today and they are living in relative separation, territorial separation in parts of London, but there's very intensive exchange going on all the time and as long as you speak about multiculturalism, you close your eyes to what's going on. (interview, Zygmunt Bauman[xxxix])

This thinking he linked integrally to the contemporary challenges of globalisation. Indeed, when, in that context, I raised the issue of the Western-centrism of the post-World War II founding documents of the current global governance regime, such as the UN Declaration of Human Rights, Bauman invoked Hannah Arendt's argument that human rights are purely an abstraction unless grounded in particular national or other contexts, pointing out that '[w]ithout a network of institutions that can defend your rights, you are nothing, and if you happen to be an illegal immigrant, you know very well what this [means]' (interview, Zygmunt Bauman[xl]).

The implications of Bauman's thinking on these issues for present-day development studies and its increasing concern with global issues are self-evident. Somewhat surprisingly, however, but perhaps because he is perceived as a 'Western' sociologist not writing about poor countries, his work has not to date received significant exposure or gained traction within the field. Bauman continued writing until days before his death on 9 January 2017 (Davis and Campbell 2017; Reisz 2017).

Reflections

Apart from the LSE connection in the context of two of the three UK-educated contingent covered in this chapter, the elements of diversity on almost every variable exceed the commonalities. One exception relates to the nature and extent of subsequent contact with their countries of birth. For most, this was limited and confined to a small number of short visits to lay ghosts, visit surviving relatives and friends, or receive restitution and/or honours from their former home towns or universities where they did or would have studied under normal circumstances. The notable exception was Zygmunt Bauman, as outlined above. His having fled (for the second time) in 1968 as a mid-career adult rather than as a child, teenager, student or very young academic may have played a role in his ability to reciprocate the warmth extended to him. The only other person in a comparable position was Michael Cernea from Romania (see Chapter 7) and he has also established some links again, albeit to a lesser extent. Since he did not continue as an academic for long in the USA before joining the World Bank, however, he didn't have the shared intellectual agenda as a vehicle in the same way as Bauman.

One point of diversity also warrants mention, namely that in the context of the disciplinary spread within this study, this is the only chapter featuring just two economists (Kari Polanyi Levitt and Irma

Adelman) but four social scientists, two of them sociologists (Emanuel de Kadt and Zygmunt Bauman) and two social anthropologists (Scarlett Epstein and Eric Wolf). That said, even in terms of their respective countries of origin, degrees of religious observance or secularism, and countries of formal education and professional practice, there is no discernible pattern apart from both the Eastern Europeans educated in their home countries after World War II having become sociologists because of the nature of the disciplines available at the time.

7 | THE YOUNGER GENERATION: INTERNATIONAL AGENCY STAFF AND INFLUENTIAL CONSULTANTS

This chapter focuses on five members of this younger age cohort who were employed by key international financial and development institutions, rather as **Hans Singer** had been among the older generation. **Shlomo Reutlinger**, **Michael Cernea** and **Ernie Stern** spent substantial parts of their careers at the World Bank, while **Gerry Helleiner** spent periods there and in UN agencies, although he was principally an academic. **John Friedmann** spent part of his early career working for USAID in Brazil and Korea and had other academic posts in Chile before moving permanently into academia in Los Angeles. He might thus just as easily have been included in Chapter 6 but appears here since he did work for these agencies, and to provide better balance of length between these two chapters. Inevitably, such boundary lines are imprecise: others among my research subjects undertook specific consultancies for international or bilateral development agencies from their university bases but never became agency employees. **Irma Glicman-Adelman** provides the boundary case by virtue of a one-year position at the World Bank. Because this short sojourn was of little significance to her overall academic career or world view, however, she fits far more naturally in Chapter 6 than here.

The five featured here are diverse in terms of original nationality (German, German/Dutch, two Austrians from Vienna who both left at an early age, and a Romanian); age (they were born over a ten-year period from 1926 in the cases of Reutlinger and Friedmann to 1936 in the case of Helleiner); religious affiliation and observance (ranging from observant orthodox Jews to baptised Christian and de facto secular) as well as professional disciplines (two economists, one economist/banker, one sociologist and one planner). Four became refugees as children or youngish teenagers and thus adjusted and completed their schooling and received their tertiary education in their countries of refuge and/or subsequent countries of settlement. Only Michael Cernea completed his formal education and had his early career in his home country of Romania since he fled only in the 1960s as a result of Cold War-era anti-Semitism. Beyond a certain *Zeitgeist* and coming from middle-class, professional homes, there is little to suggest any specific likely homogeneity within the group in terms of career choices and directions. Hence this chapter examines their decisions to work for development agencies for some or all of their careers in terms of possible commonalities of personal disposition or ethical/moral and religious beliefs.

Shlomo Reutlinger

Shlomo left Israel for the USA in 1950, ten years after arriving in the then Palestine as a refugee, in order to see his parents for the first time since their traumatic parting at Köln (Cologne) railway station in 1939 (see Chapter 2). Initially he intended to remain in the USA for only a limited time to further his education and to work as the manager of agricultural training farms sponsored by the Jewish Agency, first in Guelph, Ontario in Canada and then in Jamesburg, New Jersey. This work eventually ended as air travel made it possible for young people intending to go to Israel to receive their training there.

Faced with an ultimatum to join the US Army, then still embroiled in the final phase of the Korean War, or leave the USA and be unable to return, he enlisted a month before the end of hostilities but spent two years in the army, during which time he completed his secondary education under the so-called GI Bill. This also enabled him to pursue his tertiary studies, starting with a year in Georgia while still in the army and then a year of night classes at Brooklyn College in New York City, before completing his undergraduate degree after two years at Cornell University. That was followed by an MSc and PhD (1963) at North Carolina State College, now part of the University of North Carolina.

His MSc dissertation constructed a simulation model for evaluating costs and benefits in a risky environment. Since his studies were funded by tobacco interests, he used this model to examine the profitability of tobacco irrigation in the context of expected annual rainfall variations. His doctoral thesis in economics and statistics, entitled *Techniques of Project Analysis under Uncertainty*, evaluated the specification of alternative supply models under differing assumptions about decision making under risk and uncertainty. He retained an abiding interest in this subject throughout his career, as reflected in many of his publications (interview, Shlomo Reutlinger[i]; pers. comm.[ii]).

Shlomo became a naturalised US citizen while serving in the army. He had left Israel on a temporary Israeli passport since he had been a British subject until the end of the Mandate period and Israeli independence in 1948 but the Law of Citizenship had not yet been enacted. He should have applied after that for full Israeli citizenship but was unaware of the need to do so. That initially created some uncertainty about his citizenship status when he started returning to Israel to visit his children and then to settle there again after retirement in the early 1990s. Hence he had to apply to visit and then immigrate as a US citizen rather than as a returning Israeli with dual nationality – a status he now has. He never wanted much to do with the German postwar restitution process and, like many escapees and survivors, 'wouldn't [have] dream[t] of' applying for a German passport (interview, Shlomo Reutlinger[iii]).

Since his doctoral research had been funded by the US Department of Agriculture (USDA), and he had actually been its employee for the final year, he decided to join them longer term after completing his thesis. He and his wife, Blossom, whom he had met and married in 1957 during his time at Cornell, and their daughter, Elana, and son, Ra'anon, born in North Carolina in 1960 and 1963 respectively, thus moved to Washington DC in mid-1963, where he began work on long-run agricultural projections.

Through the UN's Food and Agriculture Organization (FAO), he was given the opportunity in 1965 to undertake a year-long economic evaluation of a UNDP watershed project in Israel, and within three weeks he and his family relocated there. He enjoyed that work within an international team, which sharpened his sense of contrast with the parochialism of most of his colleagues at the USDA. He had also clashed with an administrator there about wanting to leave early on a Friday ahead of the Jewish Sabbath. The latter insisted that he take leave for that purpose despite often working overtime, so Reutlinger lodged a formal complaint about discrimination. After returning from Israel, he therefore resolved to leave the USDA and work permanently for an international agency. The appropriate job at the FAO would have entailed too much international travel for someone with two young children, so he moved to the economic research department of the World Bank in Washington in 1966, where he was much happier and would remain until his retirement 25 years later (interview, Shlomo Reutlinger[iv]).

He had considered remaining in Israel but opportunities were hard to come by and, aged 35, he was not yet well enough established in his field to break in. Many US-trained Israelis went to work for spells in the US in order to supplement their low salaries, so he decided to do it the other way around – live in the US and spend time in Israel regularly. They had a third child in 1967 but he sadly died of a brain tumour aged 14 (interview, Shlomo Reutlinger[v]).

Shlomo's World Bank career in its Economic Policy Research Department embraced several themes. Initially he examined ways of introducing uncertainty into cost–benefit analysis, work that culminated in the publication of World Bank Staff Occasional Paper 10, *Techniques for Project Appraisal under Uncertainty* (Reutlinger 1970).

While never specialising by country or sector, Shlomo participated in several of the Bank's project appraisal missions. These provided him with invaluable insights into the issues that needed to be addressed in policy research and the applicability of theories to development practice (pers. comm.[vi]). His first country mission was to Burundi on a coffee plantation rehabilitation project. This was instructive in learning things that theory had not taught him, including 'that people, even in the poorest countries, are very much concerned with the utility of free time ... [even though] the opportunity cost in countries in this situation is zero'. The coffee growers reported their most serious problem as being waiting in queues to have their coffee washed and processed, even though it might have been expected that they would be more concerned with yields that had fallen by half since independence. He also learned what lay behind the regular changes of government and had the experience of asking top government officials and ministers (who were not formally well educated at the time) serious questions, only to have Belgian advisors emerge from behind a closed door to provide the answer (interview, Shlomo Reutlinger[vii])!

Another project appraisal mission involved a request by the Indian government to finance a grain storage project. Seeing the multitude of hungry people in India and the preoccupation of officials with expensive silos of questionable value led Shlomo for the first time to question the excessive preoccupation with supply-side interventions in addressing the problem of hunger in the world.

On return from this mission, Shlomo developed simulation models for estimating the costs and benefits of storage solutions for stabilising the supply of food grains. Noting that trading food grains (i.e. stabilisation over space) is much more efficient than storing food grains (i.e. stabilisation over time) led him to question the prevailing focus on country self-sufficiency as the central concern with food security.[1] In a further development of his thinking and work, he turned away progressively from agriculture and global food supply issues to those concerned with malnutrition and income distribution (pers. comm.[viii]).

Though concerned primarily with the financing of development projects, the World Bank made it possible for Shlomo to pursue this new line of thinking about food deprivation at local and global scales. This occurred because Robert McNamara, the Bank's president at the time, coincidentally developed a personal interest in these issues, while a member of the board of the Brookings Institution. At a seminar there, he was challenged by the social anthropologist, Margaret Mead, to explain what the Bank was doing to address widespread malnutrition and child hunger. On returning to his office, McNamara asked officials to provide him with an answer and was dissatisfied with the simple equation supplied in the resulting letter drafted by the agriculture department for his signature, stating that increased food output was the solution:

> I got to see it [the letter] somehow and took note that the contents had absolutely no relevance to malnutrition in developing countries. It said that the World Bank is doing a few projects which help increase the availability of protein. However, that doesn't really make a difference to the people because the high-priced milk and meat thus produced will have no impact on the ability of the poor to consume these foods. So that's how we [the Bank] got into this whole area of research. (interview, Shlomo Reutlinger[ix]; modified in pers. comm.[x])

Together with Marcello Selowsky, Shlomo then prepared a lengthy report on *Malnutrition and Poverty: Magnitude and Policy Options* (Reutlinger and Selowsky 1976), in which they attempted for the first time to measure the extent of global and countrywide under-nutrition, combining aggregate food consumption and income distribution data.

---

[1] This issue remains controversial today on account of international staple food price variability over time, questions over the most appropriate spatial scale(s) for food security interventions, and issues of international market dependency and food sovereignty. For instance, under structural adjustment and other liberalisation policies imposed by the IFIs, countries have sometimes been forced to sell rather than store surpluses, only to have to purchase imports a year or two later at considerably higher prices.

Simultaneously, the Bank recruited Alan Berg from the Brookings Institution to develop country action programmes to reduce malnutrition. Shlomo also spend a lot of time with others to develop the first such project in Brazil (pers. comm.[xi]).

Later in his career, Shlomo shifted his attention almost exclusively from food production to consumption issues in the segment of the population which was prone to be undernourished (pers. comm.[xii]). This is where he regards his main contribution as having been. It took a considerable time for his ideas to become widely accepted within the Bank and one key way in which he made his mark was by challenging the neoliberal deregulatory ethos dominant in the Bank while Anne Krueger was Chief Economist. This orthodoxy held that the solution to agricultural stagnation and underperformance was simply to remove the inefficient protectionist measures and increase producer prices – the essence of structural adjustment policies. Production would then boom, thereby taking care of malnutrition. Shlomo countered that, while increasing agricultural output was good, it would not in itself address malnutrition, which needed other interventions.

He expanded his ideas in *Poverty and Hunger* (Reutlinger et al. 1986), his *magnum opus*, but Anne Krueger tried to block its publication as it was not consistent with her philosophy. By a curious coincidence, the senior vice-president at the time was **Ernie Stern**, who reviewed it and supported his arguments. Shlomo recalls that Robert McNamara, then president, also favoured publication, having been exposed to the issues when challenged by Margaret Mead as mentioned above. The Bank published *Poverty and Hunger* and it became one of the most influential publications, challenging not only the Bank but also other major international agencies, such as the FAO, to refocus their food policy recommendations and action programmes.

The later part of his career was concerned increasingly with food security and international funding to achieve it. In addition to *Poverty and Hunger*, he co-authored *International Finance for Food Security* (Huddleston et al. 1984), was a principal author of *Food Aid in Africa: An Agenda for the 1990s* (World Bank and WFP 1991) and his final published paper was on 'Foreign Aid in a Period of Democratization: The Case of Politically Autonomous Food Funds', in *World Development* (Hyden and Reutlinger 1992). Altogether, Shlomo wrote or co-wrote six books or technical reports and 25 chapters or journal articles, mostly published by the Bank and journals including *American Economic*

Bulletin, American Journal of Agricultural Economics, Food Policy, Food and Nutrition Bulletin and *World Development* between 1962 and 1992, shortly before he retired as senior economist.

In contrast to some of the older generation of escapees and survivors, for whom early networks and connections with others with that background proved vital in getting established and moving on, Shlomo did not find this at all. Although he knew several of the others, including **Paul Streeten**, whom he first met at a seminar while on a four-week stint in Oxford when the latter was still warden of Queen Elizabeth House, **Michael Cernea**, with whom he shared some professional interests at the Bank, and **Ernie Stern**, then senior vice-president of the Bank, they had no special bonds. Coincidentally, also, Shlomo's late wife, Blossom, had been at college with both Ernie and his wife Zena (interview, Shlomo Reutlinger[xiii]). Shlomo's response to my question of whether their common wartime background and comparable experiences formed a subject of discussion when they were together was simply 'Never!' (interview, Shlomo Reutlinger[xiv]).

In terms of key inspirations for his career track, Reutlinger is very clear that the combination of training on the Youth Aliyah programme after arriving in Palestine coupled with his years of kibbutz experience kindled and nurtured his interest in agricultural economics and also in development. In this key sense and distinctively among my study cohort, his grounding was deeply personal and stimulated by wanting to contribute to the development of his newly established kibbutz (on land purchased piecemeal by the Jewish National Fund from its various Arab/Palestinian owners), with its collectivist ethos, and new country:

> I worked in development, very much so. We started the kibbutz [Ein Hanatziv in the Beit Shean valley] in a desert-like climate. There was nothing there. Water was there ... flowing in a well, so that was alright, but very little rainfall. Difficult, difficult conditions for agriculture – today it's blooming but when we started there was really nothing there. And we had contact with some of the Bedouin around us ... I started to develop vegetable growing.

To this end, he was sent by Ein Hanatziv to spend a year at an established kibbutz, Beit Alfa, to gain experience in vegetable cultivation (interview, Shlomo Reutlinger[xv]).

Religious or ethical commitment did not play a role. Indeed, having reflected on my questions about motivation or attraction to his chosen field, he added the importance of language learning and the idea of moving around the world as inculcated with foresight by his parents with the injunction, 'You never know what you will need or where we're going to end up'. Already at that time they had family members who had emigrated to Belgium, Palestine and both South and North America. Accordingly, Shlomo was sent to a Berlitz school aged 12 or 13 to learn some English rather than more conventionally taking piano lessons (interview, Shlomo Reutlinger[xvi]).

Michael Cernea

Michael Cernea recalls vividly the euphoria he felt as a 14-year old after the end of World War II:

> [W]e were free after the war and this was when all the accumulated rage and hope and desire to be free once and for all ... came out, and this is when I started to be really concerned and engaged in a political movement ... I joined the Organisation of Socialist Youth [in 1945–46]. I very optimistically thought about changing Romanian society into a fair society. We had a good number of Jewish colleagues coming from our Jewish school and they all faced the same problem and these theoretical conclaves at 14 and 15 [years of age were] very serious and we decided [on] the solution to the so-called 'Jewish problem'. (interview, Michael Cernea[xvii])

Influenced by propaganda about how well the Jews in Russia were doing, including from visiting Jewish Russian officials and pro-socialist and Jewish books, the idea took hold 'that if we can solve the problem of transforming Romania into a socialist country, the ethnic issue of Jews would also be solved' (interview, Michael Cernea[xviii]). His Jewish circle was his primary reference point although they made common cause with non-Jews with similar views and vice versa. They did still sometimes encounter a legacy of anti-Semitism, which they hoped would gradually disappear but 'it took just a few years to see that it was not the case'.

The Romanian king was deposed in late 1947 and from 1948 the country engaged seriously with state socialism after the Communist Party usurped political power, espousing a non-ethnic ideological posture that reinforced the ideas of Michael and his circle, and focusing instead on class. In retrospect, Michael Cernea regards the immediate postwar period, 1945–50, as formative of his broader political and social awakening. On a whim in his final year of secondary school, Michael entered and won a competition to become a journalist and, filled with enthusiasm and ideas of social change, worked in that role from 1950 to 1953/54. He studied little but managed to pass his university entry examinations. He chose to study philosophy to learn about social philosophy, social change and political issues, because sociology was no longer an option. It had been abolished by the new Communist regime on the grounds that it was not a 'legitimate' science (i.e. was a bourgeois science) and that Marxism-Leninism provided everything that people needed to know about society. Hence the entire Romanian sociological tradition was discarded, its physical infrastructure in universities was dismantled and sociologists were imprisoned if prominent enough or forced to work in anonymous jobs as librarians or worse (interview, Michael Cernea[xix]).

Naturally he was not fully aware of all that at the time but completed his BA degree. Although Communist purges against the most prominent Jews in government and public life began in 1952, thus rapidly demonstrating the gulf between socialist rhetoric and practice and also the fallacy of his and others' postwar dreams, he was keen to do a PhD. He examined the nature of emergent socialist society and sought to address its contradictions. This proved challenging because the Soviet and Romanian ideologues allowed for no such possibility or admission; instead he had to rely on the much more open Chinese position on such matters, which he gleaned from a Chinese newspaper published in Russian – which by then he could speak and read fairly well (interview, Michael Cernea[xx]).

As Michael reflected in greater detail in a subsequent interview,

> There was no encouragement for a researcher to actually look empirically at the reality and study it and report. The truth came from theory rather [than] from the facts and you had to see the facts in light of the theories ... My training in philosophy is pretty broad. At some point, I learned German to be able to read Hegel's theory and the contradictions in the original in German [are] not that easy!
>
> But ... it was precisely that over-saturation with theory which ... fed my thirst for facts, for actually what is happening on the ground, for seeing how things truly work and where they articulate ... [T]hat pushed me towards ... sociology, both from Romanian tradition and from what I could lay my hands on about empirical sociology in Western Europe and the [United] States. (interview, Michael Cernea[xxi])

He completed and successfully defended his thesis in 1958 in the Faculty of Philosophy, by when the situation for Jews had become really bad; simply being Jewish made one a suspected opponent of the regime. Although he graduated in only the second cohort of philosophy PhDs and everyone was encouraged to become a member of the academic staff, it immediately became clear that he would not be offered a job. Rather than make the reason explicit, namely that by then quotas had been set for the maximum proportion of Jews and theirs was full, the university authorities invented a spurious excuse that two members of the same family could not both be employed there. His first wife, Stella, two years his junior, whom he had married when he finished his BA in philosophy (aged 23 and 21 respectively), had been employed as a teaching assistant on finishing her BA while he was a still a doctoral student. Instead he was sent to work as a journalist again (interview, Michael Cernea[xxii])

That was his second such experience. During his final year, he wrote an article that was accepted and published in the national journal in his field, the *Journal of Philosophical Research*. He was filled with pride at this achievement and delighted to see it in print in an advance copy shown to him by a friend in the Institute of Philosophy. Normally copies reached the sales kiosks two or three days later but this time it took eight days and when he bought himself a copy, 'my article is not there – the same issue, the same date – it cannot be!' He rushed back to his friend in the Institute who refused to tell him what had happened but confirmed that his article had been removed. He then went to see the Institute's Deputy Director, who had been his boss while working as a journalist. He told Michael the story only because they knew each other well and on condition that Michael would not reveal the source of the information as that would jeopardise his (the Deputy Director's) job. As required, an advance copy had been sent to the Central Committee section of Propagit, the state's propaganda and agitation organisation. A senior figure there had subsequently phoned the Institute to challenge the composition of the authors in that issue. Michael relates the core of the conversation thus:

> Propagit (P): [D]on't you think that the way you created that issue was not very balanced?
> Prof. Breazu (of the Institute) (PB): What do you mean?
> P: Well, simply what I say. It's not balanced. How can you publish such an issue?

PB: What is not balanced?
P: Well, if you don't understand that, I have nothing to tell you. Just look at your authors and you will see what is not balanced.

That was the guidance from the Central Committee to the academic leadership of the Institute, who did understand the message. Over half the authors were Jewish so they realised that they had to remove one. Since Michael was the youngest, his article was chosen. The whole issue had then to be repaginated and printed, causing the undue delay. The impact on Michael was crushing:

> Well, if you are at the end of your PhD studies and you get such a message ... it cannot be a more tangible indicator [of how things are], measure or blow. That was what happened. I understood. I had to find my [own] way. (interview, Michael Cernea[xxiii])

After a while, he managed to get employment as an assistant researcher in the Institute until he won a competitive application to become chair of the Institute's Department of Social Philosophy. Becoming something of a 'counter-ideologist', he initiated a return to *social* empirical questionnaire-based research – carefully nuanced against sociological branding – in the tradition that had not been possible since 1948. By the time of the Khrushchev thaw, the situation had relaxed enough for the results to be published in a book subtitled 'Sociological Research in Industrial Enterprise' in 1964. Despite the title, the topic – of the cultural profile of the working class – was in vogue so there was no adverse reaction to the way in which they connected political and moral consciousness; indeed, as senior author and editor, he even won a prize from the Romanian Academy. In it, Michael also provocatively posed the question of whether there was an economic consciousness too. Only years later in the West did he discover the whole literature on *Homo economicus* and the like (interview, Michael Cernea[xxiv]).

With the more relaxed atmosphere during the 1960s, when the Romanian government also deviated somewhat from the official Soviet line, American and other Western academics and foundation representatives began to visit Romania, initially on an exploratory basis. Michael's research group was rapidly singled out for its distinctive work and he was recommended to the Center for Advanced Studies in the Behavioural Sciences at Stanford University for a visiting fellowship. In 1968, two weeks after his wife had died suddenly of a brain haemorrhage, leaving him with two children, Dana (aged 12) and Andrei (aged 6), he received an exploratory letter from the Center asking whether he might be interested in going there. Given the circumstances, he ignored the letter for some months until, urged by friends, he responded positively. Seven months later, after they had undertaken background checks, he received an invitation, including fares for his family. Getting an exit visa was problematic and he was rejected the maximum number of three times; the final time by the dictator Ceausescu's wife in person, as she was in charge of anything to do with science. Eventually, through representations at the highest governmental level – after he had told the story to one of his previous American visitors whom he had met again at a conference in Bulgaria – he received a call from the head of the Academy telling him that his visa had been approved and he should go. He was forced to leave his children behind as de facto hostages, in line with practice at the time, and they were cared for by his mother (interview, Michael Cernea[xxv]).

At the Center on the Stanford campus, he had the luxury of the 1970/71 academic year to read and study without restriction, enabling him to catch up on sociology, research methodology and the like to broaden his perspective. On arrival there, he also had an astonishing experience. His hosts told him that they had a scholar there of Romanian origin who would like to meet him, whereupon a very imposing and self-assured woman approached, introduced herself as **Irma Adelman**, and they started talking. After some initial niceties, Michael was struck by some resonances so asked her,

MC: Excuse me, may I ask you one personal question?
IA: Yes.
MC: Is it possible that your name before marriage – your family name, maiden name – was Irma Glicman?, at which she blanched and looked bewitched.
IA: Yes … how do you know? How do you know?
MC: Really?! You are really Irma Glicman?
IA: Yes …
MC: I'm Musi Katz![2] Then she blanched again.
IA: What?! Musi?!

[2] Katz was his original family name but when he entered the journalism competition in 1948 he needed a less Jewish-sounding surname and Cernea was, he says, the first that came to mind (pers. comm.).

MC: Yes, Musi – we were friends – I have your picture riding on a wooden horse.

IA: I know. I have the same picture.

MC to me: So this is how I rediscovered Irma … I had no way to suspect that she is Irma Glicman, but she was talking and from Romania and I just realised all of a sudden – and this was 1970 and we had parted in '38, so 32 years earlier.

It caused a great stir at the Center since all of a sudden, this unknown quantity from Romania was well known to one of their faculty and thereby instantly cleared of uncertainty or suspicion as to whether he might have been of dubious credentials or a regime spy. Doors immediately then opened to him (interview, Michael Cernea[xxvi]).

Since both his children had perforce remained in Bucharest, he returned at the end of his fellowship in November 1971, as the year without their widowed father had been difficult for them. Had his daughter been able to join him in California, he would have been tempted to stay and seek exit visas for his son and mother. However, he told a few friends, including Alan Dershowitz, the Harvard law professor and activist for Soviet Jewry, of his desire to leave Romania and settle in the West. On his return from Stanford, life became hard again as he was accused publicly of bringing back imported bourgeois American ideas. Soon, however, the critiques became more muted since there was a growing awareness of his international connections and reputation. His prominent American friends invited him to the 1974 World Sociological Congress and the conference of the American Sociological Association. He was again omitted from the official Romanian delegation but obtained a visa on account of his personal invitation and the fact that he had returned after his Stanford visit. He left his children behind once more but while in the USA defected and gave the Romanian embassy an ultimatum to let his children and mother join him or else he would go public. After 18 months, the children were finally allowed to leave Romania and his mother followed some time later after a campaign (interview, Michael Cernea[xxvii]).

Michael's defection was made possible by a work visa and job offer from the World Bank, although he had never formally applied for a position there. Rather, the Bank had initially approached him when they were looking to appoint their first ever social scientist – probably a sociologist or anthropologist. Some of the people he knew or had met at Stanford, including **Irma Glicman-Adelman** and **Shlomo**

Reutlinger, had suggested his name and the Bank canvassed learned societies too; the European Society for Rural Sociology also put forward his name. The Bank created a file but as an unknown Romanian in Bucharest, he was not prioritised until alternatives fell away. Then they sent someone to Bucharest but the Ministry of Finance lied that he was away and uncontactable. In fact, he reached Michael by phone so the lie was exposed but not made public. A year later the Bank tried again, just when he was in Canada for the 1974 World Congress of Sociology (see above) and Leif Christoffersen flew up to interview him. He was impressed and invited Michael down to Washington to meet his colleagues; a visa was arranged immediately. He presented the same paper on the contradiction of the peasant family on collective farms that he had delivered in Canada, was interviewed and offered the job, which he accepted, starting soon thereafter. He had not envisaged that line of work – which required a substantial gear change – but becoming an academic at a non-elite university, perhaps in the Midwest, after reaching the USA (interview, Michael Cernea[xxviii]).

In view of the often controversial role of the World Bank, as well as his undoubted achievements over the years in promoting the social dimensions of development work, most notably almost singlehandedly establishing the importance of addressing resettlement *ab initio* as an integral part of major projects involving human displacement, his retrospective reflections on his new career track bear direct quotation:

> [W]ith that background then I ended up ... at the World Bank
> equipped with a much broader, in fact, [more] theoretical outlook
> than the job ... required. But that turned out to be the best for me,
> I believe, and perhaps for the institution because I conceived my job
> from the outset ... as an ambassador for the discipline in the sense that
> I had to prove that the discipline which I represented and embodied
> has a place in the articulation of intellectual resources necessary
> for doing what we called induced development – for conceiving
> programmes, development programmes, pro-active development
> programmes. In fact, designing blueprints for change.
> ...
> Now I also had (what I've now retroactively called) an idealistic
> view on what the Bank is and could do and a very enthusiastic belief
> that good knowledge and good theory can really help change reality.
> So I've acted on that belief and I really was convinced and argued that
> we need social science knowledge not simply to advise one project or

another, [but] to draw [up] programmes, to identify what needs to be done to develop a country or to make a broader change. So that was my argument, but interestingly enough it was accepted. I mean there were many bright people in the Bank – excellent colleagues – not in sociology; in economics (microeconomics, macroeconomics) who were open to the argument that the body of knowledge can play a complementary role.

...

We dealt in bigger ideas at that time and this is what ... made my integration possible at that time when the Bank was ... altogether open to some new ideas. Poverty was coming to the Bank – the concern ... because of McNamara ... – turning around the Bank from sheer infrastructure and transportation and roads to the social issues of poverty and overcoming poverty. So in that climate of openness to that, I believed I could integrate much easier than otherwise. (interview, Michael Cernea[xxix])

Indeed, in an earlier oral history interview for the Society for Applied Anthropology (Cernea and Freidenberg 2007: 348), Michael referred to the economic or economistic hegemony within the Bank and elsewhere when he arrived as 'econo-mythical', a term that neatly captures the way in which the so-called 'magic of the marketplace' became a mantra devoid of meaning on the ground. That provided the challenge which Michael took up in his mission to socialise the Bank. One of his most notable early public contributions in that endeavour was an edited volume, *Putting People First* (Cernea 1985). Based on a series of sectorally focused invited lectures at the Bank by prominent anthropologists, its significance for the Bank and applied anthropology in general is discussed at some length in Cernea and Freidenberg (2007: 342–4) (see also Bebbington 2006: 69).[3]

His other major milestones at the Bank and his underlying strategy are explored thoroughly in Cernea and Freidenberg (2007) so will not be repeated in detail here, save to point out that his ability to invite key external speakers to buttress or advance the arguments on which he was

---

[3] I pointed out that it has many resonances with the work of Robert Chambers being undertaken around the same time and published with similar titles (Chambers 1983; 1987); indeed, Chambers contributed to this book. In response, Michael assured me that they had been working independently and in parallel. The title of Cernea's book was borrowed a few years later by Bill Clinton for his 1992 US presidential election slogan (interview, Michael Cernea, 11/4/07 @ 26–29 mins).

campaigning internally at any given time was often crucial. There were many unexpected twists, perhaps most remarkably when in 1995 the newly arrived Bank President, James Wolfensohn, 'a Wall Street mega-banker parachuted by the White House', mentioned social justice in one of his first speeches. Michael buttonholed him at a welcoming reception shortly afterwards and expressed surprise at that, to which Wolfensohn, who was also Jewish, responded that he had been trying to explain the Jewish concept of 'mitzvah' and that social justice was the closest he could get. Much to Michael's surprise, Wolfensohn then admitted that nobody had mentioned in their introductory briefings that the Bank had a Senior Advisor on social matters. Wolfensohn became a strong supporter of the social dimensions of development and increased the number of social scientists employed. This eventually led to the creation of the Social Development Department (which Cernea had proposed unsuccessfully some years earlier) and then the Social Family – a network of social specialists straddling the regional and departmental boundaries (Cernea and Freidenberg 2007: 346–8; Bebbington 2006: 70).

Two other initiatives stand out: first, work after his formal retirement from the Bank as Senior Advisor in 1997, when he was called back to lead a study that would develop Bank policy on the preservation of cultural heritage, subsequently published as a short book, *Cultural History and Development: A Framework for Action* (Cernea 2002). Second, and in many respects the body of work for which he is most widely known and through which I first met him at a conference in South Africa in 1996 (Cernea 2001), was on resettlement of people displaced by development projects. His ideas evolved over many years and were formalised in the Impoverishment Risks and Reconstruction Model for Resettling Displaced Population (IRR), itself refined through successive versions. In essence, this was his flagship effort to ensure that displacement and its consequences were considered from the outset in project planning and then right through the Bank's project cycle, with the objective of ensuring that displacees were not impoverished in the process. Indeed, appropriate and consultative processes of resettlement, training and other interventions to help them cope and rebuild their lives and livelihoods in their new homes and environment should ensure that they are no worse off afterwards (Cernea 1986; 1988; 1997; 2001; Cernea and McDowell 2000).

The approach – spawned of extensive and persistent criticism of the human costs of large-scale Bank-funded projects involving forced resettlement (see **Ernie Stern** below) – has been widely taken up around the world by other agencies and in university curricula (Cernea and Freidenberg 2007: 349–50; Bebbington 2006: 71; interview, Michael Cernea[xxx]). A related volume (Cernea and Guggenheim 1993) distinctively focused on the experience of refugees and those subject to resettlement as a counterpoint to the agency- or government-centric view of the project cycle and mitigation efforts for resettlees.

Since formal retirement, Michael has remained active as a consultant and author, with affiliations to George Washington University and at the Brookings Institution and serving on the board of the Library of Alexandria. While a member of the Science Council of the Consultative Group for International Agricultural Research (CGIAR) from 1998, he also convened a conference in 2002 and edited the ensuing volume focusing on the 'culture in agriculture' as a corrective to the dominance of economic and technical perspectives that pervaded much agricultural development research within the CGIAR and beyond (Cernea and Kassam 2006; see also Cernea and Freidenberg 2007: 351–2). His most recent edited book is an in-depth challenge to one of the longstanding fallacies in resettlement debates, namely that adequate compensation alone can avoid or mitigate impoverishment (Cernea and Mathur 2008).

His achievements have been widely recognised, perhaps most notably by his election to the Academia Română, the award of the 1988 Solon T. Kimball Prize for Public and Applied Anthropology of the American Anthropological Association and the 1995 Bronislaw Malinowski Award of the Society for Applied Anthropology. The lecture he delivered on accepting the last-mentioned was published by the World Bank (Cernea 1996).

To conclude our interview, I returned to the central theme underlying this book in order for him to reflect on it in the light of our extended discussions about his own life and career against the backcloth of two sets of such traumatic experiences:

DS: Do you think it is significant that such a ... disproportionately large group of people of Jewish origin have become involved in this field of development somehow, given your own experience and the issues we've talked about?

MC: Well frankly I don't think [of] myself as so exceptional that my case is unique. I believe that more or less the same circumstances will produce the same result so there are many other people who experienced the same type of oppression, the same type of risk and threats to their life and their condition – and worse even – ... that you don't forget ... for the rest of your life. And it ... breeds in you the need to react ... to not simply receive the punches but to return, and this is what, in my case, moved me to ... be interested in change, in social change, in modifying those old mattresses and probably that happens all over; this is why I believe it's a syndrome.

DS: [D]o you think there's anything inherent in Judaism or the Judeo-Christian philosophy that we were just talking about or the Central-Northern European cultural realm that disproportionately or somehow drives people to be concerned with these ethical and moral questions?

MC: Yes ... because *tikkun olam* (healing the world) translates so clearly and is spelled out as a commandment, this is not to be ... underestimated simply because so many people refer to it and it has almost become a ... truism to refer to it – truism but true! The true part of truism is very important. That is a fundamental value articulated as a concept. A child of 13 years who now becomes accepted in the community in the course of his Bar Mitzvah knows what *tikkun olam* is and speaks at 13, in conditions where his childhood is happy and his prospects are unthreatened, and still gets that idea that he has the duty to contribute to *tikkun olam* as part of his Jewish education. So this is a permanent value and this is a permanence in Judaism, I'd say. Another thing I remember from my father as part of what he told me ... in Hebrew which was a famous biblical saying or ... injunction: '*Shlach lechemecha al pnei hamayim*', meaning cast your bread on the face of the water; it will reach ... a hungry person – so do good even if you don't have an immediate target simply for the goodness of doing good and the hope that your good will serve somebody. I always remember that my father taught me that and he explained that to me and inculcated that into me.

DS: What a wonderful way to end off this philosophical discussion, but ... underpinning what you just said is, of course, also the balance between rights and duties or obligations, both within Judaism and more generally as a philosophical foundation. And sometimes one of the things I find missing today is that sense of balance. The emphasis all too often is on people's rights and expectations and not enough on the balancing or the countervailing duties and obligations. And it would bring us back, if we choose to go that way, to the discussion yesterday about post-structuralism or rights-based approaches to development and various other agendas which I don't propose to go into now.

MC: But you're right; in development that comes up in various ways and, of course, development has reached connectivities which are not only impoverished (economically) ... but are also deprived of power, political power. When you are both economically poor and power-poor you are much [more easily] a victim of human rights transgression than if you are not poor and if you have political power, so this is why the development enterprise – induced development – very often comes in[to] contact with issues of human rights and you have to sustain the idea of human rights. There is a tension between development and human rights because some people [push] the human rights argument too much and omit or underestimate the development of argument for people's improvement.

But one point where this [becomes] a conflict issue in development theory and in practice is the issue of dependency, when you have to emphasise both the rights of the community, which is poor, but also the duties of the community and there are often perverse incentives which push communities to demand rights and to not meet obligations and to perversely enjoy the fruits of dependency rather than assume the responsibility of independence ... I have to say, [that] I'm not happy about [this] either. (interview, Michael Cernea[xxxi])

Ernie Stern

After repatriation to Amsterdam, Ernie (aged 12) enrolled in the Jewish High School that had already been (re-)established, and his family resumed a relatively normal life. The synagogues had also been reopened after whatever repair was necessary. Their former synagogue didn't appear to have been damaged. But all their contents had been confiscated or looted, apart from some of the Jewish ceremonial silverware that had been saved for them by Christian friends. Despite having thus picked up the pieces of their lives relatively well, Ernie's father became convinced that his children would be better off outside Europe. Nevertheless, being indecisive – as Ernie described in Chapter 4 – he opted against emigration *en famile* and sent Ernie as an 'advance party' to New York in 1947 to stay with his brother (Ernie's uncle) there. His parents and brothers followed a year later and the family settled in Queens (interview, Ernie Stern[xxxii]).

Adapting to New York life was easier for Ernie's father because he continued working for the same international firm (Lissauer and Co.) as in Frankfurt and then Amsterdam. Many of the employees were of similar Germanic and predominantly Jewish backgrounds, some indeed even his former colleagues, so his work environment, at least, was to some extent familiar. Commuting from Queens to work in Manhattan's Lower East Side was, of course, very different from the quietness of Amsterdam. Ernie's mother never learnt good English, which contributed to her isolation. Overall, his parents were not very outgoing and, like many in similar situations, they tended to associate with fellow Germanic refugees and immigrants. In terms of religious observance, the family continued to observe *kashrut* and to attend a local synagogue. Services were an Americanised version of East European traditions, and eventually most of the German component of the community broke away to establish their own synagogue. His family followed a year later, in part because the new synagogue was closer to their home (interview, Ernie Stern[xxxiii]).

On arrival in New York City, Ernie enrolled in the second year of high school and completed his secondary education there before taking his undergraduate degree at Queens College. He then moved to Boston to pursue postgraduate studies at the Fletcher School at Tufts University. The eminent economist, Charles Kindleberger, became his PhD advisor, with whom Ernie described his relationship as one of 'upbringing' rather than 'camp [follower]'. After completing his coursework, he opted to leave university in favour of paid employment, although he did later complete the PhD and graduate. Having passed the civil service entry examination, he joined the Commerce Department in Washington, DC. He also married his girlfriend Zena, the daughter of prewar immigrants. They had met at Queens College [where **Shlomo Reutlinger**'s late wife, Blossom, was also a student – see above]: 'Well, she sat in front of me in English class and there was an assignment to write a critique … of a play, and a good European doesn't go to a play alone and that's how it started!' (interview, Ernie Stern[xxxiv]).

The night they bought the first piece of furniture for their new apartment, he received his military draft papers but that month's quota was full when he went to enrol, and he managed to find a local military police reserve unit in Washington after six months' basic training and some initial assignments at Fort Knox, Kentucky in 1958. As the only literate English-speaking member with arithmetic skills, he was made the company clerk, later being reassigned to a unit attached to the Pentagon. This involved little beyond a compulsory summer training camp but there was not much to do there. Ernie related with amusement how he and the one other Dutch speaker were told to go into the forest and interrogate each other! However, the sequel would have major implications for his career track:

> After a while they decided they wouldn't need Dutch interpreters for any likely invasion of Holland and they told me to learn another language. By sheer coincidence, in the language lab I picked up a Turkish tape and started to listen to Turkish. At the same time, I'd decided that the Commerce Department really wasn't where I wanted to spend my life and one day I walked past the building where the US aid agency (then called ICA [International Cooperation Agency], later USAID) was located and on the spur of the moment I went in and applied. I was accepted and, lo and behold, I was assigned to the Turkey desk. That was the start of my career in development – purely coincidental. (interview, Ernie Stern[xxxv])

Even after further discussion, Ernie insisted on this having been entirely coincidental, as were two key subsequent events some years later (see below). After training, he served in Turkey for four and a half years at a fascinating period in that country's development. The US government established the Peace Corps and all ICA missions were asked to submit proposals for deploying them; Ernie was given this task for Turkey. Since his wife was a speech pathologist who had worked in Washington linked to a contract with ICA to provide English training to Turks going to study in the USA and he had become aware of the importance of language training, he proposed recruiting Peace Corps volunteers able to teach English and prepare Turks for employment in Turkey. By chance, Hollis Chenery, then either the Chief Economist or Director of the ICA, visited at just that time and was taken with the idea. The two of them also 'hit it off' and developed a good rapport thereafter, according to Ernie. This was to prove crucial when Ernie eventually left USAID in 1972, where, after spells in India, Pakistan and again in Washington, he had risen to become Assistant Administrator (i.e. the second in command), in order 'to find a refuge at the World Bank from the Nixon White House!' By then Chenery was Vice-

President for Economics at the Bank and found Ernie a position to organise its research efforts (interview, Ernie Stern[xxxvi]).

After a year in that role, Robert McNamara, then the Bank's president (also cited above by **Reutlinger** and **Cernea**) and with whom Ernie also got on well, asked him to lead the production of a high-level policy report informed by research in order to enhance the Bank's credentials and lead wider public debate about development worldwide:

> So I ceased being Vice-President for South Asia and assembled a small team of outstanding Bank economists, including Martin Wolf and others who later became luminaries. We started work in March and were told it had to be completed in time to be issued for the Annual Meeting of the World Bank in September. So we had about six months. The first report was slim but it was the beginning of the *World Development Report*. The subsequent reports grew both in volume and sophistication.[4] The teams assigned to them grew from our staff of 6 to 15–20 people and preparation time expanded to a year or more, [to] include analysis of specific subjects which generally heralded new initiatives by the Bank in that sector. (interview, Ernie Stern[xxxvii])

Thus was born one of the most prominent, longstanding – and often controversial – series of development reports in the international arena, led by a German-Dutch-American Holocaust concentration camp survivor with economics training and field experience in Turkey and South Asia. He was not involved in subsequent reports, as his reward was to be made Vice-President and later Senior Vice-President for Operations, in which capacity he served McNamara and Tom Clausen but, as a non-Republican, fell foul of Barber Conable, who tried hard to get rid of him. Following a reorganisation of the Bank and its leadership team, however, he became Vice-President for Finance in 1987 and then helped persuade Lewis Preston, whom he had got to know as an investment banker from bond issues, to join the Bank as president. Preston reorganised the Bank again and Ernie became one of the three managing directors[5] until he left to pursue a long-desired

---

[4] See Mawdsley and Rigg (2002; 2003) for critical assessments of the thematic and ideological coverage of the entire *World Development Report* series from inception until the new millennium.

[5] A newspaper profile in 1993 suggested that this reorganisation had been in part to reduce Ernie's power as Senior Vice-President but that he soon reasserted it in the new arrangement – becoming what Bank insiders apparently dubbed the one wheel on the tricycle [of managing directors] running the show (Thomson 1993).

change of career by joining JP Morgan in 1995, shortly after James Wolfensohn had become president. He had delayed his departure during Preston's illness to maintain continuity and ensure a smooth transition. Apart from serving on the board of the Washington-based Center for Global Development, Ernie ceased his direct engagement in development work, although his role at JP Morgan and later at the Rohatyn Group centred on emerging markets and he travelled widely to many of those countries. However, he did keep track of what was happening in the development world through those travels, from other sources and through his one brother, who worked in development (interview, Ernie Stern[xxxviii]).

Given the importance of this period in the Bank's history and that institution's global reach in development debate and policy, I asked Ernie to reflect on (1) working there under McNamara, (2) the evolution of thinking and policy within the Bank and then (3) on his own role:

1   Well I thought the Bank was a great organisation. Bob, like all great men had his peculiarities, but I considered him a great manager of people, very ideas-oriented, very driven, very results-oriented, and always open to new ideas. And I experienced him as very open-minded. You could tell him that he was wrong and, if you knew the subject matter, he listened. He was happy to discuss issues – he certainly did not have a closed mind. It didn't necessarily change anything, but then those who had objections weren't necessarily right either. He was very imaginative and a creative thinker. For whatever reason, whether because of the Vietnam experience or his basic philosophy, he was very much concerned about poverty and conditions in the developing countries. He transformed the Bank, a very timely overhaul, and created the Bank as it was known in its heyday. (interview, Ernie Stern[xxxix])

2   Well, the definition of economic development changed over time from a focus on the capital/output ratio to poverty alleviation, population growth and family planning, development of domestic institutions, education, sound fiscal and monetary policies and the many elements central to increasing growth and improving productivity. But even today, the focus on financial transfers remains strong in some quarters. While finance obviously can be, and often is, a constraint, I tended to be more interested in the

implementation of changes in basic agricultural practices, basic local health care, access to credit, etc. And indeed we have seen with the technological revolution that there is a great deal of latent entrepreneurial ability, even among the poor, which can be activated with rather simple improvements.

And McNamara was conscious of that, but without de-emphasising the need for increased development financing. He was the first one to tackle health and family planning; he also emphasised the importance of agriculture at the local level, and education. I was very supportive of this since to me, having served abroad for 10 years, it was clear that while infrastructure was essential, its basic benefit was the support of growth in the productive sectors. To be sure, domestic savings in many countries did not suffice to support rapid growth, but equally important, the ability to utilise capital efficiently was hampered by bureaucracy, poor implementation capacity, and excessive government regulations and large but inefficient state enterprises. These were gradually accepted as being the central constraints to growth.

DS: But that wasn't obvious to everybody. I guess what I'm asking is did you see yourself as being in the forefront of the broadening out?

ES: Well I don't know that I'd consider myself at the 'forefront' but I certainly saw the broadening out of the Bank's areas of activity, and indeed the expanded approach to what development involved as central. I totally supported it because it seemed pretty obvious.

...

And to move beyond the emphasis on infrastructure and large-scale projects really did seem a fairly necessary change. So, I thought what Bob was doing was great. He started with health, then moved on to population. I was the first one in the World Bank who authorised procurement of condoms – to a country in East Asia. The concept created a fair amount of unhappiness from my Congressional colleagues, which was understandable. (interview, Ernie Stern[xl])

3   I'm not much of a philosopher; I tend to the pragmatic, concrete side. So, of course, you can wait until everybody has a decent income and eventually they will have fewer children. But this is a slow and multigenerational process. Moreover, it is not applicable

in all cultures. Both need to happen. And in the early days you provide incentives, such as better healthcare, so that the children that are born have a better chance of surviving. That too helps to reduce the desire for a large number of children. You provide condoms and you teach people about the importance of family planning. One of the problems with the early theories was that they were unicultural and based on the experience of the industrial countries. (interview, Ernie Stern[xli])

Since Ernie never published research or reflective pieces in academic, World Bank or media outlets and very rarely gave interviews, there is no authored literature from which to glean other insights into his thinking. One rare exception is his somewhat conciliatory yet robust defence of the Bank's environmental record in a video interview by Bob Geldof for the 1989 television series, *The Price of Progress*. These films constituted a sustained critique of Bank lending for the Trans-Amazonian Highway, large-scale hydropower dams on India's Narmada River and Indonesia's *transmigration* programme, all mega-projects involving forced resettlement (Geldof and Claxton 1989). Indeed, such sustained critique contributed in no small part to the importance attached to **Michael Cernea**'s work on resettlement policies from the mid-1980s onwards, as discussed earlier in this chapter.

We also gain insightful glimpses into Ernie's personality and of how he was perceived by some of his World Bank colleagues in a newspaper profile published in mid-1993 amid rumours that he would soon move to the European Bank for Reconstruction and Development. Terms like 'born to be a civil servant', 'low key is for him a way of life' abound and '[h]e has a civil service mandarin's obsession with operating quietly behind closed doors without publicity or fuss'. Even his physique and appearance were unexceptional but smart. Despite being described as gregarious, he kept his private life very private. Nevertheless, staff regarded him with a mixture of awe, respect and terror, reflecting his professionalism and efficiency for always having read all the documents for meetings, knowing exactly what was going on in that most complex of organisations, and of being ruthless with people who were not adequately prepared or could not keep up with him in meetings. This last, in particular, was widely resented by those at the receiving end. Overall, though, one former director is quoted as saying that 'Stern is an extraordinarily able man – one of the ablest I have ever met. He has a first-class intellect. He is a tough, even ruthless, arguer, which means that he almost always gets his way'. His genuine belief in development banking and desire to improve the world were also referred to (Thomson 1993).

In concluding my interview, we revisited my research question about the possible connections between his upbringing, socialisation and wartime experience and his move into a career in development. He said that he had puzzled over it since I initially contacted him to arrange the interview in case there had been some link that he himself had never suspected, but he remained sure that it was essentially coincidental – the Turkish language link and a sense of curiosity to live overseas and explore new horizons. He certainly felt well adjusted in the USA, not an alien, so there was no push in that respect, and also no discernible religiously inspired or ethical motive (interview, Ernie Stern[xlii]).

This was actually a very frank discussion, the more because his reputation for privacy and self-effacement – as mentioned above – was such that I had been warned in advance that my chances of getting an interview, let alone drawing him out, were slim. It was certainly one of the more challenging interviews I conducted for this project, in which I had to work hard to overcome his reticence and keep the conversation flowing. However, the issue clearly caught his attention and the similarities of our family backgrounds in the Holocaust facilitated the relaxed interaction in his own home that was essential. It became clear that he had neither considered some aspects of what we covered nor shared some of his personal history and reflections with anyone beyond his immediate circle before. Moreover, he answered my subsequent follow-up questions, including providing specific additional details, and took great care in checking and editing the interview transcript.

John Friedmann

Having chosen 'to look forward' as a planner rather than 'backwards in time' like his historian father, John Friedmann began his graduate work at the University of Chicago in the interdisciplinary Graduate Program in Education and Research in Planning in 1949. He obtained both his MA and PhD in planning, economics and geography in 1955, the latter supervised by Harvey Perloff and based on material collected while working as an industrial economist at the Tennessee Valley Authority from 1952 to 1954. Earlier, he had found Harvey Perloff's seminar on economic and social development in poor countries 'an eye opener' and teacher and student remained friends and collaborators – including decades later in Los Angeles (see below) – until the former's untimely death (Friedmann 2002: 122; 2014).

It was during this period that development studies emerged at the University of Chicago as a nascent focus of academic interest. Bertram F. Hoselitz (1913–95), an economic historian originally from Vienna and who – like Schumpeter and many others at the time – had studied law as far as Friedmann recalls (interview, John Friedmann[xliii]; Friedmann 2002: 152; 2014),[6] was a member of the Economics Department and founded *Economic Development and Cultural Change* (*ED&CC*) in 1952. This was possibly the first journal in the field and still thrives today. People like Friedmann, with an interest in economics, geography and sociology, were attracted to this emerging area because, as the journal's title suggests, its scope was broader than simply neo-classical economics, being concerned with various dimensions of socio-economic development.

In two retrospective autobiographical texts, an extended book chapter on 'Life as a Planner' and an invited public lecture in Vienna in February 2012, Friedmann (2002; 2014) reflected on 'Austrians-in-the-world' who, as émigrés or refugees, had become internationally known philosophers and social scientists and who influenced his own thinking, in several cases while studying in Chicago. Three of them were economists, including Hoselitz and also Joseph Schumpeter. Along with many others (including **Hans Singer**), Friedmann regards the latter as probably the originator of the term 'development economics' in the 1920s by virtue of his key books emphasising the role of entrepreneurship in development.[7] Hoselitz's influence on Friedmann stems from *ED&CC*: early issues on the role of cities in economic development triggered his abiding interest in the topic. This commenced with his doctoral dissertation on *The Spatial Structure of Economic Development in Tennessee Valley* (see above), followed by work

---

[6] My extensive efforts to trace a biography or any meaningful biographical details have been unsuccessful, so his family and religious background and migration history remain obscure. It is possible that he would have been eligible for inclusion in this study. Indeed, a recently added Wikipedia biography suggests that he should indeed have been included (https://en.wikipedia.org/wiki/Bert_F._Hoselitz).

[7] By contrast, Michael Lipton and others regard Rosenstein-Rodan as the originator of development economics for his work in the 1940s on industrialisation in Southern Europe (see Chapter 1).

on growth pole theory and then core–periphery structure. Thereafter he engaged professionally and academically with 'agropolitan' development over a considerable period in several parts of Latin America, East Asia and southern Africa, culminating years later in the world city hypothesis (Friedmann and Wolff 1982; Friedmann 1986; 2002; 2014: 14) – the work for which he is possibly most widely known beyond urban planning circles.

To the sociologist Karl Mannheim, Friedmann owes the insights 'that planning [can] be thought of as an intellectual pursuit in its own right, that it [is] more than merely a profession but a whole new perspective on social life', … 'that good planning [is] a pre-condition for a democratic life; and that the national state [can] and should intervene in the market for the benefit of society as a whole' (Friedmann 2014: 13). These statements grew out of John's 14-year early career in development planning, which he termed his *Wanderjahre* (years of wandering apprenticeship) during which he combined and/or alternated between roles in development agencies and academia in several countries. Punctuated by a four-year spell as associate professor in the Department of City and Regional Planning at the Massachusetts Institute of Technology (1961–65), he served successively as regional planning advisor and visiting professor at the Brazilian School of Public Administration in Rio de Janeiro and Federal University of Bahia, Brazil (funded by USAID) from 1955 to 1958; as head of the Economic Development Section of the United States Operations Mission in Korea (USAID) from 1958 to 1961; as professor in the Interdisciplinary Center for Urban Development, Catholic University of Chile from 1966 to 1969; and director of the Ford Foundation's Urban and Regional Development Advisory Program in Chile from 1965 to 1969.

During this period, he also published his first major book – on a national policy for regional development in Venezuela (Friedmann 1966) – based on work done while at MIT. In addition to a landmark book (Friedmann and Weaver 1979), several innovative and, in his own words, 'provocative' (Friedmann 2002: 133) papers also appeared about rethinking the nature of institutionalised planning, especially on the need for a very different and more actively engaged and transformative approach to planning (*ibid.*: 134) – work that would continue to occupy him over the next couple of decades.

From 1969 until his formal retirement in 1996, John Friedmann worked at the University of California at Los Angeles, having been recruited by Harvey Perloff to head and build up a new Urban Planning Program. This rapidly became a leading centre of progressive and innovative planning. Although he continued to work collaboratively with colleagues across the world and to undertake occasional consultancies such as for the United Nations Center for Regional Development (UNCRD) in Nagoya, he would not again live in the global South or be engaged directly in development practice. He wrote prolifically, however, and became increasingly critical of mainstream and conventional planning and development mantras, from growth poles to urban-biased development. For this he often attracted much criticism for apparently being anti-development and even anti-urban, which was not the case. Consultancy invitations declined markedly as a result, just as his own willingness to serve the interests of government power faded (Friedmann 2002: 139, 152).

Since Friedmann's (*ibid.*) autobiographical essay provides extensive coverage and evaluation of this period, the evolution of his thinking, his various published outputs and reactions to them, repetition of the details here is unnecessary. He reflects, among other things, on the good fortune of missing or catching the crest of breaking waves of new ideas or innovations, both of which he experienced at different times. The latter is exemplified by the world city hypothesis – 'an idea waiting to be born' (*ibid.*: 145) – and the former by the *Good Society* (Friedmann 1979), which held great personal importance to him as the philosophical and ethical basis for his future work but never attracted the same level of attention as some of his other outputs (Friedmann 2002: 142–3). This reflexive autobiographical chapter is augmented by Gaile's subsequent (2006) biographical essay, for which Friedmann provided information. Most recently, Friedmann's (2017) final autobiographical essay surveys his career and outputs, such as the challenges of writing his (1987) history of planning in the public domain, regarded by many as his *magnum opus*, and he reiterates the intensely political nature of planning. It is also more revealing than previous writings about his personal lifecourse and its influence on his thinking – ideas explored in depth during my interview with him in 2006.

Further important insights into Friedmann's *Weltanschauung* and belief in the commitment to social improvement underpinning urban planning are revealed in his trenchant critique of Manuel Castells' work on *The Information Age* (Castells 1998). Commencing the article with an open letter to Castells, Friedmann (2000: 460–1) reminds him that social science and planning are not value free and that it is impossible to 'draw a line between the authorial self and those whom you call social actors', before reprising the abiding beliefs in improved land use and quality of life that underlie the major traditions in urban planning. Mirroring the title of his earlier book, *The Good Society* (Friedmann 1979), he called this critique 'The good city: in defense of utopian thinking' (Friedmann 2000).

To me, perhaps the most eloquent and timely of his books was *Empowerment* (Friedmann 1992), a relatively short but powerful elucidation of his vision and theory for an alternative development. At its heart is the need to redress embedded inequalities in order to reduce tensions and promote more equitable development in any society. Access to knowledge, as the basis for accumulating social power, was crucial for an escape from widespread structural poverty. Although he refers to this book as a return to development studies (Friedmann 2002: 148–9), it also demonstrates a long pedigree that arises out of his earlier critiques of conventional planning and engagement with mutual learning among different stakeholders. Trained planners were one such category of stakeholder but who should be working in the service of the poor rather than with pseudo-objectivity in defence of existing power relations at all spatial scales – as evident, for instance, in the previous paragraph. Friedmann actually came to social empowerment through Karl Polanyi's focus on people's livelihoods in the household economy as a universal social institution, and the fundamental distinction 'between production of use values in the moral economy and the production of exchange values in the money economy' (Friedmann 2014: 21).

Overall, John Friedmann was distinctive in having worked on a sustained basis in different world regions, North and South, and in successfully avoiding the de facto ghettoisation of his work and its reception. Moreover, he always innovated theoretically and practically in diverse work on space, society and economy, remaining alert to new ideas and being willing to abandon once-cherished precepts if he felt them no longer valid or helpful (see e.g. Friedmann 2002: 138, 144; 2017; Gaile 2006: 104). Perhaps because of their relevance to my own work and reflection, his outputs have stimulated and inspired me since my first encounters with them during my doctoral studies.

Reflecting on his abandonment of consultancies for governments in favour of fulltime academia, Friedmann had come to regard planning as too much subject to the predilections of power and yet he could also not ignore the contradictions inherent in radical action with and for civil society that becoming a radical planner would have required.[8] Academic life thus enabled him greater freedom to express his views regardless of political considerations, while gaining satisfaction from the success of his students (Friedmann 2002: 152). During my interview, he elaborated frankly in relation to the value of the insights one obtains from working with different people in diverse contexts:

> Oh yes, I miss actually not being out there engaged in development, for want of a better word, but I don't [do it], so that makes a difference in terms of what I write. I never did much ... positivist research ... I believe in empirical research but am not very good at it, so [mainly] I rely on the research of other people as a basis for my own work. [It is] much more efficient for me to do that and at the same time to live through [the process] ... in countries that are in development of some sort, or undergoing change, as I did in Latin America. (interview, John Friedmann[xliv])

John Friedmann, widely regarded as the 'father' not just of the Urban Planning Department at the UCLA but of the discipline as a whole, remained healthy and intellectually active until taken ill a few days prior to his death at the age of 91 on 11 June 2017 (Paul 2017; Simon 2017).

In terms of the research questions underpinning this study, it is clear from this account, his autobiographical writings and my interview that his Viennese and Central European upbringing, the experience of becoming a refugee from the Nazis as a teenager and his subsequent engagement with European and Austrian philosophy and social science imbued him profoundly with his political consciousness and moral and ethical approach to development planning (see also Chapters 2 and 4). This concern with making the world a better place is shared by the members of this cohort as well as the older generation, regardless of their specific religious background, beliefs and practices.

Gerry Helleiner

Having arrived in Toronto as a small boy in a refugee family of mixed religious background – his mother was half-Jewish and his

---

[8]   See Friedmann (1987) and Douglass and Friedmann (1998) for elaborations of his view of radical planning.

father Catholic – but very largely secular in terms of observance (see above and Chapter 2), Gerry Helleiner had little religious upbringing apart from a short period of attendance at a Catholic Sunday School. Indeed, the first visit to a synagogue that he remembers was in 2004 to attend a very moving meeting of Holocaust survivors who had been compensated by the Austrian Fund.

He recalls the atmosphere in the poor area where they lived initially as very unwelcoming to immigrants; on one occasion, he and his brothers were chased home by the local bully with taunts about being 'bloody foreigners' who should go back where they came from. Consequently and also fearing further anti-Semitic or anti-German attention, his parents went to great lengths to avoid drawing attention to the family and the children were told repeatedly not to speak German in public. On one occasion, aged four or five, he drew a swastika on the pavement in front of their house without knowing what it was, causing his parents 'absolute consternation and panic', with stern follow-up for him. He assimilated rapidly, quickly losing his ease of speaking German, although it was spoken at home, especially in the years following their arrival. Indeed, he probably irritated his parents by his Canadianness. He did study German at secondary school but has never written or lectured in German, even when delivering invited lectures in Vienna or Germany, which he considers well beyond his ability. His parents considered returning to Vienna in the early 1950s but resolved to remain in Canada, where they considered their children's futures to be brighter (interview, Gerry Helleiner[xlv]; UNIHP 2007: Helleiner: 2–5; pers. comm.[xlvi]).

His career in economics came about as a result of reading a couple of books on the subject at his father's recommendation, which he found exciting. His school careers' advisor recommended accountancy so, on the strength of these stimuli and his father's encouragement (he was a political economy professor at the University of Toronto), he initially enrolled in the commerce and finance programme at the university[9] but disliked the accountancy, in particular, and switched to political science and economics after his first year. However, his real inspiration came during his summer job at the Federal Department of Labour's Economics Research Branch in Ottawa between his third

---

[9] Because of the valuable fringe benefit providing children of faculty with fee waivers (UNIHP 2007: Helleiner: 7).

and fourth undergraduate years, which he found 'wildly exciting'. In particular, he was inspired by his assigned project to try to understand the employment implications of federal expenditure on different kinds of construction project, and by discussions with older economists in the Branch. This 'gave me my head' and set him on his career path, which led towards development economics (interview, Gerry Helleiner[xlvii]; see also UNIHP 2007: Helleiner: 7–8).

Apart from the element of serendipity referred to above, he is able to relate his professional direction at least partially to 'a moral compass of some kind':

> I had a conscience and had always been interested in work relating to poverty and 'sort of Left' politics, and it really came from that. In the last two or three years of secondary school, I read more and more … and went to meetings and … had a Left political view of things and wanted to be more active … The particulars of development in Africa were probably influenced by some friends who were on study tours in Africa (while) in university … and they brought back stories and slides and in my final year of university I was active on this front in [the] student council. (interview, Gerry Helleiner[xlviii])

He graduated in 1958 and won a Woodrow Wilson fellowship to Yale, where he didn't particularly choose development courses because the main one had a poor reputation. However, the chair of the department, Lloyd Reynolds, was then launching the Economic Growth Center (EGC), a major new initiative in development economics, with funding from the Ford Foundation. This stimulated interest and discussion among the student cohort, many of whom, like Helleiner, were to become internationally renowned in development, including Richard Jolly, Don Mead, Don Snodgrass, T.N. Srinivasan and Dharam Ghai (interview, Gerry Helleiner[xlix]; UNIHP 2007: Helleiner: 12, 25; pers. comm.[l]).

In a short memoir, 'Intellectual Currents' (Helleiner n.d.: 1–2; see also UNIHP 2007: Helleiner: 12), he relates:

> In graduate school the only research essay I did on a development topic was one that argued – before Ted Schultz's paper in the *American Economic Review* made it conventional – that education and health expenditures, particularly the former, could be considered as investment rather than consumption. I mainly relied upon Indian data and sources. And I worried in this paper (and another for our student

study group on development) whether there might be such a thing as a 'premature' welfare state that spent too much on health at the expense of future growth.

Gerry also took courses with the inspirational James Tobin, who already then was addressing alternative and more meaningful ways to measure economic welfare than GDP/GNP per capita. Indeed, he and the other graduate students were fascinated by Tobin's accounts of his policy work and he vividly recalls one lecture about what he had learned in Washington by serving on Kennedy's Council of Economic Advisors. Somewhat upsettingly but instructively, Helleiner recalls – and hence it merits quoting verbatim both for its colourfulness and because of its relevance to the subsequent track of his own career embodying policy advisory work from a university base – Tobin pronounced that,

in order to be a successful economist and advisor in the policy world in the most powerful country in the world, you really didn't need anything that went beyond the first year economics textbook. But then he went further, 'Actually, there are only three concepts that you need to understand really well and that'll make you quite successful: opportunity cost, discounting the future, and fungibility – if you've got those straight, you'll be fine!' (interview, Gerry Helleiner[li])

Gerry's own thesis did not actually address development issues because his wife became pregnant around that time and he chose pragmatically to tackle a topic that enabled him to remain at Yale and complete in record time, which, he remembers proudly, he did achieve in 1961, graduating the following year. His subject was a computer-based regression analysis of connections between US and Canadian capital markets. Immediately thereafter, however, he did embark on his career in development economics as the first appointee by Lloyd Reynolds to his new centre. Helleiner refers to it as a dream appointment, with funding to go to the developing country of his choice to undertake research for a book, combined with a half-time teaching appointment (see also UNIHP 2007: Helleiner: 12–17; Helleiner 2018). He chose Nigeria and spent 13 months at the Nigerian Institute of Social and Economic Research in Ibadan (1961–62), where he taught first-year economics. By his own account, he was hooked and that cemented his career in development economics, although healthwise it proved difficult as he contracted malaria twice and viral encephalitis, the latter of which left a permanent mark. This work resulted in his first development monograph, *Peasant Agriculture, Government, and Economic Growth in Nigeria* (Helleiner 1966).

At Yale, the EGC evolved, as Reynolds had intended, into a world-leading focus for such work and attracted numerous eminent figures and young academics. This really was a period of optimism and expansion, both in the world economy and the new field of development, especially development economics, with endless opportunities for exploratory and path-defining work as decolonisation spread through Asia and Africa, with its demand for baseline research and policy advice to newly formed and often highly idealistic governments pursuing a diversity of development trajectories.

Immediately afterwards, Helleiner was sorely tempted to join the Ministry of Overseas Development in London, then just established by the newly elected Labour government, where Dudley Seers had been appointed research director and **Paul Streeten** his deputy, but family considerations led him to remain in Toronto. By contrast, he was never tempted to join the Canadian International Development Agency since its reputation was not so good and it would not have been an equivalent experience. He also came close to joining the Institute of Development Studies (IDS) at the University of Sussex when Dudley Seers became Director there, but ultimately only spent a sabbatical year there and remained based in Canada.

Later, he grew to love Tanzania even more, working as director of the newly established Economic Research Bureau at the University of Dar es Salaam initially from 1966 to 1968, with numerous return visits of varying duration thereafter. During his initial sojourn in Dar, he edited *Agricultural Planning in East Africa* (Helleiner 1968). He also got to know Lionel Cliffe, Terry Ranger, Len Berry, Bob Kates, Adolfo Mascarenhas, Reg Green, John Iliffe, John Saul, Walter Rodney and others who went on to become internationally known in their respective disciplines (interview, Gerry Helleiner[lii]; pers. comm.[liii]; Helleiner 2018).[10] He didn't always agree with them and recalls his frustrations

---

[10] Coincidentally, there are multiple points of personal intersection here. I interacted much later in the UK with Reg Green at southern African solidarity meetings and in policy debates, and worked with Lionel Cliffe while I was a post doc at Leeds University in the mid-1980s and thereafter on the editorial working group of the *Review of African Political Economy* until his death in 2014. John Saul also works on *RoAPE*. Similarly, I met Terry Ranger, then at Manchester University, at conferences as a doctoral student at Oxford, and subsequently worked with him on the editorial board of the *Journal of Southern*

with some on the Left who argued with vehemence on the basis of firm convictions but lacked supporting data or empirical evidence for their arguments. By contrast, Helleiner reflected on his career as having been influenced by the quantitative tradition of the EGC and the moral compass referred to earlier:

> I've been allergic to dogma and religion of any kind ... Others have called me a structuralist [but] I'm not sure if that means anything much. I was brought up to understand and respect neo-classical traditions and [am] somewhat excited by the innovations in that. It's not nearly as bad now as it once was ... but I'm comfortable with other broader perspectives and have lectured on deficiencies of the approach. I guess they're pragmatic and eclectic and, to the degree that I can manage it, I like to think that I'm unpredictable. I don't like to think that people know what I'm going to say in advance ... I'm thoroughly empirical and inclined to take whatever seems to work for the understanding of phenomena that I'm interested in. I don't have a solid theoretical base that makes it possible for me to put everything into ... that framework. (interview, Gerry Helleiner[liv])

Indeed, this approach brought him into conflict with some on the Left in Tanzania, especially from within the Political Science Department in the immediate wake of publication of the Arusha Declaration during his final year there in 1968. They denounced his approaches as bourgeois and thus of very little relevance to socialist Tanzania, which he found hurtful but, ironically, he was in daily demand from the government for advice, sitting on numerous official committees and boards (interview, Gerry Helleiner[lv]; UNIHP 2007: Helleiner: 22–3; Cramer 2006).

Nevertheless, he feels that his experiences in Nigeria and Tanzania left him with an enduring sense of greater humility and appreciation of non-economic issues (UNIHP 2007: Helleiner: 19–21). In 'Intellectual Currents' (Helleiner n.d.: 2), he reflected on the impact of his Nigerian and Tanzanian experience:

> It wasn't until I joined the Economic Growth Center in 1961 that I began to read voraciously and think more broadly and more seriously about development. At this time I was greatly enamoured of Dudley

African Studies from 1991 until he retired from it in 2010. He also died in 2014. Adolpho Mascarenhas' work on Dar was important to my doctoral work on decolonisation in Windhoek and, although we have never met, I serendipitously landed up as a co-author of a book chapter with him in 2014/15.

Seers' arguments on 'the limitations of the special case', the limited applicability of traditional Western economics for the analysis of developing country economies. In Nigeria my doubts about usable data and theory in the development context intensified. But so did my interest in getting better data and better economic analysis in support of development efforts. By the early 1960s, then, I was already intellectually deeply committed to the search for some 'better' form of development economics (and disenchanted with much of the mainstream material I had been taught). My experience in socialist-aspiring Tanzania moved me toward greater concern for equitable income distribution and the need to address the problems of the poorest peoples and countries; but not toward traditional socialist ideology or its key instruments of state ownership and planning which manifestly didn't work too well. Later work for UNICEF, the ILO and others strengthened these concerns for addressing poverty and income distribution as well as growth (and, later, 'adjustment') in developing countries.

These concerns were reflected in numerous monographs and edited books as well as journal articles on international trade, the role of the international financial institutions in economic development, and the impact of their policies from the 1960s until 2002 (e.g. Helleiner 1972; 1976; 1982; 1996; 2002; 2018). Probably his most widely known contributions date from a very productive period in the early 1990s, during which he undertook sustained critiques of the adverse effects of structural adjustment programmes in exacerbating poverty and inequality (e.g. Helleiner 1992; Helleiner et al. 1991) and the co-edited volume, *From Adjustment to Development in Africa: Conflict, Controversy, Convergence, Consensus?* (Cornia and Helleiner 1994). In later years he was best known, at least in official circles, for his efforts to achieve local 'ownership' of development programmes and improve aid relationships.

In his UNIHP interview, he elaborated on his commitment to the weak and poor, a perspective influenced by personal and domestic circumstances in a way, though perhaps different in detail, that is consistent with the more overtly religiously and ethically inspired value systems espoused by various others among my interviewees:

I get my kicks from backing the underdog in general. My severely handicapped son has had an impact on that as well. His struggles against the world and against all-knowing professionals, and against the idea that efficiency is everything, have all influenced me a lot, too, and have consolidated the kinds of approaches that I was already pursuing. I have been more concerned with weaker and smaller and more vulnerable people and countries. That is really what I am ... I think it is my major contribution, professionally, in the sphere of applied economics. But, analytically speaking, it may not be. When I was elected to the Royal Society of Canada, the citation said nothing about that. The citation was about my contributions to the analysis of international trade and, in particular, intra-firm trade. I was really the first to write on that as a major alternative way of thinking about a high proportion of trade. (UNIHP 2007: Helleiner: 26)

Although he had never written autobiographically until 'Intellectual Currents' and a couple of other reflective post-retirement pieces of memoir, he showed great interest in the nature of my study during our interview[lvi] and admitted that he had been conscious that a disproportionate number of development specialists were exiles, but had never related this to the Holocaust, so he looked forward to hearing about my findings since his was one of my first few interviews. He subsequently fleshed out the short memoirs into a professional autobiography, published as this book was going to press (Helleiner 2018), which contains further details of the episodes and reflections examined here.

His first encounters with the UN system came via his early work at the EGC, where he became immersed in statistical development indicators and read voluminously, including the Arthur Lewis report. Actual meetings and engagements probably commenced in 1971/72, with regular visits to Geneva while on sabbatical leave at IDS in Sussex. Over the following years, he worked extensively as technical advisor to UNCTAD, not least on the highly politicised New International Economic Order (NIEO) agenda, the ILO and later also UNICEF, but had little direct involvement with the World Bank or IMF. Linked to the NIEO process, he was instrumental in lobbying for the establishment of the North-South Institute in Canada. He also served on the UN's Committee for Development Planning (UNIHP 2007: Helleiner: 33–42) and led several research projects for the UN University's World Institute for Development Economics Research. The extensive interview transcript contains interesting insights into the intellectual and political debates bound up with these initiatives and the second UN Development Decade, as well as into Helleiner's thinking and perception of the various UN and related international initiatives. He often adopted critical stances, especially when he disagreed with analyses or found the quality of UNCTAD's and other papers weak (*ibid.*: 33ff.; Helleiner 2018).

Having worked with a slightly reduced teaching load at the university for some years while also employed as director of research for the G24, Helleiner retired officially at 62 for a combination of health-related and financial reasons since the university had a generous early retirement scheme. However, he retained an office in the Centre for International Studies (later the Munk School of Global Affairs) and worked selectively thereafter, although 'trying to retire' for some years (UNIHP 2007: Helleiner: 30; pers. comm.[lvii]; Helleiner 2018).

Conclusions

The small group of five featured in this chapter share at least as many elements of diversity as they do commonality beyond the facts of their employment for varying periods of their respective careers in bi- or multilateral agencies. Their initial motivations for doing so varied, as did their experiences of 'doing development', so to speak, and how they reflected upon those and took subsequent career decisions in that light.

On the one hand, Shlomo Reutlinger and Michael Cernea, both reasonably observant secular Jews, drew continually on moral and ethical concerns – and in Reutlinger's case also youthful kibbutz experience – to make the world a better place and were able to adapt to the evolving institutional restrictions, requirements and opportunities provided by the World Bank over long periods. John Friedmann and Gerry Helleiner, both non-Jews but lacking much active religious sentiment or practice, went into development practice for similar reasons – optimism about the value of official financial and technical assistance in promoting genuine development of poor people and countries in the post-World War II and decolonisation periods. However, they found institutional constraints and mores too constraining and ultimately opted for the greater intellectual and personal freedom to write and criticise official policies and projects afforded by university positions, which nevertheless provided a base from which to undertake select consultancies or other practitioner engagements.

By contrast, Ernie Stern, also a practising Jew, had no academic ambitions as a career and believes that he came to development and, in particular, the ICA/USAID and then World Bank by chance. Then, following his retirement as senior vice-president, he moved into the private financial sector in high net-worth asset management. Stern apart, the experiences of the other four appear consistent with those among the older generation who immersed themselves in development agencies but with one important exception. Their age difference meant that by the time the younger cohort had completed their higher education and commenced their careers, most of the postwar development and development financial institutions that the likes of Hans Singer had been engaged in establishing (see Chapter 5) were already going concerns and the scope for blue skies thinking and design was already more circumscribed. Nevertheless, by comparison with today's rule-bound and accountability-obsessed standards, they still enjoyed considerable scope to define and develop new programmes and initiatives, perhaps best exemplified by Cernea's role in overturning and reshaping the World Bank's policy on development-induced resettlement and Reutlinger's innovations in the Bank's approaches to malnutrition and income distribution.

8 | CONCLUSIONS: INTERPRETING THE MOSAIC

Pioneers in any field represent a distinctive group of people, frustrated at the status quo and imbued with a spirit of enquiry and an innovative urge to break existing conceptual, practical, technical and policy constraints or boundaries of their disciplines or communities of practice. Whether this be to fill substantive gaps or to break new ground, innovation and exploration are simultaneously challenging, exciting and often reputation-enhancing. When such landmark engagements occur in the wake of great personal and familial trauma such as the Holocaust and the experience of becoming refugees to escape genocide, it is quite remarkable. The diverse group of Holocaust escapees who form the subject of this book became pioneers in development, forging many key elements of the largely new field of endeavour that evolved into the large body of theory, policy and practice. This was known originally as economic development and more recently as development studies, international development or global development in recognition of its variegated and multifaceted nature. Several older members of the group initially engaged in postwar reconstruction and development in their native Europe, before turning their attention to the superficially similar but often profoundly different problems of poverty and 'underdevelopment' in countries of the global South. Some worked as individual advisors, consultants or academics, while others established or helped strengthen specialist multilateral agencies. Many careers involved different combinations of these roles over time. This concluding chapter pulls together the many threads and arguments running through the book. In so doing, it answers the central underlying question by demonstrating that, despite their diversity, most members of this group were indeed inspired to a greater or lesser extent by their ethical, moral or religious convictions and/or wartime experiences to help make the world a better place.

Fortunately, by pursuing multiple methods of enquiry, most importantly internet searches and snowballing, I was able to track down and include the vast majority of members of this cohort, which turned out to be far larger than anticipated at the outset. Full coverage was impossible to achieve and never intended but the extent and diversity of coverage gives the findings and analysis strong credibility. Of course, not everyone who chose a career in development achieved success or became a major figure. In addition, for reasons explained in Chapter 1, the commencement of the Nazi regime when Hitler became Chancellor in Germany in January 1933 has marked the threshold for inclusion in this study. This threshold excluded several potential candidates from Central Europe, most notably Paul Rosenstein-Rodan, Thomas Balogh and Nicholas (Miklós) Kaldor, who had commenced university studies in the UK, particularly the London School of Economics, relatively shortly beforehand and for whom that opportunity appeared the dominant motive, rather than escape from the increasingly intolerant atmosphere. Moreover, this study has not been concerned to compare the number or proportion of Holocaust escapees and survivors who entered the development field as opposed to any other academic disciplines or communities of practice.

Although representing only a modest proportion of all who played important roles in the evolution of the vibrant and diverse terrains of development theory, policy and practice during the second half of the twentieth century, the contribution of Holocaust escapees and survivors has been extraordinary. Born between 1904 and 1936 and living in those parts of continental Europe subjected to Nazism before and during World War II, they had to flee as young adults or as children with their parents at some stage between 1933 and 1943. The two Romanians fled their small towns to survive under the radar, though not actually in hiding, in the relative anonymity of Bucharest throughout the war. What became of them all after their escape and passage into exile, and how that helped shape them and influenced their later choice of career direction towards the field of development, constituted my main research focus.

One key point for this analysis is that it was not really possible for most people featured in this study to have decided at the outset, or even during their immediate postwar higher education, to embark on a career in development because no such defined field of endeavour existed. Even in anthropology, geography and planning, for instance, which had long had a focus of research in tropical and sub-tropical regions, deployment of those disciplinary skills towards something delineated as 'development' would emerge as a coherent possibility only in the 1950s. This is when **Gerry Helleiner**, the youngest in this study, and **Scarlett Epstein**, **Emanuel de Kadt** and **Kari Polanyi Levitt**, some of the latecomers to higher education among the younger cohort, obtained their PhDs. Hence, the older generation pioneers, be it in economics, the most widely represented discipline in this study, or beyond, were trained in the general or mainstream theories and applications of that time and gradually engaged in advisory work for newly independent governments or as consultants for or as employees of European and North American governments and/or new specialist international agencies. **Albert Hirschman**'s Marshall Plan experience informed his subsequent work in Colombia and elsewhere. **Hans Singer**, most notably, was instrumental in establishing several such agencies as well as serving for many years in the Institute of Development Studies (IDS) at the University of Sussex. He was also unusual in working permanently in development, first within the UN system and then at the IDS.

Perhaps because of the increasingly multidisciplinary and diverse nature of development as academic pursuit and field of policy and practice over time, the subjects of my research frequently did not know one another or act in any coherent way as a group. The main bases for personal connections were having grown up together, such as **Paul Streeten** (Hornig), **Wolfgang Stolper** and **Eric Wolf** in Vienna or **Irma Glicman-Adelman** and **Michael Cernea** (Katz) in Iaşi (Romania) (Chapter 2); being incarcerated together during internment in the UK in 1940–41 (**Hans Singer**, **Paul Streeten** and **Eric Wolf**) (Chapter 3); or having subsequently worked together professionally, as with **Alexander Gerschenkron** and **Albert Hirschman** at the Federal Reserve and then Harvard immediately after the war (Chapters 4 and 5). Professional connections within this group were most likely and strongest among the economists, who comprised by far the largest disciplinary group in this study. They were also sometimes thrown together in the challenges of immediate postwar European reconstruction and development, of establishing new United Nations agencies and/or advising the governments of newly decolonised countries on the establishment of new ministries, formulating their economic development policies and building institutional and human capacity.

Later on, with the proliferation of advisory and consultancy missions, cheaper international travel and more frequent academic conferences, for instance, the chances of meeting and collaborating increased.

With the notable exception of **Peter Bauer**, the academics, activist/practitioner–academics and practitioners alike also shared broadly progressive, left-of-centre political orientations and a general belief in the necessity of state involvement as a positive force in promoting development through greater equity, more balanced growth and reduced poverty. An assessment of the extent to which this orientation reflected their upbringings and wartime experiences was a central question addressed in my research.

The Role of Nazi-Era and Holocaust Experiences in Shaping Personalities and Careers

Seeking to distil any one particular influence in a situation of numerous interdependent variables would be futile. There were always multiple influences, in sometimes shifting combinations, for the same individual over time. Hence even a hierarchy of influences would be difficult to determine. Besides, this is no quantitative econometric study but a wide-ranging and qualitative enquiry into the lives of and formative influences on a group of people who survived one of the worst genocides of modern history through different types, extents and durations of trauma, which often left lasting legacies. To wit, in common with most Holocaust escapees and especially camp survivors, those included in this study generally suppressed or at least avoided speaking, let alone actually writing, about their experiences until late in life, often well into retirement. In part, this may have resulted from their desire to overcome their traumas, lay the ghosts to rest, and move on with their lives, but it was also a reflection of the dominant ethos of that generation not to talk about emotive or difficult topics.

The stimuli to break the silence varied. Most common were requests from family members, particularly grandchildren, and/or stirrings triggered by the high-profile commemorations to mark major anniversaries such as the fiftieth anniversary of the liberation of Auschwitz-Birkenau, or the controversial challenges to their lived experience posed by prominent revisionist and Holocaust-denying historians such as David Irving or neo-populist right-wing politicians. Sometimes this impulse found expression in writing autobiographies or in giving interviews for biographies. Some chose to reflect on their professional careers and gently interwove some more personal threads, occasionally stimulated by the interviews that I conducted. Nevertheless, therefore, both the available writings and interviews constitute recollections and perhaps selective and embellished accounts at least 50 years after the period and events concerned. As discussed in Chapter 1, this is an important caveat, even though I have sought exhaustively to verify claims and triangulate evidence from different sources wherever possible.

Age emerged as the single most important variable in explaining the effect of Nazism and the Holocaust on this group of people, in the sense of how old they were when the Nazis took power in Germany and when they annexed Austria and invaded or built client regimes in the other countries concerned. This cross-cuts all other variables because it explains how far each individual had progressed through formal education, wider socialisation and political awareness and possibly into youth activism by the critical dates. This, in turn, provides a strong indication of how vulnerable they would have been to summary arrest, dismissal from university as students or lecturers and other individualised forms of victimisation in addition to the general persecution of entire categories of people targeted by the Nazis.

This was the experience of the older generation, comprising **Alexander Gerschenkron**, **Fritz Schumacher**, **Albert Hirschman**, **Theodor Bergmann**, **Hans Singer**, **Wolfgang Stolper**, **Heinz Arndt**, **Peter Bauer** and **Paul Streeten**, as detailed in Chapter 2. Apart from Gerschenkron, a Russian who had earlier fled and settled in Vienna and then relocated rapidly from there to the USA, and Bauer, a Hungarian from Budapest who went straight to the UK in 1934, the others were German or Austrian. Several had to flee immediately the Nazis took power or invaded, escaping via various routes and devices to safety, sometimes by the skin of their teeth. They headed in different directions, e.g. like Stolper to Switzerland as the closest neutral territory, while Bergmann escaped to Palestine, before heading back to Europe to study in Czechoslovakia. Thereafter he worked as an agricultural labourer in Sweden during World War II. Uniquely in this study, he then returned to Germany shortly after the war, impelled by his ideological commitments. Singer fled to new academic pastures in Turkey before heading to study under John Maynard Keynes in the UK. Hirschman spent much of the war in Italy and France, including a spell in the Resistance, before escaping to the USA to evade capture.

The rest of this group gravitated to the UK via different routes in order to study, only to find themselves summarily and unjustly incarcerated during the mass internment of German-speakers as 'enemy aliens' in 1940–41, despite being refugees from that very enemy (see Chapter 3)![1] For some, that ironic and undignified experience was brief but for others it took months to arrange the evidence that would convince the authorities that they posed no threat. **Arndt** and **Streeten** had to mark time the longest, thanks to having been shipped to Sherbrooke camp in Canada. At the other extreme, **Hans Singer**, by then already lecturing at Manchester University – officially deemed 'useful employment' – spent only six weeks in detention. **Eric Wolf**, the only member of the younger cohort to suffer this experience, was released after 'a few' weeks. **Fritz Schumacher** was interned for three months. Making the best of their situations and refusing to let conditions degrade them psychologically, many of the highly educated and professional internees organised 'camp universities' to provide lectures and discussion and debating groups on all manner of subjects. This benefited those in this group, in several cases providing them with their first serious exposure to economics, which then stimulated a shift of discipline away from law. The privations suffered during this period proved seminal in relation to future professional engagements, such as **Paul Streeten**'s realisation on board the *Ettrick* en route to Canada just what the most fundamental human needs were. This later inspired his landmark work on basic needs during the late 1960s and early 1970s. **Fritz Schumacher**'s hardships during internment and as a wartime farm labourer provided the seeds for his later commitment to intermediate technologies (Chapter 3).

For the younger generation, experiences of living as children or teenagers under Nazi or client regime rule for varying periods of time until they were able to flee with some immediate family members – most commonly their mothers and some siblings – were no less traumatic and formative, as **Kari Polanyi Levitt**, **Scarlett Epstein** (Trude Grünwald) and **John Friedmann** attest (Chapters 2 and 3). The latter two managed to catch the final flight and voyage on their respective routes before these were cut off. The terror of being strip-searched and interrogated for three hours by the Nazis as they changed planes in Cologne, and worry that they would be detained and sent to a camp, left a deep mark on Epstein.

Precise circumstances naturally varied, as detailed in Chapters 2, 3 and 4, but the graphic accounts by **Scarlett Epstein** of her travails in

[1] As a Hungarian, Bauer avoided this fate.

occupied Vienna and by **Michael Cernea** of the brutal pogrom in Iaşi and his father's serendipitous escape and immediate need to hide until the family's flight to the relative anonymity of Bucharest, stand out. In slightly different ways, the flight, temporary incarceration and escape of **Shlomo (Fritz) Reutlinger** and the incarceration in Westerbork and then Bergen-Belsen of **Ernie Stern** and his family, and the remarkable story of how they eventually got out, constitute arguably the most harrowing experiences. Reutlinger was the only German in this study to have remained in Germany until the immediate aftermath of *Kristallnacht*, when his whole nuclear family had to flee. **Irma Glicman-Adelman**'s expulsion from school in Galatz, along with the oppressive atmosphere in the town, also propelled her family to the Romanian capital, from where they obtained exit visas to Palestine at the end of the war. **Zygmunt Bauman** and his parents fled Poznań for another part of Poland, only to have to flee the German advance again by crossing into Russia, where he completed secondary schooling before fighting for the Polish Army in Exile till the war ended. **Emanuel de Kadt** and his brother saw out the war in neutral Portugal with their grandparents after the planned voyage to Cuba became impossible and their sickly mother had then died of tuberculosis. Meanwhile, as the youngest in this cohort, **Gerry Helleiner**, who left Vienna for Canada via a short sojourn in the UK, and **Andre Gunder Frank**, who left Berlin for Switzerland and then the USA, had no direct memory of the Nazi era and World War II.

Country of birth and childhood upbringing constitute the second potentially important explanatory variable in terms of their Nazi-era experiences and their potential influence on subsequent career choices. Notwithstanding some marked differences in national identity, language and culture, the legacies of the Austro-Hungarian Empire provided some commonalities in terms of middle-class education in Latin and German and the Gymnasium secondary school system for many people in this study. Moreover, for most of those in Berlin, Vienna and some other major urban centres, in particular, life was comfortable, engaging and cosmopolitan, with many families having diverse national and sometimes also religious origins as a reflection of long histories of North/Central European mobility and modernity.

As already indicated, precise experiences varied greatly both among and within individual countries, especially for the younger generation. Hence nationality played little direct role but was more significant indirectly in terms of when people had to flee, and thus what escape routes existed or had been closed off, and what risks had to be taken. For the older generation, if they were Jewish or had Jewish ancestry, the signal to flee was usually the coming to power of the Nazis in Germany in early 1933, the *Anschluss* (annexation) of Austria in 1938 or invasion of their home countries. An exception was **Alexander Gerschenkron**, who was impelled to leave Vienna long before the *Anschluss*. For the younger generation, situations varied, with some families leaving together at the first opportunity. More common, however, was for the fathers (who, as generally the main breadwinner and hence professionally and perhaps politically most visible, were most at risk) fleeing in haste and the rest following when exit visas to join relatives or sponsors could be obtained. This was sometimes facilitated by agencies like the AAC/SPSL or the Central British Fund. Karl Polanyi, like Gerschenkron, already a refugee in Vienna, and his wife Ilona and daughter, **Kari Polanyi Levitt**, are one case in point, as are **Gerry Helleiner** and his mother and brother. When departure could be planned and undertaken with valid visas, an additional factor was how tough the exit restrictions were at the time in terms of what material possessions could be taken along, and what other assets had not yet been seized by the state and could be sold or covertly left in the hands of friends or neighbours for safekeeping.

Social and class position within the respective societies constitutes the third potential explanatory factor. This also proved insignificant as a differentiator since almost all those covered by this study grew up in broadly middle-class, well-educated semi- to fully professional families where education was highly prized. Most of the families were large and extended, often drawing members from different parts of the former Austro-Hungarian Empire, with cosmopolitan outlooks and social and professional networks reflecting that. This is particularly well exemplified by the world within which **Kari Polanyi Levitt** grew up in Vienna as the daughter of a prominent, politically engaged and mobile journalist father, Karl. **Fritz Schumacher** and **Albert Hirschman** grew up in well-established Berlin families, while **Eric Wolf** and **Paul Streeten** enjoyed relatively comfortable, cosmopolitan and politically engaged family contexts in Vienna. **Hans Singer** and **Shlomo Reutlinger** were born into comfortable smaller-town German families and **Theodor Bergmann**'s large rabbinical family would have been materially adequately provided for. **Zygmunt Bauman**'s childhood in

Poznań was also essentially middle class, his father having been a small shop-owner-turned-accountant.

In material terms, **Scarlett Epstein**, the daughter of a travelling textile salesman, had possibly the least well-off childhood, growing up in one of Vienna's working-class neighbourhoods. Nevertheless, she shared many of the other more middle-class characteristics of the others in this study, having an extended family, a wide circle of friends and progressive or socialist political outlook. By contrast, her experience of everyday anti-Semitism in the working-class areas, recounted graphically in her autobiography (Epstein 2005), appears to have been far more insidious and personal, and to have started far earlier, than for anyone else. It also intensified markedly with the *Anschluss*, with the dismissal of all Jewish children from local schools and the like. Via her brother, who was already in England, she and her mother managed to obtain British entry visas as domestic workers (Chapter 2). Scarlett later became a seamstress and then factory office manager to support her and her parents while completing her studies and eventually being able to commence further and tertiary education (Chapter 6). Anti-Semitism also cast a dark shadow in the small-town Romania of **Irma Glicman-Adelman** and **Michael Cernea**'s youth.

Religious upbringing and experiences, the fourth possible explanatory variable, also turned out to be unimportant. The overwhelmingly high levels of assimilation and the secular orientation of my sample meant that many had little if any substantive religious upbringing and training, particularly in Vienna. **Eric Wolf** and **Paul Streeten** exemplify this. Several, e.g. **Albert Hirschman** and **John Friedmann**, were brought up as Christians as a result of mixed marriages or conscious conversion to Christianity by their parents or grandparents in the hope of avoiding historically rooted stigma and obtaining social advancement. **Fritz Schumacher**, indeed, came from a longstanding Christian family but it was his social conscience and growing hatred of Nazi oppression and the claustrophobic atmosphere that propelled him eventually to leave Berlin. **Andre Gunder Frank** made no mention of Jewish content in his life. A minority, best represented by **Theodor Bergmann**, **Shlomo Reutlinger** and **Michael Cernea**, came from reasonably observant Jewish families and received considerable religious instruction, culminating in their Barmitzvah – which, in Reutlinger's case was so profoundly intruded upon by the destruction of their synagogue in Pforzheim during the *Kristallnacht*. Although less observant, **Hans Singer** attributed much of his Jewish instruction to the local rabbi. Noteworthy in this context is that none of them became either significantly more or less religiously observant as a result of their traumatic experiences. As a rabbi's son, **Theodor Bergmann** had a religious upbringing but became a Communist at an early age, even before having to flee from Berlin as a 17-year old in 1933. Nevertheless, he retained a strong secular Jewish identity and enduring engagement with research on kibbutzim and the Israel–Arab conflict.

No others in this study turned to religion as a consequence or, indeed, lost any faith and became overtly agnostic or atheistic if they had not been at least loosely of such persuasion beforehand. That said, religious values did sometimes play a role in subsequent identity (re-)formation. Having grown up in a non-observant home since her father was atheist and her mother understandably thus increasingly non-observant over time, **Epstein** resented her persecution in secondary school and everyday life in Vienna for being Jewish, something she had not experienced and did not feel as a positive identity (Epstein 2005: 20). As discrimination increased, her mother apparently regretted not having brought up her children more actively as Jewish (Chapter 2). Once she had eventually reached safety in the UK in April 1939, Scarlett actively discarded her Austrian identity, symbolically encapsulated by changing her name from Trude to Scarlett, and resolved to bring her own children up as Jewish (Chapter 3).

As the postwar socialist euphoria in Romania and Poland gave way to growing authoritarianism and anti-Semitism, **Michael Cernea** and **Zygmunt Bauman** suffered discrimination and ostracism for a second time. This contributed to political disillusionment and eventually drove them both to leave under difficult circumstances in the late 1960s, in Bauman's case to Israel, where his sister had settled much earlier, although he and his family remained there for only three years before moving permanently to the UK. Bauman evidently did not share his father's Zionist beliefs and lived a highly secular life, as he had been brought up. Indeed, they found Israel too nationalistic and struggled with the post-1967 occupation of captured Arab lands and its impact on Israeli society. Neither his nor his wife's wartime experiences in exile and in the Warsaw Ghetto respectively stimulated any religious feelings in them. Cernea maintained his previous level of observance, though more covertly at times, but brought up both his children as actively Jewish, despite all the challenges of being a widower in fulltime employment, not least the difficulties of separation from them thanks to the regime in Romania until they were all reunited in the USA.

No single personal contextual variable stands out as conspicuously important, although, in combination and in conjunction with individual personalities, they provide a good basis for understanding how members of this group fared in the face of the privations and horrors of the Nazi period to which they were subjected. It is to this that I now turn.

The actual nature of wartime experiences and their impact on the diverse individuals in this study, just as in the wider population, differed markedly. After all, they did not constitute any semblance of a coherent group, being mostly unknown to one another and scattered across continental European space–time. The only plausible basis for limited generalisation to emerge is in terms of a broad age-related division. The older generation were, perhaps, somewhat better equipped, physically and emotionally, to deal with their ordeals than the children or teenagers, although some of both cohorts did face privation, direct threats to safety, and deportation and murder of close and extended family members. Nevertheless, even direct military service during the war was not the preserve of the older group. While **Albert Hirschman** fought in the French Resistance and then US Army, and **Paul Streeten** saw action with the British commandos, **Zygmunt Bauman** of the younger cohort saw active service in the Polish Army in Exile, while **John Friedmann** served as part of the US Army occupation force in Germany after the war in Europe ended. Streeten was actually badly wounded and some shrapnel fragments have remained in his body ever since. None of the four drew direct connections between their military experience and subsequent career choices, although horror at the destruction and human cost of war and the accompanying genocide and civilian casualties would clearly have become deeply ingrained within them.

In terms of non-military aspects of the war period, two connections can be discerned. The first relates to **Fritz Schumacher**'s farm work experience in Northamptonshire alluded to above and explained in detail in Chapter 3, and the second to internment in 1940–41. During camp university sessions, Schumacher was exposed to Marx's work for the first time, and he was impressed by its relevance to conditions in both the internment camp and on the farm. This had a lasting impact on his work and writing (see below). For Streeten, too, internment and especially shipment to Canada proved a seminal experience in terms of exposure to deprivation and how it demonstrated to him what the most basic of human needs were. This had a direct influence on his subsequent work on poverty and hence his landmark contributions to the emergence of a basic needs focus in development studies in the early 1970s. Internment also left its mark on Schumacher, and together with his later experience of farm work, it fed into his pioneering work on what became known as intermediate technology. The Intermediate Technology Development Group that he established still exists under the name of Practical Action, as a major international NGO promoting intermediate or more broadly appropriate technologies in poor communities worldwide. Interestingly, despite the obvious complementarity of Streeten's and Schumacher's work in this field, they had little if any direct contact and never collaborated.

Legacies of War: The Effect of Immediate Postwar Engagements in Reconstruction and Development

Schumacher's wartime experiences then combined with intense work in mid-1945 on the American Bombing Survey of Germany, leading him to see his distinctive contribution as being to help demystify the Nazi propaganda and legacy to the German population as part of planning work for rebuilding Germany. Accordingly, he obtained employment with the British Control Commission, and used his previous experience on unemployment and the opportunity provided by the absence of the industrial barons and control of most economic assets by the Allies to plan the foundations of a future socialist state through large-scale investment and employment generation in rebuilding better, as it were. This was rejected by the postwar politicians, who instead pursued rapid capitalist redevelopment as a key bulwark against Stalinism. Although he then worked on the European Payments Union (EPU) before returning to the UK in 1949 as economic advisor to the National Coal Board, these formative experiences and his dissatisfaction with the workings of nationalised industries proved instrumental in his post-retirement career in development, on intermediate technology.

Albert Hirschman was recruited to work on the Marshall Plan from its inception in 1947 by virtue of his strong comparative advantage over most other potential candidates. This reflected his prewar and wartime experience in Germany, Italy and France and his consequent linguistic abilities, as well as his academic qualifications and work on the EPU in his previous role at the Federal Reserve Board in Washington. The latter employment had come about at **Gerschenkron**'s invitation, the two having shared an office in the University of California at Berkeley in 1941. This illustrates an important network effect among two people within this study following their initial meeting. Like Schumacher, Hirschman wanted to make a difference, and certainly did: as Adelman and Loyer (2010: 13) attest, it 'was both an ethical commitment and a practical cause'. This provides a clearer link between his exile and wartime experiences and his subsequent career path than Hirschman himself admitted at the time. In later writing (Hirschman 1998), however, he did connect his Marshall Plan experience directly with becoming involved in economic development in Colombia and then various other countries across the global South (Chapter 5).

By contrast, and despite his hasty escape from Germany in 1933, brief internment in 1940 and endless frustrations over his delayed naturalisation, **Hans Singer** appears not to have had any particular interest in development economics until immersed in the new UN Department of Economic Affairs' development section in 1947 as a result of a misunderstanding (see Chapter 5). **Wolfgang Stolper**, too, became an 'accidental' pioneer in development economics as co-author of an ILO report on industrialisation in Southeast Asia, despite no relevant theoretical or practical experience. The mere fact that he could claim to have read the entire existing development literature in a month and acquire the authority to write such a report attests both to the infancy of that literature and the dearth of actual development experience at the time. Later, advising the Nigerian Ministry of Economic Development from 1960 to 1962 'changed his life' and led him to specialise in development economics. Similarly, **Heinz Arndt** attributes the origins of his enduring academic and consultancy work on development economics not to any wartime or immediate postwar experiences but to a long conversation with Gunnar Myrdal on an intercontinental flight in the 1950s (Chapter 3) and then to having been powerfully affected by the scale of poverty he encountered in India while working with Myrdal (Chapter 5).

As an early arrival in the UK in 1934 and not having been affected by internment, **Peter Bauer** appears to have adapted fast and not suffered any particular Nazi-era impediment beyond the challenges of life as a foreigner in the wartime UK. Neither his own writings nor commentaries by his biographers and former colleagues make any specific connection between his origins and background and his later pedigree in development economics (Chapter 5). Finally, **Alexander Gerschenkron** used his Federal Reserve Board experience, together with his expertise on Russia and Austria and also the economic impacts of the war on European countries, to build his academic career. Shifting progressively towards economic history from the 1950s, his reputation rests mainly on the theory of unbalanced growth and the need for large-scale, state-led stimuli (a 'big push'), along with Rosenstein-Rodan and **Hirschman**. Having had to flee Vienna does not appear to have had a direct effect on his career direction as such.

The Role of Holocaust Experiences in Career Choices

Thomas Bergmann's career direction was strongly influenced by his experiences of anti-Semitism and anti-communism in Berlin as well as by having his interest in agriculture and agrarian issues stimulated while working on a kibbutz in Palestine right afterwards. He neatly combined his democratic communist commitment and passion for agricultural development throughout his extremely productive career. Formal retirement actually led to an increase in his written output, producing books and articles at an impressive rate until his death as a centenarian in 2017. Two additional distinctive features of Bergmann's career stand out in the context of this study. First, it was highly unusual for a committed lifelong communist not to be or become a religious agnostic or indeed atheist. By contrast, Bergmann remained a committed Jew and, indeed, drew on Jewish ethics and principles in rejecting authoritarian and inhumane communism, as practised in the Soviet Union, China and elsewhere, in favour of democratic communist ideals. This put him in a double minority, as it were, and inspired his strong commitment to the KPD-O and successor left political parties in Germany. It also probably explains his longstanding research interest in Israel's kibbutz movement, with its collectivist agricultural development origins and increasingly diverse evolutionary directions over time. Second, he deployed his considerable critical analytical skills to agricultural and rural development across a range of countries practising communism, state socialism or other forms of communalism and collectivism, often coming into conflict with intolerant and authoritarian regimes as he sought research access and demonstrated alternative, more democratic, possibilities. His extensive oeuvre in both German and English provides a particularly rich legacy in this respect.

Of the younger cohort, the two with the strongest and most direct links between their Nazi-era and wartime experiences and their subsequent career directions are **Scarlett Epstein** and **Michael Cernea** (see Chapters 7 and 6 respectively). Those experiences sharpened their strong aspirational (Epstein) or existing (Cernea) Jewish ethos and concern with issues of poverty and building better societies after the war. Epstein's Viennese background may have played a role, but her undergraduate studies in economics at Manchester University brought her into contact with kindred spirits and students and specialists on and from different parts of the global South. She then switched to social anthropology as a postgraduate and never looked back after undertaking doctoral fieldwork in India. Her entire career focused on development impacts on indigenous rural communities in South Asia and Papua New Guinea. Epstein was the only Nazi-era refugee in the UK to remain there permanently; **Emanuel de Kadt**, the other permanent UK resident, had arrived to study more than a decade after the war.

Completing his secondary schooling in the context of postwar ethnic freedom and pro-socialist sentiment in Romania, Cernea became active in the socialist youth movement and initially supported the non-ethnic and class-based focus of the Communist Party, which usurped political power in 1948. Since sociology had quickly been abolished at universities as a taboo bourgeois subject, he studied philosophy, which included Marxism-Leninism and social change. Even so, he struggled to complete his PhD amid increasing authoritarianism – in terms of which primary fieldwork was proscribed lest empirical findings might challenge ideological dogma – and a new tide of anti-Semitism during the 1950s. Thereafter, as an academic, he had to tread a fine line, seeking to promote field research-based work without incurring the regime's ire. It was only through a fellowship at Stanford and then, after his later defection, that he was invited to work for the World Bank, where he remained until retirement. There he became a development specialist, broadening his engagement with social change and rural development internationally and developing the distinctive humane approach to forced resettlement for which he is renowned (Chapter 7). Cernea draws a strong and direct line between this professional commitment and his own childhood experiences of violent oppression and becoming what today is called an internally displaced person: in March 1944, he and his family had to flee Iași for the relative safety of Bucharest in a taxi, having perforce to leave his aged grandmother, who was too ill to move, in the care of neighbours. In the process, they also lost all their property and possessions that they could take along.

For **Eric Wolf**, the link was less directly religious and more cultural. He was probably too young when he left Vienna to have been influenced directly by Austro-Marxism and broader Viennese political currents. He studied anthropology at Columbia University, where he was exposed to the diverse academic currents and many leading figures in the discipline. He rejected the dominant 'culture-and-personality' approach of the day on account of its failure to engage with political and economic context – something that he regarded as essential on the basis of his Jewish and cross-cultural upbringing in Vienna, his escape from Nazi rule and subsequent schooling in London, as well as experience of a poor community nevertheless having definite capacity. He therefore moved into the new field of cultural ecology and undertook graduate and postdoctoral research in Puerto Rico and Mexico respectively, into which he introduced a Marxian perspective. Thus commenced his career-long engagement in Marxian cultural ecology and peasant studies in different contexts, including South Tyrol. He didn't regard himself as working in or on development as such, but his incisive publications in peasant studies and on power and history do constitute important contributions to the field. Indeed, possibly his most important book, *Envisioning Power* (Wolf 1999) draws on case studies of two Latin American societies and Nazi Germany (Chapter 6).

Despite being a very private person and talking and writing autobiographically only late in life, **John Friedmann** indicated in these interventions that his moral conscience and strong desire to 'plan forwards' rather than 'look backwards' in order to contribute to making the world a better place were profoundly influenced by his Central European identity, socialisation and philosophical immersion, probably including a strand of Austro-Marxist philosophy in the sense that he wrote about late in life (Friedmann 2014), as well as his Nazi-era experiences. These included becoming a teenage refugee and then serving in Germany with the US Army after the war. After completing his postgraduate studies in the innovative cross-disciplinary planning programme at the University of Chicago, he spent successive spells of a few years in various Latin American and Asian countries in a mixture of academic and policy advisory roles before spending the rest of his career at the University of California, Los Angeles (Chapter 7).

Although his work has global reach and import, he is regarded as the father of development planning.

For several others, Jewishness or other religious/spiritual inspirations apparently played no direct role in their career choice, although – like **Epstein** and **Cernea** – their concerns with poverty and building a better world were certainly very important. **Zygmunt Bauman** was able to train in philosophy and sociology in postwar Poland, a choice of disciplines he attributed to his wartime experiences and desire to understand social agency in order to help rebuild society in a new communist order that would overcome the extensive poverty and ethnic and nationalist enmity. Having grown up in a very secular family, Jewishness or Jewish cultural values did not play a role for him. He taught sociology throughout his career, but it was only after his second flight into exile in the face of anti-Semitic purges in 1968 that he was able to read freely and develop the ideas that made him famous through prodigious published output after his retirement from Leeds University in 1990 (Chapter 6).[2] Although neither he himself nor most of the development community would regard him as having been a development specialist, his unique approach to understanding the Holocaust as a particular and perverted form of industrial modernity, rather than as a unique ideological aberration, and his distinctive analysis of 'liquid modernity' both have strong relevance to many development issues.

Irma Glicman-Adelman also attributed no particular Jewish identity or religious beliefs to her chosen career, even having spent several years in Palestine/Israel after escaping from Romania. However, a sense of 'primordial guilt' born of her Jewishness and Catholic education, exacerbated by being a Holocaust survivor, impelled her to a career in the service of humanity and especially tackling poverty (Chapter 6; Adelman 1988: 244; 1995: 4). From her doctoral studies at Berkeley, she became one of the early specialists in development economics, pioneering various quantitative approaches.

For **Kari Polanyi Levitt**, too, the motivation was socialist rather than Jewish or other religious sentiments. Indeed, she felt awkward when, after moving to Montreal, the local Jewish community tried to

---

[2] In this respect, he paralleled Theodor Bergmann, since they both increased their publication rate after retirement and remained fully active in this endeavour until their deaths.

include her family. After following her husband from the UK to Canada, she worked in diverse non-academic fields before joining the Economics Department at McGill University, where she taught and completed her MA and PhD. Her initial major field was economic planning, especially using input–output analysis and linear programming, but she became fascinated by development economics from lectures by Arthur Lewis and collaboration with Nicholas Kaldor while studying at the LSE, and then as a postgraduate. She later became engrossed with the Caribbean and thenceforth combined the two as her professional focus, inspired also by the work of Celso Furtado.

Emanuel de Kadt has always retained a strong Jewish identity, though based more in culture than religious values and rituals. He completed his schooling back in Rotterdam after the war and commenced studying for a career in business, before deciding on a different track and commencing a sociology degree at the London School of Economics. Following his MA at Columbia University in New York, he returned to the LSE to complete his PhD on radical Catholics in Brazil. This was his first experience of the global South but it whetted his appetite and he subsequently joined the IDS at the University of Sussex, where he spent the rest of his career, working mainly on health and development, along with tourism and state organisation. Following his retirement in 1994, he returned to researching aspects of fundamentalist religion in Latin America in the context of socio-political change and development.

As the youngest in this group, with no childhood memory of his first few years in Vienna or the family's escape to the UK and then Canada, nor any substantive religious upbringing, **Gerry Helleiner**'s career in development has no direct connection to prewar upbringing or wartime experience. He recalls always having a 'moral compass of some kind' and attributes his career-long engagements in development to an abiding conscience and interest in poverty issues and left-of-centre politics. The immediate stimulus was a summer job in the Economics Research Branch of the Canadian Department of Labour, while fellow students returning full of enthusiasm from study tours in Africa prompted his engagement with that continent (see Chapter 7). Although he didn't make any direct connection, his political leanings and interest in the challenges of poverty could well have stemmed from his parents and the extended family context as it evolved in Vienna. Indeed, the title of his newly published memoirs, *Towards a Better*

World (Helleiner 2018) reflects this commitment. Similarly, although born to Jewish parents, **Andre Gunder Frank** left Berlin as a four-year-old in 1933 and never referred to Judaism or its values having influenced him in any way, and he first encountered development only at university in the USA.

Ernie Stern occupies the opposite end of the spectrum from **Scarlett Epstein** and **Michael Cernea**. As detailed in Chapter 6, he had been working in the US Department of Commerce before applying on the spur of the moment to the ICA, the predecessor of USAID, where he was assigned to the Turkish desk. He adamantly maintained that this, like subsequent events that led him to the World Bank, was a pure coincidence and that no religious, ethical or other personal background factors, let alone his wartime experiences, played any role at all.

This analysis has demonstrated the variety of factors underpinning the group's career directions and shifts, often in combinations which naturally differed in relative importance. They have been arranged here in terms of a spectrum from the most to the least clearly discernible connection between youthful socialisation and Nazi-era and Holocaust experiences, and subsequent career tracks. The clearest links were often explicit in autobiographical writings and/or in interviews. Most interviewees had not previously considered the issue but articulated a response in discussion. Occasionally, when interviews were not possible, an element of deduction or conjecture on the basis of the available written evidence was required. The links were naturally mediated through the range of contextual factors summarised above.

However, two additional factors merit explicit mention. The first was the role of serendipity. This applied not only to how **Ernie Stern** stumbled into development work but has been a recurring point throughout the life stories and engagements by this remarkable group of people. At many key junctures, chance determined how particular events turned out: why one person obtained an exit visa and the next did not; why one person rounded up for detention and deportation managed or was allowed to escape by a familiar face in uniform; why one soldier was killed by a bullet or bomb while the one next to him survived; and so on. That said, only **Irma Glicman-Adelman** referred to survivor guilt but, instead of suffering it passively, she acquired appropriate skills and turned it into a force for positive change.

This, in turn, links to the second factor, namely the individual personalities involved. Although they naturally varied in terms of their degrees of extroversion or introversion, with some being decidedly reserved and private, at least about themselves, they were all imbued with perseverance and a determination to succeed and then to put their good fortune in having survived or escaped to good use for society. This probably explains the important contribution of Holocaust escapees and survivors to innumerable fields. No doubt, too, others with less good fortune and perseverance in development and other fields did not make names for themselves.

This also serves as strong evidence for the power of individual human agency, even when faced with systematic and overwhelming oppression. Refusing to accept their intended fate passively, these people found the means to survive or escape, and to find refuge in a strange country via sometimes hair-raising journeys and the ever-present risk of detection or disaster. They persevered, survived and later on succeeded against the odds.

As an aside, it is noteworthy that, albeit for different reasons, none of the four people who found refuge in Palestine/Israel, namely **Bergmann** in 1933, **Glicman-Adelman** in 1939, **Reutlinger** in 1940 and **Bauman** in 1968, remained there permanently. Given the reasons for their flight there, and the role of Palestine/Israel in fulfilling the Zionist dream of becoming a Jewish homeland, this might seem surprising in the context of this study. Despite the 35-year time difference in their arrival dates, both Bergmann and Bauman, who were communist or socialist in outlook, disapproved strongly of the ethno-religious conflict and nationalism that dominated life. Hence they left again for other parts of Europe after just a few years. Conversely, Reutlinger and Glicman-Adelman left to visit relatives and study in the USA with the intention of returning thereafter to help build the new country, but then pursued new opportunities, and met and married American spouses, so remained in the USA permanently. Reutlinger and his wife then returned to Israel after his retirement from the World Bank because their children had settled there many years earlier.

Contributions of this Study

This study has uncovered the continental European background and youthful ordeals of a sizeable group of diverse individuals in escaping or surviving the Holocaust and examined critically the extent to which these events and experiences as refugees influenced their subsequent decisions to embark on careers partly or wholly in the nascent field of development. Accordingly, this book throws important new light in at least six complementary ways on the origins and evolution of development as a coherent field of academic study and policy and practical intervention after World War II.

First, and most broadly, it draws attention to the underlying optimism of the period that poverty and underdevelopment could rapidly be overcome, and the key roles that at least one influential group of escapees from and survivors of one of the defining genocides of the twentieth century played in those endeavours. This helps to challenge the now fairly common deconstructionist contention that postwar development as a field of study and practice owes its genesis and momentum to European and American academics and bureaucrats with no experience of deprivation and essentially as exporting industrial capitalism to create newly independent states in the Western image in the name of tackling poverty. Almost all the people included in this study suffered traumatic experiences under and escaping from Nazi rule. Furthermore, two German refugees, **Fritz Schumacher** and **Theodor Bergmann**, even worked as agricultural labourers, in the UK and Sweden respectively, during the war.

Second, it demonstrates how several key individuals in this group, most notably **Alexander Gerschenkron**, **Fritz Schumacher** and **Albert Hirschman**, played important roles in the postwar surveys and then the Marshall Plan for postwar reconstruction and development in Western Europe because of their familiarity with conditions on the ground.

Third, this research reveals how these individuals, and others like **John Friedmann**, who served in the US Army in Germany after the war, inevitably drew from that experience in their initial development engagements in Latin America and Asia, and soon became all too aware of the differences, as well as of the diversity within and between even adjacent poor countries. This, in turn, stimulated many leading-edge publications, initially couched in contemporary discourses but then often undertaking 'self-subversion' (Hirschman's term) or discarding approaches no longer seen as adequate in the light of new evidence, and formulating or pushing the boundaries of alternative theories, explanatory frameworks and practical possibilities.

Fourth, it casts light on the sense of optimistic exploration and trial and error by which key individuals contributed to the evolution of theory, policy and practice, which often sat uneasily within existing bodies of knowledge, and led eventually to the identification of new sub-disciplines prefixed by 'development', most notably development economics. While a natural and welcome evolution, it also contributed over time, somewhat perversely, to the marginalisation of development economics, sociology, geography, planning and the like from what came to be regarded as the 'mainstream' of the respective disciplines. Driven by an often sub-conscious Euro- or Americocentrism, it implies a kind of ghettoisation, in terms of which everything to do with 'development' is separate from, and has little or no relevance for, 'mainstream' theory or practice (for which read the OECD countries).

Fifth, it highlights the important roles of individuals such as **Hans Singer**, **Shlomo Reutlinger**, **Michael Cernea** and **Ernie Stern**, with Holocaust backgrounds, in the establishment and/or subsequent evolution of specialist development institutions. Others, such as **Paul Streeten**, **John Friedmann** and **Gerry Helleiner** spent periods in such institutions as well as in academia, with generally positive synergies for both. Such differences reflect personal predilections and characteristics, such as degrees of curiosity and ability or willingness to moderate independent critical thought and expression to fit institutional mores and protocols.

Sixth, but no less important, it reveals the importance of individual human agency, even in the face of the institutionalised oppression of the Holocaust, and survival against great odds. Individual people can and do make a difference. Admittedly, it was far easier to make one's mark in the situations of great skills scarcity and lack of precedent and institutionalised practice then prevailing than would be the case nowadays, but this contribution enriches the history of development through an understanding of its evolution as a mesh of individual energy and endeavour interwoven with institutions and political and social processes, rather than as the familiar caricature of an amorphous and anonymous corpus of knowledge and practice.

More broadly and beyond development studies, this book also constitutes a contribution to the history of social science, triangulating among a rich blend of methods to elucidate the subject. As such, it goes well beyond volumes such as Newbold (2000) or Haselsberger (2017), which rely principally on unmediated autobiographical narratives by key figures in the respective fields (see Chapter 1). The pitfalls of selective memory or recording of recollections, which increase over elapsed time and may have the effect, knowingly or subconsciously, of embellishing records and reputations, are well known. Accordingly, this book has evolved through the research and writing into something of a critical cohort biography or ethnography, perhaps sharing some features of Zuckerman's (1977) cohort study of Nobel prize winners in the US and of the UN Intellectual History Project (Weiss et al. 2005) (see Chapter 1). This study also adds a new dimension to Holocaust studies by demonstrating how these individuals, not hitherto connected to that field of research, drew on their Nazi-era and Holocaust experiences to differing extents in opening up an entirely new field.

Epilogue

Perhaps it is no accident that so many of the luminaries of postwar development studies as an intellectual field of enquiry and as practice with the intent on making the world a better place were Holocaust escapees and survivors, and hence had been refugees who had then successfully rebuilt their lives as a platform for their professional engagements. Some expressed their career directions as explicitly linked to this, in terms of religious or associated moral/ethical commitment and/or in gratitude for having survived. In **Theodor Bergmann**'s case, the driver was a strong ideological conviction about the imperatives of working-class organisation and solidarity as the basis for revolutionary change. For others, the connection was more circumstantial or even coincidental. As already explained, my intention has not in any sense been to compare those going into development studies with those choosing other career pathways and disciplines. Rather, it has been an exploration of the extent to which a perspective stretching beyond their own eventual good fortune to the plight of 'distant strangers' suffering poverty, deprivation, discrimination and the like was evoked by their early experiences of discrimination, expulsion or flight or incarceration and then of having to pick up the pieces and forge new lives in foreign countries under often trying initial circumstances.

It would be fascinating for a similar study to examine systematically the mobility of cohorts of later emigrants and refugees from relatively or absolutely poor countries to Europe, North America and occasionally elsewhere in the OECD who have made notable contributions to development studies since the 1970s. Their numbers in and influence on development economics and postcolonial studies, to name but two specialisations, are considerable. We might also usefully think into the future in such terms.

Appropriately, therefore, the final words belong to **Zygmunt Bauman** and **John Friedmann,** who sadly both died in the first half of 2017, as this book was nearing completion. During his discussion with me about human rights and the need for institutional protection for any such rights to have meaning, an imperative that present-day illegal immigrants understand first-hand (see Chapter 6), Bauman remarked, 'So perhaps the next generation of these great thinkers of development will come from the ranks of illegal immigrants because they go through certain very interesting experiences' (interview, Zygmunt Bauman[i]).

Many of those experiences, of course, are more traumatic than 'interesting' in most lexicons, and John Friedmann's (2017: 15) final autobiographical essay is framed by the consequences of such upheavals and their legacies. He conveys a clear sense of having remained a 'perpetual outsider', of not quite belonging or succeeding 'organically to be part of the society in which I happen to be living', be it his adopted country or elsewhere after the Nazi rupture in his teens, his post-liberation experiences with the US Army in Europe, and his early career spent on successive short-term appointments in various Latin American and Asian countries. Many former refugees, including those examined in this volume, would readily recognise such feelings. Indeed, such experiences almost certainly contributed, however subconsciously or indirectly, to the power of the insights and engagements that helped launch and shape the new arenas of development theory, policy and practice after World War II.

APPENDIX | BIOGRAPHICAL SKETCHES OF PEOPLE EXCLUDED FROM THE STUDY BY VIRTUE OF THE THRESHOLD CONDITIONS

Pre-Nazi Emigrants

This section provides a brief overview of the circumstances of pre-Nazi emigrants as part of the context to the contrasting experiences of those who had to flee rapidly in 1933 or later, as addressed in Chapters 3 and 4. Two of this interwar group were Hungarian Jews who, in the manner outlined above by Frank (2009), first went to study economics in Berlin before moving to London, where they became prominent economists.

Wolf Ladejinsky (born in 1899), fled Ukraine in 1921 for Romania and then the USA in 1922 when his family's business had been nationalised after the Russian Revolution. He and his family were Jewish. He studied at Columbia University in New York, gaining his BA in just two years and then undertook graduate work but withdrew from his PhD studies during the depression. He went on to become a key agricultural development and land reform specialist in the US Department of Agriculture, in which capacity he was sent to Tokyo in 1945 as an advisor. He ultimately became the US's leading expert on Japanese land reform (Stavis 2004).

Paul Narcyz Rosenstein-Rodan was born in Kraków, Poland, in 1902[1] and studied economics under Hans Mayer at Vienna University. He obtained his PhD in 1925, so had already been practising economics for five years by the time he emigrated to Britain in 1930. In the UK, he lectured at University College London and then the London School of Economics until moving to Washington DC to work for the World Bank in 1947 (Rosenstein-Rodan 1984; New School 2006). However, none of the available sources, including his own autobiographical reflections (Rosenstein-Rodan 1984), discusses his early life and reasons for emigrating to London, although since he was Jewish, the prevailing situation was very likely a contributor.

---

[1] It has not been possible to identify the actual date.

Thomas Balogh, as he anglicised his original Hungarian name, Támás Balog, was born on 2 November 1905 and grew up in Budapest, one of the centres of the Austro-Hungarian Empire, in a middle-class Jewish family that had been badly affected by the hyperinflation, forcing them to live in much reduced circumstances. His father, a railway engineer by training, was vice-chair of the Budapest Transit Board (Morris 2007: 7) and, according to Thomas, 'a typical civil servant, cautious, moderate and shirking conflict' (*ibid.*: 8). Thomas and his younger brother were very different and much later, when both in the UK, they became estranged. Balogh was evidently a difficult personality, clashing frequently with family, friends and foe. He attended the Minta Gymnasium, which he described as 'a classical grammar school' but, which his biographer reports, has also been labelled the Winchester of Hungary (*ibid.*: 9). Around that time, many people who were to become famous Hungarian émigrés after World War II, including Nicholas Kaldor (see below) and Michael Polanyi (brother of Karl), attended that Gymnasium.

Balogh won entry to Budapest University in competitive exams, there completing a thesis on German inflation that was published by the Hungarian Academy of Sciences; he was also awarded a Fellowship of the Royal Hungarian College on the basis of which he went to study at the University of Berlin in 1927/8, where he combined study with work for the Reichsbank. Balogh was tutored by Hermann Schumacher, father of Fritz (see Chapter 3), with whose family he also lodged (*ibid.*: 9–10).

> Their friendship was to influence Balogh's thinking when he began his interest in development economics. Another tutor, Professor J.A. Schumpeter, had also taken a kindly interest in the young man and was to give him letters of introduction to J.M. Keynes, which were instrumental in getting Balogh a successful start when he came to Britain in 1930. (*ibid.*: 10)

After winning a two-year Rockefeller Fellowship to the USA, part of which was spent working in London and Paris to gain experience of their different financial and economic systems, Balogh intended to forge a career in academia and banking in Germany but, as Morris puts it, he had 'seen the omens' of the rise of Nazism and when he returned to Hamburg from the USA to take up a job he had been offered, his mother 'met him at the docks and warned him, "You can't stay in

Germany – go back". He turned around and came to England' with little money and few contacts (*ibid.*: 12; see also Streeten 2000a: 28).

Morris remarks that Balogh's notes and diaries (which he started later in life) contain very little, if anything, about his early years and what it was like growing up in interwar Budapest and then studying in Berlin. My interview with Balogh's step-daughter, Tirril Harris, and her husband, Nigel, confirmed this. She added, 'I don't think he enjoyed his time doing a doctorate in Berlin' (interview, Tirril Harris[i]).

Nicholas (Miklós) Kaldor (born 12 May 1908) lived close to and became friendly with Balogh in Budapest, where he also attended the Minta Gymnasium and then followed in Balogh's footsteps to the Humboldt University in Berlin in 1925 to study economics. He was unimpressed by that experience and came to London already in 1927, some three years ahead of his older friend. By his own admission, however, he took advantage of his fluent German and spent more time working as a foreign correspondent for a Hungarian newspaper than studying (Kaldor 1986: 29, cited in King 2009: 4). Hence this may have been a chicken and egg situation. Both men were to remain in the UK permanently and they developed a complex lifelong relationship of friendship and rivalry, both eventually becoming members of the House of Lords.

Kaldor's father was a lawyer, providing the Jewish family with a comfortable middle-class status. Nicholas graduated in 1930 with a first-class economics degree, won a research studentship and then joined the staff of the London School of Economics (LSE) in 1932 (Thirlwall 2008). Both his daughter, Frances Stewart (interview, Frances Stewart[ii]), and his most recent biographer, John King (2009: 4), explain that Kaldor's principal reason for coming to London was the opportunity to study at the LSE, which he regarded as superior to the quality of teaching in Berlin, rather than to escape the rise of Nazism. On this basis, as well as the timing of his arrival in the UK, Kaldor can – like Balogh – be taken to represent a boundary case of exclusion from the study on the basis of when they both moved to the UK, although Balogh's principal reason relates directly to the rise of Nazism, whereas Kaldor's had no explicit connection. To Tony Judt (Judt with Snyder 2013: 16), Kaldor, whom he first met in London in the 1970s, exemplified particularly well the interwar Central European assimilated Germanic cultural values that defined the age: 'he thought of himself first and above all as an educated member of the upper middle class of his native Budapest: his world was that of cultivated, German-speaking, German-educated Hungarian Jews'.

Children of Pre-Nazi Emigrants or Escapees/Survivors

This sub-section completes the portfolio by summarising briefly the essential biographical details of members of a separate sub-category of development specialists who do not satisfy the inclusion criteria for this study but whose lives and professional commitments have, to a greater or lesser extent, been influenced by the shadow of the Holocaust. It comprises five people born outside continental Europe before, during or shortly after World War II to emigrants during the Depression and early Nazi years or to escapees/survivors. As with the four pre-Nazi emigrants above, they were only excluded after careful assessment, including interviews (with all except Nicholas Stern) which provided the necessary biographical details.

Immanuel Wallerstein was born in New York in 1930 to parents who emigrated from Germany in 1921 to escape the hyperinflation. His father was a physician who had initially followed the family's long rabbinical tradition of becoming a rabbi and specialising as a Talmudic scholar and teaching at the Berlin Theological Seminary. Having left the rabbinate, he became increasingly secular and the family really only celebrated Passover (interview, Immanuel Wallerstein[iii]). Immanuel's early career was very much focused on African Studies and development issues, before moving into the broader sociological realms for which he became renowned.

Michael Lipton (Lipstadt) was born in London in 1937 to parents who had emigrated from Hamburg in 1933; his father had just qualified as a lawyer when the Nazis took power and disbarred Jewish lawyers and other professionals from practising. By various routes his immediate family avoided and survived the Holocaust, in the case of his maternal grandmother by being hidden Anne Frank-style in a basement for two years, and his maternal aunt and uncle wandering around the Hamburg area and managing to avoid detention. The family name was anglicised in 1940 to reduce the risk of internment as German-speaking potential enemy aliens, although his father was already serving in the Pioneer Corps at that time (see Chapter 3) (Michael Lipton, pers. comm.[iv]; interview, Michael Lipton[v]).

Thomas (Tom) Weisskopf was born in Rochester, NY in 1940 to a Viennese Jewish father and Danish Lutheran mother who had emigrated from Zurich (where he had worked for three years) in 1937 (telephone interview, Tom Weisskopf[vi]). Similarly, **Oded Stark** was born in Palestine in 1944 to Polish parents who had emigrated there separately in 1934 and 1935 respectively out of Zionist commitment rather than a sense of impending doom (interview, Oded Stark[vii]). **Nicholas Stern** was born in the UK in 1946 to refugee parents, and his father was interned as an enemy alien in 1940–41 (see Chapter 3) and was then sent to Australia on the *Dunera* (Inglis et al. 2018).

NOTES

1

i Montreal, 29/4/08.

2

    i London, 17/10/06 @ 32–34 and 52–53 mins.
   ii London, 17/10/06 @ 57–58 mins.
  iii 5/1/07.
  iv London, 4/7/07 @ 3–4 mins.
   v Spencertown, NJ, 7/11/06 @ 0–5 mins.
  vi Spencertown, NJ, 7/11/06 @ 8–10, 12–13 mins.
 vii Spencertown, NJ, 7/11/06 @ 13 mins.
viii Spencertown, NJ, 7/11/06 @ 4.00–6.40 mins.
  ix Spencertown, NJ, 7/11/06 @ 13 mins.
   x Spencertown, NJ, 7/11/06 @ 10.00–12.25 mins.
  xi Spencertown, NJ, 7/11/06 @ 14.40–20.00 mins.
 xii 25/4/12, 14/2/13.
xiii email, 25/4/12.
xiv email, 14/2/13.
 xv Hove, 11/10/06 @ 20–30 mins.
xvi Irvington, NY, 5/11/06 @ 0–15 mins.
xvii Irvington, NY, 5/11/06 @ 0–15 mins.
xviii Irvington, NY, 5/11/06 @ 12–13 mins.
xix Vancouver, 22/6/06 @ 1–3 mins.
 xx Vancouver, 22/6/06 @ 3.30–10.00 mins.
xxi email, 24/1/13.
xxii Vancouver, 22/6/06 @ 7–11 mins.
xxiii Vancouver, 22/6/06 @ 9–14 mins.
xxiv London, 8/11/07 @ 3–15 mins.
xxv 4/08/13.
xxvi London, 8/11/07 @ 0–4 mins.
xxvii London, 8/11/07 @ 4–5 mins.
xxviii London, 8/11/07 @ 18.50–27.00 mins.
xxix email, 29/1/13.
xxx Leeds, 12/10/07 @ 46–47 mins.
xxxi email, 29/1/13.
xxxii Leeds, 12/10/07 @ 36–37 mins.
xxxiii Berkeley, CA, 16/4/07 @ 2.00–4.50 and 10 mins.
xxxiv Berkeley, CA, 16/4/07 @ 4.50–6.50 mins.
xxxv Berkeley, CA, 16/4/07 @ 16–18 mins.
xxxvi Bethesda, MD, 2/11/06 @ 1–3 mins.

xxxvii   Bethesda, MD, 2/11/06 @ 5–8 mins.
xxxviii New York City, 4/11/06 @ 0–3 mins.
xxxix   Spencertown, NJ, 7/11/06.
xl   London, 12/1/07 @ 48–53 mins.

3

i   email, 5/2/12.
ii   Spencertown, NY, 7/11/06.
iii   email, 18/1/12.
iv   Spencertown, NJ, 7/11/06 @ 42 mins.
v   Spencertown, NJ, 7/11/06 @ 42–43 mins.
vi   Montreal, 29/4/08.
vii   Spencertown, NJ, 7/11/06 @ 32–44 mins.
viii Spencertown, NJ, 7/11/06 @ 32–35 mins.
ix   Hove, 11/9/06 @ 23–31 mins.
x   Spencertown, NJ, 7/11/06 @ 52–53 mins.
xi   Spencertown, NJ, 7/11/06 @ 63–64 mins.

4

i   London, 8/11/07 @ 16–17 mins.
ii   London, 8/11/07 @ 17–18 mins.
iii   London, 8/11/07 @ 13 mins.
iv   London, 8/11/07 @ 31 mins.
v   London, 8/11/07 @ 28–31 mins.
vi   London, 8/11/07 @ 34–37 mins.
vii   London, 8/11/07 @ 37–42 and 75–76 mins.
viii London, 8/11/07 @ 42–43 mins.
ix   Vancouver, 22/6/06 @ 8–10 mins.
x   Vancouver, 22/6/06 @ 10–19 and 27–28 mins.
xi   email, 30/4/12.
xii   Irvington, NY, 5/11/06 @ 64–66 mins.
xiii London, 12/1/07 @ 62–66 mins.
xiv   London, 12/1/07 @ 56–57 mins.
xv   London, 12/1/07 @ 57–58 mins.
xvi   London, 12/1/07 @ 60–61 mins.
xvii London, 12/1/07 @ 41–42 mins.
xviii New York City, 4/11/06 @ 3–5 mins.
xix   New York City, 4/11/06 @ 5–8 mins; text edited by Ernie Stern September 2007, with dates inserted from his late father's unpublished memoir.
xx   email, 9/5/12.
xxi   Leeds, 12/10/07.
xxii email, 9/5/12.
xxiii Berkeley, CA, 16/4/07 @ 5–10 mins.
xxiv Berkeley, CA, 16/4/07 @ 14–15 mins.
xxv   Berkeley, CA, 16/4/07 @ 25–26 mins.
xxvi Bethesda, MD, 2/11/06 @ 8–10 mins.
xxvii Bethesda, MD, 2/11/06 @ 11–15 mins.

xxviii Bethesda, MD, 2/11/06 @ 16–25 mins.
 xxix Bethesda, MD, 2/11/06 @ 38–41 mins.
  xxx Bethesda, MD, 2/11/06 @ 45–50 mins.

5

    i 18/9/13.
   ii email, 4/3/13.
  iii London, 17/10/06 @ 8 mins.
   iv 5/5/14.
    v London, 17/10/06 @ 32–34 mins.
   vi London, 17/10/06 @ 85–87 mins.
  vii London, 4/7/07 @ 44 mins.
 viii Spencertown, NJ, 7/11/06 @ 64–65 mins.
   ix Spencertown, NJ, 7/11/06 @ 71–78 mins.
    x Spencertown, NJ, 7/11/06 @ 65–69 mins.
   xi 7/11/06 @ 139 mins.
  xii 7/11/06 @ 78–82 mins.
 xiii Spencertown, NJ, 7/11/06 @ 101–103 mins.
  xiv Spencertown, NJ, 7/11/06 @ 144–146 mins.
   xv Spencertown, NJ, 7/11/06 @ 128–135 mins.
  xvi Spencertown, NJ, 7/11/06 @ 132–133 mins.
 xvii Spencertown, NJ, 7/11/06 @ 133–134 mins.
xviii Spencertown, NJ, 7/11/06 @ 147–152 mins.
  xix Spencertown, NJ, 7/11/06 @ 95–98 mins.
   xx Spencertown, NJ, 7/11/06 @ 158–161 mins.

6

    i Hove, 11/10/06, notes.
   ii Hove, 11/10/06, notes.
  iii Hove, 11/10/06, notes.
   iv Hove, 11/10/06, notes.
    v Hove, 11/10/06 @ 21.50 mins.
   vi Hove, 11/10/06, file 13 @ 2.25 mins.
  vii 18/12/06 @ 48.30–51.00 mins.
 viii Montreal, 29/4/08 @ 1 hr 11–12 mins.
   ix Montreal, 29/4/08 @ 53–55 mins.
    x Montreal, 29/4/08 @ 1 hr 2–3 mins.
   xi email, 7/3/14.
  xii Montreal, 29/4/08 @ 1 hr 3–6 mins.
 xiii email, 7/3/14.
  xiv Montreal, 29/4/08 @ 1 hr 12, 18 and 24 mins.
   xv email, 7/3/14.
  xvi Montreal, 29/4/08 @ 1 hr 8–11 mins.
 xvii Montreal, 29/4/08 @ 1 hr 18 and 22–23 mins.
xviii London, 12/1/07 @ 6–8 mins, 1 hr 10–12 mins.
  xix London, 12/1/07 @ 31–34 mins.
   xx London, 12/1/07 @ 1 hr 19–22 mins.

xxi   8/1/16.
xxii   Irvington, NY, 5/11/06 @ 62–63 mins.
xxiii   5/11/06 @ 96–102 mins.
xxiv   5/11/06 @ 90–93 mins.
xxv   Berkeley, CA, 16/4/07 @ 30–34 mins.
xxvi   Berkeley, CA, 16/4/07 @ 33–34 and 42–43 mins.
xxvii   Berkeley, CA, 16/4/07 @ 74–79 mins.
xxviii   Berkeley, CA, 16/4/07 @ 34–42 mins.
xxix   Berkeley, CA, 16/4/07 @ 43–46 mins.
xxx   Berkeley, CA, 16/4/07 @ 63–68 mins.
xxxi   Berkeley, CA, 16/4/07 @ 56–61 mins.
xxxii   Berkeley, CA, 16/4/07 @ 68–74 mins.
xxxiii   Berkeley, CA, 16/4/07 @ 68–74 mins.
xxxiv   Leeds, 12/10/07 @ 39–42 and 50–51 mins.
xxxv   Leeds, 12/10/07 @ 49–51 mins.
xxxvi   Leeds, 12/10/07 @ 42–46 mins.
xxxvii   Leeds, 12/10/07 @ 54–57 mins.
xxxviii   Leeds, 12/10/07 @ 17–24 mins.
xxxix   Leeds, 12/10/07 @ 25–29 mins.
xl   Leeds, 12/10/07 @ 30–34 mins.

7

i   London, 8/11/07 @ 42–53 mins.
ii   8/9/14.
iii   London, 8/11/07 @ 54–56 mins.
iv   London, 8/11/07 @ 59–69 mins.
v   London, 8/11/07 @ 69–76 mins.
vi   8/9/14.
vii   London, 8/11/07 @ 86–91 mins.
viii   8/9/14.
ix   London, 8/11/07 @ 94–101 mins.
x   8/9/14.
xi   8/9/14.
xii   8/9/14.
xiii   London, 8/11/07 @ 94–95 mins.
xiv   London, 8/11/07 @ 102 mins.
xv   London, 8/11/07 @ 81–83 mins.
xvi   London, 8/11/07 @ 83–86 mins.
xvii   Bethesda, MD, 2/11/06 @ 65–69 mins.
xviii   Bethesda, MD, 2/11/06 @ 69–70 mins.
xix   Bethesda, MD, 2/11/06 @ 69–83 mins.
xx   Bethesda, MD, 2/11/06 @ 82–85 and 90–95 mins.
xxi   Bethesda, MD, 11/4/07 @ 3–5 mins.
xxii   Bethesda, MD, 2/11/06 @ 82–85 mins.
xxiii   Bethesda, MD, 2/11/06 @ 85–90 mins.
xxiv   Bethesda, MD, 2/11/06 @ 95–100 mins.
xxv   Bethesda, MD, 2/11/06 @ 100–120 mins.

xxvi Bethesda, MD, 2/11/06 @ 124–129 mins.
xxvii Bethesda, MD, 2/11/06 @ 131–140 mins.
xxviii Bethesda, MD, 11/4/07 @ 11–19 mins.
xxix Bethesda, MD, 11/4/07 @ 6–12 mins.
xxx Bethesda, MD, 12/4/07 @ 21–27 mins.
xxxi Bethesda, MD, 12/4/07 @ 19–28 mins.
xxxii New York City, 3/9/07 @ 16–22 mins.
xxxiii New York City, 3/9/07 @ 19–20 mins.
xxxiv New York City, 3/9/07 @ 16–23 mins.
xxxv New York City, 3/9/07 @ 25–29 mins.
xxxvi New York City, 3/9/07 @ 29–35 and 39–40 mins.
xxxvii New York City, 3/9/07 @ 35–36 mins.
xxxviii New York City, 3/9/07, Part 2 @ 10–21 mins.
xxxix New York City, 3/9/07, Part 1 @ 37–38 mins.
xl New York City, 3/9/07, Part 1 @ 3–6 mins.
xli New York City, 3/9/07, Part 1 @ 9–10 mins.
xlii New York City, 3/9/07, Part 1 @ 4–9 mins.
xliii Vancouver, 22/6/06 @ 29–31 mins.
xliv Vancouver, 22/6/06 @ 83–84 mins.
xlv Toronto, 1/11/06 @ 8–34 mins.
xlvi 27/8/15.
xlvii Toronto, 1/11/06 @ 29–34 mins.
xlviii Toronto, 1/11/06 @ 34–36 mins.
xlix Toronto, 1/11/06 @ 36–39 mins.
l 27/8/15.
li Toronto, 1/11/06 @ 40–42 mins.
lii Toronto, 1/11/06 @ 49 mins.
liii 27/8/15.
liv Toronto, 1/11/06 @ 57–60 mins.
lv Toronto, 1/11/06 @ 60–61 mins.
lvi Toronto, 1/11/06 @ 66–67 mins.
lvii 27/8/15.

8

i Leeds, 12/10/07 @ 33–34 mins.

Appendix

i London, 7/9/07 @ 21 mins, p. 6.
ii Oxford, 24/4/08.
iii Yale, New Haven, CT, 8/11/06 @ 0–4 mins.
iv email, 6/10/06.
v Brighton, 11/10/06 @ 5–8 mins.
vi 13/12/07 @ 0–5 mins.
vii Klagenfurt, 25/6/07 @ 0–8 and 35–37 mins.

REFERENCES

Adelman, I. (1961) *Theories of Economic Growth and Development*. Palo Alto: Stanford University Press.

Adelman, I. (1969) *Practical Approaches to Development Planning: Korea's Second Five Year Plan*. Baltimore: Johns Hopkins University Press.

Adelman, I. (1974) On the state of development economics, *Journal of Development Economics* 1(1): 3–5.

Adelman, I. (1975) Development economics: a reassessment of goals, *American Economic Review* 65(2): 302–9.

Adelman, I. (1978) *Redistribution before Growth: A Strategy for Developing Countries*. The Hague: Martinus Nijhof.

Adelman, I. (1988) Confessions of an incurable romantic, *Banca Nazionale del Lavoro Quarterly Review* 166, September: 243–62.

Adelman, I. (1995) Introduction, *Institutions and Development Strategies: The Selected Essays of Irma Adelman*, vol. 1. Aldershot: Edward Elgar, 3–22 (reprint of Adelman 1988).

Adelman, I. (n.d.) Research versus policy in the life of an academic economist, unpublished ms.

Adelman, I. and Morris, C.T. (1967) *Society, Politics, and Economic Development: A Quantitative Approach*. Baltimore: Johns Hopkins University Press.

Adelman, I. and Morris, C.T. (1973) *Economic Growth and Social Equity in Developing Countries*. Palo Alto: Stanford University Press.

Adelman, I. and Robinson, S. (1978) *Income Distribution Policy in Developing Countries: The Case of Korea*. Palo Alto: Stanford University Press.

Adelman, J. (2012) Jeremy Adelman on Albert Hirschman, *YouTube*. www.youtube.com/watch?v=lDjVoA2NfH4, accessed 1 March 2013.

Adelman, J. (2013) *Worldly Philosopher: The Odyssey of Albert O. Hirschman*. Princeton: Princeton University Press.

Adelman, J. and Loyer, E. (2010) Between worlds: the life and work of Albert O. Hirschman: introduction, *The Tocqueville Review* 31(2): 9–18.

Agarwala, A.N. and Singh, S.P. (1958) *The Economics of Underdevelopment: A Series of Articles and Papers*. Bombay: Oxford University Press.

Alacevich, M. (2016a) Albert O. Hirschman and the rise and decline of development economics, in Fiorito, L., Scheall, S. and Suprinyak, C.E. (eds) *Including a Symposium on Albert O. Hirschman*. Research in the History of Economic Thought and Methodology, 34B. Bingley, UK: Emerald, 13–39.

Alacevich, M. (2016b) Albert O. Hirschman, in Ghosh, J., Kattel, R. and Reinert, E. (eds) *Handbook of Alternative Theories of Economic Development*. Aldershot: Edward Elgar, 456–74. https://papers.ssrn.com/sol3/papers.cfm?abstract_id=2659846, accessed 6 August 2017.

Amin, S. (1970) *The Maghreb in the Modern World: Algeria, Tunisia, Morocco*. Harmondsworth: Penguin.

Amin, S. (1973) *Neocolonialism in West Africa*. Harmondsworth: Penguin.

Amin, S., Arrighi, G., Frank, A.G. and Wallerstein, I. (1982) *Dynamics of*

Global Crisis. New York: Monthly Review Press, and London: Macmillan.

Anderson, L.R. (2001) *Autobiography*. London and New York: Routledge.

Arestis, P. and Sawyer, M. (eds) (2000) *A Biographical Dictionary of Dissenting Economists*, 2nd edn. Cheltenham, UK and Northampton, MA: Edward Elgar.

Arksey, H. and Knight, P. (1999) *Interviewing for Social Scientists*. London: Sage.

Arndt, H.W. (1944) *The Economic Lessons of the Nineteen-thirties*. New York: Oxford University Press (reprinted in 1963 by Frank Cass and in 1994 by Gregg Revivals).

Arndt, H.W. (1985) *A Course Through Life: Memoirs of an Australian Economist*. History of Development Studies, 1. Canberra: National Centre for Development Studies, Australian National University.

Arndt, H.W. (1987) *Economic Development: The History of an Idea*. Chicago and London: University of Chicago Press.

Arndt, H.W. (1997) Economist down under, in Hagemann, H. (ed.) *Zur deutschsprachigen Wirtschaftswisse nschaftlichen Emigration nach 1933*. Marburg: Metropolis-Verlag, 151–76.

Bauer, J. (2017) Widerstandskämpfer aus Stuttgart: Theodor Bergmann ist tot, Stuttgart Nachrichten, 13 June. www. stuttgarter-nachrichten.de/inhalt. widerstandskaempfer-aus-stuttgart-theodor-bergmann-ist-tot.556e2a67-d1be-4f71-96df-3658ca27bfac.html.

Bauer, P.T. (1948a) *The Rubber Industry*. Cambridge, MA: Harvard University Press.

Bauer, P.T. (1948b) *Report on a Visit to the Rubber-Growing Smallholdings of Malaya*.

Bauer, P.T. (1954) *West African Trade*. Cambridge: Cambridge University Press.

Bauer, P.T. (1971) *Dissent on Development*. London: Weidenfeld and Nicolson.

Bauer, P.T. (1984) Remembrance of studies past: retracing first steps, in Meier, G.M. and Seers, D. (eds) *Pioneers in Development*. New York: Oxford University Press for the World Bank, 27–50 (with commentary by T.N. Srinivasan, 51–5).

Bauer, P.T. (1985) Interview with Lord Bauer, *The Caian* 1 Oct 1984 – 30 September 1985 (Magazine of Gonville and Caius College, Cambridge).

Bauman, J. (1986) *Winter in the Morning: A Young Girl's Life the Warsaw Ghetto and Beyond 1939–1945*. London: Virago.

Bauman, Z. (1989) *Modernity and the Holocaust*. Cambridge, UK and Maldon, MA: Polity.

Bauman, Z. (1991) *Modernity and Ambivalence*. Cambridge, UK and Maldon, MA: Polity.

Bauman, Z. and Tester, K. (2001) *Conversations with Zygmunt Bauman*. Cambridge, UK and Maldon, MA: Polity.

Beaud, M. and Dostaler, G. (1995) *Economic Thought since Keynes: A History and Dictionary of Major Economists*. Aldershot: Edward Elgar (subsequently published by Routledge).

Bebbington, A. (2006) Michael Cernea (1934–), in Simon, D. (ed.) *Fifty Key Thinkers on Development*. London and New York: Routledge, 67–73 (a revised and updated version of the essay will appear in Simon, D. (ed.) (2019) *Key Thinkers on Development*, 2nd edn. London and New York: Routledge).

Beckford, G. with Levitt, K. (2000) *The George Beckford Papers, Selected and Introduced by Kari Levitt*. Mona, Jamaica: Canoe Press, UWI.

Bentwich, N. (1953) *The Rescue and Achievement of Refugee Scholars:*

The Story of Displaced Scholars and Scientists 1933–1952. The Hague: Martinus Nijhoff.

Bergmann, T. (1960) Die landwirtschaftliche Bevölkerung im System der Sozialversicherung: ein internationale Vergleich. Göttingen: Agrarsoziale Gesellschaft.

Bergmann, T. (1966) Stand und Formen der Mechanisierung der Landwirtschaft in den asiatischen Ländern. Teil 2 – Südasien. Stuttgart: Klett.

Bergmann, T. (1971) Die Genossenschaftsbewegung in Indien: Geschichte, Leistungen, Aufgaben. Frankfurt am Main: Knapp.

Bergmann, T. (1975) Farm Policies in Socialist Countries. Farnborough, UK: Saxon House.

Bergmann, T. (1977) The Development Models of India, the Soviet Union and China: A Comparative Analysis. Assen: Van Gorcum.

Bergmann, T. (1979) Agrarpolitik und Agrarwirtschaft sozialistischer Länder, 2nd rev. edn. Saarbrücken: Breitenbach.

Bergmann, T. (2000, 2016) Im Jahrhundert der Katastrophen. Autobiographie eines kritischen Kommunisten. Hamburg: VSA-Verlag (2nd expanded edn 2016).

Bergmann, T. (2004a) Rotes China im 21. Jahrhundert. Hamburg: VSA-Verlag.

Bergmann, T. (2004b) Die Thalheimers. Geschichte einer Familie undogmatischer Marxisten. Hamburg: VSA-Verlag.

Bergmann, T. (2007a) China entdeckt Rosa Luxemburg. Berlin: Dietz.

Bergmann, T. (2007b) 'Klassenkampf und Solidarität'. Geschichte der Stuttgarter Metallarbeiter. Hamburg: VSA-Verlag.

Bergmann, T. (2009a) Internationalismus im 21. Jahrhundert. Lernen und Niederlagen – für eine neue internationale Solidarität. Hamburg: VSA-Verlag.

Bergmann, T. (2009b) Internationalisten an den antifaschistischen Fronten. Spanien, China, Vietnam. Hamburg: VSA-Verlag.

Bergmann, T. (2011) Der 100-jährige Krieg um Israel. Eine internationalistische Position zum Nahostkonflikt. Hamburg: VSA-Verlag.

Bergmann, T. (2012) Strukturprobleme eder kommunistischen Bewegung. Irrwege – Kritik – Erneuerung. Hamburg: VSA-Verlag.

Bergmann, T. (2014) Sozialisten Zionisten Kommunisten: Die Familie Bergmann-Rosenzweig – eine kämpferische Generation in 20. Jahrhundert. Hamburg: VSA-Verlag.

Bergmann, T. (2016) Im Jahrhundert der Katastrophen: Autobiografie eines kritischen Kommunist, 3rd updated and expanded edn. Hamburg: VSA Verlag.

Bergmann, T. (2017) Der chinesische Weg. Versuch, eine ferne Entwicklung zu verstehen. Hamburg: VSA-Verlag.

Bergmann, T., Gey, P. and Quaisser, W. (eds) (1984) Sozialistischer Agrarpolitik. Cologne: Bund-Verlag.

Bergmann, T. and Gräff, E. (1987) Gegen den Strom: die Geschichte der Kommunistischen-Partei-Opposition. Hamburg: VSA-Verlag.

Bergmann, T. and Liegle, L. (2002) Krise und Zukunft des Kibbutz. Weinheim and Munich: Juventa.

Bergmann, T. and Ogura, T. (1985) Cooperation in World Agriculture: Experiences, Problems and Perspectives. Tokyo: Food and Agriculture Policy Centre.

Berkeley Department of Agricultural and Resource Economics (2017) In Memoriam: Irma Adelman, March 1930 – February 5, 2017. https://are.berkeley.edu/news/2017/02/memoriam-irma-adelman, accessed 12 October 2017.

Best, L. and Levitt, K. (1975) Character of plantation economy, in Beckford, G.L.

(ed.) *Caribbean Economy: Dependence and Backwardness*. Mona, Jamaica: Institute of Social and Economic Research, UWI, 34–60.

Best, L. and Levitt, K. (2010) *Essays on the Theory of Plantation Economy*. Mona, Jamaica: UWI Press.

Beveridge, W.H. (1959) *A Defence of Free Learning*. London, New York and Toronto: Oxford University Press.

Binns, T. (2006) E.F. (Fritz) Schumacher, in Simon, D. (ed.) *Fifty Key Thinkers on Development*. London and New York: Routledge, 218–23 (a revised and updated version of the essay will appear in Simon, D. (ed.) (2019) *Key Thinkers on Development*, 2nd edn. London and New York: Routledge).

Blaug, M. (1998) Great Economists since Keynes: An Introduction to the Lives and Works of One Hundred Modern Economists, 2nd edn. Cheltenham, UK and Northampton, MA: Edward Elgar (1st edn 1985).

Bondi, H. (1990) *Science, Churchill and Me: The Autobiography of Hermann Bondi, Master of Churchill College Cambridge*. Oxford: Pergamon.

Braga, S. (2019) Celso Furtado (1920–2004), in Simon, D. (ed.) *Key Thinkers on Development*, 2nd edn. London and New York: Routledge (in press).

Brohman, J. (2006) Albert O Hirschman (1915–), in Simon, D. (ed.) *Fifty Key Thinkers on Development*. London and New York: Routledge, 126–32 (a revised and updated version of the essay will appear in Simon, D. (ed.) (2019) *Key Thinkers on Development*, 2nd edn. London and New York: Routledge).

Buchanan, J.M. (2002) Obituary: the sayer of truth: a personal tribute to Peter Bauer, *Public Choice* 112 (3–4): 233–4.

Buchanan, N.S. and Ellis, H. (1955) *Approaches to Economic Development*. New York: The Twentieth Century Fund.

Buergenthal, T. (2015) *A Lucky Boy: A Memoir of Surviving Auschwitz as a Young Boy*, expanded edn. New York, Boston and London: Back Bay Books (originally published in German in 2007 as *Ein Glückskind* by Fischer Verlag, and in English in 2009 by Profile Books, London and Little, Brown and Company, New York).

Bunting, M. (2003) Passion and pessimism, *The Guardian*, 5 April. www.theguardian.com/books/2003/apr/05/society, accessed 3 March 2006, 17 January 2016.

Burletson, L. (1993) The state, internment and public criticism in the Second World War, in Cesarani, D. and Kushner, T. (eds) *The Internment of Aliens in Twentieth Century Britain*. London: Frank Cass, 102–24.

Castells, M. (1998) *The Information Age: Economy, Society and Culture*, vol. 3: *End of the Millennium*. Oxford: Blackwell.

Cernea, M.M. (ed.) (1985, 1991) *Putting People First: Sociological Variables in Development*. New York: Oxford University Press for the World Bank (2nd edn 1991).

Cernea, M.M. (1986) *Involuntary Resettlement in Bank-Assisted Projects: A Review of the Application of Bank Policies and Procedures in FY79–95 Projects*. Operations Policy Staff, World Bank.

Cernea, M.M. (1988) *Involuntary Resettlement in World Bank Projects: Policy Guidelines for Bank-Finance Projects*. Washington, DC: World Bank.

Cernea, M.M. (1996) *Social Organisation and Development Anthropology: The 1995 Malinowski Award Lecture*. Environmentally Sustainable Development Studies and Monographs Series, 6. Washington, DC: World Bank.

Cernea, M.M. (1997) The risks and reconstruction model for resettling displaced people, *World Development* 25(10): 1569–88.

Cernea, M.M. (2001) Eight main risks: preventing impoverishment during population resettlement, in De Wet, C. and Fox, R. (eds) *Transforming Settlement in Southern Africa.* Edinburgh: Edinburgh University Press for the International African Institute, 237–52.

Cernea, M.M. (2002) *Cultural Heritage and Development: A Framework for Action in the Middle East and North Africa.* Washington, DC: World Bank.

Cernea, M.M. and Freidenberg, J. (2007) Michael Cernea 'Development anthropology is a contact sport': an oral history interview with Michael M. Cernea by Judith Freidenberg, *Human Organization* 66(4): 339–53.

Cernea, M.M. and Guggenheim, S. (eds) (1993) *Anthropological Approaches to Resettlement: Policy, Practice and Theory.* Boulder, CO: Westview Press.

Cernea, M.M. and Kassam, A.H. (eds) (2006) *Researching the Culture in Agriculture: Social Research for International Development.* Wallingford, UK and Cambridge, MA: CABI Publishing.

Cernea, M.M. and Mathur, H.M. (eds) (2008) *Can Compensation Prevent Impoverishment?: Reforming Resettlement through Investments and Benefit-Sharing.* New York: Oxford University Press.

Cernea, M.M. and McDowell, C. (eds) (2000) *Risks and Reconstruction: Experiences of Resettlers and Refugees.* Washington, DC: World Bank.

Cesarani, D. (1993) An alien concept? The continuity of anti-alienism in British society before 1940, in Cesarani, D. and Kushner, T. (eds) (1993) *The Internment of Aliens in Twentieth Century Britain.* London: Frank Cass, 25–52.

Cesarani, D. and Kushner, T. (eds) (1993) *The Internment of Aliens in Twentieth Century Britain.* London: Frank Cass.

Chambers, R. (1983) *Rural Development: Putting the Last First.* Harlow: Longmans.

Chambers, R. (1987) *Whose Reality Counts? Putting the First Last.* Rugby: Intermediate Technology Development Group.

Chappell, C. (2005) *Island of Barbed Wire: The Remarkable Story of World War Two Internment on the Isle of Man.* London: Robert Hale (1st edn 1984).

Chenery, H., Ahluwalia, M.S., Bell, C.L.G., Duloy, J.H. and Jolly, R. (1974) *Redistribution with Growth.* Oxford: Oxford University Press.

Coleman, P., Cornish, S. and Drake, P. (2007) *Arndt's Story: The Life of an Australian Economist.* Canberra: Asia Pacific Press, Australian National University, and Singapore: Institute of Southeast Asian Studies.

Cooper, R.M. (1992) *Refugee Scholars: Conversations with Tess Simpson.* Leeds: Moorland Books.

Cooper, R.M. (ed.) (1996) *Retrospective Sympathetic Affection: A Tribute to the Academic Community.* Leeds: Moorland Books.

Cornia, G.A. and Helleiner, G.K (eds) (1994) *From Adjustment to Development in Africa: Conflict, Controversy, Convergence, Consensus?* London: Macmillan.

Cowen, M.P. and Shenton, R.W. (1996) *Doctrines of Development.* London and New York: Routledge.

Cramer C. (2006) Gerald K. Helleiner (1936–), in Simon, D. (ed.) *Fifty Key Thinkers on Development.* London and New York: Routledge, 121–6 (a revised and updated version of the essay will appear in Simon, D. (ed.) (2019) *Key Thinkers on Development*, 2nd edn. London and New York: Routledge).

Davis, M. and Campbell, T. (2017) Zygmunt Bauman obituary, *The Guardian*, 15 January. www.theguardian.com/education/2017/jan/15/zygmunt-bauman-obituary.

Dawidoff, N. (2002) *The Flyswatter: How My Grandfather Made His Way in the World*. New York: Pantheon.

De Kadt, E. (1964) *British Defence Policy and Nuclear War*. London: Frank Cass.

De Kadt, E. (1970) *Catholic Radicals in Brazil*. London: RIIA/Oxford University Press.

De Kadt, E. (1980) Some basic questions on human rights and development, *World Development* 8(2): 97–105.

De Kadt, E. (1985) Of markets, might and mullahs: a case for equity, pluralism and tolerance in development, *World Development* 13(4): 549–56.

De Kadt, E. (1994) Getting and using knowledge about the poor, *IDS Bulletin*, 25(2): 100–9.

De Kadt, E. (2006) Ch 1 Jewish background: the impact of a life history. Unpublished manuscript originally intended for inclusion in De Kadt (2013).

De Kadt, E. (2009) A time of distress. A personal chronicle of 1933–1945. Unpublished manuscript.

De Kadt, E. (2013) *Assertive Religion: Religious Intolerance in a Multicultural World*. New Brunswick, NJ and London: Transaction Publishers.

De Kadt, E. and Williams, G. (eds) (1974) *Sociology and Development*. London: Tavistock.

Desai, V. and Potter, R.B. (eds) (2014) *The Companion to Development Studies*, 3rd edn. Abingdon and New York: Routledge.

Dimand, R.W., Dimand, M.A. and Forget, E.L. (eds) (2000) *A Biographical Dictionary of Women Economists*. Cheltenham, UK and Northampton, MA: Edward Elgar.

Douglass, M. and Friedmann, J. (eds) (1998) *Cities for Citizens: Planning and the Rise of Civil Society in a Global Age*. Chichester: John Wiley & Sons.

Dove, R. (ed.) (2005) *Totally Un-English? Britain's Internment of 'Enemy Aliens' in Two World Wars*. Yearbook of the Research Centre for German and Austrian Exile Studies, Institute of Germanic and Romance Studies, University of London. Amsterdam and New York: Editions Rodopi.

Economist, The (2012) Exit Albert Hirschman: a great lateral thinker died on December 10th. www.economist.com/news/business/21568708-great-lateral-thinker-died-december-10th-exit-albert-hirschman, accessed 16 January 2013.

Ekbladh, D. (2010) *The Great American Mission: Modernization and the Construction of an American World Order*. Princeton and Oxford: Princeton University Press.

Elias, N. (1939) *Über den Prozeß der Zivilisation. Soziogenetische und psychogenetische Untersuchungen*. 2 vols. Basel: Haus zum Falken (2nd edn 1969 Bern: Francke Verlag; 3rd edn 1976 Frankfurt am Main: Suhrkamp) (English translation, *The Civilising Process*, 1994a, Oxford: Blackwell).

Elias, N. (1994b) *Reflections on a Life*. Cambridge: Polity Press.

Emmerij, L., Jolly, R. and Weiss, T. (2001) *Ahead of the Curve? UN Ideas and Global Challenges*. Bloomington and Indianapolis: Indiana University Press.

Engerman, D. (2017) Development politics and the Cold War, *Diplomatic History* 41(1): 1–19.

Engerman, D., Gilman, N., Haefele, M.H. and Latham, M.E. (eds) (2003) *Staging Growth: Modernization, Development, and the Global Cold War*. Amherst: University of Massachusetts Press.

Epstein, T.S. (1962) *Economic Development and Social Change in South Asia*. Manchester: Manchester University Press.

Epstein, T.S. (1973) *South India: Yesterday, Today, and Tomorrow: Mysore Villages Revisited*. London: Macmillan, and Teaneck, NJ: Holmes and Meier.

Epstein, T.S. (1998) *Village Voices: Forty Years of Rural Transformation in South India*. New Delhi and Thousand Oaks, CA: Sage.

Epstein, T.S. (2005) *Swimming Upstream*. London and Portland, OR: Vallentine Mitchell.

Epstein, T.S., Firth, R. and Madan, T.N. (1980) *Capitalism, Primitive and Modern: Some Aspects of Tolai Economic Growth*. Delhi: Hindustan Publishing Corp.

Epstein, T.S. and Jackson, D. (1977) *The Feasibility of Fertility Planning: Micro Perspectives*. Oxford: Pergamon.

Escobar, A. (1995) *Encountering Development: The Making and Unmaking of the Third World*. Princeton: Princeton University Press.

Escobar, A. (2006) Dudley Seers (1920–83), in Simon, D. (ed.) *Fifty Key Thinkers on Development*. London and New York: Routledge, 224–30 (a revised and updated version of the essay will appear in Simon, D. (ed.) (2019) *Key Thinkers on Development*, 2nd edn. London and New York: Routledge).

Evans, R. (ed.) (1996) *Register of Rhodes Scholars 1903–1995*. Oxford: Rhodes Trust.

Ferry, G. (2007) *Max Perutz and the Secret of Life*. London: Chatto and Windus.

Feuchtwanger, L. (1982) *Der Teufel in Frankreich. Erlebnisse*. Berlin: Aufbau.

Frank, A.G. (1967) *Capitalism and Underdevelopment in Latin America*. New York. Monthly Review Press (2nd edn 1969).

Frank, A.G. (1969) *Latin America: Underdevelopment or Revolution*. New York: Monthly Review Press.

Frank, A.G. (1980) *Crisis: In the World Economy*. London: Heinemann.

Frank, A.G. (1981a) *Crisis: In the Third World*. London: Heinemann.

Frank, A.G. (1981b) *Reflections on the World Economic Crisis*. London: Hutchinson.

Frank. A.G. (1991a) Transitional ideological modes: feudalism, capitalism, socialism, *Critique of Anthropology* 11(2): 171–88.

Frank, A.G. (1991b) Underdevelopment of development: an autobiographical essay, *Scandinavian Journal of Development Alternatives* 10, 1–150.

Frank, A.G. (1996) The underdevelopment of development: an autobiographical essay, in Chew, S.C. and Denemark, R.A. (eds) *The Underdevelopment of Development: Essays in Honor of Andre Gunder Frank*. Thousand Oaks, CA: Sage, Chapter 2. (This is an updated and shortened version of a 1991 essay of the same title in the *Scandinavian Journal of Development Alternatives*).

Frank, A.G. (1997) The Cold War and me, *Bulletin of Concerned Asian Scholars* 29(3): 79–84.

Frank, A.G. (1998) *ReOrient: Global Economy in the Asian Age*. Berkeley, CA: University of California Press.

Frank, T. (2009) *Double Exile: Migrations of Jewish-Hungarian Professionals through Germany to the United States, 1919–1945*. Bern: Peter Lang.

Friedman, J. (1987) An interview with Eric Wolf, *Current Anthropology* 28(1): 107–18.

Friedman, M. and Sowell, T. (2005) Reflections on Peter Bauer's contributions to development economics, *The Cato Journal* 25(3): 441–7.

Friedmann, J. (1966) *Regional Development*

Policy: A Case Study of Venezuela. Cambridge, MA: MIT Press.

Friedmann, J. (1979) *The Good Society.* Cambridge, MA: MIT Press.

Friedmann, J. (1986) The world city hypothesis, *Development and Change* 17(1): 69–84.

Friedmann, J. (1987) *Planning in the Public Domain: From Knowledge to Action.* Princeton: Princeton University Press.

Friedmann, J. (1992) *Empowerment.* Oxford: Blackwell.

Friedmann, J. (2000) The good city: in defense of utopian thinking, *International Journal of Urban and Regional Research* 24(2): 460–72.

Friedmann, J. (2002) *The Prospect of Cities.* Minneapolis and London: University of Minnesota Press.

Friedmann, J. (2014) Austrians-in-the-world: conversations and debates about planning and development, *European Spatial Research and Policy* 21(1): 11–22.

Friedmann, J. (2017) Planning as a vocation, in Haselsberger, B. (ed.) *Encounters in Planning Thought:16 Autobiographical Essays from Key Thinkers in Spatial Planning.* Abingdon and New York: Routledge, 15–34.

Friedmann, J. and Weaver, C. (1979) *Territory and Function: The Evolution of Regional Planning.* London: Edward Arnold, and Berkeley: University of California Press.

Friedmann, J. and Wolff, G. (1982) World city formation: an agenda for research and action, *International Journal for Urban and Regional Research*, 6(3): 309–44.

Fry, V. (1945) *Surrender on Demand.* New York: Random House.

Fry, V. (1968, 1993) *Assignment: Rescue – An Autobiography.* New York: Scholastic Books (reprinted 1993, with an Introduction by Albert Hirschman, in conjunction with the

US National Holocaust Museum. That Introduction is reprinted as Chapter 10 in Hirschman 1995).

Gaile, G. (2006) John Friedmann (1926–), in Simon, D. (ed.) *Fifty Key Thinkers on Development.* London and New York: Routledge, 101–5 (a revised and updated version of the essay will appear in Simon, D. (ed.) (2019) *Key Thinkers on Development,* 2nd edn. London and New York: Routledge).

Geldof, B. and Claxton, N. (1989) *The Price of Progress.* Oley, PA: Bullfrog Films and Central Independent Television.

George C. Marshall Foundation (2013) *The Marshall Plan.* www. marshallfoundation.org/ TheMarshallPlan.htm, accessed 14 February 2014.

Gerschenkron, A. (1943) *Bread and Democracy in Germany.* Berkeley and Los Angeles: University of California Press.

Gerschenkron, A. (1945) *Economic Relations with the USSR.* New York: The Committee on International Economic Policy in cooperation with the Carnegie Endowment for International Peace.

Gerschenkron, A. (1947) The Soviet indices of industrial production, *Review of Economics and Statistics* 34: 217–26.

Gerschenkron, A. (1962) *Economic Backwardness in Historical Perspective.* Cambridge, MA: Harvard University Press.

Gerschenkron, A. (1968) *Continuity in History and Other Essays.* Cambridge, MA: Harvard University Press.

Ghani, A. (1987) A conversation with Eric Wolf, *American Ethnologist* 14(2): 346–66.

Gillman, P. and Gillman, L. (1980) *'Collar the Lot!' How Britain Interned and Expelled Its Wartime Refugees.* London: Quartet Books.

Gilman, N. (2003) *Mandarins of the Future: Modernization Theory in*

Cold War America. Baltimore: Johns Hopkins University Press.

Gonzalez, A. (2015) The political ecology of voice (PEV): an innovative approach to examining environmental pollution and the accountability of economic actors, *Journal of Political Ecology* 22: 466–85.

Goody, J. (2002) Elias and the anthropological traditions, *Anthropological Theory* 2(4): 401–12.

Goody, J. (2003) The 'civilising process' in Ghana, *European Journal of Sociology* 44(1): 61–73.

Grady, T. (2011) *The German-Jewish Soldiers of the First World War in History and Memory*. Liverpool: Liverpool University Press.

Grossbard-Shechtman, S. (2002) Explorations: Irma Adelman: a pioneer in the expansion of economics, *Feminist Economics* 8(1): 101–16.

Gwynne, R. (2006) Alexander Gerschenkron (1904–78), in Simon, D. (ed.) *Fifty Key Thinkers on Development*. London and New York: Routledge, 116–21 (a revised and updated version of the essay will appear in Simon, D. (ed.) (2019) *Key Thinkers on Development*, 2nd edn. London and New York: Routledge).

Hagemann, H. (1997a) Einführung, in Hagemann, H. (ed.) *Zur deutschsprachigen wirtschaftswisse nschaftlichen Emigration nach 1933*. Marburg: Metropolis, 7–36.

Hagemann, H. (ed.) (1997b) *Zur deutschsprachigen wirtschaftswisse nschaftlichen Emigration nach 1933*. Marburg: Metropolis.

Hagemann, H. (2006) German-speaking economists in British exile 1933–1945, *Newsletter of the Royal Economic Society* 134(July): 17–20.

Hart, Keith (1973) Informal income opportunities and urban employment in Ghana, *The Journal of Modern African Studies* 11(1): 61–89.

Haselsberger, B. (ed.) (2017) *Encounters in Planning Thought: 16 Autobiographical Essays from Key Thinkers in Spatial Planning*. Abingdon and New York: Routledge.

Hedeler, W. and Kessler, M. (eds) (2015) *Reformen und Reformer in Kommunismus. Für Theodor Bergmann eine Würdigung*. Hamburg: VSA-Verlag.

Helleiner, G.K. (1966) *Peasant Agriculture, Government, and Economic Growth in Nigeria*. Homewood, IL: Richard D. Irwin.

Helleiner, G.K. (ed.) (1968) *Agricultural Planning in East Africa*. Nairobi: East Africa Publishing House.

Helleiner, G.K. (1972) *International Trade and Economic Development*. Harmondsworth: Penguin.

Helleiner, G.K. (ed.) (1976) *A World Divided: The Less Developed Countries in the International Economy*. Cambridge: Cambridge University Press.

Helleiner, G.K. (1982) *For Good or Evil: Economic Theory and North–South Negotiations*. Oslo: Universitetsforlaget, and Toronto: University of Toronto Press.

Helleiner, G.K. (1992) The IMF, the World Bank and Africa's adjustment and external debt problems: an unofficial view, *World Development* 20(6): 779–92.

Helleiner, G.K. (ed.) (1996) *The International Monetary and Financial System: Developing Country Perspectives*. London: Macmillan.

Helleiner, G.K. (2002) *Non-Traditional Export Promotion in Africa: Experience and Issues*. New York: Palgrave.

Helleiner, G.K. (2018) *Towards a Better World: Memoirs of a Life in International and Development Economics*. Toronto, Buffalo and London: University of Toronto Press.

Helleiner, G.K., Cornia, G.A. and Jolly, R. (1991) IMF adjustment policies and approaches and the needs of children, *World Development* 19(12): 1823–34.

Helleiner, G.L. (n.d.) Intellectual currents. Unpublished MS.

Herod, A. (1999) Reflections on interviewing foreign elites: praxis, positionality, validity, and the cult of the insider, *Geoforum* 30: 313–27.

Higgins, B. (1959) *Economic Development: Problems, Principles and Policies*. New York: W.W. Norton.

Hill, A.V. (1996) Memories and reflections, in Cooper, R. (ed.) *Retrospective Sympathetic Affection: A Tribute to the Academic Community*. Leeds: Moorland Books, 171–238.

Hindu, The (2014) Magala remembers Scarlett 'Kempamma', *The Hindu*. www.thehindu.com/news/cities/bangalore/mangala-remembers-scarlett-kempamma/article5960260.ece, accessed 4 August 2014. (This is an obituary of Scarlett Epstein).

Hirschfeld, G. (1988) German refugee scholars in Great Britain, 1933–1945, in Marcus, M.R. and Bramwell, A.C. (eds) *Refugees in the Age of Total War*. London: Unwin Hyman, 152–63.

Hirschman, A.O. (1958) *The Strategy of Economic Growth*. New Haven, CT: Yale University Press (reprinted 1978 by Norton Library; 1988 by Westview Press).

Hirschman, A.O. (1963) *Journeys toward Progress: Studies of Economic Policy-making in Latin America*. New York: Twentieth Century Fund (reprinted 1973 by Norton Library with new preface).

Hirschman, A.O. (1967) *Development Projects Observed*. Washington, DC: Brookings Institution (re-edited with new author's preface 1995).

Hirschman, A.O. (1970) *Exit, Voice, and Loyalty: Responses to Decline in Firms, Organizations, and States*. Cambridge, MA: Harvard University Press.

Hirschman, A.O. (1977) *The Passions and the Interests: Political Arguments for Capitalism before Its Triumph*. Princeton: Princeton University Press.

Hirschman, A.O. (1981a) The rise and decline of development economics, in Hirschman, A.O., *Essays in Trespassing*. New York: Cambridge University Press, 1–24.

Hirschman, A.O. (1981b) *Essays in Trespassing*. New York: Cambridge University Press.

Hirschman, A.O. (1984) A dissenter's confession: 'The Strategy of Economic Development' revisited, in Meier, G.M. and Seers, D. (eds) *Pioneers in Development*. New York: Oxford University Press for the World Bank, 85–111 (with commentaries by C.F. Diaz Alejandro and Paul P. Streeten, 112–18).

Hirschman, A.O. (1995) *A Propensity to Self-subversion*. Cambridge, MA and London: Harvard University Press.

Hirschman, A.O. (1996) University of Southern California Shoah Foundation Institute, Interview no. 11536, 29 January. http://vha.usc.edu, accessed 1 May 2012.

Hirschman, A.O. (1998) *Crossing Boundaries: Selected Writings*. New York: Zone Books (paperback edition 2001).

Hogan, M.J. (1987) *The Marshall Plan: America, Britain, and the Reconstruction of Western Europe, 1947–1952*. Cambridge: Cambridge University Press.

Huddleston, B., Johnson, D.G., Reutlinger, S. and Valdes, A. (1984) *International Finance for Food Security*. Baltimore and London: Johns Hopkins University Press for the World Bank.

Hughes, H. (2002) A tale of two refugees: Heinz Arndt and Peter Bauer, *Policy* 18(2): 63–4.

Hyden, G. and Reutlinger, S. (1992) Foreign aid in a period of democratization: the case of politically autonomous food funds, *World Development* 20(9): 1253–60.

Inglis, K., Spark, S. and Winter, J. with Bunyan, C. (2018) *Dunera Lives; A visual history*. Melbourne: Monash University Publishing.

Institute of Economic Affairs (IEA) (2002) *A Tribute to Peter Bauer*. London: IEA in association with Profile Books.

International Commission on the Holocaust in Romania (ICHR) (2004) *Final Report*. President: Elie Wiesel; eds: Tuvia Friling, Radu Ioanid, Mihail E. Ionescu. Iaşi: POLIROM. www.ushmm.org/research/center/presentations/features/details/2005-03-10/, accessed 24 April 2012, and www.jewishvirtuallibrary.org/jsource/Holocaust/romaniareport.html, accessed 11 May 2012.

Ioanid, R. (2000) *The Holocaust in Romania: The Destruction of Jews and Gypsies under the Antonescu Regime, 1940–1944*. Chicago: Ivan R Dee in association with the United States National Holocaust Museum.

Ioanid, R. (2017) *The Iaşi Pogrom, June– July 1941*. Bloomington: Indiana University Press in association with the United States Holocaust Memorial Museum and the Eli Wiesel National Institute for the Study of the Holocaust in Romania.

Jolly, R. (2006) *Hans Singer: The Gentle Giant. A Memorial Lecture by Richard Jolly*. Geneva: International Institute for Labour Studies.

Judt, T. with Snyder, T. (2013) *Thinking the Twentieth Century*. London: Vintage Books.

Kaldor, N. (1986) *Recordi di un economista: a cura di Maria Cristina Marcuzzo*. Milan: Garzanti.

Kamp Westerbork (2012) www.kampwesterbork.nl/geschiedenis/doorgangskamp/transporten/, accessed 7 May 2012. This is the official website of the Westerbork Camp Memorial Centre.

Kaplan Centre for Jewish Studies and Research, and South African Jewish Museum (2012) *The Jews of District 6: Another Time, Another Place*. Cape Town: Kaplan Centre for Jewish Studies and Research, University of Cape Town, and South African Jewish Museum.

Kavanagh, D. (2012) Obituary: Albert Hirschman, economist, *The Financial Times*, 13 December. www.ft.com/cms/s/0/6a25ba34-4544-11e2-858f-00144feabdco.html#axzz2I83XbRWT, accessed 16 January 2013.

Kay, C. (2006) Raúl Prebisch (1901–86), in Simon, D. (ed.) *Fifty Key Thinkers on Development*. London and New York: Routledge, 199–205 (a revised and updated version of the essay will appear in Simon, D. (ed.) (2019) *Key Thinkers on Development*, 2nd edn. London and New York: Routledge).

Kessler, M. (2017) 'The strongest fight their entire lives': in memory of Theodor Bergmann (7 March 1916 – 12 June 2017), *Historical Materialism* (translated by L. Balhorn from the original German text, 'Die Stärksten kämpfen ein Leben lang. Theodor Bergmann (7.3.1916 – 12.6.2017)' in a supplementary issue of *Sozialismus* dedicated to Bergmann. www.bw.rosalux.de/fileadmin/ls_bw/dokumente/Nachruf_Theo_Bergmann_Sozialismus_Kessler.pdf, accessed 7 August 2017), www.historicalmaterialism.org/blog/strongest-fight-their-entire-lives-memory-theodor-bergmann-7-march-1916-12-june-2017, accessed 9 August 2017.

King, J.E. (2009) *Nicholas Kaldor*. Basingstoke: Palgrave Macmillan.

Klein, K.L. (2000) On the emergence of memory in historical discourse, *Representations* 69: 127–50.

Kochan, M. (1993) Women's experience of internment, in Cesarani, D. and Kushner, T. (eds) *The Internment of*

Aliens in Twentieth Century Britain. London: Frank Cass, 147–66.

Kössler, R. (1998) *Entwicklung.* Münster: Westphalisches Dampfboot.

Kössler, R. (2011) Zweierlei Amnesie und die komplexe postkoloniale Lage Namibias, *Die Friedens-Warte* 86(1–2): 73–99.

Kössler, R. (2012) Review article: Genocide in Namibia, the Holocaust and the issue of colonialism, *Journal of Southern African Studies* 38(1): 233–8.

Kössler, R. and Schiel, T. (2006) Eric R. Wolf (1923–1999), in Simon, D. (ed.) *Fifty Key Thinkers on Development.* London and New York: Routledge, 270–5 (a revised and updated version of the essay will appear in Simon, D. (ed.) (2019) *Key Thinkers on Development*, 2nd edn. London and New York: Routledge).

Kothari, U. (ed.) (2005) *A Radical History of Development Studies*, London: Zed Books and Cape Town: David Philip.

Kreft, G. (2011) Dedicated to represent the true spirit of the German nation in the world: Philip Schwartz – founder of the Notgmeinschaft, in Marks, S., Weindling, P. and Wintour, L. (eds) *In Defence of Learning: The Plight, Persecution and Placement of Academic Refugees 1933–1980s.* Proceedings of the British Academy, 169. Oxford: Oxford University Press, 127–42.

Kregel, J.A. (1989) *Recollections of Eminent Economists*, vol. 2. London: Macmillan.

Kreienbaum, J. (2015) *Ein trauriges Fiasko. Koloniale Konzentrationslager im südlichen Afrika 1900–1908.* Hamburg: Hamburger Edition.

Krinsky, C.H. (1985) *Synagogues of Europe: Architecture, History, Meaning.* London: Constable & Co; Cambridge, MA: MIT Press; New York: Architectural History Press.

Kushner, T. (1989) *The Persistence of Prejudice: Anti-Semitism in British Society during the Second World War.* Manchester: Manchester University Press.

Kushner, T. (1993) Clubland, cricket tests and alien internment, 1939–40, in *The Internment of Aliens in Twentieth Century Britain.* London: Frank Cass, 79–101.

Lafitte, F. (1988) *The Internment of Aliens*, 2nd edn. London: Libris (1st edn 1940 Harmondsworth: Penguin).

Latham, M. (2011) *The Right Kind of Revolution: Modernization, Development, and U.S. Foreign Policy from the Cold War to the Present.* Ithaca: Cornell University Press.

Laurie, N. (2010) Finding yourself in the archives and doing geographies of religion, *Geoforum* 41(2): 165–7.

Lee, R.M. (1993) *Doing Research on Sensitive Topics.* London: Sage.

Lerner, D. (1958) *The Passing of Traditional Society: The Modernization of the Middle East.* New York: Free Press of Glencoe.

Levitt, K.P. (1970) *Silent Surrender: The Transnational Corporation in Canada.* Montreal: McGill-Queen's University Press.

Levitt, K. (2005) *Reclaiming Development: Independent Thought and Caribbean Community.* Kingston, Jamaica: Ian Randle.

Levitt, K. and McIntyre, A. (eds) (1967) *Canada–West Indies Economic Relations.* Montreal: Centre for Developing-Area Studies, McGill University.

Lewis, W.A. (1949) *Economic Survey 1919–1939.* London: George Allen and Unwin.

Leys, C. (1996) *The Rise and Fall of Development Theory.* London: James Currey.

Loeffler, J. (2018) *Rooted Cosmopolitans: Jews and Human Rights in the Twentieth Century.* New Haven, CT and London: Yale University Press.

London, L. (2000) *Whitehall and the Jews 1933–1948.* Cambridge: Cambridge University Press.

Lösch, A. (1954) *The Economics of Location*. New Haven and London: Yale University Press (originally published in German as *Die räumliche Ordnung der Wirtschaft* (1940/1944)).

Mackie, J. (2001) In memoriam: Professor Benjamin Higgins, 1912–2001, *Bulletin of Indonesian Economic Studies* 37(2): 183–8.

Marcus, A. (2003) Review article: Imaginary worlds. The last years of Eric Wolf, *Social Anthropology* 11(1): 113–27.

Marks, S. (2011) Introduction, in Marks, S., Weindling, P. and Wintour, L. (eds) *In Defence of Learning: The Plight, Persecution and Placement of Academic Refugees 1933–1980s*. Proceedings of the British Academy, 169. Oxford: Oxford University Press, 1–26.

Mawdsley, E. and Rigg, J. (2002) A survey of the World Development Reports I: discursive strategies, *Progress in Development Studies* 2(2): 93–111.

Mawdsley, E. and Rigg, J. (2003) The World Development Report II: continuity and change in development orthodoxies, *Progress in Development Studies* 3(4): 271–86.

McPherson, M.S. (2000) Albert O. Hirschman (born 1915), in Arestis, P. and Sawyer, M. (eds) *A Biographical Dictionary of Dissenting Economists*, 2nd edn. Cheltenham, UK and Northampton, MA: Edward Elgar, 298–305.

Meadows, D.H., Meadows, D.L., Randers, J. and Behrens, W.W. III (1972) *The Limits to Growth: A Report for the Club of Rome's Project on the Predicament of Mankind*. New York: Universe.

Meier, G.M. (2005) *Biography of a Subject: An Evolution of Development Economics*. New York: Oxford University Press.

Meier, G.M. and Seers, D. (eds) (1984) *Pioneers in Development*. New York: Oxford University Press for the World Bank.

Menzel, U. (2006) Walt Whitman Rostow (1916–2003), in Simon, D. (ed.) *Fifty Key Thinkers on Development*. London and New York: Routledge, 211–17 (a revised and updated version of the essay will appear in Simon, D. (ed.) (2019) *Key Thinkers on Development*, 2nd edn. London and New York: Routledge).

Merton, R.K. (1973) *The Sociology of Science: Theoretical and Empirical Investigations*, Norman W. Storer (ed.). Chicago, IL: University of Chicago Press.

Merton, R.K. (1979) *The Sociology of Science: An Episodic Memoir*. Carbondale and Edwardsville: Southern Illinois University Press, and London and Amsterdam: Feffer & Simons.

Millikan, M.F. and Rostow, W.W. (1957) *A Proposal: Key to an Effective Foreign Policy*. New York: Harper & Bros.

Mintz, S. (2007) Andre 'Gunder' Frank (1929–2005), *American Anthropologist* 109(1): 232–7.

Morris, C.T. and Adelman, I. (1988) *Comparative Patterns of Economic Development, 1850–1914*. Baltimore: Johns Hopkins University Press.

Morris, J. (2007) *The Life and Times of Thomas Balogh: A Macaw among Mandarins*. Brighton: Sussex Academic Press.

Mosse, W.E. (ed.) (1991) *Second Chance: Two Centuries of German-speaking Jews in the United Kingdom*. Tübingen: JCB Mohr.

Myrdal, G. (1953) *The Political Element in the Development of Economic Theory*. London: Routledge and Kegan Paul.

Myrdal, G. (1968) *Asian Drama: An Inquiry into the Poverty of Nations*. Harmondsworth: Penguin.

New School (2006) Paul N. Rosenstein-Rodan, 1902–. www.cepa.newschool.edu/het/profiles/rrodan.htm, accessed 5 December 2006.

Newbold, H. (ed.) (2000) *Life Stories: World-renowned Scientists Reflect on Their Lives and the Future of Life on Earth*. Berkeley, Los Angeles and London: University of California Press.

Olusoga, D. and Erichsen, C. (2010) *The Kaiser's Holocaust: Germany's Forgotten Genocide and the Colonial Roots of Nazism*. London: Faber and Faber.

Panayi, P. (1993) An intolerant act by an intolerant society: the internment of Germans in Britain during the First World War, in Cesarani, D. and Kushner, T. (eds) *The Internment of Aliens in Twentieth Century Britain*. London: Frank Cass, 53–75.

Paul, S. (2017) John Friedmann, the 'father of urban planning' dies at 91. http://luskin.ucla.edu/john-friedmann-father-urban-planning-dies-91/, accessed 15 June 2017.

Perelman, M. (2002) Obituary – Wolfgang Stolper, *PEN-L mailing list archive*, 4 April. http://archives.econ.upenn.edu/archives/pen-1/2002m04.1/msg00147.htm, accessed 4 January 2007.

Pinto, N. (n.d.) About Jewishness Amsterdam. http://jewishness.bellevueholidayrentals.com/amsterdam.html, accessed 4 May 2012.

PNG Institute of National Affairs (2014) Late Dr Trude Scarlett Epstein. www.facebook.com/permalink.php?story_fbid=636976123057782&id=349915851763812, accessed 4 August 2014. This is the PNG Institute of National Affairs' obituary of Scarlett Epstein.

Polanyi Levitt, K. (n.d.) *Biography*. www.karipolanyilevitt.com/bio.shtml, accessed 18 April 2008.

Polanyi Levitt, K. and Witter, M. (eds) (1996) *The Critical Tradition of Caribbean Political Economy: The Legacy of George Beckford*. Kingston, Jamaica: Ian Randle.

Ramras-Rauch, G. (1994) *Aharon Appelfeld: The Holocaust and Beyond*. Bloomington: Indiana University Press.

Reisman, A. (2006) *Turkey's Modernization: Refugees from Nazism and Atatürk's Vision*. Washington, DC: New Academia Publishing.

Reisz, M. (2017) Zygmunt Bauman: visionary sociologist dies aged 91, *Times Higher Education*, 19 January, 12. www.timeshighereducation.com/news/zygmunt-bauman-visionary-sociologist-dies-aged-91, accessed 25 July 2017.

Renzetti, C.M. and Lee, R.M. (eds) (1993) *Researching Sensitive Topics*. London: Sage.

Reutlinger, S. (1970) *Techniques for Project Appraisal under Uncertainty*. World Bank Staff Occasional Papers, 10. Baltimore: The Johns Hopkins University Press. http://documents.worldbank.org/curated/en/1970/01/1558326/techniques-project-appraisal-under-uncertainty.

Reutlinger, S. (2005) My Bar Mitzva a few days after Kristallnacht, unpublished ms, 2 May.

Reutlinger, S. and Selowsky, M. (1976) *Malnutrition and Poverty: Magnitude and Policy Options*. World Bank Staff Occasional Papers, 23. Baltimore: The Johns Hopkins University Press.

Reutlinger, S., Van Holst Pellekaan, J. with Lissner, C., Pendred, C. and Roberts, C. (1986) *Poverty and Hunger: Issues and Options for Food Security in Developing Countries*. A World Bank Policy Study. Washington, DC: World Bank.

Rist, G. (1997, 2001) *The History of Development: From Western Origins to Global Faith*. London: Zed Books.

Rosenstein-Rodan, P. (1943) Problems of industrialisation of Eastern and South-Eastern Europe, *The Economic Journal* 53(210/211): 202–11.

Rosenstein-Rodan, P. (1984) Paul N. Rosenstein-Rodan, in Meier, G.M. and Seers, D. (eds) *Pioneers in Development*. Washington, DC: World Bank, 205–21.

Rostow, W.W. (1953) *The Process of Economic Growth*. Oxford: Oxford University Press.

Rostow, W.W. (1960) *The Stages of Economic Growth: A Non-Communist Manifesto*. New York. Norton.

Sachs, W. (1992) *Zur Archäologie der Entwicklungsidee*, Acht Essays. Mit Karikaturen aus der 'Dritten Welt' Frankfurt am Main: Verlag für Interkulturelle Kommunikation.

Safran, E. (2011) The Iaşi Pogrom; my father was the chief rabbi where one of the most violent pogroms in Jewish history took place. www.aish.com/ho/p/The_Iasi_Pogrom.html, accessed 24 April 2012.

Saija, L. (2017) Autobiography as method of enquiry, in Haselsberger, B. (ed.) *Encounters in Planning Thought: 16 Autobiographical Essays from Key Thinkers in Spatial Planning*. Abingdon and New York: Routledge, 8–12.

Sarkin, J. (2011) *Germany's Genocide of the Herero: Kaiser Wilhelm II, His General, His Settlers, His Soldiers*. Cape Town: UCT Press, and Woodbridge, Suffolk and Rochester, NY: James Currey.

Schiavo-Campo, S. and Singer, H. (1970) *Perspectives in Economic Development*. Boston: Houghton-Mifflin.

Schumacher, E.F. (1966) Buddhist economics, in Wint, G. (ed.) *Asia: A Handbook*. London: Anthony Blond.

Schumacher, E.F. (1974) *Small Is Beautiful: A Study of Economics as if People Mattered*. London: Abacus (hardback, London: Blond and Briggs 1973).

Schumacher, E.F. (1977) *A Guide for the Perplexed*. London: Jonathan Cape.

Schuurman, F. (ed.) (1993) *Beyond the Impasse: New Directions in Development Theory*. London: Zed Books.

Seabrook, J. (2009) *The Refuge and the Fortress: Britain and the Flight from Tyranny*. Basingstoke: Palgrave Macmillan.

Seers, D. (1983) *The Political Economy of Nationalism*. New York: Oxford University Press.

Shatzkes, P. (2002) *Holocaust and Rescue: Impotent or Indifferent? Anglo-Jewry 1938–1945*. Basingstoke: Palgrave.

Shaw, D.J. (2002) *Sir Hans Singer: The Life and Work of a Development Economist*. Basingstoke: Palgrave Macmillan.

Shaw, D.J. (2006a) Hans Wolfgang Singer (1910–), in Simon, D. (ed.) *Fifty Key Thinkers on Development*. London and New York: Routledge, 242–7 (a revised and updated version of the essay will appear in Simon, D. (ed.) (2019) *Key Thinkers on Development*, 2nd edn. London and New York: Routledge).

Shaw, D.J. (2006b) Professor Sir Hans Singer: a tribute, *Food Policy* 31: 272–4.

Shaw, D.J. (2006c) The life and work of Professor Sir Hans Singer: an appreciation, *Canadian Journal of Development Studies* 27(3): 403–13.

Sichel, F. (1966) *From Refugee to Citizen: A Sociological Study of the Immigrants from Hitler-Europe Who Settled in Southern Africa*. Cape Town and Amsterdam: A.A. Balkema.

Silverman, S. (2002) Eric R Wolf: a political life in anthropology, unpublished lecture to mark the inauguration of the Eric Wolf Memorial Lecture Series, University of Vienna, 4 November.

Simon, D. (1998) Development revisited: thinking about, practising and teaching development after the Cold War, in Simon, D. and Närman, A. (eds) *Development as Theory and Practice*. Harlow, Essex: Addison Wesley Longman, 17–54.

Simon, D. (2003) Dilemmas of development and the environment in a globalizing world: theory, policy and praxis, *Progress in Development Studies* 3(1): 5–41.

Simon, D. (ed.) (2006) *Fifty Key Thinkers on Development*. London and New York: Routledge (a revised and updated edition will appear as Simon, D. (ed.) (2019) *Key Thinkers on Development*, 2nd edn. London and New York: Routledge).

Simon, D. (2009) From the Holocaust to development: reflections of surviving development pioneers, *Third World Quarterly* 30(5): 849–84.

Simon, D. (2012) To and through the UK: Holocaust ethnographies of escape, education, internment and careers in development, *Contemporary Social Science: Journal of the Academy of Social Sciences* 7(1): 21–38.

Simon, D. (2017) Obituary: John Friedmann, 1926–2017, *International Development Planning Review*, 39(3): v–vii. https://doi.org/10.3828/idpr.2017.14.

Simon, D. and Dodds, K. (1998) Introduction: rethinking geographies of North–South development, *Third World Quarterly* 19(4), 595–606.

Singer, H. (1984) The terms of trade controversy and the evolution of soft financing: the early years in the UN, in Meier, G. and Seers, D. (eds) *Pioneers in Development*. New York: Oxford University Press for the World Bank, 273–303 (with commentary by Bela Belassa, 304–11).

Singer, H. (1997) The influence of Schumpeter and Keynes on the development of a development economist, in H. Hagemann (ed.) *Zur deutschsprachigen Wirtschaftswissenschaftlichen Emigration nach 1933*. Marburg: Metropolis-Verlag, 127–50.

Singer, H. (2000) Hans Wolfgang SINGER (born 1910), in Arestis, P. and Sawyer, M. (eds) *A Biographical Dictionary of Dissenting Economists*, 2nd edn. Cheltenham, UK and Northampton, MA: Edward Elgar, 606–12.

Singer, H., Wood, J. and Jennings, T. (1987) *Food Aid: The Challenge and the Opportunity*. Oxford: Clarendon Press.

Smith, D. (1999) *Zygmunt Bauman: Prophet of Postmodernity*. Cambridge, UK and Malden, MA: Polity Press.

Sponza, L. (1988) *Italian Immigrants in Nineteenth Century Britain: Realities and Images*. Leicester: Leicester University Press.

Sponza, L. (1993) The British government and the internment of Italians, in Cesarani, D. and Kushner, T. (eds) *The Internment of Aliens in Twentieth Century Britain*. London: Frank Cass, 125–44.

Srinivasan, T.N. (1984) Comment, in Meier, G.M. and Seers, D. (eds) *Pioneers in Development*. New York: Oxford University Press for the World Bank, 51–5.

Staples, A.L.S. (2006) *The Birth of Development: How the World Bank, Food and Agriculture Organization and the World Health Organization Changed the World*. Kent, OH: Kent State University Press.

Stavis, B. (2004) Wolf Ladejinski, tireless (and frustrated) advocate of land reform. http://astro.temple.edu/~bstavis/courses/215-ladejinsky.htm, accessed 17 July 2007.

Stent, R. (1980) *A Bespattered Page? The Internment of His Majesty's 'Most Loyal Enemy Agents'*. London: Andre Deutsch.

Stern, G. (2000) Exile studies and exile literature, in *Leo Baeck Institute*

Yearbook XLV. London: Leo Baeck Institute, 226–7.

Stolper, W.F. (1966) *Planning without Facts: Lessons in Resource Allocation from Nigeria's Development*. Cambridge, MA: Harvard University Press.

Stolper, W.F. (1997) Facts without planning, in Hagemann, H. (ed.) *Zur deutschsprachigen wirtschaftswisse-nschaftlichen Emigration nach 1933*. Marburg: Metropolis, 95–125.

Stolper, W.F. (1998) Joseph A. Schumpeter: the man and the economist, in Sapsford, D. and Chen, J. (eds) *Development Economics and Policy: The Conference Volume to Celebrate the 85th Birthday of Professor Sir Hans Singer*. Basingstoke: Macmillan, 511–23.

Stone, D. and Moses, D.A. (2008) The first genocide of the twentieth century: the German war of destruction in southwest Africa (1904–8) and the global history of genocide, in Bergen, D.L. (ed.) *The Holocaust: Lessons and Legacies*. Evanston, IL: Northwestern University Press.

Stone, L. (1971) Prosopography, *Daedalus* 100(1): 46–79.

Streeten, P. (1961) *European Integration: Aspects and Problems*. Leiden: A.W. Sythoff.

Streeten, P. (1972a) *Aid to Africa: A Policy Outline for the 1970s*. New York: Praeger.

Streeten, P. (1972b) *The Frontiers of Development Studies*. London: Macmillan.

Streeten, P. (1974) Alternatives in development, *World Development* 2(2): 5–8.

Streeten, P. (1984) Basic needs: some unsettled questions, *World Development* 12(9): 973–8.

Streeten, P. (1985a) Balliol men in fact: an autobiographical fragment, *Balliol College Annual Record 1985*. Oxford: Balliol College, 44–56.

Streeten, P. (1985b) Obituary notices: Lord Balloch (1905–1985), *Balliol College Annual Record 1985*. Oxford: Balliol College, 17–19 (This was one of four such obituaries, the others being by Michael Posner, Roger Opie and Andrew Graham).

Streeten, P. (1986a) An autobiographical fragment, *Aberdeen University Review* 51(4), 176(autumn): 395–409.

Streeten, P. (1986b) Aerial roots, *Banca Nazionale del Lavoro Quarterly Review* 157(June): 135–59.

Streeten, P. (1995) *Thinking about Development*. Cambridge: Cambridge University Press.

Streeten, P. (1997) An autobiographical sketch, in H. Hagemann (ed.) *Zur deutschsprachigen Wirtschaftswisse-nschaftlichen Emigration nach 1933*. Marburg: Metropolis-Verlag, 177–205.

Streeten, P. (2000a) Thomas Balogh (1905–1985), in Arestis, P. and Sawyer, M. (eds) *A Biographical Dictionary of Dissenting Economists*, 2nd edn. Cheltenham, UK: Edward Elgar, 28–35.

Streeten, P. (2000b) Paul Streeten (born 1917), in Arestis, P. and Sawyer, M. (eds) *A Biographical Dictionary of Dissenting Economists*, 2nd edn. Cheltenham: Edward Elgar, 636–42.

Streeten, P. and Burki, S.J. (1978) Basic needs: some issues, *World Development* 6(3): 411–21.

Streeten, P. and Lipton, M. (eds) (1968) *The Crisis of Indian Planning: Economic Policy in the 1960s*. London: Oxford University Press.

Streeten, P. with Burki, S.J., ul Haq, M., Hicks, N. and Stewart, F. (1981) *First Things First: Meeting Basic Human Needs in the Developing Countries*. New York: Oxford University Press for the World Bank.

Taylor, J.E. and Adelman, I. (1996) *Village Economies: The Design, Estimation and Use of Villagewide Economic Models*.

New York: Cambridge University Press.

Thirlwall, A.P. (2008?) Kaldor, Nicholas [Miklós], Baron Kaldor (1908–1986), economist, *Oxford Dictionary of National Biography*, online edition, Oxford University Press. www.oxforddnb.com/index/39/101039977/, accessed 27 November 2012.

Thomson, R. (1993) Profile: Principal lender to the poor: Ernie Stern gets things done at the World Bank, writes Richard Thomson. He may soon be muscling in on Jacques Attali at the EBRD, *The Independent*, 20 June. www.independent.co.uk/news/business/profile-principal-lender-to-the-poor-ernie-stern-gets-things-done-at-the-world-bank-writes-richard-thomson-he-may-soon-be-muscling-in-on-jacques-attali-at-the-ebrd-1492802.html, accessed 14 August 2014.

Toye, J. (2006a) Obituary: Hans Singer and international development, *Journal of International Development* 18(6): 915–23.

Toye, J. (2006b) Obituaries: Sir Hans Singer, *Newsletter of the Royal Economic Society*, 133: 16–17.

Toye, J. (2012) The world improvement plans of Fritz Schumacher, *Cambridge Journal of Economics* 36(2), 387–403.

Tribe, K. (2006) Bauer, Peter Thomas, Baron Bauer (1915–2002), *Oxford Dictionary of National Biography*, online edition, Oxford University Press. www.oxforddnb.com/view/article/76873, accessed 1 February 2007.

Uitto, J. (2006) Hollis B. Chenery (1918–94), in Simon, D. (ed.) *Fifty Key Thinkers on Development*. London and New York: Routledge, 78–83 (a revised and updated version of the essay will appear in Simon, D. (ed.) (2019) *Key Thinkers on Development*, 2nd edn. London and New York: Routledge).

United Nations Intellectual History Project (UNIHP) (2007) *The Complete Oral History Transcripts from* UN Voices. New York: UNIHP, Ralph Bunche Institute for International Studies, Graduate Center, City University of New York.

Vanas, A. (2012) *In the Lion's Den: Subverting the Nazis from within Westerbork Transit Camp 1942–1945*. Caulfield South, Victoria: Makor Jewish Community Library.

Wallerstein, I. (1991) World System versus World-Systems: A Critique, *Critique of Anthropology* 11(2): 189–94.

Watts, M. (2006) Andre Gunder Frank, in Simon, D. (ed.) *Fifty Key Thinkers on Development*. London and New York: Routledge, 90–6 (a revised and updated version of the essay will appear in Simon, D. (ed.) (2019) *Key Thinkers on Development*, 2nd edn. London and New York: Routledge).

Weiss, T., Carayannis, T., Emmerij, L. and Jolly, R. (2005) *UN Voices: The Struggle for Development and Social Justice*. Bloomington and Indianapolis: Indiana University Press.

Wikipedia (2013) Judensau, *Wikipedia*. http://de.wikipedia.org/wiki/Judensau, accessed 22 January 2013.

Wikipedia (2016) *Struma* disaster, *Wikipedia*. https://en.wikipedia.org/wiki/Struma_disaster, accessed 11 January 2016.

Wikipedia (2017a) Bert F. Hoselitz, *Wikipedia*. https://en.wikipedia.org/wiki/Bert_F._Hoselitz, accessed 8 August.

Wikipedia (2017b) Theodor Bergmann (agronomist), *Wikipedia*. https://en.wikipedia.org/wiki/Theodor_Bergmann_(agronomist), accessed 6 August.

Wikipedia (2017c) Andre Gunder Frank, *Wikipedia*. https://en.wikipedia.org/wiki/Andre_Gunder_Frank, accessed 10 August.

Wilson, F. (2006) Paul Patrick Streeten (1917–), in Simon, D. (ed.) *Fifty Key Thinkers on Development*. London and New York: Routledge, 252–8 (a revised and updated version of the essay will appear in Simon, D. (ed.) (2019) *Key Thinkers on Development*, 2nd edn. London and New York: Routledge).

Wolf, E.R. (1959a) Specific aspects of plantation systems in the new world: community subcultures and social class, *Plantation Systems in the New World*. Social Science Monograph, 7, Pan American Union, Washington, DC, 136–46.

Wolf, E.R. (1959b) *Sons of the Shaking Earth*. Chicago: University of Chicago Press.

Wolf, E.R. (1966) *Peasants*. Englewood Cliffs: Prentice Hall.

Wolf, E.R. (1969) *Peasant Wars of the Twentieth Century*. New York: Harper and Row.

Wolf, E.R. (1982) *Europe and the People without History*. Berkeley and Los Angeles: University of California Press (reprinted with updated Preface in 1997).

Wolf, E.R. (1992) Thoughts about a boyhood in Vienna, *Mitteilungen der Anthropologischen Gesellschaft in Wien (MAGW)*, 122: 5–7.

Wolf, E.R. (1999) *Envisioning Power: Ideologies of Dominance and Crisis*. Berkeley and Los Angeles: University of California Press.

Wolf, E.R. and Minz, S.W. (1957) Haciendas and plantations in middle America and the Antilles, *Social and Economic Studies* 6: 380–412.

Wolf, E.R. with Silverman, S. (2001) *Pathways of Power: Building an Anthropology of the Modern World*. Berkeley, Los Angeles and London: University of California Press.

Wood, B. (1985) *Alias Papa: A Life of Fritz Schumacher*. Oxford: Oxford University Press (1984 hardback edition published by Jonathan Cape, London).

World Bank and World Food Program (1991) *Food Aid in Africa: An Agenda for the 1990s. A Joint Study by the World Bank and World Food Program*. Washington, DC and Rome.

Yamey, B.S. (1987) Peter Bauer: economist and scholar, *The Cato Journal* 7(1): 21–7.

Yardley, W. (2012) Albert Hirschman, optimistic economist, dies at 91, *The New York Times*, 23 December. www.nytimes.com/2012/12/24/business/albert-o-hirschman-economist-and-resistance-figure-dies-at-97.html?_r=0.

Ziai, A. (2016) *Development Discourse and Global History*. Abingdon, UK and New York: Routledge.

Zilberman, D. (2017a) Irma Adelman (1930–2017): A leading economist and outstanding Berkeley faculty member, *Berkeley Blog*, 29 March. http://blogs.berkeley.edu/2017/03/28/irma-adelman-1930-2017-a-leading-economist-and-outstanding-berkeley-faculty-member/, accessed 12 October 2017.

Zilberman, D. (2017b) Obituary: Irma Adelman 1930–2017, Newsletter of the Agricultural and Applied Economics Association, 37, March. www.aaea.org/publications/the-exchange/newsletter-archives/volume-39---2017/march-2017-issue-7/obituary, accessed 12 October 2017.

Zilberman, D. (2019) Irma Adelman (1930–2017), in Simon, D. (ed.) *Key Thinkers on Development*, 2nd edn. London and New York: Routledge (in press).

Zimmerer, J. (2011) *Von Windhuk nach Auschwitz? Beiträge zum Verhältnis von Kolonialismus und Holocaust*. Berlin: Lit.

Zionism and Israel (2009) Iasi pogrom. www.zionism-israel.com/dic/iasi_pogrom.htm, accessed 24 April 2012.

Zuckerman, H. (1977) *Scientific Elite: Nobel Laureates in the United States*. New York: Free Press and London: Collier Macmillan.

INDEX